THE WORD AS TRUE MYTH

THE WORD AS
TRUE MYTH

Interpreting Modern Theology

Gary Dorrien

Westminster John Knox Press
Louisville, Kentucky

Scripture quotations from the New Revised Standard Version
of the Bible are copyright © 1989 by the Division of Christian Education
of the National Council of the Churches of Christ in the U.S.A.
and are used by permission.

Book and cover design by Jennifer K. Cox
Images © 1997 PhotoDisc, Inc.

First edition
Published by Westminster John Knox Press
Louisville, Kentucky

This book is printed on acid-free paper that meets the
American National Standards Institute Z39.48 standard. ∞

PRINTED IN THE UNITED STATES OF AMERICA
97 98 99 00 01 02 03 04 05 06 — 10 9 8 7 6 5 4 3 2 1

Library of Congress Cataloging-in-Publication Data

Dorrien, Gary J.
        The Word as true myth : interpreting modern theology / Gary
Dorrien. — 1st ed.
        p.   cm.
    Includes bibliographical references.
    ISBN 0-664-25745-3 (alk. paper)
        1. Theology, Doctrinal—History—19th century.   2. Theology,
Doctrinal—History—20th century.   3. Word of God (Theology)
4. Myth in the Bible.   5. Postmodernism—Religious aspects—
Christianity.   6. Theology—Methodology.   I. Title.
BT28.D67   1997
2309.099034—dc21   97-16941

For Greg, Robyn, and Hope with love.

Contents

Introduction

Modern theology has been in crisis for most of its history. Notwithstanding its deep and distinctive concern with the social meaning of Christianity, the crisis of modern theology is now and has always been first a crisis of belief. What kind of Christian belief is possible after modern science and Enlightenment criticism have desacralized the world? Is it possible to sustain Christian faith in the absence of any personal or collective sense of the sacred? How should Christian theology relate to the mythical aspects of Christianity?

These questions are peculiar to modern theology and its postmodern offshoots. Secularization was inconceivable to Thomas Aquinas; Martin Luther and John Calvin did not ask themselves whether Christian myth should be demythologized. The very notion of "Christian myth" would have struck them as absurd. These questions have played a central role in modern theological discussion, however. The fact that modern theologians regard Christian myth as mythical is a distinguishing feature of the modern tradition. One way to interpret the history of modern theology is therefore through its attempts to deal with the cluster of questions that the myth question contains. Should theologians try to isolate or minimize the role of myth in Christianity? Should they assign a normative theological role to myth? Should they attempt to transcend Christian myth by translating the mythical aspects of Christian faith into the language of Neoplatonism or idealism or existentialism or some other philosophy? Is it necessary to demythologize the gospel faith before any credible program of philosophical translation can be carried out? What is at stake for the Christian understanding of God, the incarnation, history, and providence in the debate over Christian myth? Should theologians seek to recover a mythical sense of the world as infused by divine grace? Is it possible or desirable to create new forms of religious awareness through remythologization?

This book pursues these questions and others related to them as it recounts and assesses the history of Protestant theology since Friedrich Schleiermacher. It focuses on the three most influential types or movements of theology during this period—liberalism, crisis theology/neoorthodoxy, and liberationism/postmodernism—but in a way that brings other theological positions into view. My previous book, *Soul in Society: The Making and Renewal of Social Christianity,* employed a similar structure in addressing the social meaning of Christianity. In that book, the three dominant paradigms were social gospel Christianity (which correlates with part of theological liberalism), Christian realism (which correlates with part of neoorthodoxy), and liberation theology. The narrative in *Soul in Society* was driven toward my prescriptive discussion of the theory and future of economic democracy, however, while the present work is both more consistently historical and theological.

My account of theological liberalism begins with Immanuel Kant and Friedrich Schleiermacher and moves to G. W. F. Hegel and the Hegelians before taking up an extended discussion of David Friedrich Strauss's epochal left-Hegelian program of demythologization. The narrative then traces the historicist turn in liberal theology represented by Albrecht Ritschl, Adolf von Harnack and the Ritschlian movement, which dominated Protestant theology in the late nineteenth and early twentieth centuries. The Ritschlian school directly influenced and provided much of the theology for the social gospel movement; during the same period a group of scholars associated with the Ritschlians branched out to form a new school of religious interpretation, the *Religionsgeschichtliche Schule.*

At the height of its influence in the early twentieth century, liberal theology appropriated all of these Romanticist, idealist, mediating, and historicist approaches to Christianity. Major theologians such as Adolf von Harnack, Ernst Troeltsch, and William Adams Brown variously blended the insights of the past century of theological liberalism and created new dogmatic systems. Thinkers such as Shailer Mathews and Douglas Clyde Macintosh tried to move liberal theology into an empiricist direction, adopting the methods and spirit of the natural sciences. With all of its differences in philosophy, sensibility, historical interpretation, and theological strategy, however, theological liberalism spoke with one voice in assuming that the mythical aspects of Christianity must be transcended or otherwise overcome. This was part of what it meant for theology to be modern and progressive. Those who first took seriously the problem of Christian myth took it for granted that myth belongs to a primitive stage of consciousness. Theological liberalism proposed various strategies for making Christianity adapt to an Enlightened myth-negating consciousness.

My discussion of the succeeding major movement in modern theology tracks familiar ground, for it includes the most influential theologians of this century, especially Karl Barth, Rudolf Bultmann, Emil Brunner, Paul Tillich, Friedrich Gogarten, Dietrich Bonhoeffer, and Reinhold Niebuhr. The early names that this movement embraced—"crisis theology" and "dialectical theology"—carried stronger overtones of the revolution in theological consciousness that it represented than the more restrictive name it later acquired, "neoorthodoxy." By whatever name, however, the liberal-blasting theological movement launched by Barth in the closing months of the Great War eventually produced the most creative and profound Protestant theology of this century. Neoorthodoxy reclaimed the biblical language of grace, evil, divine transcendence, and judgment in opposition to the accommodating optimism of liberal theology. In its protest against the pretensions of modern liberal culture, crisis theology anticipated much of the critique of modernity that recent postmodern criticism has put forward.

Moreover, despite the provincial sound of its label, it is the neoorthodox tradition that has produced the most exotic mix of viewpoints in modern theology concerning the problem of Christian myth. With neoorthodoxy the myth question comes to the forefront. Nothing about the question is taken for granted or assumed away as in liberal theology; Barth, Bultmann, and Niebuhr define the problem differently and propose radically contrasting approaches to it. This diversity was too great to hold Barth, Brunner, Bultmann, Niebuhr, and Tillich into anything like a common theological movement; the differences between Barth and Tillich were ultimately greater than the agreements that made them allies against theological liberalism. Barth, Brunner, and Tillich produced massive theological systems that accentuated their distinctiveness, while Bultmann and Niebuhr towered over the fields of New Testament studies and social ethics, brandishing their own alternatives to liberal theology. For nearly four decades these thinkers dominated modern theology while finding common accord mostly in their negations. From Barth's perspective all of them eventually reverted to liberalism, especially Tillich. The commonalities between Tillich, Bultmann, and Niebuhr became difficult to remember or discern when these figures were at the height of their influence in the 1950s, but with the eruption of new social movements and critical perspectives that appeared in the 1960s, the shared limitations of the "neoorthodox" generation were exposed. Neoorthodoxy lost its dominant position in theology with the same suddenness by which it displaced liberal theology in the 1920s.

How could such an accomplished and formidable generation of theologians lose their persuasive force so quickly? The giants of twentieth-century theology had expected their students to revise their theological systems to fit the circumstances of a new generation. What they witnessed instead in their closing years was an outburst of "death of God" theologies and an explosion of new theologies of hope, ecumenism, black power, and women's liberation. Established assumptions about what theology is and how it should be carried out were abruptly discarded. Liberation theology subverted the progressive self-image of theological liberalism and neoorthodoxy. It challenged the universalist pronouncements of a privileged white male academic establishment. It also engendered a host of deconstructionist, ecological, gay liberation, and other decentering theological critiques.

One theologian in particular bridges the transition from the era of neoorthodox domination to the splintered multiplicity of contemporary theological postmodernism. Langdon Gilkey studied under Niebuhr and Tillich at Union Theological Seminary in the late 1940s and began his theological career as an ardent proponent of a Niebuhr/Tillich/Brunner blend of neoorthodoxy. For ten years he defended this position while accumulating a cluster of private doubts about its coherence. In 1961 his forceful presentation of these doubts shook the foundations of the neoorthodox establishment in biblical studies. Though his own writings were filled with standard neoorthodox references to the "mighty acts of God" in biblical history, Gilkey admitted that he could not explain what the phrase actually meant. He suspected that neoorthodoxy had no answer beyond the answer it inherited from the liberal theology it rejected. Neoorthodox theology took its stand on a principle that vanished upon close inspection.

Gilkey's reflections on this problem and his exposure to the cultural upheavals of the 1960s pushed him to rethink his relation to theological liberalism. In response to the spectacle of death of God theology, his theology took a more deeply Tillichian turn, but this identification with the religiophenomenological approach of his teacher also opened his thought to further influences, especially process philosophy, mythography, Ricoeurian hermeneutical philosophy, philosophy of science, and history of religions scholarship. The middle chapters of the present work offer a close reading of Gilkey's thought and theological career because more than any theologian of the past generation, he has sought to bring the renewable resources of theological liberalism and neoorthodoxy to the problems faced by theology in a postmodern context. His work addresses nearly all of the issues and theological positions that drive the narrative of this book, especially the question of the role of myth in theology. His theology exemplifies the possibility of a different kind of theological liberalism that affirms its rootage in Christian myth. In Gilkey's mature thought the mythical impulse of Tillich's theology is brought forward into a religious situation that is far more chaotic than the contexts in which Tillich wrote, but also more open to the insights of the mythical imagination.

This is the verdict toward which my chapter on postmodernism moves. The spirit of postmodernism is notoriously fragmenting and secular, as chapter 6 shall elaborate; deconstructionist criticism has specialized in Nietzschean pronouncements about the death of presence, meaning, and even truth. In a postmodern situation in which Christendom is a fading memory and the death of the sacred is widely proclaimed, one viable option for theology is the original liberal strategy of seeking to overcome the mythical/sacral consciousness. Stripped of its former home in a sacred cosmos, theology has the option of translating its faith claims into the language of a credible philosophy. Process theology represents this option in my account of the postmodern situation.

The postmodern attack on all forms of foundationalism and stable meaning opens other possibilities for theology, however. Enlightenment rationalism taught that conceptual reason is inherently superior to the mythic imagination as a form of understanding. But with the dethronement of the Enlightenment ideology of universal reason, the way is open for theology to completely overturn the rationalist denigration of myth, imagination, and fictive representation. Here theology affirms and appeals to the mythic imagination as a distinctively generative and revelatory mode of understanding. My account of the trend toward myth-creative approaches to theology focuses on Jungian theory and on recent developments in feminist and ecofeminist theology, especially post-structuralist feminism.

Because so much of Christian myth has been harmful to women and the natural world, some form of myth-criticism is inherent to feminist theology. Feminist theologies expose not only the immorality and injustice of sexist myth, doctrine, and practice, but also the inadequacy of "inclusive" theologies that merely clean up the language of patriarchal religion. Feminist proposals to remythologize Christian teaching are fueled by the recognition that the mythic imagination is both a source of evil in Christianity and the key to a Christian faith that is liberating and life-sustaining. I shall argue that in the form represented by Sallie McFague's metaphorical remythologizing of Christianity, ecofeminist theology also partly mediates a fundamental disagreement in theology that for the past century has fueled other disagreements over the proper role of myth in theology. This deeper disagreement concerns the nature of divine transcendence. Though I shall argue that McFague's approach does not sufficiently recognize the transcendent mystery of God or God's power over nonbeing, it has the considerable virtue of being a fresh and compelling alternative to a long-stalemated debate in theology.

The strange concoction that constitutes my own position is signaled by the title of the last chapter. The postmodern dialectic that I am interested in developing would be a theology of Word and Spirit that is philosophically and discursively pluralistic. It would affirm the mythical character of the gospel while holding fast to the myth-negating message that is implicit in the gospel condemnation of idolatry and the gospel appeal to history. Put differently, it would develop a Barthian argument in a direction quite different from Barth's own purpose, affirming much of his dialectic of Word and Spirit, while rejecting his antifeminism, his reductionistic approach to myth, and his biblicist restriction of the Word to scripture and preaching.

This interpretive work makes no claim to historical completeness, even within its modern Protestant narrative frame. Because the book focuses on problems related to the myth question in theology, it generally excludes theologians who do not address this question. By organizing the narrative according to the paradigms of theological liberalism, crisis theology/neoorthodoxy, and liberationism/postmodernism, it also tends to exclude positions that do not fit into this narrative frame. At the same time, however, one of my purposes in offering a close reading of Gilkey's work is to show how fluid these ruling paradigms can be. Gilkey's theological corpus exemplifies for me the possibility (though not the realization) of a theological perspective that draws upon all of these currents of thought and others, especially history of religions scholarship, without losing its center in the crucified and risen Christ.

The Problem of Biblical Myth

I shall argue for a positive approach to Christian myth, but one problem with this project must be noted at the outset. This is that scripture assumes an explicitly pejorative understanding of myth. The word occurs five times in the New Testament, and never in a positive light. 1 Timothy 1:4 and 4:6–7 equate myth with "old wives' tales" and other vain speculation; 2 Timothy 4:4 warns against the temptation to turn away from truth "and wander away to myths"; Titus 1:14 similarly warns against "paying attention to Jewish myths." Though the latter reference might open the door slightly to the problem of myth in Hebrew scripture, the attitude of the later epistles toward myth as a whole is plainly summarized in 2 Peter 1:16: "For we did not follow cleverly devised myths when we made known to you the power and coming of our Lord Jesus Christ, but we had been eyewitnesses of his majesty."

Here the early church's motive for denouncing the very category of myth is made clear. On the few occasions when the New Testament writers explicitly refer to myth at all, they dismiss it categorically in order to heighten their claim that the message of salvation is grounded in factual occurrence.[1] Acts 26:26 proclaims that God's saving acts in Christ were "not done in a corner." The traditional Christian tendency to regard myth as a primitive mode of discourse devoid of value for teaching truth is thus grounded in the appeal of Jewish and Christian scripture to history as the theater of God's saving action.

Modern theology has not been lacking in movements that embrace this biblical emphasis on the historical character of revelation. The "Biblical Theology" movement of the 1940s through the 1950s was prominent among them. Modern theology has also produced movements that matched the New Testament's disdain for myth as a category. Liberal theology typically derided myth as primitive and unreal. One of the distinguishing marks of modern theology as a whole, however, has been its willingness to recognize that scripture contains at least some mythical material. Even by its own negative conception of myth as fable, some New Testament accounts are plainly mythical. Acts 19:11–12 refers to healings of the sick made possible by contact with pieces of cloth that touched Paul's body; 1 Corinthians 10:4 mentions a rock that followed Moses in the wilderness; Matthew 17:24–27 tells a story about a coin turning up in a fish's mouth. Moreover, the Hebrew scriptures contain ample material of this kind. The biblical stories of the flood and the Tower of Babel are reworked from mythical Babylonian texts; Psalm 74:13–14 recounts that Yahweh smashed the sea monster in two "and broke the heads of the dragons in the waters"; Psalm 95:3 calls the Lord "a great King above all gods." According to Genesis 5:1–32, the antediluvian patriarchs lived an average of 857 years, and in Judges 9:7–15 the prophet Jotham speaks of the trees going forth to anoint a king over them. Elsewhere Hebrew scripture mentions night hags (Isa. 34:14), a day when the sun went backward (Isa. 38:8), and a day when the sun stood still (Josh. 10:13). It contains the wild and crudely legendary exploits of Samson (Judg. 13:1–16:31).

Evangelical theologian Clark Pinnock observes that if we read any of these accounts anywhere else, we would have no difficulty assigning them to the categories of myth and legend.[2] Christian orthodoxy has pretended for too long that because they are contained in scripture, they must be something else. What does it mean for Christian theologians to recognize that scripture contains plainly mythical elements and accounts? What should theologians assume about the possible worthiness of myth as a literary vehicle for God's Word? How should they rethink the possible truth-value of myth or the relation of myth to history? In the course of addressing these questions I shall argue that these questions provide a uniquely instructive guide to the pilgrimage of modern theology.

Myth and the History
of *Religionsgeschichtliche*

There is one approach to these questions that my argument frequently mentions but does not include in its structural scheme. This is the history of religions school of interpretation. The *Religionsgeschichtliche* tradition is formally excluded from my schematism because, despite Troeltsch's efforts to make it one, it has not developed into a normative theological approach. On the other hand, my numerous references to it reflect the considerable influence that this tradition has exercised over modern theological understandings of myth and the sacred. A special word about this tradition is therefore warranted at the outset. The *Religionsgeschichtliche Schule* began as a Göttingen-centered offshoot of the Ritschlian movement in the 1880s and soon developed into a distinctive interpretive school that affirmed its linkages with earlier forms of mythography and world religions comparativism.[3] In its early years it was led by Hermann Gunkel, William Wrede, Wilhelm Bousset, Ernst Troeltsch, and Johannes Weiss. Against Ritschl's liberal/social understanding of the teaching and mission of Jesus, Weiss argued that the historical Jesus had no concept of historical salvation but was fixated instead on the expectation of a history-ending apocalypse from above, the kingdom of God.[4]

By the time that Barth and Bultmann were students at the turn of the century (both studied at Berlin and Marburg), the *Religionsgeschichtliche Schule* was an ascending intellectual movement with strong views about the nature and history of religion in general. Recent converts to its approach included Julius Wellhausen, Rudolf Otto, Ulrich von Wilamowitz-Moellendorff, and Albrecht Dieterich. The history of religions movement argued that cult and liturgy form the experiential center of every religious tradition, not theology; that religious knowledge is transmitted mainly by folklore and oral tradition; that religious experience is essentially irrational in its character; and that most religions (especially early Christianity) are syncretistic blends of various sources and traditions. It taught that religions must be understood according to criteria that do not belong to or derive from any particular religious tradition. It further claimed that when the Christian Bible is approached from an objective, historical perspective, the essentially mythical/eschatological character of biblical religion shows through. Biblical faith is not primarily historical or moral, but mythical, with a strong expectation of the end of history.[5]

Every form of twentieth-century theology has been forced to grapple either directly or indirectly with the impact of this structuralist/historicizing perspective. The *Religionsgeschichtliche* picture of Christianity in the context of world religious history shows up directly in the theologies of Troeltsch, Mathews, Bultmann, Tillich, and Gilkey; indirectly it informs or challenges numerous other theological positions, especially Barthian neoorthodoxy and process theology. Bultmann's early interest in the Hellenistic background to Christianity was inspired by his training under Gunkel (at Berlin) and Weiss (at Marburg); more than a half-century later, Gilkey based much of his revised theological outlook on his appropriation of an approach to myth pioneered by Tillich, Niebuhr, and Mircea Eliade.

The differences in the approach to myth taken by Bultmann and Gilkey are partly attributable to this generational difference between them. In its early years the *Religionsgeschichtliche Schule* spoke of myth primarily as fable or invention; like most nineteenth-century intellectuals, the founders of *Religionsgeschichtliche* criticism generally treated myth as a form of primitive explanation. The seeds of a more positive approach to myth were already present, however, in Wrede's understanding of myth as the use of imagery to express the otherworldly in terms of human relationships. This definition treated myth as a mode of understanding constitutive of religion itself. It prefigured the twentieth-century turn toward a more appreciative sense of myth as a true story that discloses exemplary or sacred truths. This idea of myth as a particular mode of truthful understanding was adopted in various forms of twentieth-century psychology, philosophy, literary criticism, and anthropology. Carl Jung regarded myths as expressions of the deepest truths of the personal and collective unconscious. Ernst Cassirer and Claude Levi-Strauss understood myths as fundamental forms of world-constructing thought.

In theology, Tillich made a powerful case in the 1920s (and afterward) for an understanding of myth as the essential mode of encounter with the sacred. Myth is the universal category of religion as such, he argued; it is an essential component of *all* human thought that takes expression in human concern over the ground and meaning of life. This turn toward the meliorative sense of myth was bolstered in history of religions scholarship by Eliade's epochal works on comparative religion and world religious history. Speaking from a *Religionsgeschichtliche* perspective, he described myth as the narration of a sacred history that "relates an event that took place in primordial Time, the fabled time of the 'beginnings.'" Put differently, myth tells how a reality came into existence through the agency of divine beings, "be it the whole of reality, the Cosmos, or only a fragment of reality." Myth is always a creation account of the true or "real" story behind how something came to *be*, he explained: "In short, myths describe the various and sometimes dramatic breakthroughs of the sacred (or the 'supernatural') into the World. It is this sudden breakthrough of the sacred that really *establishes* the World and makes it what it is today."[6]

Gilkey's definition of myth draws upon these formulations, especially the idea of myth as sacred narrative that relates the "real story" behind the world's reality. Myth is a mode of language that features a distinctive set of elements, referent, and meanings, he proposes. The elements of myth are multivalent symbols that refer in some way to the sacred or transcendent realm and that address the ultimate existential questions of human living and death.[7] As Tillich and Niebuhr maintained, myth is the essential language of religion. Though the present work is careful to explain why certain theologians do not accept or employ this description of myth, my own discussions of Christian myth assume this general understanding.

This is hardly a conventional way to assess or account for the history of modern theology. I keep writing about modern theology not only because I love it and because I have ideas about the direction it should move next, but also because I fear that much of this remarkable tradition will be forgotten if we do not find new ways of telling its story. If the promise of a postmodern theology of Word and Spirit (by whatever name) is to be fulfilled in the next generation, it must critically appropriate not only its biblical and patristic past, but also its modern past. The way beyond modernity is through it.

1

Theology Beyond Myth:
Liberal Christianity

The first Christian thinkers to recognize the mythical aspects of Christian teaching were determined to overcome them. Modern liberal theology was born in the recognition by such thinkers as Immanuel Kant, G.W.F. Hegel, and Friedrich Schleiermacher that the mythical worldview of biblical and orthodox Christian theism was no longer credible as the basis of Christian belief. Kant sought to reestablish the basis of Christianity in moral reason; Hegel developed a philosophy of Absolute Spirit in which the Christian idea was presented as the highest form of religious truth; Schleiermacher located the essence of religion in religious "feeling" *(Gefühl)* or intuition.[1] Liberal theologians afterward variously built upon or appropriated Kant's moralism, Hegel's metaphysical system, and Schleiermacher's theology of religious experience.[2] Many of them argued that the Enlightenment/Romanticist founders of liberal theology gave insufficient attention to the kingdom of God and the social meaning of Christianity. But for nearly two centuries, theological liberalism spoke with one voice in proclaiming that modern Christianity must overcome its mythical inheritance. Liberal theology embraced the modern deprecation of religious myth while claiming that the essence of true Christianity is not mythical. Though they never used the term, the founders of liberal theology thus carried out an epochal program of demythologization.

Liberal theology is the heir of Enlightenment criticism and modern science. Enlightenment thinkers throughout the eighteenth century proposed that the inductive, empirical methodologies of modern natural science should be applied to all fields of knowledge. Many of them argued that religion should not be exempt from the tests of autonomous critical reason. If reason is the only valid authority in science or philosophy, it followed that no respectable claim to religious truth can be based upon any appeal to an authoritative scripture, church, or tradition. Near the end of the self-designated "Age of Reason," Kant declared that to be "enlightened" is to be liberated from a self-incurred tutelage or immaturity. "This immaturity is self-imposed when its cause lies not in lack of under-standing, but in lack of resolve and courage to use it without guidance from another," he asserted. The slogan of the Enlightenment was, therefore, "Have courage to use your own understanding."[3]

To apply the test of "pure" or speculative reason (science) to religion was not only to rule out all "revealed" or authority-based theologies, but also to discard all "natural theologies" that sought to provide a rational groundwork for Christian theism. These included the classical traditions of Christian nat-ural theology as well as the various deist and rationalist theologies recently propounded by Enlightenment defenders of religion. These strategies ap-pealed to reason rather than revelation in making their case for the existence of God, the soul, and eternal life, but Kant argued in the *Critique of Pure Reason* (1781) that unaided theoretical reason is unable to establish the ex-istence of such transcendent realities as God or immortality. Scientific rea-son knows no reality outside the web of sense experience within the space/time continuum, he observed, but the spiritual realities posited by nat-ural theology transcend space and time. The existence of an unconditioned divine being therefore cannot be known or proven by appealing to limited, conditioned, sense-bound theoretical reason.[4]

At the same time, Kant believed that the moral dimension of human ex-perience provides a secure foundation for religion. He observed in *Religion Within the Limits of Reason Alone* (1793) that human beings are not merely creatures of sense experience, but moral agents. Human experience includes a sense of moral obligation that cannot be subsumed or explicated by sense-bound theoretical reason, but which discloses the existence of a constitu-tively human realm of moral value. Kant proposed that this was the true home of religion. Before the Enlightenment, no Christian theologian or philosopher had ever thought of "morality" as a realm independent from re-ligion, but Kant insisted that the sacred narrative of Christianity "must at all times be taught and expounded in the interests of morality." True religion consists "not in the knowing or considering of what God does or has done for our salvation, but in what we must do to become worthy of it."

Kantianism thus saved a place for religion by proposing that the heart of religion is morality. Having subjected the myths and dogmas of Christianity to rational criticism, the enlightened consciousness found little value in the-ology, but it ascribed great value to the function of religion as a source, in-spiration, and guarantor of ethical behavior. Subjectively regarded, Kant argued, true religion is the recognition of all moral duties as divine coun-sels. True religious doctrines emerge from our experience of the moral law and through our struggles to obey it: "They who seek to become well-pleasing to Him not by praising Him (or His envoy, as a being of divine origin) according to revealed concepts which not every man can have, but by a good course of life, regarding which everyone knows His will—these are they who offer Him the true veneration which He deserves."[5]

Religion as Spiritual Feeling:
Schleiermacher

The father of modern liberal theology made a similar, but more creative move. Six years after Kant's great work on religion proposed to provide a home for religion in moral reason, Schleiermacher countered that the wellspring of true religion is spiritual feeling. His great work, *On Religion: Speeches to Its Cultured Despisers* (1799), was addressed immediately to his circle of youthful, highly cultured Romanticist friends in Berlin, where he was a hospital chaplain. Schleiermacher sought to persuade them that true religion is not rooted in doctrine or morality but consists of an immediate relation to the source of life. His background in Moravian piety inspired and shaped his contention that religious experience is the heart of religion. His father was a Reformed church chaplain in the Prussian army who sent his children, during their adolescence, to the Moravian boarding school at Niesky. Friedrich never saw either of his parents again, though he corresponded frequently with his father for many years afterward. He later recalled, in the opening chapter of *On Religion,* that piety was "as it were, the maternal womb in whose sacred obscurity my young life was nourished and prepared for a world still closed to it. Before my spirit had found its distinctive sphere in the search for knowledge and in the mature experience of life, it found its vital breath in piety."[6]

The warm-hearted communal spirituality of the Moravians left its mark on him long after Schleiermacher relinquished their biblical literalism and their belief in Christ's substitutionary atonement. As a student at the Moravian seminary at Barby, he began to question the religious beliefs of his teachers and received an impassioned rebuke from his father for "no longer obeying the truth." Gottlieb Schleiermacher had sent his son to the Moravian Brethren to keep him in the faith, only to learn that Friedrich was reading Goethe on the side and devising his own theology. In his sensitive but pointed reply to his father, Friedrich wrote, "You say that the glorification of God is the end of our being, and I say the glorification of the creature; is not this in the end the same thing?" Schleiermacher later resumed his theological studies at Halle, where he embraced much of Kant's philosophy, but he retained his protoromanticist belief that the glorification of God and the creature are the same thing. In 1790 he was ordained a Reformed minister; six years later, after working at a variety of tutorial and pastoral posts, he began his appointment as Reformed chaplain at Charite hospital. He later recalled that it was religious feeling that sustained him through periods of loneliness and intellectual uncertainty: "As I began to sift out the faith of my fathers and to clear the rubbish of former ages from my thoughts and feelings, piety supported me," he explained. "As the childhood images of God and immortality vanished before my doubting eyes, piety remained." He told his beloved friends that it was only through true religion that he was truly capable of friendship and love.[7]

On Religion made a clean break with all theologies that tied religion to scientific reason or morality. "At the very outset, religion waives all claims to anything belonging to the two domains of science and morality," Schleiermacher declared. "It would now return all that has been either loaned or pressed upon it from those sources."[8] True religion gave up any claims to knowledge about science or morality in order to sustain its distinctive source, realm, and character. Schleiermacher conceived this source as a deep prereflective awareness of reality that underlies all thought and sensation. That is, he believed that religious feeling is a deeper aspect of human experience than theoretical reason, practical reason, or even sensation. His interpretation of feeling thus sought to establish a mediating position between the continental rationalist and Kantian perspectives.

The rationalist tradition regarded feeling as a self-transcending, intentional form of knowledge, but ascribed little value to it. Rationalists such as Leibniz interpreted feeling as a confused and relatively primitive form of knowledge. Kant's attempt to put feeling in its place took the opposite strategy. For Kant, feeling was not a form of knowledge at all, but an autonomous faculty. It was neither self-transcending nor intentional, but consisted of an emotive, noncognitive mode of consciousness that 'knows' no truth beyond psychological experience. Schleiermacher's mediating position ascribed greater value to feeling than either of these perspectives. With the rationalist tradition, he maintained that feeling is a direct, self-transcending apprehension of reality. As Robert Williams observes, Schleiermacher believed that feeling is the general organ of the subject's receptivity and is therefore not reducible to a psychological state. As the preconceptual organ that underlies and makes possible all thought and experience, feeling brings the self into apprehension of the world as a whole; feeling is the immediate presence of "undivided being" that unites the self to his or her world.[9]

At the same time, Schleiermacher argued that feeling is not a lowly form of cognition; it is not a mode of knowing or doing, or even a third faculty alongside the theoretical and practical faculties. Knowing and doing are determinate, mediated modes of consciousness; moreover, Schleiermacher rejected Kant's faculty psychology of the self because it obscured the fundamental *unity* of the self as a whole agent.[10] For Schleiermacher, feeling was self-consciousness as such; it was the autonomous, unifying dimension of the self that prereflectively apprehends the world as a whole. "Feeling" was his term for the prerational apprehension of reality affected by the self in its immediate self-consciousness.[11] This understanding of consciousness as essentially intentional and Schleiermacher's persistent privileging of concreteness over the abstract prefigured the concern of Husserlian phenomenology with "consciousness as such."[12] For Schleiermacher, true religion was essentially contemplative, "the immediate consciousness of the universal being of all finite things in and through the infinite, of all temporal things in and through the eternal." True religion is rooted in an awareness of "the infinite nature of the whole, in the one and all, in God."[13]

This emphasis on totality precluded any suggestion that religion is not related to science and praxis; though he sought to liberate religion from outside pressure and assistance, Schleiermacher did not divorce religious feeling from knowledge or morality. "For what else is science than the existence of things within you, within your reason?" he wrote. "What else is art and culture than your existence in things on which you bestow measure, form, and order? And how can either science or art and culture spring to life for you except insofar as the eternal unity of reason and nature, the universal being of all finite things in the infinite, thrives within you?" Religion is the unifying ground of science and culture, he argued; while it maintains its own life in spiritual experience, it gives life to all regenerative intellectual, cultural, and moral action. "True science is perspective fully achieved; true praxis is art and culture created of oneself; true religion is sense and taste for the infinite," he explained.[14] The irreducible ground of religion is the self's prereflective awareness of its absolute dependence on the eternal ground of being: "To seek and to find this infinite and eternal factor in all that lives and moves, in all growth and change, in all action and passion, and to have and to know life itself only in immediate feeling—that is religion."[15]

True religion therefore does not include beliefs or knowledge about the nature of reality, but consists of the process of appropriating the effects of "the amazing plentitude of life." Schleiermacher's metaphors for the religious life were unfailingly organic, totalistic, relational, and affective. He warned that as soon as one attempts to isolate or break down the particular factors that represent the infinite, one moves out of the religious sphere. All attempts to synthesize religion and science inevitably reduce religion to mythology or mysticism. To be religious is "to feel all that moves us in our feeling, in the supreme unity of it all, as one and the same, and to feel all that is individual and particular as mediated only through that unity," he explained. That is, to be religious is "to feel our being and life as a being and life in and through God."[16]

This organic, totalizing, relational understanding of the religious field excluded all theologies that conceptualized God as a separate being or a "bit of knowledge." Schleiermacher insisted that it was "vain mythology" to make God an object of thought. He rarely used the term "mythology" without an accompanying "vain" or "empty" qualifier. With regard to the divine object of religious experience, he argued, it was "absolutely empty mythology" to conceive God as one object of knowledge among others.[17] God is not an hypostatized being outside the world of human experience and natural causality, he urged; God is the power of all being and ultimate unity of the world. The God who is known in true religion is therefore not known "in any other way than through these stirrings which the world brings forth in us."[18] Put differently, it is "vain mythology" to separate God and the world: "We do not feel ourselves dependent on the whole insofar as it is a collocation of mutually conditioning parts of which we are ourselves one," he contended. "We feel the dependence only insofar as a unity determining everything, including our relation to every other part, underlies the coinherence of the world."[19] True religion is "a sense and taste for the infinite" that finds the eternal factor at work in all that lives and has being.

By removing religion from the field of contested claims about theoretical knowledge and morality, Schleiermacher sought to extricate true religion from the confusions and pretensions of myth. He defined mythology as "a purely ideal object explicated in the form of history."[20] For the past century, Enlightenment thinkers had assumed that mythical forms should be interpreted as erroneous attempts to explain or describe matters of fact. Immanuel Kant and David Hume routinely denigrated mythical language for its promotion and sacralization of superstition, misinformation, and immorality. To the Enlightenment rationalist mind, enlightenment was synonymous with the debunking and correction of all mythical forms. Schleiermacher's deprecation of myth shared much of the spirit of this tradition, but his experiential interpretation of religion opened modern theology to the possibility of a more sympathetic understanding of myth than he or his Enlightenment forerunners could sanction.

He observed that Christian mythology and the myths of ancient polytheistic religion were basically similar in their essential claims and forms. Monotheistic and ancient polytheistic mythologies both claimed to possess knowledge about something that is happening or has happened within the divine being, "notably, divine decrees touching something going on in the world or modifying previous divine decrees, to say nothing of those special divine decrees that enter into the notion of answered prayer." This is the heart of mythical religion, he instructed; any religious perspective that conceives God as an outside being who interferes in history or natural events is by definition mythological. Schleiermacher did not propose that all of the mythical aspects of traditional Christian teaching should be expunged from theology; what was needed in theology was simply a recognition that the mythical aspects of Christian language and doctrine are mythical. "There is no particular danger in using mythological language in scientific discourse about religion, since, on the whole, the standard procedure there is to move away from the form of temporality and the specific contents of history anyway," he reasoned.[21]

Scientific understanding is inherently demythologizing in its spirit and impact. The mere recognition that Christian teaching is to some extent inevitably mythical is a crucial protection against superstition in Christian teaching and practice, Schleiermacher argued. Moreover, mythical language is indispensable in poetic and rhetorical forms of discourse. If the heart of religion is in religious experience rather than any doctrinal or scientific account of religion, it follows that doctrinal and scientific forms of discourse are severely limited in their capacity to grasp, judge, or express religious truth. Poetic and rhetorical modes of language are much better suited to express the truths of religious experience, even though these forms of discourse inevitably employ language about God's "will" and historical "actions" that are mythical. Schleiermacher argued that the best approach to the problem of myth is therefore not to censure all mythical language, but to use it with a critical awareness of its limitations and evocative capacities. He believed that the wisdom of this approach would be evident to all genuinely religious and discerning people, for in such persons "the tendency to make allowances for defective expressions is already built in."[22]

He lamented at the turn of the century that such people could be found only among "the cultured sons and daughters of Germany." His early writings were addressed to the liberal, well-educated, aesthetically sensitive despisers of religion, not only because his closest friends were numbered among them, but further because he judged that only they were capable of attaining true religion. The English were too greedy and power-seeking to be religious, he opined; they cared only about things that enhanced their wealth and position; moreover, their corrupt state religion was religiously antiquated and morally bankrupt. As for the French, he reported, "One who honors religion can scarcely bear to look their way." The French were unspeakably rude, arrogant, and flippant; their self-absorbed incapacity for piety was confirmed in "their every word almost." Schleiermacher thus invested his hope for an awakening of the sacred in the highly cultured children of Goethe, Kant, and Beethoven, in the midst of perhaps the greatest flowering of cultural achievement in German history. "Only here in my native land do we find a climate suitable enough for everything meaningfully human to grow and flourish, if only in scattered fashion," he wrote in 1799. "Here all that humanly prospers somewhere attains its finest form, in a few individuals at least."[23]

Schleiermacher called them to recognize the religious source of their life and art; he invited them to open themselves to the "glorious feeling of our relationship to the whole."[24] The cultured children of modern Germany were predisposed to reject Christianity because the church identified Christianity with the vain mythology of the West's prescientific past. In a scientific age, true Christianity can be recovered only if one begins with the recognition that Christian myth is mythical, Schleiermacher urged. Though myth is indispensable as an evocative mode of language that gives expression to ineffable religious experiences, the heart of true religion itself is not mythical. True religion is the sacred human longing for relation to the whole. It is the highest development of feeling, the fulfillment of all that is good in the human spirit. Put differently, Schleiermacher argued in his later dogmatics, the fulfillment of true religion comes about only through the realization and mobilization of God-consciousness, as epitomized by Jesus, the embodiment of constantly potent God-consciousness.[25]

Schleiermacher as
Church and University Theologian

This spiritual perspective was maintained and developed with remarkable consistency throughout Schleiermacher's theological career. After a brief period as a pastor in Stolpe, Pomerania, he was appointed professor and university preacher at Halle in 1804, only to witness the destruction and humiliation of Halle by Napoleon's army two years later. Schleiermacher's university was dissolved; his church was turned into a grain store; and his house was ransacked and occupied by French troops. His Prussian patriotism soared in response.

Though he vowed at first to remain in Halle as long as he had potatoes and salt, the futility of this gesture soon became apparent to him (as Halle was granted to Westphalia), and Schleiermacher returned to Berlin, the Prussian capital, in 1807. Two years later he became pastor of Berlin's prestigious Trinity Church, where he remained an every-week preacher for the rest of his life. This pulpit became the focal point of his numerous academic, political, and ecclesiastical efforts to renew Prussian life and culture. Schleiermacher used his pulpit unabashedly as a forum for Prussian resistance to Napoleon, and in 1813, when Napoleon's forces retreated from Russia in defeat, Schleiermacher exhorted his students on to Breslau to join the rout of the vanquished invaders.[26]

His students came from the University of Berlin, which Schleiermacher helped to found in 1810 and which he served as professor and dean of the theological faculty. In 1815 he was appointed rector of the university. The work of establishing a new university moved him to rethink how theology should be taught at a post-Enlightenment university. Some influential thinkers, notably the philosopher J. G. Fichte, strongly questioned whether theology deserved its own department in a modern university. Schleiermacher's response was published a year after the university opened. This slender volume, *Brief Outline of the Study of Theology* (1811), presented a rigorous argument for the teaching of theology as a unified, integral academic discipline that, as he insisted, surely belonged in the curriculum of a modern university. It proposed that the discipline of theology should be divided into three distinct but interrelated fields, which he called philosophical theology, historical theology, and practical theology.[27] For many German universities afterward, Schleiermacher's curriculum at Berlin presented the model of how theological knowledge should be organized and taught.

As a theologian who was also a university dean and rector, he was compelled to explain why Christianity should be privileged over other religious traditions as the object of academic study and personal faith. The same question arose in his work as a pastor. Schleiermacher's sermons occasionally touched on this question, but his developed answer to it was presented in his dogmatic system, *The Christian Faith* (1821, 1830), which appealed to a stage theory of religious consciousness. He graded religions in the same way that he identified stages of animal life and grades of consciousness. Schleiermacher argued that Christianity is superior to other religions not because all other religions are false, but because they represent less-developed forms of religious truth. "Only the true, and not the false, can be a basis of receptivity for the higher truth of Christianity," he instructed. Some religions are too similar to Christianity to be entirely false. Moreover, he reasoned, if the more primitive religions contained nothing but error, how was it possible for human communities of the past to move from these religions to Christianity? "The whole delineation which we are here introducing is based rather on the maxim that error never exists in and for itself, but always along with some truth, and that we have never fully understood it until we have discovered its connexion with truth, and the true thing to which it is attached," he explained. All religions are true insofar as they are rooted in piety, which is the consciousness of absolute dependence, "or, which is the same thing, of being in relation with God."

In any moment or state of consciousness, we are aware not only of our unchanging identity, but also of its changing, variable character. Schleiermacher argued that this experience discloses the two main constitutive elements of self-consciousness. Self-consciousness always includes a self-caused element (ein Sichselbstsetzen) and a non-self-caused element (ein Sichselbstnichtsogesetzthaben), which he called, respectively, the Ego and the Other. The first element of self-consciousness expresses the subject for itself, while the second element expresses the coexistence of the ego with an other. It is this double constitution of self-consciousness that makes possible the feeling of absolute dependence.

Schleiermacher explained that the conscious self is constituted only in relation to an other; the ground of self-consciousness is the element of its openness to an other. We exist as affective, active, self-conscious creatures only in coexistence with an other. On the one hand, therefore, the feeling of dependence is common to all determinations of self-consciousness that express predominantly an affective condition of receptivity, but on the other hand, he observed, the feeling of freedom is common to all determinations that express predominantly movement and change. The feelings of dependence and freedom are thus ultimately one "in the sense that not only the subject but the corresponding Other is the same for both."[28] The totality of all moments of the feelings of dependence and freedom comprise a single reality that corresponds in reciprocal relation to an other that makes self-consciousness possible. "Hence a feeling of absolute dependence, strictly speaking, cannot exist in a single moment as such, because such a moment is always determined, as regards its total content, by what is given, and thus by objects towards which we have a feeling of freedom," Schleiermacher argued. But self-consciousness is also always awareness of absolute dependence, "for it is the consciousness that the whole of our spontaneous activity comes from a source outside of us in just the same sense in which anything towards which we should have a feeling of absolute freedom must have proceeded entirely from ourselves."[29]

This was the basis of his language about divine reality. Rather than begin with some notion of God's actuality derived from scripture, tradition, or reason, he proposed that theology should secure a stronger ground for its theorizing by focusing on God's possibility and the limits of the human spiritual relation. For Schleiermacher, Christian theology was human reflection necessitated by the Christ-relation that reposes in a person's feelings of utter dependence on God. Theology begins with and reads off of piety; it presupposes the affective condition of persons in their feeling or innermost self-consciousness. Just as religion is immediate self-consciousness, the dependency and actualization of a self that is grounded in feeling and involved in thinking and willing, so is Christian theology the positive self-conscious employment of language by the subject of religious feeling. Religion stands for a person's position as the being on whom God and world converge. God is not a being, but rather that which holds all being together, giving integrity to all things.

Theology of Experience

The doctrine that God is knowable as the power and unity of being is an experiential claim. It is also the only kind of claim that belongs in a system of Christian doctrine, Schleiermacher argued. God-language is credible only as a report from experience. That is, the business of theology is to explicate those religious claims that are generated and supported directly by piety. Schleiermacher took this principle seriously enough to consign the Trinity to the epilogue of his dogmatics.[30] He allowed that classical Christian theism was not necessarily wrong in its claims about the nature or inner life of divine reality, but he insisted that the classical/orthodox tradition was certainly wrong to base its doctrinal claims on scripture, tradition, or metaphysical argument. With remarkably little discussion of premodern Christian theology, he therefore set aside its dogmatic and metaphysical claims about God. Theology properly explicates only that with which it has direct knowledge, he urged, which is religious experience. Neither revealed doctrine nor metaphysical reason brings us into genuine contact with the original signification of the word "God," but through piety God is knowable as the *Whence* of our receptive and active awareness of existence. As an idea, "God" expresses the feeling of absolute dependence. "In the first instance God signifies for us simply that which is the co-determinant in this feeling and to which we trace our being in such a state; and any further content of the idea must be evolved out of this fundamental import assigned to it," he explained.[31]

There is no difference between feeling one's absolute dependence and being conscious of one's relational existence with God, because all possible relationships are included in the fundamental relation of absolute dependence. Schleiermacher allowed that revelational language could still be used to speak of the God known through feeling, but only if it is understood to mean that human beings are given immediate self-consciousness of the absolute dependence of all temporal existence, which becomes God-consciousness. He measured piety by the constancy and intensity of a person's consciousness of the Whence of all existence. Though his dogmatics adopted much of the classical symbolism and style that his earlier writings spurned, *The Christian Faith* insisted even more stringently than his early writings that to worship God as a being given to thought is idolatry. Schleiermacher renounced all attempts to prove the truth of Christianity. God is not a being about whom we possess bits of information apart from feeling, he repeatedly cautioned; God is rather the unifying ground of all relations known through the experience of absolute dependence. As the Whence of utter dependence, God is the presupposition of all searching for truth. Schleiermacher's theology thus developed a novel form of the ontological approach to religion, in which the identical relation between God and truth makes God the necessary presupposition of all truth.

But he did not believe that the experience of God as the Whence of utter dependence is the sole ground of Christian certainty. Christianity is more than one example among others of true religion. Like every nineteenth-century liberal after him, Schleiermacher resorted to an "essence of Christianity" argument to explicate what this "more" might be. He taught that the essence of any faith is discernible only by finding the affective element that is both distinctive to it and constant within all variable expressions of it. This criterion posed special problems for interpreters of Christianity. Schleiermacher observed that the essence of Christianity has been distorted by centuries of dogmatic teaching and obscured by the bewildering profusion of rival confessional traditions within the Christian tradition. He argued that a spiritual center was nevertheless discernible in the welter of Christian overdefinition, distortion, and multiplicity, which he called the "redeeming influence" of Christ. Every form of Christianity is rooted not merely in Christ, he explained, but in some experience and understanding of the redemptive influence of Christ. Every form of Christianity speaks in some way of Christ aiding or making possible the passage from sin or captivity to righteousness.

He gave short shrift to the various juridical models of salvation advanced by patristic and medieval Christianity. For Schleiermacher, sin was anything that interferes with or arrests God-consciousness; in its extreme form, evil is not a state of disobedience to God, but a state of God-forgetfulness. "We must not think this means a state in which it is quite impossible for the God-consciousness to be kindled," he cautioned. "For if that were so, then, in the first place, the lack of a thing which lay outside of one's nature could not be felt to be an evil condition; and in the second place, a re-creating in the strict sense would then be needed in order to make good this lack, and that is not included in the idea of redemption."[32] The possibility of being transformed from a state of arrested God-consciousness to a state of potent God-consciousness remains in reserve even for those who by their wickedness suppress the truth and worship idols (Rom. 1:18, 23).

It is in its focus and emphasis upon redemption through Christ that Christianity is fundamentally distinguished from other world religions, he argued. In other religions, redemption always appears as a derivative aspect of a controlling doctrine or institution, but in Christianity "the redeeming influence of the Founder is the primary element, and the communion exists only on this presupposition, and as a communication and propagation of that redeeming activity."[33] Christianity is distinguished by the preeminence it ascribes to the redeeming work of Christ and the corresponding value it gives to the experience of redemption in piety. As the unique embodiment of constantly potent God-consciousness, Jesus creates and embodies the possibility of salvation. The first desire of every uncorrupted heart is to become good, Schleiermacher explained elsewhere, "but to become good, we need an example we can always rely on." Only a perfect example of the good can adequately guide our feeling and inspire our reason in the direction of the good. "And it is Christ who gives us this sublime example," he claimed. "His whole life was nothing but an unbroken series of deeds for the good of humankind, reaching as far as the circle of influence in which his circumstances placed him. He spent the best years of his life going around among the fallen, though for the most part they were ungrateful, to preach the truth to them and

to practice virtue among them. Never discouraged by mockery, disdain, persecution, or misinterpretation of his purest motives, his virtue remained ever constant. Everywhere he sought out misery to alleviate it with his gentle healing
hand, as he alone always could."[34]

Christ the redeemer was for Schleiermacher the image of perfected humanity, "the image of a soul constantly at one with God." Because Christ gave himself for us and became ours, we are able through his indwelling presence to
become one with him "and his righteousness is seen as ours, so that we are
justified through faith in him."[35] Schleiermacher understood redemption as the
removal of sin from our consciousness by divine love. This was the key to his
understanding of Christ as redeemer. The love that Christ bears for us is divine,
he observed, "and it is this very divine love that he ignites in our hearts"
through his perfectly God-conscious influence.[36] Because Christ is "the real origin of constant living unhindered evocation of the God-consciousness,"
Schleiermacher argued that it is appropriate and necessary that Christ should
be exalted exclusively over others. At the same time he cautioned that an essential likeness between Christ and all others must exist "because otherwise
what He has to impart could not be the same as what they need."[37]

What they need is fellowship with God, which God-consciousness does not
assure. While others may be truly religious through their awareness of dependence, true fellowship with God is possible only through the mediating influence of the redeemer. "The distinctive feature of Christian piety lies in the fact
that whatever alienation from God there is in the phases of our experience, we
are conscious of it as an action originating in ourselves, which we call Sin; but
whatever fellowship with God there is, we are conscious of it as resting upon
a communication from the Redeemer, which we call Grace," he explained.[38]
Following Calvin, Schleiermacher taught that sin-consciousness comes into existence only through God-consciousness. Human beings come into awareness
of their sin only after their God-consciousness has been awakened. But to
Christian experience, there is no relation to God (and therefore no awareness
of sin) that is not bound up with Christ's redeeming influence: "In the actual
life of the Christian, therefore, the two are always found in combination: there
is no general God-consciousness which has not bound up with it a relation to
Christ, and no relationship with the Redeemer which has no bearing on the
general God-consciousness."[39] Thus we owe to Christ the salvation from sin
that his redeeming influence has brought to our awareness. "If in our weakness we are aware of the consolation that God is mighty in the weak, that he
aids us in manifold ways, and that he promotes our salvation, then it is because
of the religion that Jesus gives us."[40]

Because we experience Christ as love, we know that God is love. Because
we experience Christ as redeemer, we know that we are sinners under God's
judgment and grace. This was the basis of Schleiermacher's theological method.
To him, the church was called not to be the institutional guardian of revealed
doctrine, but the Christ-following community in which God-consciousness is

the determining power. "Christ was sent to us so that we should follow in his footsteps: to him belongs a heart that he alone can fill," he claimed.[41] Schleiermacher lamented that so many children of the Enlightenment were scorning "the element of mystery that seems to be inseparable from the religion of Jesus." He countered that it is better to remain faithful to Christ than to mock what we do not understand. In their "proud delusions," the cultured despisers of Christianity were failing to acknowledge that even their weaker lights were borrowed from Christ. "The truths which they attribute to reason's own speculations have been spread abroad only through Christianity," he admonished.[42] A liberal Western culture that was serious about moving forward would not try to leave behind its formative spiritual center.

Liberal Theology as a Modernist Strategy

David Friedrich Strauss later remarked that Schleiermacher's theology was held together by a single doctrine, the dogma of the person of Christ.[43] Like much else that Strauss wrote in his withering critiques of Schleiermacher, this assertion was both discerning and not quite right. Though he died shortly before the publication of Strauss's *Life of Jesus Critically Examined* (1835) set off an explosive debate about the historical foundations of Christianity, Schleiermacher's theology was carefully constructed to appropriate the most radical historical criticism of his generation. He was well acquainted with the past century of critical-biblical scholarship, beginning with H. S. Reimarus's pioneering essays of the 1750s through the 1760s, which were published anonymously after Reimarus's death by G. E. Lessing after Lessing discovered them in the Wolfenbuttel library. Reimarus's *Wolfenbuttel Fragments* went beyond the usual rationalist critiques of the biblical miracle stories; he presented Jesus as a misguided prophet who mistakenly predicted the immanent arrival of the kingdom of God and whose brief career ended in tragic defeat.[44] Modern New Testament criticism began with Reimarus's radical deconstruction of the gospel narrative. By the time that Strauss began to work on his epochal critique of Christian origins more than a half-century later, a substantial literature of rationalist and mythical criticism of the Bible existed, especially in the writings of Johann Gottfried Eichhorn, Wilhelm Martin Leberecht de Wette, Gottlieb Philipp Christian Kaiser, Heinrich August Wilhelm Meyer, J. F. Leopold George, Johann Carl Ludwig Gieseler, and Strauss's teacher, Ferdinand Christian Baur.[45]

Schleiermacher developed his theology during the very period when this body of critical literature became too substantial for any serious theologian to ignore. Though his deeper concern was always to mitigate rationalist critiques of the Trinity, the incarnation, the atonement, and other Christian doctrines, Schleiermacher's theology was carefully gauged not to come into conflict with the negative results of contemporary biblical criticism. It was his distinction between the religious reality of living faith and its outmoded doctrinal expressions that gave Christian theology a new beginning in the face of its various challenges from modern science, Enlightenment philosophy, and historical criticism. By expounding piety as the essence of religion, he found a home for religion that was safe from the blasts of scientific and rationalist criticism. By expounding Christianity as a religion based on the experience of redemption through Christ, he saved the heart of the gospel faith without committing Christianity to any particular doctrinal or historical claims.

His theology invested no importance or necessity in the historicity of God's miraculous deliverance of the Hebrews from slavery, or God's audible words to the prophets, or God's literal resurrection of Jesus from the dead. Though he clung to the tradition that the author of his favorite gospel, the gospel of John, was John the son of Zebedee, Schleiermacher was otherwise prepared to accept the negative historical results of contemporary scholarship.[46] His statements on the resurrection of Jesus were so obscure that Albert Schweitzer later interpreted him as teaching that Christ's resurrection was a case of "reanimation after apparent death."[47] This reading was mistaken, for Schleiermacher never doubted that Jesus died on the cross. Against various rationalist believers in the resuscitation theory, he countered that "we cannot represent him as those do who maintain the hypothesis of an apparent death. We cannot think of him as spending this time with his life force at a low ebb."[48] As Schweitzer rightly perceived, however, Schleiermacher did not believe that anything important was at stake in the question whether Jesus was raised from the dead. To him, the crucial claim of the gospel was the spiritual significance of Christ's redeeming death rather than any claim about the historicity or meaning of the Easter appearances. Christianity needed no other foundation than the experience of Christ's redeeming influence and example.

Contrary to Strauss, however, Schleiermacher was not a thoroughgoing Christocentrist in his defense of this doctrine. For him, Christianity was the ultimate or absolute religion; Schleiermacher never understood Christ in any way as the negation of religion. B. A. Gerrish aptly observes that in the precise sense of the term, Christocentrism was therefore never an option for Schleiermacher.[49] Throughout his dogmatics, Schleiermacher persistently argued that the Christian life is sustained by a general religious God-consciousness and a special relation to Christ. Though he was always concerned to persuade his readers that the religion they needed was Christianity, Schleiermacher's theology was generally stronger as a defense of religion than as a persuasive argument for choosing Christianity. Though he unfailingly claimed that Christianity is the highest religion, his theology was based upon a particular argument about the integrity of religious experience.

His definition of theology in *Brief Outline on the Study of Theology* (1810) put the matter plainly. "Theology is a positive science, whose parts join into a cohesive whole only through their common relation to a particular mode of faith, i.e., a particular way of being conscious of God," he wrote.[50] Theology is a *positive* science because it follows from the *given* of God-consciousness—an essence that is "positive" because it takes historical forms. Schleiermacher thus found a secure home for theology in the reality of religious experience, but at the price of making his argument for Christianity secondary to his defense of religion. A century later, near the end of the reign of theological liberalism in the United States, Yale theologian D. C. Macintosh objected that Schleiermacher's theology thus unwittingly implied that Christianity is merely one religious option among others.[51] On Schleiermacher's terms, Christianity should be chosen only if it brings greater spiritual edification than the alternatives.

This approach to theology was so influential in liberal Protestantism that by 1865 Strauss observed that even ecclesiastical authorities were taking refuge in it. It was also the kind of religious halfway house that Strauss abhorred. In his early writings, Strauss sought to destroy all theologies that mediated between supernatural Christianity and the modern consciousness. His pursuit of this project in the mid-1830s cost him any hope of attaining an academic position in theology. For several years, Strauss defended his perspective in a furious barrage of articles and books—and then turned away from theology. For 20 years he wrote no theology at all. When Schleiermacher's lectures on the life of Jesus were published belatedly in 1865, however, 33 years after he had delivered them at Tübingen, Strauss found a reason to return to his first passion. This was where he had come in. He found that little had changed in three decades. He declared that Schleiermacher's theology was significant because it was the last great attempt "to make the churchly Christ acceptable to the modern world."[52]

Liberal theology was still living off this achievement. Strauss observed that Schleiermacher's picture of Christ as 'a soul constantly at one with God' was surviving the assaults of modern historical criticism upon the gospel texts, "but only because it does not originate with these texts."[53] The liberal picture of Christ as the image of perfected humanity is not a biblical image, he explained, but a modern substitute for the biblical picture prefigured by Plato, Spinoza, and Kant. Strauss was incredulous that Schleiermacher could have recognized so much of the mythical character of Christianity while retaining his desire "for a personal Christ who existed historically." This remnant of the old faith kept him confused and conflicted. Schleiermacher knew that modern criticism was right; he wrote with great feeling about spiritual freedom; but he chose to cling to a fantasized Redeemer. "He senses the danger which, coming from the power of the modern ideas which he permitted to permeate himself, threatens the fragment of faith which he has carried over from the past and does not want to give up for anything," Strauss explained. Schleiermacher's Christ was only a memory from a long-forgotten time, like the light of a burned-out star that still appears to the eye.[54] Stronger souls would not seek to save a mythical Christ after the historical Jesus was demythologized, Strauss assured: "We may no longer, like Schleiermacher, speak of a redeemer after we have given up the God-man who offered himself as a sacrifice for the sins of the world."[55]

Lessing once complained that the pressure to make Christianity reasonable was turning many of his contemporaries into bad philosophers.[56] Nearly a century later, in the later years of his own stormy intellectual career, Strauss embraced Lessing's view that the real choice was between orthodox Christianity and rational science; liberal Christianity was a contradiction in terms. Strauss's last book finally repudiated Christianity altogether. In *The Old Faith and the New* (1872), he argued that we do not know enough about Jesus to make him an object of faith, and what we *do* know is that he was an apocalyptic prophet who cannot be our model. "The evangelists have overlaid the picture of his life with so thick a coat of supernatural coloring, have confused it by so many cross lights of contradictory doctrine, that the natural colors cannot now be restored," he observed. But even if the historical Jesus could be recovered, it wouldn't matter. The important questions today deal with science, technology, the fine arts, and practical politics, Strauss contended, but Jesus has no relevance to any of this. By every reckoning, liberal Christianity was therefore losing its claim to coherence. The old faith was absurd, but at least it didn't contradict itself; liberal Christianity was doubly absurd because it contradicted both reason and itself.[57]

Thus did Strauss finally dispense with Schleiermacher's Christianity, a generation after his first book on the life of Jesus made Schleiermacher's lectures on this subject obsolete. If his assessment of Schleiermacher's theological achievement suffered from more than a bit of jealous resentment, his scorching critique of Schleiermacher's relation to biblical Christianity showed nonetheless why Schleiermacher's subjectivism would not be enough to sustain liberal theology. Strauss suffered for his demolition of biblical history; in light of the bitter disappointments that he suffered for deconstructing the sacred narrative, it is surprising only that his repudiation of Christianity took so many years to complete. Strauss was slow to reject Christianity altogether because during the crucial period of his intellectual career, when the controversy over his biblical criticism made him notorious, he was deeply committed to another kind of liberal Christianity. The wellspring of his early biblical criticism was his attachment to the promise of Hegelian theology. He believed that the truths of Christianity were absorbed and transcended in Hegelian philosophy. It would take nearly forty years for Strauss to give up the last remnant of his hope that Hegelian philosophy might salvage some part of Christian myth. Strauss undoubtedly realized that his best works were inspired by this conviction, that the meaning of history is never historical, but philosophical.

David Friedrich Strauss and
the Radical Hegelian Alternative

Strauss gleaned some of his convictions from his teacher, F. C. Baur, with whom he studied at the Wurrtemberg lower seminary in Blaubeuren from 1821 to 1825. The following year, Baur accepted a teaching position at Tübingen, where Strauss was again his most promising student. For a brief period during his studies at Tübingen, Strauss identified with Schleiermacher's theology; he was closely involved with a group of Romanticist-leaning, poetry loving, intellectually intense friends at both Blaubeuren and Tübingen who looked to Schleiermacher for religious guidance. Aside from Baur, this group took little instruction from the faculty, which was mediocre. Strauss studied the mystical writings of Jacob Boehme and Friedrich Christian Oetinger, as well as the idealism of J. G. Fichte and the idealistic nature philosophy of Baur's favorite philosopher, Friedrich Schelling. His turning point occurred in 1829, however, when he and his friends made a close study of Hegel's *Phenomenology of Spirit* and resolved to become Hegelians.[58]

This conversion threw them into uncharted territory. None of their professors knew Hegel's philosophy, including Baur. Did they know what they were doing? If they became Hegelians, what would it mean for their theological and clerical careers? Was Hegelian idealism a substitute faith? Was it a preachable faith in Christian pulpits? Strauss's friends struggled with these questions for several years, especially after they became pastors, but Strauss told them not to worry. He was serving a church in Kleiningersheim and his sermons were going well. Though he tried to minimize his use of traditional Christian language, he realized that his congregation wasn't ready for Hegel. He therefore used as much of the traditional picture language of Christianity as seemed necessary to the task, while introjecting as much of its Hegelian meaning as seemed prudent into his sermons. "When I considered how far even in intellectual preaching the expression is inadequate to the true essence of the concept, it does not seem to me to matter much if one goes even a step further," he reported. "I at least go about the matter without the least scruple, and cannot ascribe this to a mere want of sincerity in myself." Schweitzer later found this a showcase example of Hegelian logic.[59]

Strauss was not as sure of his position as he made out, however. One of his letters to Christian Märklin conceded that Märklin's troubled conscience over "this whole game with images instead of concepts" might be justified.[60] Strauss's doctoral dissertation on the doctrine of immortality contained other clues. Though he identified himself as a "radical Hegelian" in the dissertation, his argument for a monistic identity between God and the world was closer to Schelling's idealism or Spinoza's pantheism than to Hegel's forward-looking historical dialectic. Strauss later claimed to a friend that he stopped believing in the dissertation's argument for immortality at the moment he penned its final period.[61] In September 1831, after less than a year in parish ministry and after winning the faculty prize at Tübingen for a dissertation he didn't believe, Strauss took a sabbatical in Berlin to attend Hegel's lectures. He sought to resolve the various tensions between his confused philosophical worldview and his religious vocation by speaking with Hegel directly. But on November 15th, after only one meeting with Hegel and a few lectures, Strauss met Schleiermacher for the first time—who told him that Hegel had died of cholera the night before. Strauss was devastated, though he may not have cried out, as in the often-told tale about him, that he had come to Berlin only to study with Hegel. Schweitzer later remarked that if the story was true, it showed a certain want of tact on Strauss's part, considering the identity of his informant.[62] In either case, there is no doubt that Strauss went to Berlin as an aspiring Hegelian.[63] In his disappointment, he made contacts with Hegel's leading disciples, especially Philipp Marheineke and Leopold Henning, and established friendships with younger Hegelians such as Karl Michelet, Agathon Benary, and Wilhelm Vatke.[64] He also attended Schleiermacher's lectures and sermons through the spring term. It was during this period of creative dislocation that Strauss conceived the idea for a radical book on the historical Jesus and the future of theology.

As a student Strauss had been exposed to Baur's work on symbolism and myth in antiquity, as well as Baur's developing perspective on biblical criticism and Christian history. He accepted Baur's credo that without philosophy, history is "eternally dead and mute."[65] The death of Hegel drove Strauss to find his own perspective within the conflation of sources that he already possessed. Through Baur he had been exposed to Schelling's philosophical idealism, which conceptualized history as "a continuous, gradually self-disclosing revelation of the absolute."[66] The possibility that philosophy might absorb and improve Christian doctrine thus appealed to Strauss initially through his teacher's enthusiasm for Schelling's idealism. If history was the processive revelation of the divine will or absolute ideal, it followed that all of the subject matter of religion belonged also to philosophy. Baur's *Symbolik und Mythologie* embraced this conclusion, proclaiming that religion and philosophy share the same content and absolute.[67] Strauss relinquished this belief in his later career, when he rejected Christianity altogether, but it was the idealism of Schelling, Baur, and especially Hegel that provided the basis for the constructive religious philosophy that he sought to develop in his early writings.

Hegel's distinction between *Vorstellung* (image or religious imagery) and *Begrif* (philosophical Concept) defined the heart of the matter for young Strauss. By classifying all religious thinking as representational in nature, he reasoned, Hegel had explained why religious thought is inevitably lower and less sophisticated than philosophical thinking. Moreover, this distinction established the reason why philosophy must seek to save theology by replacing it. Strauss's exposure to the Hegelian theologians at Berlin soon convinced him that they were not prepared to carry out the superrogatory mission of philosophy in its relation to theology, however. To many of his leading disciples, whom Strauss later dubbed "the right-wing Hegelians," Hegel's idealism was a speculative appropriation and reinterpretation of the Christian doctrine of the incarnation. Hegelian theologians such as Philipp Marheineke, Karl Rosenkranz, and Carl Friedrich Göschel understood Hegelianism to be a philosophical interpretation of the Christian teaching that by entering history in the crucified Christ, God has taken on the suffering of the world in order to redeem it. Strauss shared the "right-Hegelian" belief that Hegel's idealism contained the key to the future and credibility of Christian theology, but he was critical of the theologies that Marheineke and others were producing. This dissatisfaction was the stimulus to his early work.[68]

The Hegelian Idea

Hegelianism sought to answer the ancient fundamental question of what constitutes human knowledge of the particulars of the world external to consciousness. Kant's critical idealism was the last great "rationalistic" attempt to answer the question; it was the problem analyzed in his theory of the categories and further explicated in the schematism of the *Critique of Pure Reason*. Kant's philosophy attempted to explain how such diverse entities as the particulars of the external world and the pure concepts of mind could be related. He found the relationship in the universal applicability of time, for both the particulars of the external world and the pure concepts of the mind exist in time. Space and time are not realities that reason apprehends in the world, but the essential preconditions of thought itself. Human reason makes sense of the world by applying its a priori categories to all phenomena perceived by the senses.[69]

Hegel did not so much dispute this solution to the problem of the possibility of knowledge as contend that the question itself, as posed by Kant, was inappropriate. In Kantian philosophy, he observed, the question only arises in a relatively primitive mode of self-consciousness that sees the distinction between form and content as real and true in the world. Hegel countered that the proper form of consciousness is one that recognizes in the Category the complete unity of particularity and universality, for the concepts of the mind are universals. It followed for Hegel that there is no rational basis for dichotomizing between subject and object, or form and content; rather, the world only exists as the externalization of self-consciousness, and conversely, self-consciousness only exists as a recognized shape of this world as Spirit. As he observed in the *Phenomenology of Spirit*, "Reason is spirit, when its certainty of being all reality has been raised to the level of truth, and reason is *consciously* aware of itself as its own world, and of the world of itself."[70]

Hegel's phenomenology traced the process by which the meanings of representations are taken up into the Concept through the dialectical movement of Spirit to disclose their ultimate meaning or truth. Spirit empties itself into the world of sensuous particularity in its 'creation' of that reality as an experience of itself. He argued in the *Phenomenology of Spirit* that because this action of self-consciousness is a spiritual function, and not an individual act, it transcends the peculiar actuality of the dualism of subject and object that existed in Kantian philosophy. The world is known totally as Spirit.

With Hegel's vigorous support, theologians such as Marheineke and Rosenkranz sought to appropriate this philosophical vision for theology. Though Hegel gently distanced himself from his most conservative followers, such as Carl Friedrich Göschel and Kasimir Conradi, when they hypostatized divine reality as self-conscious apart from the world, he strongly endorsed the efforts of "right-Hegelians" to develop a theology out of his philosophical system. Within a year of Hegel's death in 1832, Marheineke edited and published a first edition of Hegel's lectures on the philosophy of religion, in which Hegel often sounded exactly like his theological followers. Against theological subjectivism, Hegel declared that as Absolute Spirit, God is "not only the Being who keeps Himself within thought, but who also manifests Himself, and gives Himself objectively." Against those who tried to drive a wedge between religion and philosophy, he countered that "there cannot be two kinds of reason and two kinds of Spirit; there cannot be a Divine reason and a human, there cannot be a Divine Spirit and a human, which are absolutely different." Human consciousness is the manifestation of divinity in humankind, he lectured, "and Spirit, insofar as it is the Spirit of God, is not a spirit beyond the stars, beyond the world. On the contrary, God is present, omnipresent, and exists as Spirit in all spirits. God is a living God, who is acting and working." It followed for Hegel that religion must not be denigrated as an inferior product of reason, for "religion is a product of the Divine Spirit; it is not a discovery of man, but a work of divine operation and creation in him."[71]

The right-Hegelians constructed new theological systems out of this philosophical vision. Virtually all of them defended the doctrine of immortality; most of them insisted that the gospel history is necessarily constitutive to Christian truth (though Rosenkranz affirmed this belief only on speculative grounds); some of them spoke of the Absolute Spirit as self-conscious apart from the world. Though Hegel reaffirmed his panentheist conception of Spirit whenever followers such as Göschel or Conradi interpreted God as hypostatized apart from the world, he strongly endorsed the "right-Hegelian" view that philosophical truth is dependent upon religious truth. He warmly praised the "rare excellence" of Göschel's theological philosophy, which he judged to be "thoroughly imbued" with the realization that Christian truth and rational truth are fundamentally unified.[72] Hegel never taught that philosophy should replace religion, or that the historical core of Christianity was dispensable. He believed that philosophy was dependent upon and continued to be fed by religious experience.

This kind of argument was troublesome to Strauss, however. He did not dispute that the theological Hegelianism of the right-Hegelians had a basis in the master's work; in his later career Hegel clearly endorsed and contributed to the development of a Marheineke-style theological school. The religious conformism and historical naïvete of the Hegelians bothered Strauss very much, however. He believed that Hegel's distinction between representational and conceptual thinking was more revolutionary than anything the well-established Hegelians had in mind, even if Hegel himself rejected this conclusion. He further questioned whether Hegel's philosophy should not be able to leave behind the myths and doctrines of Christian theology. Strauss encountered that the mythic imagination of Christianity had nothing to contribute to the credible religious philosophy that was needed. What was needed was a system that absorbed and transcended the truths of Christianity. As Peter Hodgson observes, instead of developing a hermeneutics of religious myths and symbols, Strauss "proposed to *destroy* them, together with the historical tradition in which they were imbedded."[73]

Left Hegelianism Against Myth

Strauss's scholarship was marked by its persistent attention to the mythical elements of biblical narrative and his unremitting hostility to them. Baur had introduced Strauss to the past half-century of mythography, especially the rationalist and idealist interpretations of myth. In this area, as in his early philosophy, Baur was influenced chiefly by Schelling. According to Schelling, myths should not be taken as factual reports, but should be understood as ideas presented in pictorial form that are meant to persuade observors of some higher truth. His view of myth may have been influenced by Johann Gottfried Eichhorn and other critical scholars, to whom Strauss gave ample tribute in the introductory section of his book on the historical Jesus. In either case, under Schelling's influence, Baur taught that myth is "the most perfect form in which the ideas of the absolute make themselves palpable" (*Versinnlichen*). The difference between symbol and myth is that symbols are static images, Baur argued, whereas myth is a "visual presentation of an idea by means of an action."[74]

The elements of a liberal theology that interpreted myth critically but appreciatively were therefore present in Baur's hermeneutic, but Strauss adopted only its critical aspects. His exposure to theological Hegelianism gave him the idea for his scorchingly negative first book. The right-Hegelians maintained that the historical data pertaining to Jesus was inherent in the *content* of Christianity, meaning the idea of divine-human unity. They denied that the historical data pertaining to Jesus was reducible entirely to imagination (*Vorstellung*); to the contrary, they reaffirmed Hegel's claim that *Vorstellung* and *Begriff* are interrelated in the development of religious truth.[75] The truth of the divine-human unity is necessarily rooted in the historical Christian source of this ideal, they argued, which is the basis upon which the ideal is known to the religious consciousness.

But Strauss was unsettled by their seemingly mystifying and historically uncritical treatment of the relation between historical Christianity and the Concept. As he later explained in a letter to Christian Märklin, the crucial issue for him was that the Hegelians were obscuring the negative aspects of the relation of the Concept to history: "Does the historical character adhere to the content, thus demanding recognition from the Concept as well as the imagination, since the content is the same for both, or is it reduced to the mere form [of imagination], to which conceptual thinking is not bound?"[76] Strauss's thesis was that the Hegelians overemphasized the affirmative relationship between the Concept and Christian history and thus produced a metaphysical system that bolstered, or in some cases even embraced, traditional orthodoxy. Theologians such as Philipp Marheineke, Karl Rosenkranz, and Karl Daub were presenting Hegelianism as a sophisticated form of revisionist Christianity, but to their right, religious thinkers such as Carl Friedrich Göschel, Kasimir Conradi, and Isaak Rust were using Hegelian philosophy to bolster traditional forms of Christian supernaturalism, arguing that God can be known as fully self-conscious independently of the world.[77]

In his politics, Strauss had nothing in common with the radical Hegelians who soon outflanked him on the left; Strauss's politics were fervently right-wing, aristocratic, and pro-Prussian monarchist. In his critique of the comfortable, self-satisfied religion of the right-Hegelians, however, Strauss was the first left-Hegelian. His critique of Hegelian theology provided the starting point for the left-Hegelianism of Ludwig Feuerbach and Bruno Bauer. Less than a year after Hegel's death, Strauss published a critique of Rosenkranz's theology that contained the essential clue to his break with the established Hegelians. According to Strauss, the problem with Hegelian theology was that it reconciled the Absolute Idea to the history of Christianity by taking an uncritical approach to Christian history. Theologians such as Marheineke and Rosenkranz presented Hegelianism as a philosophical expression of historical Christian truth. But the relationship between philosophical reason and historical Christianity is not simply a relation of essence to appearance, Strauss objected. The right-Hegelians moved too easily from the historical forms of imagination to the Concept, as though historical truths could be established or validated on systematic grounds.[78]

Deconstructing the Gospel Narratives

This was the crucial intellectual background to Strauss's *Life of Jesus Critically Examined*. He originally conceived the book as a three-part work that would establish the negative relation between historical Christianity and the Concept. Strauss believed that Christianity was true as a religion that affirmed the idea of the unity between God and the world, or, at least, the immanent relation of divine reality to the world. He believed that God is incarnate in humanity as a whole, not only in Jesus or any other figure. His proposed constructive theology sought to explicate and defend this position. In order to clear the field for his theological philosophy, however, it was necessary to show why traditional Christianity was not historically credible. Strauss set out to present an opening section that described orthodox Christian teaching and spirituality, a second section that destroyed the historical basis of traditional Christianity, and a third section that contained his constructive theology.[79]

But his sprawling critical research soon overwhelmed the entire project; he dropped the first section entirely and ended the book with only a brief appendix on the "dogmatic import" of the historical Jesus. The first edition of his masterwork was published in two volumes in 1835, when its author was 27 years old. In 1,500 pages it relentlessly exposed the mythical elements of the New Testament gospels. Nothing like it had ever been published. Rationalist scholars for the past century had wrestled with the Bible's internal contradictions and miracle stories, and other forms of critical scholarship had exposed various historical problems in the biblical narratives, but no one before Strauss had marched straight through the gospel narratives armed with a command of the entire critical scholarship on scripture and a persistent focus on the Bible's mythical foundations. He noted at the outset that the church fathers typically assumed "that the gospels contained a history, and secondly, that this history was a supernatural one." More recently, rationalist scholars such as Johann Gottfried Eichhorn and Heinrich Eberhard Paulus had rejected the latter presupposition, "but only to cling the more tenaciously to the former, maintaining that these books present unadulterated, though only natural, history."[80]

Rationalist scholars eschewed the supernatural theism of orthodox Christianity, but then sought to provide naturalistic explanations for biblical events. Paulus, the pre-eminent biblical scholar of the rationalist school, explained the transfiguration as an autumnal sunrise that transfixed the three disciples in their early-morning drowsiness; he explained the raising of Lazarus as a deliverance from a coma and similarly described the resurrection of Jesus as a resuscitation.[81] The rationalists assumed that God does not intervene in history, but also assumed that biblical history is historical. But this half-measure is not credible either, Strauss retorted: "the other presupposition also must be relinquished, and the inquiry must first be made whether in fact, and to what extent, the ground on which we stand in the Gospels is historical." This is the natural next step for scholarship to take, he assured, and thus "the appearance of a work like the present is not only justifiable, but even necessary."[82]

What was needed was a method that deconstructed the historical pretenses of the sacred narrative and accentuated the mythical character of Christianity. Strauss sought to establish the necessity of his mythical interpretive method by playing off the supernaturalist and rationalist methods against each other. The Life of Jesus Critically Examined moved straight through the gospel narratives to show that in the interpretation of one gospel event after another, the literalistic orthodoxy of the supernaturalists and the naturalistic revisionism of the rationalists refuted each other. It is not possible for a modern educated person to make sense of the New Testament by accepting literally its accounts of angel appearances, Mary's virginal conception, numerous miracle stories, and the many places (most notably the genealogical tables and passion narratives) where the gospel narratives are unbelievable and contradictory, Strauss maintained. Rationalist criticism rightly belabored many of these problems over the past century.

But Strauss repeatedly turned the tables on the rationalists, who typically sought to make sense of unbelievable accounts by providing naturalistic explanations for them, including, as a last resort, the suggestion that some accounts owed their defects to faulty reporting by witnesses. Strauss was unsparing in his ridicule of what he called the "unnaturalism" of naturalistic biblical criticism. By comparison to the tortuous and convoluted attempts of rationalists to explain what must have really happened, he generally preferred the straightforward exegesis of the supernaturalists, who at least remained in contact with the biblical text. Strauss noted with regret that the rationalist dispositon was deeply ingrained in modern biblical criticism. Though he admired and drew upon the scholarship of the "mythical school" biblical critics, especially Wilhelm Martin Leberecht de Wette, Gottlieb Philipp Christian Kaiser, and

Baur, Strauss observed that even they overused naturalistic explanations.[83] Baur explained the angelic appearance at the birth of Jesus as a meteoric phenomenon; he suggested that the baptism of Jesus was accompanied by thunder and lightning and the accidental descent of a dove; he thought the transfiguration was caused by a storm; and he identified the angels at the tomb of the risen Jesus as gatekeepers wearing white graveclothes.[84]

Strauss did not always reject naturalistic explanations, and he did not always find biblical history to be in error. His accounts of some of Jesus' healing miracles and his interpretations of the resurrection appearances relied heavily upon psychological explanations. Moreover, he believed that the New Testament contained an ample core of reliable historical material pertaining to Jesus. In his reading, Jesus was a follower of John the Baptist who launched his own messianic ministry in Galilee after John was imprisoned. Jesus remained John's disciple through most of his messianic career, called disciples of his own, and proclaimed that the appearance of the messianic Son of Man was immanent. His teachings were preserved in generally reliable form in the synoptic gospels, including the predictions of the apocalypse. Strauss believed that Jesus identified himself with the Son of Man in his later career and was subsequently arrested, tried, and crucified.[85] He thus found a stronger core of historical material in the gospels than many neoorthodox theologians after him. Because he was generally uninterested in the teachings of Jesus, Strauss ascribed little importance to his judgment that the recorded synoptic accounts of Jesus' teaching were basically reliable. Liberal theologians afterward invested considerably more importance in this judgment. Strauss's biblical criticism was thus neither as insistently antinaturalistic nor as purely negative as it has been repeatedly portrayed.

Myth Criticism

But Strauss's dominant mode of interpretation was mythical criticism. The need for a mythical understanding of scripture was proven by the inadequacies of the dominant supernaturalist and rationalist approaches, he argued. Supernaturalism made unbelievable historical claims and thus negated genuine history, while rationalism distorted the historical texts by removing the miraculous from them. If theology is to have a credible future, Strauss insisted, it must face up to the mythical character and origins of Christianity. With the Hegelian distinction between *Vorstellung* and *Begriff* firmly in mind, he claimed that the "eternal truth" of Christianity was not affected by his deconstruction of the gospel narratives. "The supernatural birth of Christ, his miracles, his resurrection, and ascension, remain eternal truths whatever doubts may be cast on their reality as historical facts," he assured.[86] Rationalist criticism subverted the religious truth of Christianity by distorting the biblical accounts and by failing to address the mythical character of Christian faith. By contrast, he asserted, it is the mythical approach that promises to liberate the truths of Christianity from their undeveloped original forms. The true meaning of the incarnation is not tied to any putative historical event. Rather, the truth of the essence of Christianity is maintained and refined in Hegelian philosophy, but it can be recognized as such only after one leaves behind the mythical thought forms of traditional Christianity.

Strauss's presentation of mythical criticism was rather unwieldy, a fact that he sought to correct in the second edition by adding a section on criteria by which unhistorical material may be perceived.[87] His conception of myth emphasized its representational, unconscious, and collective character. Myths are not fables concocted by individuals, he stressed; rather, myths are narrative descriptions of events or ideas that express a community's partly unconscious self-understanding and experience. In his reading, the infancy narratives in Matthew and Luke were almost entirely mythical, as were the gospel accounts of relations between Jesus and John the Baptist, most of the miracle stories, the transfiguration, most of the passion narrative accounts, and virtually all of the resurrection and ascension accounts.

He gave short shrift to arguments for the historicity of the resurrection. Strauss conceded that "something extraordinarily encouraging" must have happened to the disciples after the death of Jesus that transformed their "deep depression and utter hopelessness" into religious enthusiasm. He judged that the encouraging "something" must have begun after the disciples returned to Galilee "where they gradually began to breathe freely, and where their faith in Jesus, which had been temporarily depressed, might once more expand with its former vigour." It was in this place and mood, far from the grave of Jesus, that the disciples first formed the idea of his resurrection. Within several weeks, their intense desire to see Jesus raised to life produced visions in which he appeared and spoke to them. Some of these visions occurred even "before whole assemblies in moments of highly wrought enthusiasm," in which the disciples believed they heard Jesus "in every impressive sound, or saw him in every striking appearance."[88]

Once the idea of a resurrection of Jesus was established in the hearts and minds of his followers, Strauss explained, the great event was quickly "surrounded and embellished with all the pomp which the Jewish imagination furnished."[89] The angels became the "chief ornaments" of the primitive church's Easter myth; they opened the grave of Jesus, kept watch over it, and delivered the tidings of Jesus' resurrection to the women. Baur's dictum applied strongly to the resurrection narratives, that whenever you see reports about angel activities, you're dealing with myth.[90]

Strauss followed Baur in defining myth as "the representation of an event or of an idea in a form which is historical, but, at the same time characterized by the rich pictorial and imaginative mode of thought and expression of the primitive ages." Myths typically present historical accounts of events that "are either absolutely or relatively beyond the reach of experience," such as events pertaining to the spiritual realm, or events which by their particular nature preclude historical witnesses. Myths also·typically depict fantastic or marvelous events in the form of highly symbolic language. Strauss followed Baur in distinguishing among historical myths ("narratives of real events colored by the light of antiquity" in which the natural and supernatural realms are mixed); philosophical myths (in which an idea is clothed "in the garb of historical narrative"); and poetic myths (in which historical and philosophical myths are partly blended together "and partly embellished by the creations of the imagination").[91]

Strauss conceded that it was often a question of judgment whether a particular biblical myth should be classified as historical, philosophical, or poetic, "since the mythus which is purely symbolical wears the semblance of history equally with the mythus which represents an actual occurrence." He accepted Baur's rule that the essential difference between historical and philosophical myths is that the latter seek to advance, symbolize, or otherwise support some particular truth claim; in philosophical myths, a legend is invented to serve a dogmatic or persuasive purpose, whereas no such purpose is apparent in historical myths. Strauss observed that biblical myths often piece together the elements of both kinds of myth, but the kind of blend that constitutes the third type of myth obscures the original fact or idea of the narrative "by the veil which the fancy of the poet has woven around it." Poetic myths are too strong on fantasy or marvel to be historical and too lacking in ideas to be philosophical. Strauss thus endorsed Schelling's judgment that myths are generally "unartificial and spontaneous" in their origin. The biblical writers and other mythicists of antiquity expressed their ideas in historical narratives not only because they sought to accommodate these ideas to popular consciousness, but also because their philosophical self-understanding was too undeveloped not to resort to religious imagery.[92]

Strauss conceded that biblical mythology is more restrained and historical than the myths of Greek, Roman, and other cultures. Though he routinely placed the angel narratives, theophanies, and miracle stories of the Bible in the same mythical category as the fables of Jupiter, Hercules, and Bacchus, he allowed that biblical myths are generally less incredible than their pagan counterparts: "Vishnu appearing in his three first avatars as a fish, a tortoise, and a boar; Saturn devouring his children; Jupiter turning himself into a bull, a swan, etc.—these are incredibilities of quite another kind from Jehovah appearing to Abraham in a human form under the terebinth tree, or to Moses in the burning bush." Even here he cautioned that numerous biblical stories approach pagan levels of fancy, such as the tales of Balaam, Joshua, and Samson, "but still it is here less glaring, and does not form as in the Indian religion and in certain parts of the Grecian, the prevailing character."[93]

Moreover, in pagan mythologies the gods have a history; they are subjected to time, change, opposition, and suffering; but in the Hebrew scriptures God is the absolute I Am. Hebrew religion is therefore not mythological in the narrow sense of the term, Strauss allowed. It contains no history of the gods, for in the Hebrew Bible only God's people have a history, not God himself. Strauss suggested that this difference explains the superiority of Jewish/Christian mythologies over pagan mythologies. The ultimate fruit of Christian myth is the idea of the divine-human unity expounded in Hegelian philosophy. But his stronger concern was to drive home the point that the difference is a matter of degree, not kind. Biblical myth is undoubtedly closer to reality than the pagan fables, but it is mythical nonetheless.

This is what we should expect, Strauss counseled; because Christianity is a religion, it inevitably apprehends reality in the form of mythic imagery. "If religion be defined as the perception of truth, not in the form of an idea, which is the philosophic perception, but invested with imagery; it is easy to see that the mythical element can be wanting only when religion either falls short of, or goes beyond, its peculiar province, and that in the proper religious sphere it must necessarily exist," he explained.[94] The biblical writers should not be demeaned for expressing their ideas in prephilosophical images, for myth is necessarily constitutive to religion. The peculiar province of religion is the mythical imagination, which is less rational and self-conscious than the scientific mind.

Strauss therefore adopted Ottfried Müller's understanding of myth as necessary and (partly) unconscious, but he rejected Müller's thesis that myth is never intentionally deceptive. An expert on Greek mythology and history, Müller claimed that the notion of myth as a deliberate fabrication is entirely false; in the strict sense of the term, he argued, it is a mistake even to speak of myths as being "invented," because the mythic imagination lacks the requisite self-awareness to "create" a self-consciously true or false narrative. "It is this notion of a certain necessity and unconsciousness in the formation of the ancient mythi, on which we insist," he declared. The inventor of myth is not a rational or individuated interpreter of the world, but merely "the mouth through which all speak, the skillful interpreter who has the address first to give form and expression to the thoughts of all."[95]

This was also Baur's view of how myth should be understood. In response to Müller and Baur, Strauss conceded that the characterization of myth as necessary, unconscious, and communal is correct, but potentially misleading. As usual, his counterargument began with a mild objection; he cautioned that the distinguishing line between intentional and unintentional fiction is not so easily drawn as Müller and Baur contended. Many of the New Testament narratives that depict Jesus as the Messiah were ambiguous in this regard. For example, the gospel narratives often portray Jesus as saying or doing something that fulfills the details of a messianic prophecy. These accounts are clearly contrived, Strauss observed; the pertinent question is not whether they were invented to show that Jesus was the Messiah, but whether the gospel writers perceived them as inventions. It is quite possible that the gospel writers believed that these recent inventions were historically true and not recently invented; after all, they believed that Jesus was the Messiah. If Jesus was the Messiah, they may have reasoned, he must have said and done the messianic things that the church's oral tradition attributed to him. Strauss argued that the messianic fulfillment texts were therefore too ambiguous to make a judgment upon; the gospel writers may have realized that these accounts were unhistorical, but quite possibly they did not.

Strauss insisted that another class of biblical narratives clearly crossed the line, however. Baur's claim that myth is never intentionally contrived was itself a pious fiction. The authors of the Homeric songs surely did not believe that every event in their accounts of the history of the gods had actually happened. By the same token, Strauss argued, the writer of the Chronicles surely recognized that his account contradicted Samuel and Kings, partly by introjecting later material into the narrative; just as surely, the author of Daniel must have realized that his account was modeled on the Joseph story and that it made "prophecies" of events already past. To recognize that the ancient authors must have been conscious at times of inventing myths is not necessarily to charge them with "evil design," Strauss allowed; the ancient writers had little concept of the difference between history and fiction and no concept at all of the rights or morality of authorship. That their fictions were entirely undesigned, however, is not credible. Scripture mixes history and fiction in ways that even the biblical writers must have recognized, Strauss argued. These inventions became myth as they were received in faith by religious communities, thus confirming that they were the fruit "not of any individual conception, but of an accordance with the sentiments of a multitude."[96]

He quickly disposed of the objection that the forty-year interlude between the death of Jesus and the destruction of Jerusalem was not long enough to give birth to a rich body of sustainable myth. Strauss suggested that this objection would be convincing if the background to Christianity had not included several centuries of Jewish messianic myth. New Testament Christianity was too complicated and developed to have sprung from nothing, he agreed. At the same time, early Christianity was too deeply mythical to be categorized as a merely historical religion. The historical explanation for the rapid development of Christian myth is not that early Christianity was not mythical, he argued, but that it was based upon the long-developing Jewish myth of messianic deliverance. With this structure of religious teaching in place, early church leaders needed only to transfer the messianic legends, "almost all ready formed, to Jesus, with some alterations to adapt them to Christian opinions."[97] Strauss acknowledged that there was a second historical source of Christian myth—the strong impression that Jesus left on his followers—but he argued that the primary source, the tradition of Jewish messianic expectation, provided most of early Christianity's mythical core.

Three Kinds of Gospel Myth

Strauss's deconstruction of the gospel narratives sorted out three kinds of gospel myth, which he described in a typological section added to the third and fourth editions of the book. He defined *evangelical* myths as narratives about Jesus that are not based in fact, but are products of an idea *(religiose Vorstellung)* about him promulgated by his followers. This idea, such as the idea of Jesus as Messiah, may have some relation (often unrecoverable) to something that Jesus said or did, but in either case it is the idea that is determinative. *Pure* myths have no direct historical basis at all, but flow directly from the religious imagination. Strauss classified the Transfiguration and the story of the rending of the Temple veil after Jesus's death as examples of pure myth, because neither of these stories appeared to have any historical basis in the life of Jesus. The gospel story of the Transfiguration is a slightly reworked messianic redeemer myth and the temple veil account reflects the hostile relationship between first-century Judaism and the early Christian church. Strauss identified *historical* myths as a third type, in which a definite historical fact is "twined around with mythical conceptions culled from the idea of the Christ."[98] In his reading, the gospel accounts of the baptism of Jesus, the calls to the disciples, the barren fig tree story, and some of the healing stories are historical myths; each of these stories presents mythically embellished accounts of events that probably had some historical basis.

While arguing that the gospels are loaded with all three kinds of myth, Strauss found little evidence of the legendary in the New Testament. In this case, the relatively brief time span between the death of Jesus and the writing of the gospels was a crucial factor. He defined legends as products of oral tradition in which the originating mythical idea (presuming it ever existed) has been lost. Mythical accounts are both unhistorical and fictional, but legends are merely unhistorical. Legends are characterized by "indefiniteness and want of connexion," Strauss observed; they are often strange, confused, and pointless, "the natural results of a long course of oral transmission."[99] If the New Testament is filled with mythically overdetermined and embellished accounts about Jesus, for the same reason it contains relatively few legends. The idea of Christ as Lord and redeemer fills the gospel narratives, just as it shaped the early church's recollections and interpretations of Jesus.

But these interpretations were the products of a mythical consciousness that we cannot pretend to share or aspire to. Time after time, Strauss drove home this reminder. The biblical writers viewed all of history "down to the minutest details" in mythical terms. In biblical religion, it is God "who gives the rain and sunshine; he sends the east wind and the storm; he dispenses war, famine, pestilence; he hardens hearts and softens them, suggests thoughts and resolutions." It is precisely this view of reality that modern science has torn apart, Strauss exhorted. Modern educated people, "after many centuries of tedious research," no longer attribute everything that happens to the immediate agency of a divine ruler, but rather believe "that all things are linked together by a chain of causes and effects, which suffers no interruption." What is needed, therefore, is a theological philosophy that brings the conceptual truths of Christianity forward into a world that knows no miracles or angels. Theology must reestablish on speculative grounds "that which has been destroyed critically."[100]

The Straussian Controversy

Strauss became instantly notorious for these arguments, not because any of them were new, but because no one before him had so extensively or aggressively marshaled the evidence for the mythical nature of Christianity. Though he never developed a coherent theory of myth or even related his two typologies of myth to each other, his work outstripped everything before it in the literature of mythical criticism. Moreover, his blend of mythical, rationalist, and Hegelian themes produced a distinctive intellectual vision that placed him in a category by himself. In 1835, this was a vulnerable place indeed. Though he begged for their support, none of Strauss's friends or teachers came strongly to his defense after his book set off an explosion of outrage; in one of his numerous rebuttals to book reviewers (in this case, a group of Hegelians), Strauss aptly summarized the situation by categorizing himself as the only left-Hegelian.[101]

By 1837, having lost nearly any hope of attaining a teaching position as a theologian, Strauss was sufficiently chastened by his isolation and the critical reaction to his work to reconsider his position. He was deeply wounded by Baur's critique of the relentlessly negative character of his work, and he admitted to friends that he was terrified at the prospect of never landing a teaching post. In December 1837 he admitted to Adolf Rapp that he was no longer determined to fight for principle; the world could believe what it wanted, and if his only alternative was exile, he would agree to "believe" unbelievable things.[102]

This was the mood in which his accommodating third edition was written. Strauss's third edition toned down the aggressive sarcasm of his original text and made nearly one hundred substantive changes in the book's arguments, including a reconsideration of his negative judgment on the historicity of the fourth gospel. John was the favorite gospel of the post-Enlightenment German theologians, who loved its eloquent discourses and its deemphasis on miracles. In the third edition, Strauss meekly offered that the authenticity of the fourth gospel was uncertain; more important, he reworked his earlier portrait of Jesus as a misguided apocalyptic prophet and presented Jesus as the embodiment of the divine-human idea. Though he characterized his new Christology as Hegelian, Strauss's emphasis on the intense God-consciousness of Jesus placed his third edition within the orbit of Schleiermacher's liberalism. He remarked in the preface that while the book's argument had lost much of its unity in the course of being revised, he was hopeful that it had gained in truth.[103]

But he was soon embarrassed by it. Strauss didn't believe in the book's revisions enough to defend them, and Baur sharply questioned his defense of the possible authenticity of the Johannine discourses. For a brief moment, Strauss had reason to hope that the third edition would restore his reputation and career. In 1839, he was appointed to a theology position at the University of Zurich, partly on the strength of his accommodations to liberal orthodoxy, but the news of his appointment sparked a firestorm of outrage in the local churches. Bowing to popular pressure, the Zurich city council quickly ended this controversy by pensioning Strauss off at half salary before he ever taught a course. His life turned a corner with this incident. Under the pressure of his desire for a theological career, he had sought to be reconciled with the academic establishment, but his forced "retirement" from Zurich ended his yearning for academic respectability. Strauss no longer cared what the well-appointed professors and ecclesiastics thought of him. With the loss of his desire to please and succeed, he began admitting to friends that he didn't believe in any of the third edition's concessions. He regarded its mythologization of the spiritual consciousness of Jesus as a religious evasion. He regretted his attempt to salvage anything from historical Christianity, he told Christian Märklin in November 1839; the religion that was needed has no need of an outside savior.[104]

At last he was free to speak the truth as he knew it. Strauss prepared a final edition of the *Life of Jesus* during the same months that he completed his massive two-volume historical theology, *Die Christliche Glaubenslehre* (1840), which examined the history of Christian doctrine from its biblical origins to its current conflicts with modern science. The latter work declared that "the true criticism of dogma is its history."[105] This was the spirit of the final edition *Life of Jesus* as well, which restored the book's original tone and arguments. Strauss explained in the preface that the "intermingling voices of opponents, critics, and fellow labourers, to which I held it a duty attentively to listen, had confused the idea of the work in my mind; in the diligent comparison of divergent opinions I had lost sight of the subject itself."[106] Now he was finished with paying his respects to Christian apologists and careerists. He was at last free from the influence of those who could not face up to the mythical nature of Christianity.

This included most of the Hegelians. At the height of the controversy over the first edition, when various right-Hegelians were correcting him with quotes from Hegel, Strauss admitted that Hegel was "no friend of historical criticism" and that if he had lived to read the book, Hegel would not have liked it. Part of the problem was Hegel's "undeniable vagueness" regarding Christology, which gave license to supernaturalists and other "followers" to his right. There was also the fact that in his later years, Hegel was personally inclined to emphasize the positive, reconciling function of the dialectic rather than its negative function. His lectures on religion made it clear that he regarded Jesus' life and death as part of the content of religious truth, and his objective panentheistic God-language was indistinguishable from Marheineke's. Having conceded that the right-Hegelians were closer to Hegel in some respects than he was, Strauss countered that his own critical theology was nonetheless ultimately truer to the spirit of Hegel's revolutionary dialectic than the religious philosophies of Marheineke, Rosenkranz, and the rest.[107]

This argument gained an impressive following over the succeeding decade. It was embraced by a new generation of left-Hegelians, led by Bruno Bauer (who converted from right-Hegelianism) and Ludwig Feuerbach, who soon surpassed Strauss in their radical rejection of Christianity.[108] But Strauss did not persist in his claim to being the true Hegelian. Merely five years after his first edition *Life of Jesus* sought to clear the way for a philosophical appropriation of Christianity, his two-volume interpretation of Christian doctrine relinquished the dream of the Hegelian synthesis. *Die Christliche Glaubenslehre* observed that Hegelian philosophy had promised to bring about a new order of peace in which reason and faith would live together. But this promise was a pretentious illusion. No philosophy could hold Christianity and the modern consciousness together, Strauss insisted, because modernity is a revolution. Modernity is a fundamental transformation of consciousness that renders premodern philosophies and theologies irrelevant. Contrary to what Hegel wanted to believe in his last years, the present historical moment is not a time for restoration or reconciliation, but for "pulling down a structure" that has lost its credibility. The polemics and crushing disappointments of recent years had devoured Strauss's faith that any philosophy could bridge the chasm between premodern faith and modern reason.[109]

Rationalism and Hermeneutics

Though he regarded his work as an elaboration of the implications of mythical criticism and Hegelian philosophy, it was Strauss's rationalism that was finally determinative for his theology. His negative criterion for the identification of unhistorical material put the matter bluntly. An account is not historical, he asserted, "when the narration is irreconcilable with the known and universal laws which govern the course of events." These universal laws included the law of cause and effect, which ruled out all supernatural interventions, prophecies, apparitions, and unexplainable miracles. "The intermingling of the spiritual world with the human is found only in unauthentic records, and is irreconcilable with all just conceptions," he insisted.[110] Strauss's criteria for historical authenticity included other tests as well, including the law of succession, various "psychological laws," and the law of internal consistency, but these laws merely reinforced his adherence to a narrowly rationalist understanding of history. Though he repeatedly attacked rationalist exegesis for its evasions and distorted reconstructions, he took no interest in the hermeneutical movements of his time that sought to advance beyond rationalism.

These innovations in interpretation theory included Schleiermacher's reconstructionist hermeneutics of understanding, in which the meaning of a text is grasped through identifying with the author in such a way that one relives the experience out of which the author wrote. The task of hermeneutics, Schleiermacher taught, is "to understand the text at first as well as and then even better than its author."[111] Though Strauss's deconstructive project sought to clear the way for a Hegelian theophilosophy, his rationalism also blinded him to the import of Hegel's hermeneutic of understanding, in which the work of interpretation is ultimately carried out by the self-penetration of spirit. Hans-Georg

Gadamer observes that Hegel's theory of understanding was profoundly inte-grationist in its spirit and execution. Hegel conceived the work of historical un-derstanding not as a destruction or restoration of the past, but as a "thoughtful mediation with contemporary life." That is, to Hegel the work of philosophical mediation was not an external operation conducted after the fact, but dialecti-cally on the same level as the truth it explicated.[112]

But Strauss's commitment to rationalism was too deep for him to counte-nance any kind of postrationalist hermeneutical approach to history, myth, or understanding. He had no interest in developing a hermeneutics of religious myth or symbolism, because for him the purpose of historical understanding was to destroy religion. His use of historical criticism was controlled by an a priori positivism that disallowed the possibility of miracles before he even looked at any particular miracle story. Strauss's negation of biblical history was made possible not so much by historical interpretation as by his commitment to a rationalist positivism that defined miracles out of possibility (and thus "dis-credited" the text) before any kind of historical, literary, or theological inter-pretation could begin. Moreover, he insisted that any judgment about the credibility of biblical history "must be founded on the nature of its particular narratives" and not upon any consideration of its literary history or character. This explained his disinterest in the teaching of Jesus and his disregard for the literary and religious purposes of the gospels. As Baur noted, Strauss gave no attention to the gospels themselves as integral literary works; his attention was consumed by his interest in destroying the credibility of the individual gospel stories.[113] His method broke each gospel into independent literary units and then compared these pericopes with parallel stories in the other gospels. In this procedure, to his considerable credit, Strauss anticipated much of what would later be called form criticism.[114]

As Peter Hodgson observes, however, contemporary form criticism isolates the gospel stories in order to define their literary forms and describe their keryg-matic functions in early Christianity. For Strauss, the purpose of this method was solely to disclose the mythical nature of these stories in order to dismiss them. His driving concern was to show that the gospel stories contradicted each other, violated universal laws of history, and mythologized the life and meaning of Jesus. Strauss's use of a prefigurative form of form criticism was fueled and shaped by his rationalistic abstraction of the gospel stories from their literary, his-torical, and religious contexts. Hodgson rightly remarks that his persistently neg-ative results were thus predetermined by a method that paid little attention to context.[115] In this, he was merely the first, if extreme, example of the dangers that attend a one-sided use of any critical methodology, especially form criticism.

The Legacy of Strauss

Schweitzer once remarked that "in order to understand Strauss one must love him," to which Karl Barth aptly replied that while we should feel sympathy for

Strauss, he was not a tragic figure.[116] Strauss was too moody, vain, undisciplined, and self-absorbed to be a great scholar, Barth observed. As Strauss repeatedly confessed, the subject of his historical scholarship was never the historical material as such, but "the dream-image of his own existence." Strauss's self-description put the matter exactly: "I am not a historian; with me everything has proceeded from dogmatic (or rather anti-dogmatic) concerns."[117] If he was known and judged nonetheless primarily on the basis of his historical scholarship, Barth suggested, this was the fate he created and deserved, all the while protesting that his higher contribution was ignored.

But Strauss's higher contribution—his theology of monistic idealism—was a more serious alternative than Barth allowed, and his critical challenge to Christianity defined the issues over which liberal theology was subsequently forced to make choices and define itself. Though liberal theology did not adopt his dogmatic perspective, pieces of it have been retrieved repeatedly over the past century. His Christology is a chief example. Since religion is the form in which the truth presents itself to the popular consciousness, he argued, the truth of the divine-human unity was first disclosed to the senses: "In other words, there must appear a human individual who is recognized as the visible God. "The reality of the incarnation was proven when Christ was tortured to death on Calvary, for this death revealed that the God-man knew "how to find a way of return into himself." The unity of the divine and human in Christ subsequently becomes "a part of the general consciousness; and the church must repeat spiritually, in the souls of its members, those events of his life which he experienced externally."[118]

The problem occurs when the church restricts the incarnation to Jesus. When the church made Jesus the sole bearer of the incarnation, Strauss argued, it confined the great truth of divine-human unity to the blinkered consciousness of the religious imagination. "Is not the idea of the unity of the divine and human natures a real one in a far higher sense, when I regard the whole race of mankind as its realization, than when I single out one man as such a realization?" he implored. "Is not an incarnation of God from eternity, a truer one than an incarnation limited to a particular point of time?" This was the crucial issue that all of his critical labors sought to raise. To liberate the truth in Christian myth, the myth had to be broken open. "This is the key to the whole of Christology, that, as subject of the predicate which the church assigns to Christ, we place, instead of an individual, an idea; but an idea which has an existence in reality, not in the mind only, like that of Kant," Strauss urged.[119]

Traditional Christianity left the church with impossible contradictions. How could a single historical person have a fully human nature and a fully divine nature? Did Christ possess one will or two? Either answer undermined the church's theology of the incarnation, Strauss believed, but in the idea of humanity, these contradictions disappeared: "Humanity is the union of the two natures—God becomes man, the infinite manifesting itself in the finite, and the finite spirit remembering its infinitude; it is the child of the visible Mother and the invisible Father, Nature and Spirit." Humanity is the worker of miracles in

the course of the spirit's mastery of nature; it is the redeemer of sin, which af-
flicts individuals but "does not touch the race or its history." Through its triumph over nature and individual evil, humanity realizes its spiritual nature.[120]
The doctrine of the union of divinity and humanity is the great truth of Christianity, Strauss proclaimed, but Christianity has obscured and distorted its truth
by referring it only to Jesus: "It is Humanity that dies, rises, and ascends to
heaven, for from the negation of its phenomenal life there ever proceeds a
higher spiritual life; from the suppression of its mortality as a personal, national,
and terrestrial spirit, arises its union with the infinite spirit of the heavens."

The miracle of humanity's spiritual transformation is infinitely more important than the historicity of the biblical miracle stories. What is needed, Strauss
urged, is a generation of theologians and clerics that proclaims the reality of
the incarnation, death, and resurrection as "the infinitely repeated pulsation of
the divine life." The church confines the incarnation to the historical Jesus, but
critical theology must recognize that the idea "only attains existence in the totality of the individual." The church regards the gospel narratives as history, but
critical theology regards them "for the most part as mere myth." The crucial reality for theology is not any single fact or part of the process, Strauss argued,
but the process that gives meaning to facts. "Our age demands to be led in
Christology to the idea in the fact, to the race in the individual." Any theology
of Christ that stops at the historical Jesus is thus no theology at all, he concluded, but a sermon.[121]

Having sought to present critical theology with a choice between Schleiermacher's mystifying romanticism and his own rationalistic monism, Strauss later
renounced Christianity when it became hopelessly clear that liberal Protestantism was choosing Schleiermacher. Though his constructive position was
later appropriated by various process, panentheist, and feminist theologians, it
has remained a marginal perspective in modern theology. But it was Strauss's
critical assault on Christianity that set the agenda for liberal theology afterwards.
His critical influence exceeded that of every nineteenth-century figure except
Darwin. His deconstructive method prefigured the development of form criticism. Though his polemics against mediating theologies were often skewed
and always self-serving, his depiction of the pertinent theological alternatives
dominated the field for decades. His wedge between the Jesus of history and
the Christ of faith opened a major theological debate that has carried into the
present. His exposure of the extensive mythical content in Christian scripture
and tradition forced modern theologians afterward to struggle with the relationships between theology and myth.[122]

Barely six years after he burst upon the scene as a religious radical far ahead
of his time, Strauss found himself outflanked and often ridiculed by a Hegelian
left that regarded all religion as wish projection. The attacks on his position by
Bruno Bauer and other recent converts to left-Hegelianism were so disre-
spectful that Strauss broke off all relations with them. His religion of humanity
and his reactionary politics made him an object of ridicule to the Hegelian
left.[123] At the same time, he witnessed the development of new mediating

theologies that sought with greater sophistication to hold together modern historical consciousness and the historical claims of Christianity. A. E. Biedermann's neo-Hegelian theology of the incarnation was an especially influential perspective in the middle and later decades of the nineteenth century. For Biedermann, the essence of Christianity did not include the church's mythological accounts or doctrines about Jesus, but consisted of the incarnational *principle* that is revealed uniquely in Christ.[124] Isaak Dorner and Richard Rothe also developed highly creative, strongly metaphysical theological systems that drew upon Schleiermacher and Hegel (among other sources) and appropriated Baur-style biblical criticism. Dorner's neo-Hegelian reinterpretation of the idea of divine immutability became a classic text in its field.[125]

In the early 1860s, Strauss flirted with the possibility of making his peace with Schleiermacher's epigones. He published a popular revision of the *Life of Jesus* that restored many of the liberal-leaning compromises of the third edition. The success of Ernst Renan's *Life of Jesus* (1863) made Strauss hope that a more attractive version of his own book might find a welcome audience. The book got rough treatment from numerous reviewers, however, and Strauss soon went back to deriding liberal theology as *Speck* (fat) and mediating theology as *Wurst* (sausage). He scolded that it was futile to tie the Christ of faith to the Jesus of history. It was not credible to substitute a modern "Christ principle" or experience of redemption for the church's historic doctrine of vicarious atonement. Liberal theology was "like a sheet of transparent paper which, when laid on an old picture, shows the outlines of a figure, but which appears blank when removed from it." Schleiermacher's theology of Christian experience was true only as a reflection of his personal experience, Strauss argued: "It changed nothing in substance." Christian theology could progress beyond its present impasse only by letting go of historical Christianity, for "the ideal of the dogmatic Christ on the one hand and the historical Jesus of Nazareth on the other are separated forever."[126] He claimed in 1865 to be waiting for Christian theologians to face up to the epochal task of reconstructing the ideal Christ figure apart from the mythical/dogmatic Christ of Christian history. Seven years later, in *The Old Faith and the New,* he concluded that this theological project wouldn't be worth the trouble, either. Christianity is not true and is therefore not worth saving.[127]

History and Liberal Faith

As Strauss expected, liberal theology struggled mightily with the Jesus of history/Christ of faith problem. As he expected, liberal theologians also echoed Strauss's insistence that theology must overcome its mythical elements. What Strauss could not have expected, but only witnessed with astonishment in the closing years of his life, was the emergence of a dominant theological liberalism that took his criticism seriously while contradicting all of his conclusions about its meaning. Leander Keck once remarked that if Strauss had lived to see the triumph of Ritschlian theology in nineteenth-century Protestantism, he would have regarded Albrecht Ritschl the way that Herod regarded Jesus: "John, whom I beheaded, has been raised."[128] With Ritschl's acceptance of the Straussian split between the Jesus of history and the Christ of faith, liberal Protestantism found a way to overcome the mythical inheritance of Christianity while claiming fidelity to the true Jesus.

Albrecht Ritschl was the son of George Karl Ritschl, a bishop of the Prussian Protestant church in Stettin (now Szezczin, in Poland bordering Germany). A deeply pious ecclesiastic and member of the Prussian establishment, the elder Ritschl was devoted to the cause of the Prussian Union Church, the state church that united the Lutheran and Calvinist communions in the face of intense opposition by confessional Lutherans. Though Albrecht Ritschl discovered during his seminary training that he could not accept his father's theological conservatism, he retained his father's Lutheran piety, his practical concern for the life of the church, his ecumenism, and his moralism, which included his upper-class sense of social responsibility. Ritschl's educational itinerary was characteristic for students of his background and generation who became liberal Christian leaders. He began his theological studies at Bonn, where he studied under dogmatic theologian Immanuel Nitzsch, the conservative mediationist. Next he studied at Halle under Julius Müller and the influential neopietist, F. A. Tholuck, where he sought to find a basis for his increasingly revisionist beliefs.[129]

Ritschl earned his doctorate at Halle in 1843, but was generally dissatisfied with his theological teachers. He found Baur's work in historical theology more compelling than anything he heard at Bonn or Halle. When Ritschl expressed an interest in pursuing graduate studies with Baur at Tübingen, however, his father persuaded him to study instead under Richard Rothe at Heidelberg. A former student of both Hegel and Schleiermacher, Rothe was a creative proponent of a conservative-leaning mediation theology. He taught that while theology is obliged to appropriate the results of historical criticism, it must begin with a strong concept of revelation. Rothe's highly distinctive blend of supernaturalist and modernist beliefs helped Ritschl put together the elements of his own theology, but also confirmed his desire to study with Baur. In 1845 his father relented.

Ritschl's relationship with Baur was short-lived, stormy, and unfortunate, but also crucial to his theological development. It was under Baur's influence that he learned to use the tools of historical criticism as a means to interpret Christianity as a total historical reality. Baur taught that the nature of Christianity can be grasped only by subjecting its original sources and its total historical development to critical scrutiny.[130] In the process of appropriating Baur's historicism, Ritschl fashioned his own theological perspective and located the boundary of his use of negative criticism. His first book, *The Gospel of Marcion and the Gospel of Luke* (1846), was a pure example of Tübingen school historical theology. Ritschl argued for the priority of Luke's gospel, a position that he later rejected just before Baur became its leading advocate.[131] His next book, *The*

Emergence of the Old Catholic Church (1850), used Baur's method to trace the historical transition from New Testament Christianity to Catholicism, but it also contained the first signs of his immanent break with Baur. Beyond various smaller points of disagreement, Ritschl declared at the outset that historical criticism is properly a "pure art" unto itself and must not be used as the servant of any dogmatic or philosophical system, whether liberal or conservative.[132]

These were fighting words. Baur's commitment to philosophical idealism was well known. In the 1830s, following the example of his students (especially Strauss), he turned increasingly to Hegel for the "orienting idea" that he claimed all historical work requires. Baur never became a strict Hegelian, but his interpretation of Christianity featured a strongly Hegelian emphasis on the self-disclosure of Spirit in and through historical process.[133] Moreover, his analysis of Christian history and his interpretations of such Christian doctrines as the atonement and the divine Trinity became heavily influenced by a rather one-dimensional understanding of Hegel's dialectic. The method by which Baur traced the manifestation of Spirit through historical change was a simplified application of Hegel's dialectic in which the conflict between a dominant historical "thesis" and its contrasting "antithesis" generates historical change in the form of a new thesis (the "synthesis").[134] His major work, *Das Christenthum und die christliche Kirche der drei ersten Jahrhunderte* (1853), provided a showcase example of the kind of philosophically controlled historiography that Ritschl rejected. Baur interpreted early Christian history as primarily a struggle between the "Judaizing" and "Hellenizing" factions of the early church, represented respectively by the Jerusalem-based apostles (especially Peter) and the Hellenistic Gentile converts to Christianity, whose perspective was championed and symbolized in the New Testament by Paul. In this scheme, the Johannine literature was viewed as a synthesis of the Jewish-Hellenistic conflict, which led to Catholicism.[135]

In the second edition of his book on early Christianity, Ritschl strongly criticized Baur's method and conclusions. He argued that Baur's dialectical model distorted Christian history by forcing the pieces of a complex, unwieldy historical process into a simplistic three-part schematism. He further insisted that Catholicism was not a product of the early church's Judaizing-Hellenizing conflict, but the product entirely of a triumphant hellenistic faction that redefined Christianity in its own image. Catholicism represented the negation of early Christianity's Jewish character, language, and identity.[136] The seed of a central liberal Protestant thesis was thus planted with Ritschl's break from the Tübingen school. Liberal theologians had routinely denigrated the Jewish aspects of Christianity as being more primitive and legalistic than its non-Jewish aspects. Schleiermacher claimed that all of the "higher elements" in Christianity derived from its non-Jewish sources.[137] This prejudice resurfaced in the writings of numerous liberal theologians afterward, notably Adolf von Harnack.[138] But with Ritschl's critique of Baur-style historicism, liberal Protestantism also began to argue that the real problem in Christianity was its lack of Jewish influence. Ritschl characterized Catholicism as an alien, paganized religious tradition that was in error precisely because of its dissociation from the Jewish biblical roots of Christianity. As in much of his later theology, he emphasized his continuity with Luther in making this argument about the "Babylonian captivity" of the Catholic tradition.[139] A generation later, part of this critique of hellenized Christianity was deepened and extended by Harnack, though in the name of a "simple gospel" that was less sympathetic to Judaism and less historical in its theological underpinnings than Ritschl's liberalism.

In his concern to uphold the integrity and independence of historical criticism, Ritschl sometimes exaggerated Baur's reliance on Hegelian philosophy, a mistake that led numerous observers afterward to identify Baur as a Hegelian. Ritschl also tended to underestimate the extent to which Baur's historical theology was grounded in historical research. The source of the break between Baur and Ritschl was deeper than their misinterpretations of each other, however. Baur did believe that an alternative metaphysical system was needed to provide the orienting idea for a credible modern Christianity. He did not conceive historical theology as an alternative to metaphysics, but as a component of the work of systematic theological reflection that requires a systematic metaphysical ground. For Ritschl, however, the virtue of the historical approach to Christianity was precisely that it offered a possible alternative to metaphysical speculation. As his perspective became more sharply defined in the 1850s, he often defended historical conclusions that were more conservative than Baur's. These disagreements were not insignificant, but it was Ritschl's adoption of a thoroughgoing historicism that marked the crucial difference between them. The key to his break from Baur and the source of his enormous influence in late nineteenth-century theology was Ritschl's insight that unaided historical interpretation might recover the historical essence of Christianity that transcends passage. Through his influence, liberal theology learned to speak the biblical language of justification, reconciliation, and the kingdom of God again with a confident voice.

Liberal Theology as Social Historicism

Ritschl taught at Bonn from 1846 to 1864 and then at Göttingen for twenty-five years. As a theologian in the age of Darwin, he was pressed to explain what kind of work theology should be doing while science increasingly explained the world. As a theological liberal and pro-Bismarck defender of the Prussian state, including the state union church, he was also embroiled for much of his career in battles with conservative confessionalists and pietists. These two major challenges situated Ritschl's approach to theology. His influence as a theologian derived not so much from his origination of any particular theory or argument as from his use of historical interpretation to reestablish the credibility of liberal theology in the face of its pressing cultural, political, scientific, and religious challenges. Ritschl's social vision was generally conservative, though with a reformist tinge; his interpretation of the kingdom of God was strongly ethical, but ethically grounded in his concern for the preser-

vation of social order and authority. In the name of building the kingdom of
God, he attributed great importance to the maintenance of existing social institutions and the cultivation of authority-respecting personal habits, especially
the self-acceptance of each person's vocational role. He was thus highly critical of modern individualism, secularism, and the weakening of Christianity's
moral and social authority. Ritschl looked with horror at the spectacle of a theologian such as Strauss, whom he judged to be "helplessly entangled in the
monstrous world-machine" and thus a proponent of secularization.[140] Ritschl's
concern to save the soul in the social order was a distinguishing feature of his
theology, even if his politics had little in common with his social gospel successors.

His chief concern as a theological servant of the church was to define the
field of religious knowledge in relation to scientific knowledge. Ritschl's answer was influenced by Kant's proposal to expunge metaphysics from theology and, especially, by Kant's moral interpretation of Christianity. He argued
that science describes the way things are, or appear to be, but theology is properly about the way things should be. Put differently, religious knowledge is
never disinterested, but always consists of value judgments about reality, especially judgments that contribute to personal and social good. As he explained
in his dogmatics, *The Christian Doctrine of Justification and Reconciliation*
(1874): "Religious knowledge moves in independent value judgments, which
relate to man's attitude to the world, and call forth feelings of pleasure and
pain, in which man either enjoys the dominion over the world vouchsafed him
by God, or feels grievously the lack of God's help to that end."[141] The heart
and goal of true religion is the attainment of the highest possible good.

Ritschl argued that the content of this good in Christianity cannot be gleaned
from an infallible text or doctrine, but must be derived from the "apostolic circle of ideas" as established by historical critical research. The ultimate object of
historical theology is not so much to establish what Jesus really said or did as
to establish the collective Christian experience of value inspired by Jesus. As
he declared at the outset of his dogmatics, "It would be a mistaken purism were
anyone, in this respect, to prefer the less developed statements of Jesus to the
forms of apostolic thought."[142] Because Christianity is a form—the highest
form—of true religion, it is concerned essentially with value; moreover, Ritschl
argued, historical research discloses that the essence of Christianity is the kingdom of God as valued by the Christian community. But the kingdom is valued
as absolute only by those who follow Jesus, he observed; to others it is a matter
of indifference what Jesus taught about sin, redemption, or the kingdom. It followed for Ritschl that the significance or truth of Christianity cannot be grasped
from outside the Christian community, but can be comprehended only within
the inner history of the church's life and practices. The value of the kingdom
can become a matter of knowledge only within the inner history of the church's
historical life. From this perspective, Ritschl taught, Jesus becomes knowable
as the embodiment of humanity's highest ideal; he is the redeemer of humankind who incarnates and inaugurates the realization of the kingdom.[143]

Schleiermacher defined Christianity as a monotheistic faith belonging to the teleological (moral) type of religion which derives its distinction from other religions "by the fact that in it everything is related to the redemption accomplished by Jesus of Nazareth."[144] This starting point made him the first theologian to define Christianity in terms of its relation to the history of religion. Ritschl believed that this innovation was the key to Schleiermacher's crucially important interpretation of religion, even though Schleiermacher's explication of it was ultimately unconvincing. The problem with his definition of Christianity was that it failed to express clearly the relation between Christianity's generic religious qualities and its distinctive characteristic, Ritschl argued: "For if the Divine final end is embodied in the Kingdom of God, it is to be expected that the redemption which has come through Jesus should also be related, as a means, to this final end." But Schleiermacher never developed this relation; he construed Christian God-consciousness sometimes in relation to redemption and elsewhere by reference to the kingdom, but he never explained the relation between the redeeming work of Christ and the kingdom. The upshot is that he failed to account for the teleological nature of Christianity, which is "constantly crossed by the neutral idea of religion by which he is guided, by the abstract Monotheism which he follows, and finally by everything being referred solely to redemption through Jesus." Though he took a pass at working outward from the history of religion, Schleiermacher's obscure interpretation of religion disclosed that he did not really take instruction from its history. His prejudice against the Hebrew scriptures made him unable to recognize or affirm the connections between Judaism and Chistianity. This was a serious shortcoming, Ritschl observed, for in Hebrew religion "the concrete conception of the one, supernatural, omnipotent God is bound up with the final end of the Kingdom of God, and with the idea of a redemption."[145]

Ritschl hastened to note that the kingdom idea was purged of its nationalism in Christianity: "In Christianity, the Kingdom of God is represented as the common end of God and the elect community, in such a way that it rises above the natural limits of nationality and becomes the moral society of nations." As the religion of perfect moral value, Christianity presents the possibility of justification and renewal through relation to Christ. "We have in Christianity a culmination of the monotheistic, spiritual, and teleological religion of the Bible in the idea of the perfected spiritual and moral religion," he declared. In Christianity, the spiritual realities of redemption and the final end are essential and mutually related. Christ's redemption and kingdom condition each other in the historical experience of the church. Ritschl acknowledged that Protestantism often reduced Christianity to a religion of redemption, with little recognition of its kingdom-bearing ethical meaning. This distortion of the faith of Jesus must be corrected by those who remember what it means to pray "thy kingdom come," he suggested, for the kingdom "is the very purpose of God in the world, as Jesus himself recognized."[146]

True Christianity does not resemble a circle described from a single center, he asserted, "but an ellipse which is determined by two foci." Christ is made known to his followers as the redeemer, but the center of the redeemer's teaching and the moral end of his existence is the kingdom of God. "Now it is true that in Christianity everything is 'related' to the moral organisation of humanity through love-prompted action; but at the same time everything is also 'related' to redemption through Jesus, to spiritual redemption, *i.e.,* to that freedom from guilt and over the world which is to be won through the realised Fatherhood of God." The moral end of individual existence is freedom in God, just as the final end of all existence is the kingdom of God. This does not mean that Christian theology should be based on redemption while Christian ethics is based on the kingdom, Ritschl cautioned. The mark of true Christianity is its mutually relational double character, in which the "perfectly religious and perfectly ethical" dimensions of Christian faith perpetually interact and advance through history. This criterion yielded Ritschl's definition of Christianity: "Christianity, then, is the monotheistic, completely spiritual, and ethical religion, which, based on the life of its Author as Redeemer and as Founder of the Kingdom of God, consists in the freedom of the children of God, involves the impulse to conduct from the motive of love, which aims at the moral organisation of mankind, and grounds blessedness on the relationship of sonship to God, as well as on the Kingdom of God."[147]

For Ritschl, Christianity was not a doctrine, but a movement; it was the forward-moving and communal faith of those who know Christ as redeemer and live out his ethic of the kingdom. Ritschl's emphasis on the practical, historical, ethical mission of Christianity was inspiriting to a generation of Christians that found much of their religion under assault. In response to serious challenges from modern science, Enlightenment philosophy, and an increasingly secular culture, most liberal and mediating theologians felt compelled to distinguish between the variously defined "essence" of Christianity and its disposable secondary elements. Ritschl's version of this strategy acknowledged its close relation to Schleiermacher while seeking to give the Christian movement a more active social-ethical character than Schleiermacher's romanticism had provided. It appropriated Rothe's understanding of the kingdom as the moral end of history while eschewing Rothe's emphasis on revelation.

Though he was not oblivious to the strengths of romanticism, pietism, and confessionalism as strategies to cope with the deracinating, secularizing pressures of modern civilization, Ritschl persistently maintained that these strategies were too reductionist to represent the fullness of Christian conviction. Though his theology was carefully devised to avoid conflicts with modern science and philosophy, Ritschl insisted that Christian faith is not merely subjective or communitarian, but outward-moving, public, historical, and socially engaged. For him, theology was not concerned with objects or questions studied by science, but only with "states and movements of man's spiritual life." On the other hand, he maintained that theology must not conceptualize the spiritual life as self-enclosed or protected from public criticism. "We know nothing of a self-existence of the soul, of a self-enclosed life of the spirit above or behind those functions in which it is active, living, and present to itself as a being of special worth," he declared.[148] So-called "metaphysical" reason cannot justify its distinctions between physical and spiritual realities and therefore has nothing to contribute to the Christian interpretation of God's relation to the world. Theology has no metaphysical knowledge of the nature of the soul or the interrelations of the divine being, Ritschl argued; what it does have is knowledge of God's redemptive and ethical *effects* in history. It is the manifestation of God's presence through the redemptive and kingdom-bringing effects of God's action in history that theology explicates.[149]

The "positive theology" that Ritschl sought to provide expounded the double character of Christianity without commiting Christian faith to any metaphysical system; it combined a reinterpretation of the Lutheran emphasis on redemption with the modern recovery of the kingdom idea; it blended Schleiermacher's theology of religious experience with Kant's insistence on the moral character of Christianity, while restoring more of the language and feeling of biblical Christianity than either Schleiermacher or Kant. This strategy was enormously influential; it created a dominant theological school and made Ritschl one of the giant figures of modern theology. For all of his influence over his theological generation, however, it was Ritschl's fate to become relatively forgotten afterward. In the twentieth century, his work received little attention in either Europe or America, chiefly for two reasons. The first is that those who carried out the "neoorthodox" revolution of the 1920s and afterward set themselves against Friedrich Schleiermacher, Adolf von Harnack, and Wilhelm Herrmann, but gave short shrift to Ritschl. In a typical and brutally dismissive assessment, Barth claimed that Ritschl was merely a religious apologist for nineteenth-century bourgeois German society.[150] The second reason for Ritschl's relative neglect is that he produced a school that surpassed its founder. One measure of his influence is that many of his followers became major theologians; his disciples utterly dominated Protestant theology in the late nineteenth and early twentieth centuries, some of them producing works that surpassed Ritschl's for scholarly depth, originality, relevance, and lasting influence. They included Adolf von Harnack, Ernst Troeltsch, Wilhelm Herrmann, and Walter Rauschenbusch.

The Ritschlian School

Ritschl's works fell into relative obscurity as the writings of his successors broke new ground in historical theology, history of religion, and social theology. Modern theology became a distinctively social-ethical enterprise in the late nineteenth century in ways that made Ritschl's bourgeois Prussian conservatism seem quaint at best.[151] As a response to the question of how Christianity should deal with the mythical elements of Christianity, however, liberal Protestantism produced a stronger line of continuity from Schleiermacher to the Ritschlians to the liberal modernists. Liberal theologians readily acknowledged that much of the Hebrew scriptures and parts of the gospels are mythical. They also agreed with Strauss that a credible theology must have a nonmythical basis.

The Ritschlians disputed Strauss's characterization of the central gospel narratives as mythical, however; with ample warrant, they claimed that Strauss misconstrued the distinctive kind of literature that the gospels represent. They further insisted that Christian theology has no need to relate its myth-transcending faith to any philosophical system or theory. Christian theology has all that it needs, they argued, in the life, teaching, and influence of Jesus.

Ritschl's greatest disciple faced the issue directly in the opening pages of his classic work on the essence of Christianity. Harnack taught church history at the University of Berlin from 1888–1921 and also served as a close advisor and friend of Kaiser Wilhelm, as Director General of the Royal Library, and as president of the Kaiser Wilhelm Gesellschaft. His writings included the monumental three-volume *History of Dogma*, the three-volume *History of Ancient Christian Literature*, and more than a thousand articles on Christian history. He also wrote the Kaiser's speech to the German people in 1914 that announced the beginning of the Great War.[152] In his most influential work, *What Is Christianity?* (1900), Harnack declared that true Christianity "is something simple and sublime; it means one thing and one thing only: Eternal life in the midst of time, by the strength and under the eyes of God."[153] Though he surpassed Ritschl and Baur (and everyone else) as a scholar of Christian history, his normative theology took comparatively little instruction from the total Christian tradition.

Christianity is a religion, he reasoned, and religion pertains fundamentally not to doctrine, ethics, or social order, but to the existing human self. Goethe once remarked that although humanity is always advancing, human beings remain the same. This perception was crucial to Harnack's conception of Christianity as the true religion. Religion pertains to the life and condition of the human self that never changes while living in the midst of change, he argued. True religion is always concerned with the fundamental human problems of living, suffering, meaning, and death. And what is the basis of the highest form of religion known to human history? Harnack replied that the answer is both simple and exhaustive; it is "Jesus Christ and his Gospel."

In the spirit of Baur and Ritschl, he cautioned that this answer is exhaustive because it includes the history of Christianity as a whole. Christianity is not fundamentally a doctrine, but a life, "again and again kindled afresh, and now burning with a flame of its own." To grasp the nature of this dynamic object, one must pay attention to its history. "Just as we cannot obtain a complete knowledge of a tree without regarding not only its root and its stem but also the bark, its branches, and the way in which it blooms, so we cannot form any right estimate of the Christian religion unless we take our stand upon a comprehensive induction that shall cover all the facts of its history," he explained.[154] This conviction animated his massive historical scholarship. In response to Cardinal Manning's dictum that the church must overcome history by dogma, Harnack replied that the very opposite is true; it is only through historical criticism that dogma can be purified. The vocation of the historical theologian is precisely to "break the power of the traditions" that are fossilizing Christianity into something alien to the gospel of Jesus.[155]

As a cultural Protestant associated in spirit, though not in fact, with the free church tradition, Harnack never doubted that genuine Christianity is incompatible with the bureaucratic ecclesiastical systems maintained by the Roman Catholic, Eastern Orthodox, and various Protestant state churches. On account of this belief, as well as his general theological liberalism, his appointment at Berlin in 1888 was opposed by the Prussian state church and approved by Chancellor Bismarck and Emperor William II only over vehement church opposition. During the controversy over his call to this position, Harnack argued that the purpose of historical criticism is not to destroy biblical faith and church tradition, but to "build up" the Christian faith on its most credible and compelling basis, which happened to be its original basis.[156]

His subsequent studies of Christian doctrine reinforced this judgment—and the view of theological liberalism—that the kerygmatic core of Christianity is simple, sublime, and historically credible. Harnack set liberal Protestantism squarely against Strauss in making the argument for its credibility. "Sixty years ago David Friedrich Strauss thought that he had almost entirely destroyed the historical credibility not only of the fourth but also of the first three Gospels," he recalled. But Strauss's form of gospel criticism failed to comprehend the kind of literature that he attacked. Strauss dismissed as mythical every gospel account that could be questioned on historical grounds, but the gospel writers made no pretense of presenting disinterested historical accounts, Harnack observed. The gospels are not works of history in the modern sense of the term; but testimonies of faith "composed for the work of evangelization." Their purpose is to inspire faith in the person and mission of Jesus.

Harnack noted that all four of the gospels were products of Jewish didacticism composed under the short-lived conditions of first-century Jewish Christianity. They were written by representatives of a diminishing religious community that was in the last stages of its absorption by the Hellenistic church. To treat the gospels as primarily history or myth is to miss their unique character as the faith literature of a disappearing community of memory, he argued: "This species of literary art, which took shape partly by analogy with the didactic narratives of the Jews, and partly from catechetical necessities—this simple and impressive form of exposition was, even a few decades later, no longer capable of exact reproduction." That is, with the triumph of Hellenistic Christianity, the peculiar gospel blend of history recounted from the perspective of Jewish Christian faith and tradition became alien to the church. It was no longer a living possession. "The style of the evangelists was then felt to be something strange but sublime," Harnack remarked. The question of how to interpret these alien texts became problematic for the early church, and has remained so.[157]

Though he emphasized the distinctive literary character of the gospels, Harnack did not dismiss the importance of reading the gospels as historical sources. "They are not altogether useless as sources of history, more especially as the object with which they were written is not supplied from without, but coincides in part with what Jesus intended," he argued. He judged that in their main lines, the gospels present a historically reliable picture of Jesus' life and teaching. Harnack disputed Strauss's contention that the gospels are riddled with myth, "even if the very indefinite and defective conception of what 'mythical' means in Strauss's application of the word, be allowed to pass." In Harnack's reading, only the infancy and childhood narratives were truly mythical. Strauss treated every miracle story as a mythical invention, but Harnack noted that the modern concept of "miracle" as a violation of the laws of nature was unknown in the ancient world. The gospel writers lived at a time in which marvelous events seemed to happen nearly every day. They lived in a world filled with the sights and sounds of wonder, in which they held little conception of the difference between what is naturally possible and impossible. At this level of awareness, Harnack observed, miracles do not exist, for no one "can feel anything to be an interruption of the order of Nature who does not yet know what the order of Nature is."[158]

It followed that the gospel writers could not have attributed as much significance to their miracle stories as did their supernaturalist, rationalist, and mythical-school interpreters. Moreover, even in the hyperrationalistic age of modernity, Harnack cautioned, our understanding of nature is incomplete and our knowledge of psychic forces is very poor. The discerning gospel reader must keep in view not only the gulf that separates the modern and ancient worlds, but the limitations of modern understanding. He explained, "Miracles, it is true, do not happen; but of the marvellous and the inexplicable there is plenty. In our present state of knowledge we have become more careful, more hesitating in our judgment, in regard to the stories of the miraculous which we have received from antiquity. That the earth in its course stood still; that a she-ass spoke; that a storm was quieted by a word, we do not believe, and we shall never again believe; but that the lame walked, the blind saw, and the deaf heard, will not be so summarily dismissed as an illusion."[159]

In his effort to establish a philosophical substitute for Christianity, Strauss reduced Christianity to myth; but Harnack argued that neither the Bible's genuinely mythical elements nor its miracle stories are central to Christianity. "It is not miracles that matter; the question on which everything turns is whether we are helplessly yoked to an inexorable necessity, or whether a God exists who rules and governs, and whose power to compel Nature we can move by prayer and make a part of our experience," he explained. Just as Ritschl said very little about the nature of divine reality apart from God's effects upon people in their formation of value judgments, Harnack eschewed all metaphysical speculation about God, Jesus, and the nature of reality in order to emphasize that the heart of Christianity consists of a threefold kerygmatic message that he called the Gospel. The essence of Christianity is the gospel of Jesus, which he identified as the proclamation of the kingdom of God, the reality of the infinite value of the human soul under the rule and love of God the Father, and the promise of righteousness and eternal life.[160]

This core of Christian teaching and identity is summarized in the Lord's Prayer, he observed. Jesus pointed not to himself, but to the providential care of the Father. His teaching was centered on the reality of the coming kingdom, which Harnack defined as the prospect of a cooperative social order in which human beings live under the rule of love and conquer their enemies by gentleness. The kingdom begins in the heart of an individual, he explained, "by entering into his soul and laying hold of it." The kingdom is the rule of God, "but it is the rule of the holy God in the hearts of individuals." This meant for Harnack that there is ultimately no distinction between the God of Jesus Christ and the kingdom proclaimed by him, for "God" and "kingdom" are signifiers for the same spiritual reality: The question of the kingdom "is not a question of angels and devils, thrones and principalities, but of God and the soul, the soul and its God."[161] The work of theology is to faithfully separate this unchanging "kernel," the gospel of Jesus, from the "husk" of its various cultural and doctrinal forms as expressed in the New Testament, ante-Nicene Christianity, and subsequent church history.

Harnack's reputation as perhaps the greatest church historian in Christian history gave considerable authority to these constructive proposals. He was prepared to accept a highly mythical reading of the Hebrew scriptures because he found very little of the gospel in them. Neither did he deny that the New Testament infancy narratives are purely mythical, or that mythical elements are also present in other stories that feature angels, devils, absolute miracles, and foretellings of the apocalypse. What he firmly denied is that any of the early church's mythical trappings affected its gospel core. The gospel of Jesus is not about devils or virgin births, but about "the soul and its God." A sentence such as "I am the Son of God" is not a gospel statement, but an addition to the gospel. For Harnack, the point was not to condemn the church for adding to the gospel, but only to keep the essential distinction clear. It was only natural for the church to remember Jesus in the light of its faith in him, he explained, for "here the divine appeared in as pure a form as it can appear on earth." What was crucial was that Christianity not be identified with any of the church's mythical or doctrinal expressions of its faith in Jesus.

This included doctrinal statements about the historicity of the resurrection of Jesus. Harnack distinguished between "the Easter faith" that belongs to the gospel and "the Easter message" that, despite its rootage in the earliest forms of Christian preaching, does not belong to the gospel kernel. "The Easter *faith* is the conviction that the crucified one gained a victory over death; that God is just and powerful; that he who is the firstborn among many brethren still lives," he asserted. The Easter faith is not the end of an argument or a conclusion drawn from historical evidence, but faith in God's sustaining power over death. This faith is upheld in the gospel story of doubting Thomas, in which those who have not seen are exhorted to believe. It is assumed when the disciples on the road to Emmaus are chastised for not believing in the resurrection, "even though the Easter message had not yet reached them." The Easter message, on the other hand, is the church's effort to substantiate and codify its faith in the risen Christ. It contains vivid accounts of Jesus' resurrection appearances and lists of witnesses to them. Harnack placed 1 Corinthians 15 and most of the resurrection accounts in Luke, Matthew, and John into this category, as well as any apologetic argument for the resurrection that draws on this evidence.

The problem with the Easter message is the problem with all of the church's attempts to rationalize or prove its faith claims, he argued. To believe in God on the basis of evidence is to believe in the evidence, not God. In the case of the Easter message, it is to base Easter faith on some reconstruction of the evidence. But the various New Testament accounts are too fragmented and inconsistent to bear the weight of this colossal question of faith, Harnack insisted. How can we base Easter faith on the Easter message when it isn't even clear which account or conflation of accounts is the right one? "Either we must decide to rest our belief on a foundation unstable and always exposed to fresh doubts, or else we must abandon this foundation altogether, and with it the miraculous appeal to our senses," he declared. Though it is true to say that the Easter faith arose from historical experiences, only one thing about the nature of these experiences is certain to us, which is that the grave of Jesus "was the birthplace of the indestructible belief that death is vanquished, that there is a life eternal."[162] This is gospel kernel; the rest is mythical, apologetic, or doctrinal husk. Harnack cautioned that all forms of gospel husk inevitably become antiquated over time; every attempt to rationalize, codify, or prove Christianity eventually becomes an obstacle to Christian faith. But the gospel itself is timeless, he argued. It is never falsified or rendered irrelevant by an "advanced" age, for its constitutive elements are eternal. Though variable in form and expression, the truth of the gospel is unchanging; it is a message of spiritual truth to human beings who are themselves unchanging in the midst of historical change.

This was the defining voice of liberal Protestant theology. Harnack was too liberal to receive the support or recognition of the Prussian state church, but he was easily the most influential Christian scholar and teacher of his generation. Along with his friends, Troeltsch and Herrmann, he dominated liberal theology at the turn of the century; thousands of his students became pastors (though he was not permitted by the church to examine them); several of his students became major theologians, including William Adams Brown, Karl Holl, Walter Rauschenbusch, Dietrich Bonhoeffer, and Karl Barth.[163] Harnack's immense authority as a critical scholar bolstered the self-confidence of liberal Christians that the mediating approach was the true one. He taught liberal theologians to judge Christian history by its relationship to the gospel kerygma and by its results. With Baur, he insisted that the Hellenization of Christianity beginning with Paul was the central problem of Christian history; with Ritschl and against Baur, he maintained that the heart of Christianity is not an idea but a spiritually and socially redemptive way of life.[164]

Harnack did not dispute that the church requires an institutional structure; his massive volumes on the development of Catholicism even expressed a grudging respect for the institutional and religious genius of the Catholic system.[165] His conception of what it means to "continue the Reformation" was far-reaching nonetheless: Harnack set Paulinism and "early Catholicism" against the gospel, he questioned the authority of the ecumenical councils on account of their Greek philosophical bent, he maintained that the Apostles' Creed should not be a test of Christian belief, and late in his career he urged that the Old Testament should be expunged from the Christian scriptures.[166] He allowed that it would have been a mistake for the second-century church to endorse Marcion's exclusion of the Old Testament from the Bible, and in the sixteenth century, the Reformers were too weighed down by "the power of a fateful heritage" to fully recover the gospel faith; but in the twentieth century it was only a "paralysis of religion and the church" that kept the church from getting rid of the Old Testament.[167] To Harnack, the purpose of modern liberal theology was to complete the kerygma-recovering work of the Reformation, which required the elimination of all pregospel and postgospel traditions that obscured the face of Christ.

Liberal theology in its dominant voice was thus an evangelical tradition that persistently based its message on its image of Christ. With ample warrant, Henry Van Dusen later remarked that modern liberal Protestantism was the most Christocentric theological tradition in Christian history.[168] Liberal theologians repeatedly declared their readiness to discard any doctrine, institution, or tradition that impeded their commitment to know and follow Christ. William Adams Brown proclaimed this faith for forty years at Union Theological Seminary without having to deal with his teacher's ecclesiastical interference.[169] His inaugural lecture at Union in 1898 was characteristically titled, "Christ the Vitalizing Principle of Christian Theology."[170] Walter Rauschenbusch similarly claimed that the heart of modern progressive Protestantism was its recovery of Christ's theology of the kingdom. Though his economic radicalism caused Rauschenbusch to adopt a far more revolutionary understanding of the kingdom than Harnack, and though this difference also moved Rauschenbusch to find much more of the gospel in the traditions of Hebrew prophetism than Harnack ever recognized, Rauschenbusch's appeal to the faith and way of Jesus was Harnackian nonetheless.[171]

Evangelical Liberalism and the Social Gospel

"The eclipse of the kingdom idea [in Christian history] was an eclipse of Jesus," Rauschenbusch declared in *Christianizing the Social Order* (1912). "We had listened too much to voices talking about him, and not enough to his own voice. Now his own thoughts in their lifelike simplicity and open-air fragrance have become a fresh religious possession, and when we listen to Jesus, we cannot help thinking about the Kingdom of God."[172] He later insisted that for this reason, the social gospel was neither alien nor novel, but a recovery of the kingdom-bringing religion of Jesus. "We shall not get away again from the central proposition of Harnack's *History of Dogma,* that the development of

Catholic dogma was the process of the Hellenization of Christianity; in other words, that alien influences streamed into the religion of Jesus Christ and created a theology which he never taught nor intended," Rauschenbusch wrote. "What would Jesus have said to the symbol of Chalcedon or the Athanasian Creed if they had been read to him?"[173]

The same church that heaped Greek titles on Jesus forgot what it means to seek the kingdom. Rauschenbusch exhorted the church to recover the full meaning of the kingdom ideal, which consisted, in his reading, not only of heaven and eternal life, but also of the church as the collective kingdom-prefiguring body of Christ *and* of the eschatological kingdom that is always breaking into the present from the future.[174] As the foremost proponent of social gospel Christianity, Rauschenbusch emphasized that the kingdom includes, but is not exhausted by, moral and political efforts to live out the way of Christ. As a passionate proponent of antimilitarism and democratic socialism, he accentuated the split between the radical and liberal currents of modern social Christianity. Social gospel leaders such as Brown and Shailer Mathews emphasized the social character of Christianity without accepting Rauschenbusch's claim that the socialist, trade union, and antiwar movements were signs of the coming kingdom. American liberal Protestantism expended much of its energy in the Progressive era debating its political realism and efficacy. Many of its leaders were upper-class liberals, like Brown, or bourgeois moralists, like Mathews and Harry Emerson Fosdick, who taught that liberal Protestantism should avoid taking sides in the class struggle.[175]

For all of its debates over politics and social ethics, however, the religious self-understanding of liberal Protestantism was affected more deeply by its basic disagreements over theological orientation than by its arguments over politics, economics, and social change. Harnack's liberal evangelicalism was the dominant perspective. It sought to restore the credibility of Christianity by refounding Christian theology on the faith and person of Jesus. "The new school raises the old cry, 'Back to Christ,'" Brown declared in 1898. "Let no theology call itself Christian which has not its center and source in Him."[176] Evangelical liberals such as William Adams Brown, Walter Rauschenbusch, Harry Emerson Fosdick, and William Newton Clarke thus resolved the Straussian Jesus of history/Christ of faith problem by identifying with their image of Jesus. That is, they opted for the Christ of faith, but then identified this figure with the historical Jesus.

The Ritschlians were adept at appropriating various critical challenges that did not threaten this touchstone of faith; Rauschenbusch embraced evolutionary theory, modern democratic theory and forms of historical criticism that supported his understanding of progressive Christianity. But he fiercely resisted the David Friedrich Strauss/Johannes Weiss/Albert Schweitzer thesis that the historical Jesus was nothing like the liberal sage and justice-seeking prophet depicted in liberal theology. Schweitzer's *Quest of the Historical Jesus* (1906) gave epochal expression to the view that Jesus was an apocalyptic prophet whose teaching centered on a mistaken belief about the immanent end of history. In

order to establish a religious basis for their already-established moral and religious beliefs, Schweitzer argued, liberal theologians disregarded the apocalyptic character of Jesus' teaching while projecting their own liberal progressivism
onto it.[177] As Rudolf Bultmann later remarked, echoing Schweitzer, "Harnack
somehow never clearly saw nor understood the eschatological character of the
appearance of Jesus and of his preaching of the immanent advent of the Kingdom of God." Bultmann added that Harnack also underestimated the apocalyptic character of Paulinism and early Christianity: "In fact, Harnack never even
caught a glimpse of the utter strangeness of the image of primitive Christianity
disclosed by the religious-historical school."[178]

Evangelical liberalism coped with this attack on its fundamental claims by
attributing the apocalyptical sections of the gospels to the early church, rather
than to Jesus. Following Harnack and Herrmann, Rauschenbusch argued that
pericopes such as Mark 13 were retrojections of the early church's apocalyptic
expectations onto the historical sayings of Jesus. In his reading, the gospel parables of the sower, the tares, the net, the mustard seed, and the leaven were crucial clues to the mind of Jesus; in these parables, Rauschenbusch observed, the
kingdom is not a sudden, world-shattering intervention from above, but an organic, developing, inner-historical reality. The parables of Jesus were protests
against the worldview of late Jewish apocalypticism rather than products of it,
he claimed: "It is thus exceedingly probable that the Church spilled a little of
the lurid colors of its own apocalypticism over the loftier conceptions of its
Master."[179]

Evangelical liberalism was (and is) defined by its insistence that the Christ
worthy of being followed is the Jesus of history. The longtime liberal theologian and president of Union Theological Seminary, Henry Van Dusen, continued to proclaim this faith long after theological liberalism lost its hegemonic
influence. "For normative Evangelical Liberals, the Jesus of History and the Living Christ are a single, organic, indissoluble personal reality," he explained.
"That reality is defined in the life, words, deeds, mind, spirit, faith of Jesus of
Nazareth; it is known in present power in the Living Christ."[180] Evangelical liberalism was affirmative of modern science, culture, and historical criticism as
long as its religious center was immune from the acids of modern criticism. In
Fosdick's phrase, it conceived theology as the work of explicating the meaning of "abiding experiences in changing categories."[181] Liberal theologians in
the Ritschl/Harnack tradition assumed that Christianity had to be reinterpreted
to retain its life and credibility in the modern age, but they insisted that this
project of reinterpretation neither caused nor required any negation of the core
of historic Christianity.

This was a highly adaptable and forward-looking faith. American theologians such as William Newton Clarke and Theodore Munger reinterpreted
Christian doctrine in relation to evolutionary theory. Others such as A. C. Knudson and Eugene Lyman maintained the evangelical liberal emphasis on Christ
while seeking to refurbish the explanatory and apologetic roles of metaphysical reasoning in theology.[182] Brown blended the insights of Schleiermacher,

Ritschl, and Harnack to show that "the new theology" was hospitable to modern science.[183] Evangelical liberals in England and France were generally less influenced than the Americans by German theology, but made similar claims with regard to the nature of revelation, the essence of Christianity, and the relation of religion and science. Auguste Sabatier wrote in his influential *Outlines of a Philosophy of Religion* (1910) that Christianity is a revealed mystery "which has become evident to pure hearts and pious souls through the public preaching of it." It is nonsense to demand of this faith any verification other than "its own truth, beauty, and efficiency," he claimed. Revelation is not a communication of immutable doctrines, but consists "of the creation, the purification, and progressive clearness of the consciousness of God in man—in the individual and in the race."[184] Sabatier observed that if the gospel of Jesus had been an immutable doctrine, it would have lost its power of life centuries ago. This insight was the clue to his understanding of the function of historical criticism. Far from being destructive to faith, he argued, historical criticism is necessary to the attainment of faith in the true Christ. "It is not doubtful that the teaching and the work of Christ, having been preserved in the simple oral tradition for half a century, have not been transmitted to us without some corruptions and some legendary elements," he observed. This was why historical criticism was needed, to purify the tradition, remove its veils, and "set forth more certainly the authentic soul of Christ."[185]

Liberal theologians were sensitive to the charge that their work was overly critical and destructive. "How can it be otherwise?" Brown asked in 1911. "The new theology is the outgrowth of a rational movement, and thought is necessarily critical, destructive, sceptical." He observed that the new theology that was needed was only beginning to be built. This new theology began by assuming that life is an organic, interrelated, unified system. It presupposed that nature and the supernatural "are not two different kinds of reality, but two different aspects of one and the same reality." What we call "nature" is the law of natural process, whereas the "supernatural" is the end of natural process. "Nature has to do with cause, the supernatural with meaning and value," Brown explained. It followed for him that the traditional Christian dichotomy between rational knowledge and revealed knowledge was also mistaken. There are not two kinds of knowledge, Brown continued, but two aspects of knowledge, "the knowledge of the causes which produce effects and the knowledge of the purpose which the effects are designed to serve." Revelation is related to this second aspect of knowledge, as the divine disclosure of the meaning of natural processes. Among liberal theologians, Brown was comparatively conservative in his retention of traditional Christian language and apologetic forms, yet even he gave strong emphasis to the modern understanding of God as the immanent divine power of being, "an ever-present spirit guiding all that happens to a wise and holy end." God is knowable through nature, he affirmed, as well as through history, scripture, the lives of faithful people, "and supremely in Jesus, the ideal man, through whom he has given us the clearest revelation of his character and purpose."[186]

Evangelical liberalism assured an increasingly secularized generation that the way of Christ is the way to certainty and righteousness. "For God is the name we give to the reality which is most excellent in the universe, the basic fact on which our faith in all other good depends," Brown asserted.[187] Instead of playing down its religious beliefs in the face of modernist criticism, liberal theologians claimed to have recovered the true essence of Christianity through the use of modern critical methodologies. While acknowledging that the gospels contained mythical elements and other "corruptions and distortions," they insisted that the gospel itself is God's revealed truth and the heart of any Christian faith worthy of the name.

The Liberal Modernist Alternative

This faith in the compatibility of modern culture and the religion of Jesus was routed from the field by the stupendous horror of the Great War and the subsequent emergence of what came to be called "neoorthodox" theology. Karl Barth's early "crisis theology" poured devastating ridicule on the efforts of his theological teachers, especially Harnack, to synthesize Christianity and liberal culture. In their own way, however, another group of liberal theologians sought to forestall the neoorthodox revolution by giving up their claims to an evangelical basis. This movement was centered in the United States, where neoorthodoxy was slow to take root, partly because the Great War was experienced as something less than the death of progress. Liberal modernists such as Shailer Mathews, D. C. Macintosh, and Henry Nelson Wieman relinquished the Ritschlian claim that modernist criticism always yields and confirms the liberal Christ of faith. The modernists sought to preempt outside attacks on liberal theology by acknowledging that their theologies were based on *modern* liberal beliefs and procedures. Modern criticism creates and requires new forms of religious belief, they argued. It does not leave untouched a kerygmatic core of Christianity, but requires wholesale reinterpretations of the religious and moral meaning of Christianity in the light of modern criticism. Modernist theologians usually sought to salvage as much of the religious and moral content of traditional Christianity as they found credible, but they did not exempt any aspect of Christianity from the tests of credibility. They relinquished the evangelical claim that the norm of religious truth must be found within the Christian tradition. They countered that the only theology that might survive the onslaught of modern criticism and culture was a theology that put modernism in the driver's seat.

Mathews's theological career exemplified the shift that many liberally trained theologians felt compelled to make. For nearly 20 years, while serving as a dean and theology professor at the University of Chicago Divinity School, Mathews was a leading American proponent of evangelical liberalism. His first book, *The Social Teachings of Jesus* (1897) was the first major work in English to make a case for the sociopolitical significance of Jesus' teaching. This highly influential manifesto for social gospel Christianity presented Jesus as the preacher of a historically attainable kingdom and exemplar of the Christian moral ideal. Mathews interpreted the kingdom as the "goal of social evolution" to be brought about by the mobilization of humanity's possibilities for good as inspired by the teaching and example of Jesus.[188] His early writings equated Jesus' understanding of the kingdom with his own faith in social progress or "process."

The first crack in his evangelicalism appeared in 1905, however, when he reluctantly conceded in *The Messianic Hope in the New Testament* that Jesus' understanding of the kingdom was much more vertical and catastrophic than the progressive ideology favored by modern social theology.[189] This acknowledgment was a partial concession to Weiss's apocalyptic interpretation of early Christianity. It was also the beginning of Mathews's turn to the modernist alternative, a transformation that took more than twenty years to complete. Between 1907 and 1914, which was the high tide of the social gospel movement, Mathews poured out a stream of books that presented true Christianity as a progressive social movement inspired by the peacemaking and redemptive way of Jesus. "The real significance of the historical Jesus lies in the fact that in him the Spiritual Life for which humanity has searched was perfectly brought in terms of time and human relationships," he asserted.[190] For the religious movement that he founded, Jesus was the perfect symbol and agent of spiritual regeneration; in the historical experience of this religious movement, "the Jesus of history became the Christ of experience."[191] For Mathews, as for Harnack, the gospel was a message "that seeks to transform human lives into conformity with the ideals of Jesus by bringing them into regenerating relations with God."[192] He proclaimed that "the very heart of the Social Gospel" is the faith that Jesus can save the world by transforming it into the kingdom of God.[193]

But by the end of this period Mathews was no longer claiming that the social gospel movement was recovering the essence or core of original Christianity. The Harnackian method of stripping historical Christianity to its ostensible kernel was no longer credible to him, because it distorted the relativizing, historical, forward-moving character of "social process." Jesus and Paul believed many things that are now unbelievable, Mathews increasingly cautioned. Modern theologians needed to absorb the implications of the differences between the social mind of early Christianity and the rationalist consciousness of our time. What is needed in theology is not to identify some immutable core that transcends historical passage, he argued; rather, what modern theology needs is to recognize the radical dissociation between the modern mind and all earlier forms of consciousness, including the prescientific, mythical, apocalyptic consciousness of early Christianity.

The historicist/sociological concept of a "social mind" was crucial to Mathews's modernist turn. He defined a social mind as a "more or less general community of conscious states, processes, ideas, interests, and ambitions which to a greater or less degree repeats itself in the experience of individuals belonging to the group characterized by the community of consciousness."[194] He observed that in Christian history, the self-understanding of the Christian movement has been shaped and defined successively by the Semitic, the Greco-Roman, the imperialist, the feudal, the nationalistic, the bourgeois, and the modern democratic social minds.[195] Historical progress is made possible by the fact that each social mind generates from its own experience the conceptions that fulfill current religious needs, he noted. Hellenistic Christianity needed to be assured that true salvation is mediated through Christ, and thus the logos and Neoplatonist essence theologies were created; the Christian movement of the Middle Ages needed a theology of divine sovereignty in the midst of social breakdown and chaos, and thus the authoritarian theologies of the imperialist and feudal social minds were created. In the modern world, the theology that is needed would "not only save individuals but society in accordance with the laws of the universe," Mathews argued.[196] The defining features of the modern mind were its commitments to democracy and scientific reason. If Christian theology is to meet the needs of modern educated people, he urged, it must reinterpret Christianity according to the two great social forces that have liberated modern people from political and cultural backwardness.

Mathews's later works sought to develop a theology of the modern mind. His transitional work, *The Faith of Modernism* (1924) declared that a credible and morally inspiring Christianity is needed to channel the immense powers given to humanity by modern science and democracy. If these social forces are used rightly, Mathews argued, science and democracy are powerful instruments for good, but neither of these instruments is *morally* regenerative. For this reason, the Christian movement was needed more than ever. Without the inspiriting and chastening moral influence of Christianity, he warned, science and democracy were perfectly capable of producing immense new forms of evil. A new Christianity was needed to help create the kind of free society in which freedom would be a blessing. But it must be a Christian movement that does not appeal to any claim or authority removed from the realm of scrutiny, he insisted. Nothing is sacred to the scientific mind. It followed that for any authentically modern theology, "there can be no God behind a veil too sacred to be touched." Though he still appealed to the example and spirit of Jesus in making his moral claims, Mathews frankly admitted that for the modernist theologian, historical criticism trumped theology, and method trumped any appeal to faith, ideology, or results.[197]

He cautioned that he was not seeking to accommodate Christianity to a new creed. Modernism is not a philosophical or ideological system, he explained, but "the use of the methods of modern science to find, state and use the permanent and central values of inherited orthodoxy in meeting the needs of a modern world."[198] Modernism is not a creed, but a method, the method of scientific discovery. It followed for Mathews that the modern age was right to exalt scientific knowledge over all other forms of knowledge and belief, because scientific knowledge is empirical, rational, and universalist. It explains the processes of nature and events, including the dynamics of religious evolution, with superior analytic power. Under the pressure of his concern to reinterpret Christianity from the standpoint of this superior form of knowledge, Mathews gradually relinquished the last vestiges of his conception of God as a transcendent power. His later works developed a form of religiously tinged naturalism in which God was conceptualized as an aspect of the evolutionary process.

The account of reality that modern natural science presents is the account that modern theologians are obliged to presuppose in their theologizing, he argued. This account precludes any kind of supernaturalism, but it does not preclude a religious explanation of consciousness. If the evolutionary process brought human beings into being, he reasoned, "then there must be activities within the cosmos sufficient to account for the evolution of the human species with its personal qualities." In other words, "there must be personality-evolving activities in the cosmos."[199] This was the key to Mathews's later theology. He argued that "God" is the name that religion gives to the mystery of the personal character of natural process. Unlike his Chicago colleague, Henry Nelson Wieman, he did not attempt to develop his religious naturalism into a metaphysical system.[200] Unlike the Chicago school of process theologians that succeeded him and Wieman, Mathews had no interest in the doctrines of the Trinity, the incarnation, or the atonement beyond whatever functional significance he was able to discover within them.[201] His method of theological interpretation after he converted to modernism was always to discern the apparent function that a particular doctrine played in past social minds and then translate its meaning into the modern idiom. "If we properly interpret the patterns in which the idea of God has been successively expressed, we see that they stand for conceptions of the personality-evolving and personally responsive activities of the universe upon which human beings depend," he explained.[202] To believe in God is to hold in faith that the human struggle for a better world is aided by an immanent life-giving force within the cosmic process.

Like most liberal theologians, Mathews presented Christianity as an account of how the divine power immanent within the world is working to bring about the fulfillment and perfection of nature, history, and finite spirit. His theology was distinctive among liberals only in the extent to which he allowed his understanding of the natural and social sciences to displace the normative functions of Christian history and experience. Mathews believed that by embracing scientific reason, modern theology could bring about the complete triumph of theological liberalism over myth. In his later career, he decided that this project required him to relinquish any appeal to Christ as the source or necessary embodiment of the religious ideal. Though he still referred to Jesus as the perfect exemplar of religious truth, his theology made no investment in normative claims about Christ and worked perfectly well without him. Mathews's overriding concern was to give religious meaning to the account of reality produced by modern science.

Making Theology Empirical

This concern to synthesize theology and science was shared by liberal modernists who didn't share Mathews's naturalistic conception of divine reality or his social science/historicist orientation. The most significant thinker in this group was a Yale theologian who studied under Mathews and G. B. Foster at Chicago.[203] D. C. Macintosh insisted throughout his long career at Yale that theology must adopt the empirical methods of science if it is to regain its intellectual credibility. He agreed with Mathews that the starting point for theology must be "a relationship with the universe described by the scientist."[204] Instead of putting a religious spin on naturalistic forms of explanation, however, Macintosh proposed that theology should use empirical methods to examine the constellations of experience that provide knowledge of God. He argued that God is not merely a personality-enhancing factor in the evolutionary process, but the Object of religious experience described (however fallibly) in Christian theism. That is, it is not necessary for theologians who embrace empirical methods of investigation to give up a theistic understanding of God as a personal transcendent power.

Macintosh's ambition for theology was that it would become scientific "in the full, modern sense of the word," which meant that it would be based upon the results of empirical, inductive investigation "within limits set only by human experience itself."[205] He did not believe that the entire content of valid Christian theology could be verified scientifically, because theology necessarily draws upon faith and knowledge. "There is an element of reasonable, practically defensible *faith* and an element of speculative *surmise* in our theological theory, as well as a nucleus of scientifically verified (or at least verifiable) religious *knowledge*," he explained.[206] But he did believe that Christian theology could regain its credibility only by basing itself on empirically established truths. The crucial challenge for modern theologians was to make theology objective. Toward this end, Macintosh devoted much of his work to the explication and defense of epistemological realism.[207] His theology sought to objectivize Schleiermacher's concern with religious consciousness and Ritschl's emphasis on moral value. As he explained near the end of his career, "In religious experience at its best there is a revelation (discovery) of a dependable reality, divine in quality and function, which promotes the good will in man on condition of his maintenance of the right religious adjustment."[208] This thesis fueled all of his works.

Though he shared the emphasis of his tradition on religious experience, Macintosh's method was not to base theology upon religious experience, but to describe the Object known through it. Though he acknowledged that subjective factors are constitutive to all experience, he believed that theology should attend primarily to that which is apprehended in religious experience rather than to the dynamics of religious consciousness itself. "All religious experience is material for the psychology of religion; it has no criterion for distinguishing between true and false religions; it cannot say the first thing about the existence or nature of God," he observed in his major theological work, *Theology as an Empirical Science* (1927). These were tasks for theology proper. Macintosh argued that theology should be related to psychology of religion in the same way that the physical sciences are related to psychology. "Psychology of religion is simply a department of psychology, and psychology is the science which describes mental activity and experience as such," he reasoned. "Empirical theology, like the physical sciences, would be a science descriptive not of experience but of an object known through experience."[209]

He lamented that liberal theology typically settled for much less than scientific credibility. Schleiermacher's theology marked a crucial step toward the ideal of making theology empirical, but his one-sided concern with religious feeling left his theology stuck in mere subjectivism. Schleiermacher's approach was too subjective to determine which doctrines correctly express the Christian consciousness or even to explain why Christianity should be chosen over other religions, he observed; from the standpoint of the religious experience of absolute dependence, it is unclear why Buddhism and Islam are not equally true religions. Macintosh noted that the Ritschlians set out to correct this problem by appealing to Christian history. Ritschl objectivized liberal theology by appealing to the historical Jesus as the founder of the Christian experience of redemption from sin. As the founder of the Christian experience of salvation, the historical Jesus (an objective norm) acquires the religious value of divinity from those who follow him. "And so, while religious knowledge has to do with objective facts of human history, it is nevertheless not made up of judgments of historic fact, but of value-judgments, expressions of appreciation of the worth of these facts for practical religious experience," Macintosh observed. Ritschl's confidence in this blend of objective historicity and subjective experience moved him to reject metaphysical speculation altogether, on the grounds that theology has nothing to gain by attaching itself to any metaphysical system.[210]

Macintosh allowed that the Ritschlian movement made some progress toward the ideal of empirical theology. Ritschl's emphasis on the historical core of Christianity regained some objective control over Schleiermacher's appeal to experience, and his doctrine of religious value-judgments established that the process of giving value to particular experiences is fundamentally constitutive to religion. But the Ritschlian theological tradition is still subjective, Macintosh argued. The Ritschlians invested a great deal in their claims about the historical Jesus and the "kernel" of kerygmatic Christianity without acknowledging that these claims are highly subjective. Historical science cannot be counted upon to confirm their account of Christian origins. Moreover, their choice of Christianity over other religions was never really defended, but simply assumed at the outset. Macintosh rejected the "unscientific dogmatism" of the Ritschlian presumption that Christianity is the singularly true religion.

He also criticized the Kantian structure of the Ritschlian approach to theology on the grounds that it heightened the subjective character of Ritschl's religious claims. Kant's epistemological agnosticism laid the groundwork for Ritschl's distinction between theoretical knowledge and value judgments. Macintosh objected that this theory of knowledge reduced philosophy to the description and evaluation of appearances. If experience does not gain access to the Kantian "thing-in-itself" or ultimate reality, but only to appearances, he observed, then knowledge is limited to the realm of appearances. This account of knowledge secured a seemingly unassailable basis for Ritschl's theology by restricting theology to value statements, but at the cost of making theology merely subjective. The Ritschlians distrusted metaphysical reason ostensibly on account of their desire to protect the integrity of Christian faith, Macintosh observed, but their metaphysical agnosticism actually undermined their ability to explicate or defend Christianity. One form of epistemological agnosticism leads to another. The Ritschlians failed to secure the objective validity of their religious claims because "with their doctrine of the inaccessibility of ultimate Reality, divine or other, to human experience, they have excluded the idea of a scientific verification of religious judgments."[211]

Macintosh noted that Troeltsch's recent work was redressing some of the faults of the Ritschlian school. Troeltsch expanded the purview of Ritschl's historicism to include the history of all major world religions. He was seeking to develop a universal theology of religion that would be rational as well as historically and experientially empirical. He departed radically from Ritschl in affirming that a credibly rationalized Christianity would have to take the form (in its final form) of a metaphysical system.[212] But despite all of these objectivistic, historical, and universalist elements, Macintosh observed, Troeltsch was ultimately as subjective as his liberal forerunners. He defended Christianity as merely the historical religion best suited for modern Western culture. His historicism was so thoroughgoing that he excluded the idea of making theology "a part of real science" at the outset. "He cannot even claim that it is knowledge; strictly speaking, he has to confess to an ultimate agnosticism," Macintosh remarked. "His eclectic approval of Christianity, as valid for our time and place and culture, is symptomatic of the incurable subjectivity which remains in his religious system."[213]

The upshot was that theology was not yet scientific, but had the potential to become so. Progressive theology in the eighteenth century was rationalistic; progressive theology in the nineteenth century variously blended romanticist, pietist, socioethical, and historicist elements. The next stage of progress would make theology scientific, Macintosh argued. Philosophical pragmatism became scientific when it finally submitted without equivocation to the test of empirical verification. Theological empiricism would work the same way. When theologians finally embraced the distinction between empirically verified and unverified claims, he declared, "then we shall have alongside of the *novum organum* of inductive logic in general a *novum organum theologicum,* a new instrument for the criticism of religious thought and the discovery of religious truth, which will transform theology from mere religious common sense into an inductive empirical science." Just as Thomas Aquinas transformed the "external-authority religion" of the middle ages by using Aristotelian metaphysics, empirical theology would transform the "undogmatic experience-religion" of modern liberal theology by using the inductive empirical methodology of modern science.[214]

Macintosh observed that every science assumes the existence and knowability of its object: Chemistry assumes the existence of matter; psychology assumes the existence of states of consciousness; and psychology of religion assumes the existence of religious experience. In the spirit of scientific inquiry, theology must also assume the existence and knowability of its object as a working hypothesis, he reasoned: "On the basis of knowledge of God through religious experience, one can scientifically assume *that* God is, although he may have as yet very little knowledge as to *what* God is."[215] The work of empirical theology is not to prove the existence of the object of religious experience, but to study the effects of this "working hypothesis" upon its human subjects.

Empirical theology gave primary attention to the laws "of the divine response to the right religious adjustment." Macintosh defined theological laws as generalizations about what the divine being can be expected to do in human experience under particular conditions. His emphasis on "religious adjustment" signaled that these laws were fundamentally volitional, as in the case of answers to prayer. "Experience will show that the indispensable element in prevailing prayer is not a matter of mere words or formal petitition, nor of the name or national mythology associated with the deity, whether Jewish, Grecian, Mohammedan, Hindu or Christian," he observed. "It is the character of the religious adjustment that is all-important, and this will be influenced by the belief as to the character and power of the religious Object."[216] The same procedure uncovered the meanings of more complex or composite experiences, such as the experiences of regeneration, sanctification, fullness of the Spirit, and salvation.

Macintosh envisioned that this procedure might someday be applied to other kinds of emotional, intellectual, and even sociological aspects of religious experience, but his own work focused on understanding religious experience in relation to its conditions and primary referent. The conditions are subjective, he acknowledged, but the referent is objective and divine. In order to understand the nature and character of God, theology studies the effects of its hypothesized divine Object in human experience, especially in the experiences of attention to God, surrender to God, dependence on God, moral responsiveness to the divine will, and persistence in religious attitude.[217] A certain kind of "religious adjustment" evokes the most gracious and life-giving responses from the divine cause, he argued. Macintosh's name for this kind of faith was "the gospel of moral optimism," which he explicated in his major work of constructive theology, *The Reasonableness of Faith* (1925). He defined moral optimism as "a fundamental attitude of confidence in the cosmos, together with a full sense of man's moral responsibility." Moral optimism expresses "and is expressed in the conviction that if only a person's will is right, he need have no fear of anything the universe can do to him; no absolute or final disaster can come to him whose will is steadfastly devoted to the true ideal." The gospel of moral optimism assumes that if a person's will is right, "the Supreme Power on which he is dependent will do whatever else needs to be done."[218]

These assurances were written in the immediate aftermath of the premature death of Macintosh's brother and, shortly afterward, his wife. He later confirmed that "moral optimism" was another name for religious faith, "only this should be added, that it was for me as I wrote not faith as a mere assumption or working hypothesis, but faith as a religious experience, an inner certitude."[219] *The Reasonableness of Faith* was indirectly a report on his inner experience of divine providence and grace in the midst of his grieving for his wife and brother. Macintosh argued that moral optimism is reasonable, healthy, and necessary: "It is what the strong good will says must be true. It is the faith of the virile and pure." It is moral optimism that inspires people to live ethically wholesome lives in persistent devotion to the highest spiritual ends, he claimed. In this capacity especially, moral optimism characterizes the Christian life and constitutes the essence of Christianity as a religion. "Anything in traditional Christianity which conflicts with this is rightly to be discarded as nonessential and outgrown," he declared.[220]

His list of worn-out beliefs included "any number of ancient creeds," belief in miracles that violated laws of nature, and all doctrines that prescribed particular conclusions about historical events. Macintosh found it "preposterous" that any theologian should suppose "that a mere change in one's historical opinions, honestly arrived at, could necessarily make one cease to be a Christian."[221] Christianity is not a doctrine or opinion about historical events, he insisted, but a life, the life of Christ-following, God-conscious moral optimism.[222] His teacher, George Burman Foster, never tired of noting that the essence of a living Christianity cannot belong only to the past. Macintosh quoted Foster throughout his career, while struggling to avert Foster's periodic lapses into "the slough of epistemological subjectivity."[223]

His apologetic for the life of faith began with the supposition that there ought to be a God to give spiritual meaning and moral direction to life. It proceeded to the consideration that there may be a God, since modern science is compatible with the notion of a rational, indwelling, purposive divine mind at work in nature and history. It moved to the tentative conclusion that there must be a God if the life of moral optimism is to be affirmed as a valid, reasonable, healthy, and necessary approach to living. "We have a moral right to believe as we must in order to live as we ought," he explained.[224] That such a God does exist is the knowledge gained through the experience of moral/spiritual transformation, in which we learn that the Object of religious desire is objectively real. Responding to Reinhold Niebuhr's recent assault on theological liberalism, Macintosh conceded that "there is indeed good reason to believe that the Kingdom of God is 'impossible of realization, except by God's grace,' but this does not mean that the world, groaning and travailing in pain, must wait for some spectacular miracle; the grace of God is accessible now, and awaits only 'the revealing of the sons of God,' bearing to every man and to all nations God's 'word of reconciliation.'"[225]

Spirit and Nature

Theological modernism thus retained the moralizing thrust of the Ritschlian tradition, the Hegelian insistence that myth must give way to a higher mode of reasoning, and the focus on religious experience emphasized by Schleiermacher, but always with a difference. Earlier forms of theological liberalism had merely coped with the various challenges to Christianity posed by modern science and historical criticism, but the modernists sought to erase the conflicts between religion and science by making religion scientific. They would not necessarily defend the claims of classical, biblical, or even kerygmatic Christianity from modern criticism, but claimed that Christianity has no investment in any particular claims about history or nature. They presented liberal Christianity as a healthy, credible, necessary complement to modern culture and thus invested everything in a strategy of cultural accommodation. They believed that Christianity could survive only by keeping pace with the progress of modern culture and science. Words such as process, evolution, and progress functioned as virtual God-terms in the vocabulary of theological modernism; having dispensed with the burden of securing a religious norm from the past, liberal modernists saw no reason not to make Christianity as palatable, culture-affirming, and self-affirming as possible.

In this they differed only in degree from earlier forms of liberal theology, however. For two centuries liberal theologians of all kinds persistently conceptualized the fundamental problem of human life in terms of the conflict between spirit and nature. They gave religious meaning to evolution by interpreting divine reality as a creative personalizing factor in the evolutionary process. They explained the reality of human evil as a residue of the bestial impulses of humankind's animal nature. Liberal theology taught that while human beings are finite spirits created in the image of the divine Spirit, they are also evolutionary products of the lower organic forms of natural existence.

This conflict between the bestial impulses of humankind's animal nature and the creative, loving impulses of humankind's God-given spiritual nature set the framework for the liberal understanding of sin, redemption, and the kingdom of God. Liberal theology interpreted the good news of the gospel as the promise of the triumph of spirit over nature as mediated by the example and teaching of Jesus. Under the influence of Jesus, the perfectly God-conscious redeemer, human beings are liberated from the selfish, abusive impulses of their animal nature and transformed into right relation with God. To be saved in Christ is to experience this fulfillment of one's moral and spiritual personality through the triumph of the indwelling Spirit of Christ over nature. To follow Christ in spiritual freedom is to build the kingdom.

Virtually every liberal theologian adopted some form of this interpretive model. The remarkable uniformity of liberal theology during its period of religious hegemony contributed to its dissolution, however, in the generation that followed the First World War. The vaunted relevance and credibility of liberal theology in Europe swiftly disintegrated in the face of the horrendous violence, destruction, and suffering of the Great War. Its rhetoric of cultural progress and moral idealism was blasted with shattering contempt by Karl Barth and his followers in the immediate aftermath of the war. Liberal theology uneasily sustained its hegemony for another half-generation in the United States, where the war was not experienced as a fatal blow to liberal hopes. This was the period in which Macintosh's attempts to make liberal theology more realistic, objective, and scientific were written. American theological liberalism in the 1920s toned down its social gospel politics while struggling to sustain its religious influence and coherence.

In the early 1930s, at the low point of the world depression that did belatedly make Americans question the superiority and goodness of their civilization, a former student of Macintosh's unleashed a devastating assault on American liberal Protestantism from which it never recovered. Reinhold Niebuhr blasted liberal theology for its moralism, its neopacifist perfectionism, and its sacralization of the pretensions of modern liberal culture. Having begun his career as a social gospel liberal, Niebuhr turned on the social gospel with vengeful insight. So-called neoorthodox theologians never matched the collective coherence or consistency of the liberal movement they replaced, nor did they ever seek to attain such a uniform vision. Niebuhr had as much in common with his liberal teachers as he shared with Barth. But with the rise of Barthian crisis theology, Niebuhrian realism, and other "neoorthodox" perspectives, liberal theology went into eclipse. Its defining faith in science, progress, and moral optimism became alien and unreal to a theological generation that did not believe the world was getting better.

The assurance that liberal theology had surpassed or overcome the mythical elements of Christianity was rejected with particular force. This is not to suggest that the generational movement that grew out of crisis theology propounded a single alternative to the liberal view. Among all of the major theological movements of this century, neoorthodoxy produced the most profound and profoundly diverse interpretations of the significance of Christian myth. The only position it shared in common with the others was that the liberal faith was wrong. The notion that Christian myth has been superceded by liberal Christian romanticism, kerygmatic theology, metaphysics, or empiricism was a liberal Christian conceit. Neoorthodox theologians countered that the meaning in Christian myth needed to be liberated from the pretensions of modernity's cultured Christian apologists.

2

The Word as Myth: Neoorthodoxy

No theological movement in Christian history has effected a more dramatic transformation of its inherited landscape than modern neoorthodoxy. For two centuries the pressure of modern science and historical criticism made the liberal strategy in theology seem imperative. Christian theology could not have secured a place in the modern academy if liberal theologians had not defused the conflict between science and religion and relinquished their claims to an infallible text. Theological liberalism was a creative, often idealistic, sometimes courageous movement that sought to make modern Christianity face up to modernity. To its practitioners, liberal theology was an utterly necessary project that saved Christianity by making it credible.

As a theology student at Berlin under Harnack and later at Marburg under Herrmann, young Karl Barth accepted these assurances as gospel truth. He later recalled that he was inclined to follow Schleiermacher "blindly all along the line," despite the strenuous efforts of his father, Fritz Barth, to keep him in the orthodox faith.[1] Fritz Barth was a Swiss Reformed pastor and lecturer at the University of Bern for whom the doctrine of verbal biblical inspiration was a living article of faith. His son would later declare, to the bewilderment of his teachers, that if he had to choose between the doctrine of verbal inspiration and the historical-critical method, he would choose the former without hesitation.[2] During his early career as a student and Reformed pastor, however, Barth embraced the liberal culture-faith of his teachers with the fervor of a convert.

At Berlin, he hung on Harnack's every word; at Tübingen, where he studied under Adolf Schlatter at his father's behest, Barth sneered at Schlatter's theological conservatism; at Marburg he embraced Herrmann's Christocentric blend of Kant and the younger Schleiermacher. "I absorbed Herrmann through every pore," he later recalled. The strength of Herrmann's warm-hearted devotion to Christ reassured Barth that liberal theology retained the essential gospel faith. "One of the best remedies against liberal theology and other kinds of bad theology is to take them in bucketsful," he later remarked. "On the other hand, all attempts to withhold them by strategem or force only causes people to fall for them even more strongly, with a kind of persecution complex." By allowing his son to attend the wrong theological schools, Fritz Barth saved him from a lifelong fascination with theological liberalism. As a young pastor, however, when Karl Barth began to discard his acquired liberalism, his father's conservatism was never an option. "Only much, much later did I find my way out of this liberal swamp of my own accord, by quite a different route," he wrote. The modern orthodoxy that was needed would have to overcome the challenges of modern criticism rather than refuse to address them.[3]

As an assistant pastor in Geneva and then a pastor in Safenwil, young Barth filled his lengthy sermons with hortatory liberal moralisms. He exhorted his congregation to "think seriously about yourselves," to strive for the highest ideals, and to "try to become valuable." As a country pastor in Safenwil, Barth preached this form of culture-affirming religiosity to a perilously small congregation that was rarely inspired or even present during his sermons. The experience of preaching to a mostly empty sanctuary gave him his first glimmerings of doubt about the meaningfulness of the liberal gospel.[4] At the same time, through his acquaintance with the Zurich pastor and Christian socialist, Hermann Kutter, Barth became seriously involved in the Religious Socialist movement. The prophetic social passion of Kutter and other Christian socialists such as Leonhard Ragaz and Christoph Blumhardt was inspiriting to Barth, but he was equally moved by the religious character of their social witness.

The Religious Socialists were religiously serious in a way that was new to him. They spoke and behaved as though it made all the difference in the world whether one believed in God. "From Kutter I simply learnt to speak the great word 'God' seriously, responsibly, and with a sense of its importance," Barth later recalled. From Kutter's eloquent and prophetically powerful preaching and writing he learned "that the sphere of God's power really is greater than the sphere of the church."[5] Barth embraced the Religious Socialist credo that the Christian and socialist movements needed each other. In 1911, he declared in a lecture that true socialism is "the true Christianity for our time." He observed that Jesus identified in a special way with those who are poor and oppressed; the church has no right to call itself Christian, he asserted, if it does not preach and practice a gospel of justice for the poor. On the other hand, there is no prospect that a secularized kingdom movement would be either desirable or successful, Barth explained: "I regard socialist demands as an important part of the application of the gospel, though I also believe that they cannot be realized without the gospel." It was the deeply religious and socially radical Christianity of the Religious Socialists that first shook him loose from his acquired culture-religion. The Religious Socialists were not ashamed of the gospel and not impressed with the achievements of capitalist civilization. Though he later withdrew from active political involvement, Barth remained a democratic socialist for the rest of his life, and a sharp critic of the idolatry and injustice of bourgeois society.[6]

Barth's involvement in the Religious Socialist movement triggered his first serious misgivings about the theological integrity of liberal Protestantism. In the two years that preceded the outbreak of World War I, he became increasingly critical of the liberal emphasis on divine immanence and its accommodation of the gospel to bourgeois culture. God is not in our possession, he warned. God is neither the guardian of bourgeois civilization nor merely the "inner light within." Herrmann viewed religion in almost exclusively positive terms, but Barth's commitment to Religious Socialism drove him to a more critical perspective on religion, especially the bourgeois religiosity of his teachers. He told his congregation that without a commitment to a kingdom-bringing social justice, their religion was a pack of lies. Armed with a socialist critique of the church's acquiesance to injustice, he sought to blend the most attractive aspects of liberal theology with the prophetic gospel of Religious Socialism. He still assumed, with Schleiermacher and Herrmann, that religious experience must be the generative ground of theology. Barth resisted the disturbing suspicion that his own theological formation had been subverted by the cultural chauvinism and nationalism of his teachers.[7]

Theology and the Great War

Barth's suspicion that his theological principles were tainted by his teachers' cultural and political views became undeniable to him in the early weeks of the Great War, however. Barth was sickened by the eagerness of his German teachers to provide religious support for the Kaiser's war. Though his former mentor, Martin Rade, was careful not to claim that God had willed the war, Rade and other German theologians claimed that God was the "only possible ground and author" of the surge of war enthusiasm that the German people experienced. This appeal to the phenomenon of a "religious war experience" became a Christian warrant for German militarism in the hands of the German theologians. On October 1st, 1914, Barth told Rade that his long-felt respect for the "German character" was being destroyed in the process. The Christian part of German liberal theology is breaking into pieces under the pressure of a war psychosis, he complained to Rade. Two days later, on October 3rd, 93 prominent German intellectuals issued a ringing manifesto of support for the Kaiser's war policy. The war boosters included Adolf von Harnack, Wilhelm Herrmann, and Rudolf Eucken. "To my dismay, among the signatories I discovered the names of almost all my German teachers," Barth later recalled. He compared the experience to the twilight of the gods.[8]

The spectacle of seeing his theological mentors promote the Kaiser's militarism was deeply alienating to him. Their appeal to a religiously normative "war experience" made him doubt their entire theology of experience. The moral failure of Harnack and Herrmann to even raise the question of national idolatry proved to Barth that "their exegetical and dogmatic presuppositions could not be in order." If liberal theology was so easily pushed aside by political expediency or so easily turned into an instrument of patriotic hubris, what good was it? The question answered itself: "A whole world of exegesis, ethics, dogmatics and preaching, which I had hitherto held to be essentially trustworthy, was shaken to the foundations, and with it, all the other writings of the German theologians."

It pained Barth deeply to think that he no longer belonged to a tradition that included Schleiermacher and Herrmann. It took him several more years to accept that Schleiermacher really would not have approved of the change in his thinking. Barth was appalled that his teachers were so deeply compromised by their ties to the dominant order that they could not imagine any other response to the Kaiser's call to war. In his bewilderment and disgust with them, he reread Schleiermacher with a frenzied intensity, trying to resist the verdict that Schleiermacher had started German theology down a fatal sub-Christian path. This was precisely the verdict to which he was driven, however. The cultural conformism of Schleiermacher's tradition led straight to Harnack's war-boosting. The claims for a new "war experience" were not distorted manipulations of liberal theology, but its logical outgrowth. Referring to Schleiermacher, he later wrote that "in a decisive way all the theology expressed in the manifesto and everything that followed it . . . proved to be founded and governed by him."

The World of the Bible

These events and Barth's deep ambivalence about the worth of his liberal preaching set into motion a theological revolution. He confessed to his close friend and fellow pastor, Eduard Thurneysen, that his ministry was in danger of coming to a dead end if he didn't rethink his entire theology. The previous year Barth had begun to speak of God as "wholly other" as an antidote to liberal immanence-language. Thurneysen concurred that "what we need for preaching, instruction, and pastoral care is a 'wholly other' theological foundation."[10] In their precarious Swiss refuge from the horror and destruction of the Great War, Barth and Thurneysen looked for this alternative in what Barth called "the strange new world within the Bible."[11]

The world of the Bible became a fresh discovery to him in the months after he stopped using the tools of historical criticism to find it. By putting aside the critical methodologies that, in his reckoning, had prevented him from coming into contact with scripture on its own terms, Barth was awakened to the spiritual power and majesty of the biblical witness. In his perception, he was awakened to the Word in the words. He remarked to Thurneysen in January 1916 that he was becoming "frightfully indifferent" to historical questions.[12] As Barth conceded, this was not an entirely new development for him. He had never been comfortable with the Ritschl/Harnack tradition of historicist apologetics. Under Herrmann's influence, he had viewed historical criticism not as a constitutive element or form of theology, but merely as a means of attaining intellectual freedom in relation to the history of Christian dogma. For the rest of his theological career, Barth would continue to insist that he valued this function of historical criticism. He never disputed the legitimacy of historical criticism for the purpose of historical understanding. He repeatedly asserted that historical criticism has important work to do in biblical scholarship.

Yet his massive writings made almost no use of the results of modern biblical criticism, for the reason that he identified at the outset of the "neoorthodox" revolution. "If we wish to come to grips with the contents of the Bible, we must dare to reach far beyond ourselves," he declared in 1916. To his own astonishment, one of his father's favorite biblical scholars, J. T. Beck, was becoming an invaluable guide to the content of scriptural teaching. "As a biblical expositor he simply towers far above the rest of the company, also above Schlatter," he told Thurneysen. Beck's respect for the canonical integrity of the biblical text opened his scholarship to a world of religious meaning unknown to modern criticism. Barth explained elsewhere that biblical criticism seeks to establish the meaning of scripture by deconstructing the Bible's literary and religious history, but this procedure is oblivious to the driving spiritual force that makes the Bible holy scripture to Christianity. "It is the Bible itself, it is the straight inexorable logic of its on-march which drives us out beyond ourselves and invites us," he asserted. To read scripture on its own terms is to reach "for the last highest answer," the strange new world, the world of God, to which scripture uniquely attests. "The Holy Scriptures will interpret themselves in spite of all our human limitations. We need only dare to follow this drive, this spirit, this river, to grow out beyond ourselves toward the highest answer," he urged. In a word, the Bible must be read not with modesty or restraint, but in faith. Faith is a daring desire to reach out beyond oneself. "And the invitation to dare and to reach toward the highest, even though we do not deserve it, is the expression of *grace* in the Bible: the Bible unfolds to us as we are met, guided, drawn on, and made to grow by the grace of God."[13]

Barth cautioned that the Bible rarely offers what people are looking for. Readers come to scripture looking for guidance on some practical or moral problem and are usually disappointed. With regard to the difficult questions of business life, marriage, civilization, and statecraft, the Bible is almost entirely deficient in offering guidance to the modern reader, he conceded. The question of war is a crucial example: "How unceremoniously and constantly war is waged in the Bible! Time and again, when this question comes up, the teacher or minister must resort to various kinds of extra-Biblical material, because the New as well as the Old Testament almost completely breaks down at this point." To read the Bible for guidance on such questions is to read it wrongly, Barth argued. The Bible is not about how we should find our way to God, but about how God has sought and found the way to us.[14]

Liberal theology reduced Christianity to "the weak, pitiably weak tones of today," but the biblical Word is strong, assertive, and disruptive, he declared. The biblical Word does not affirm or accommodate the conceits of modern culture, but stands in judgment upon them. It followed for Barth that Schleiermacher's opponents had been right to cling to the doctrine of biblical revelation.

"And our fathers were right when they guarded warily against being drawn out upon the shaky scaffolding of religious self-expression."[15]

During the final weeks of the war, Barth fretted that his conversion to biblical Christianity had come too late. "If only we had been converted to the Bible *earlier* so that we would now have solid ground under our feet!," he sighed to Thurneysen. But in fact, his turn against the theologians was perfectly timed. In July 1916 he had reported to Thurneysen that he was putting together a notebook "in which I summarize everything in my own language."[16] By then the German theologians had stopped exulting in the religious fervor of the "war experience." The horror of the war and its staggering death toll were chastening even to the most enthused culture-theologians. In the closing months of the war, Barth's "copy-book" turned into a strange but full-blown "commentary" on Romans. *The Epistle to the Romans* was published in December 1918 and caused a stir among a small but ultimately influential circle of readers. Having discovered only recently that Paul was greater than Luther and Calvin, Barth presented Paul's theology of the gospel as a history-transcending message of redeeming grace and glory.[17]

Theology of Crisis

So-called crisis theology was, at the outset, a message of hope. The book sustained a forward-looking, joyful, exuberant tone that made Barth's later works seem dispirited by comparison. He reported that it was written "with the joy of a discoverer." It reverberated with the Pauline proclamation that through his resurrection from the dead, Jesus has inaugurated a new world-embracing aeon of the Spirit. With Jesus, Barth proclaimed, a new creation begins; as the redeeming "hinge of history," Jesus has inaugurated a new aeon of real history that is distinct from the old unreal aeon of sin and death.[18] In the old aeon, God was hidden to "the old Adam" on account of humankind's bondage to sin; in the new aeon of Christ's triumph over sin, God's sovereign grace works not only upon faith, but upon all unbelief and sin to bring about God's purpose. Through Christ's redeeming death and resurrection, God has inaugurated the salvation of the entire world.[19] For Barth, the Pauline faith was thus the true "essence of Christianity" that Pietism and liberal theology claimed to look for, but never found. Privately he was still assuring himself that at least the younger Schleiermacher would have agreed.

Hans Urs von Balthasar later called this rendering of the gospel message a theology of "dynamic eschatology" with Platonist overtones.[20] For Paul, as for Plato, salvation is about the restoration of a broken existing ideal. Through Christ's intervention in the fallen order of sin and death, the broken temporal order is restored to true history. Paul really believed that true history is made only through the inbreaking power of the Spirit, Barth explained. The truth of the Pauline gospel therefore cannot be known by cutting Paul's theology to fit the worldview of modern academic culture. It can be known only by presenting Paul in all of his strangeness. In Barth's presentation, Paul was an apostle of the kingdom of God who speaks to all people of every age. It is not religiously significant that Paul lived long ago, Barth insisted, because we share with Paul in the same new aeon of the Spirit. The value of historical criticism is that it demonstrates that the historical differences between the early Christian context and our context are "purely trivial." For Barth this was the crucial clue to the weakness and superficiality of liberal theology; liberal theology is weak because it historicizes the truth of the gospel. He proposed instead that theology should "see through and beyond history into the spirit of the Bible, which is the Eternal Spirit."[21]

Like the Expressionist writers and painters that he admired at the time, Barth urged that "real reality" lay beneath the surface of the so-called real world that presents itself to the senses. True reality can be glimpsed only by disrupting or breaking up the world of appearances that conventional historiography treats as "real." In his reading, Paul's message of salvation presented a disruptive, idol-breaking critique of the pretensions of all merely human strategies of salvation. These included every known form of religion, liberalism, idealism, and political activism. Barth's first edition *Romans* was especially critical of liberal theology, Pietism, conventional church religion, and Religious Socialism as inadequate vehicles of salvation. It presented Pauline Christianity as a kingdom-bringing message of emancipation from the illusions and evil of the so-called real world. The new world of the kingdom is not a second world standing apart from the existing "real" world, Barth repeatedly cautioned. It is rather this existing world made new through the inbreaking power of the Spirit. The true meaning of what historians call "history" can be known only through the Spirit's penetration of history. Put differently, Barth explained, the hidden motor that drives "so-called history" is the "real history" of the kingdom. The meaning of ordinary history is disclosed and fulfilled by the revelation of God's meaning for it in the "real history" of the new aeon.[22]

Karl Adam later remarked that *Romans* "exploded like a bomb on the playground of the theologians." More precisely, as Adam recognized, it was the book's second edition that set off a history-turning explosion in theology, but the first edition laid much of the groundwork for this epochal turn. The book's alternately soaring, lyrical, volcanic prose made the reigning liberal theology seem sterile by comparison. Its torrential flow of metaphor made several academic reviewers doubt whether they were supposed to take the book seriously as theological scholarship. Barth was forced to warn others that the book was meant to be an exercise in critical scholarship and not a source of religious inspiration or enthusiasm. Though he considerably heightened the Expressionist style of his work in its second edition, especially by adding a host of explosive images, the book's first edition already made heavy use of repetition, exaggeration, hyperbole, exclamation points and dashes, and other Expressionist rhetorical techniques. The emotional reactions to both editions of the book took Barth by surprise. He later compared himself to someone groping up the dark stairs of a church tower, who thinks he is clutching the handrail but finds that he is accidently ringing an immense church bell. At the very moment when his Expressionistic Spirit-filled Paulinism was being celebrated and blasted by reviewers, however, Barth was having second thoughts about the book's message. It bothered him that so many reviewers (especially Emil Brunner) appeared to misunderstand his argument, but he also recognized that his first edition was overloaded with "organic" and "seed" metaphors and that his age of Adam/age of Christ schematism was misleading. In fact, his reading of Kierkegaard and, especially, Franz Overbeck made him question whether his fundamental dialectic was not theologically and historically misguided.[23]

Barth was deeply affected by Overbeck's posthumously published critique of Christian history, which was extreme, eccentric, eschatological, and to Barth intoxicating. Overbeck believed that the entire history of postapostolic Christianity was fatally distorted and corrupt. As a professor of New Testament and early Christian history at Basel from 1870–1897, he taught that "Christianity" was in its final stage of degenerative disintegration; his closest friend at Basel was Friedrich Nietzsche. Overbeck regarded himself as a practitioner of Ferdinand Christian Baur's historical criticism who rejected Baur's philosophical idealism and, especially, Baur's "Hegelian" interpretation of early Christian history. His writings sought to present a rigorously objective account of Christian history that stripped away all apologetic interests. What was needed was to apply the tools of historical criticism to Christian history without introjecting any religious or philosophical commitment into the picture.

Overbeck's "objective" analysis of early Christian literary forms prefigured twentieth-century form criticism, as well as the form-critical picture of early Christianity as an intensely eschatological faith. In his reading, apostolic Christianity was a world-denying faith that lived in the expectation of an immanent apocalyptic intervention from above. He invented the term *Urgeschichte* (primal history) to describe the early church's relation to historical process. The first Christian communities lived in history but were not part of it, he explained; their world was a counter-world to the dominant order. The source of their inspiration and expectation was transhistorical. But with the loss of the early church's apocalyptic expectation, he contended, the so-called Church Fathers began to accommodate "Christianity" to the dominant order. Patristic Christianity turned an antihistorical apocalyptic faith into a rationalized institutional religion. Overbeck found early signs of this Christ-negating turn in the book of Acts. In the triumphant bourgeois culture-Protestantism of his time, he believed that he was witnessing the final stage of this degenerative process. Modern Christianity was totally corrupt.[24]

Overbeck never resolved his doubts about whether he should call himself a Christian, but upon reading his electrifying writings, Barth had no doubts that Overbeck was a Christian ally in the struggle against Christendom. Barth was also reading Kierkegaard at the time, and he tended to read Overbeck in the light of Kierkegaard's earlier attack upon modern Christianity.[25] Together they blew apart Barth's lyrical mythologizing of the new aeon. The Pauline dialectic of Adam and Christ was still the answer to the problem of Christianity, but

under the influence of Overbeck, Kierkegaard, Dostoevsky, and Christoph
Blumhardt, Barth perceived that if the cross is the meeting point between the
old and new creation, then human history in its entirety must live under
the judgment of death. The new aeon of the Spirit becomes possible through
the cross of the kingdom-inaugurating Redeemer, Barth reasoned, but in the
light of Overbeck's shattering account of Christian history, it was nonsense to
describe the new creation as a new world that becomes a "life process" in our
history. All human history, including all Christian history, stands under the sign
of sin, death, and judgment. After he paid a visit to Overbeck's widow in 1920,
who confirmed Barth's somewhat eccentric reading of Overbeck, Barth enthused to Thurneysen that "it is clear that the idol totters."[26]

Liberal theology taught that history has an inner capacity for renewal because God is an aspect of the temporal order. Brunner thought that Barth also
promoted a liberal conception of divine indwelling—a "divine reservoir in us."
But in 1920, in his address at the Aarau Student Conference, Barth made it clear
that he was breaking entirely from the liberal tradition. He declared that God
is not an object or process within or among other objects, "but the Wholly
Other, the infinite aggregate of all merely relative others."[27] Theology is like trying to draw a bird in flight, he explained. The object of its gaze eludes human
perception and control. For this reason good theology has no standpoint; apart
from the movement, theology has no purpose or ground. That is, apart from
the movement of the Spirit that transcends and yet penetrates human history,
theology "is absolutely meaningless, incomprehensible, and impossible." What
the theologian must avoid is the temptation to make the movement itself an
objectified thing. Aside from the history-transforming movement of God in history, "a movement which has neither its origin nor its aim in space, in time, or
in the contingency of things," he insisted, theology is nothing but idolatry.[28] As
he declared elsewhere, the only basis for a nonidolatrous affirmation of God
and the world is "the possibility of a new order absolutely beyond human
thought," which is the partially realized possibility of the kingdom. But for the
kingdom to become an actual possibility to theology, "there must come a crisis that denies all human thought."[29]

The Gospel as Dialectic

Barth's second edition Romans was written under the pressure of this history-
subverting crisis. It described the gospel message as "the fire alarm of a coming new world."[30] It described all known religions as monuments to the
"no-God." From Blumhardt, Barth interpreted Christianity as a kingdom faith
that proclaims the transformation of the present from beyond. From Overbeck,
he presented Christian history as an unavoidably degenerative process. From
Dostoevsky, he adopted the judgment that the church prefers to give people
what they want—mystery, authority, and miracle—rather than preach freedom
through Christ. From Kierkegaard he refashioned Romans around the dialectic

of time and eternity, and adopted the notion of the "moment" as a transhistorical divine act through which God breaks into history from beyond.[31] These sources gave weight and fire to Barth's presentation of the "crisis" as a universal, permanent condition that nullifies all human strategies of salvation. The war was not the cause, but merely a symptom of the crisis under which contemporary history stands, Barth contended. This crisis is the presupposition of Paul's message. In Barth's rendering, Paul sought above all to make visible the reality of the history-nihilating void. The gospel is not an event, an experience, or an emotion, Barth insisted, but rather "the clear and objective perception of what eye hath not seen nor ear heard."[32]

If all history stands under the crisis of divine judgment and death, a different fundamental dialectic was needed. The vestigially liberal dialectic of the first edition *Romans* turned the gospel into a progress report. Barth's second edition *Romans* set the stage for his subsequent turn to Luther and Calvin, by putting Kierkegaard's dialectic at the heart of his argument. In the Hegelian and Marxist traditions, dialectic is a critical process; it is the dynamic of history that makes history move. In the form of an exposition of Pauline theology, Barth affirmed the movement but also its dissolution. Paul did not think of God as an aspect of the historical or evolutionary process, Barth observed. To Paul, God was a personal supracosmic reality, absolute in power, who cannot be free for us unless he is free from us. The infinite qualitative difference between God and humanity was presupposed. To absorb this presupposition, Barth contended, is to understand the Pauline dualism of Adam and Christ not as an equilibruim of opposing forces; rather, Paul's dialectic of Adam and Christ must be affirmed in order to be dissolved by the all-negating glory of God's grace.[33]

Negation is always implicit in affirmation; at every point there is an other. Barth's second edition featured a stronger use of the language of paradox as a consequence of his turn to the Kierkegaardian dialectic of time and eternity. For Barth, as for Kierkegaard, God was an impossibility whose possibility cannot be avoided. "God is pure negation," he characteristically asserted. "He is both 'here' and 'there.' He is the negation of the negation in which the other world contradicts this world and this world the other world. He is the death of our death and the non-existence of our non-existence."[34] Then how can God's relation to history be known? Barth responded by distinguishing between two kinds of history. History is humanity's inauthentic history under judgment, which bears the footprint of divine wrath, he argued; but "history" also refers to God's eternal history independent of human history.[35] Human history has no meaning apart from its relation to divine history. Human history is qualitatively limited at both ends by the reality of God's history, which is not an aspect of human experience but "the ground of all elements, by whom they are measured and in whom they are contained."[36] One reads the Bible properly not to learn about human history, but to deepen one's historical relation to divine history. Faith is not a matter of grasping a revelation that cannot be held, but a matter of being open to being held in God's ever-gracious hands.

Barth's explication of this theme heightened the first edition's sense of the existential crisis of faith. Faith is the miraculous possibility of constantly new beginning, he argued. There is no way to faith, for faith is its own presupposition. "Faith is conversion: it is the radically new disposition of the man who stands naked before God and has been wholly impoverished that he may procure the one pearl of great price; it is the attitude of the man who for the sake of Jesus has lost his own soul," he declared. In this sense, Kierkegaard was right to claim that faith is never an assured possession or the end of an argument, but "always a leap into the darkness of the unknown, a flight into empty air."[37] Faith in Christ is the radical Pauline "nevertheless!" spoken in the crisis of human contingency and divine silence.

Barth was unsparing in his depiction of the risk and scandal of Christian faith. "In Jesus the communication of God begins with a rebuff, with the exposure of a vast chasm, with the clear revelation of a great stumbling block," he warned. "Faith in Jesus is to feel and comprehend the unheard of 'love-less' love of God, to do the ever scandalous and outrageous will of God, to call upon God in his incomprehensibility and hiddenness. To believe in Jesus is the most hazardous of all hazards."[38] The gospel is the antithesis of reasonable, self-affirming religion. It worships an unknown source of revelation. It sees the idol in all religions.

Barth's language in describing this "fire alarm of the kingdom" resounded with the metaphors of disruption, paradox, cleavage, and nihilation.[39] The new world of the Spirit touches the old world of the flesh "but touches it as a tangent touches a circle, that is, without touching it," he proclaimed. "And, precisely because it does not touch it, it touches it as its frontier—as the new world."[40] The grace of God was likened to an explosion that blasts everything away without leaving a trace.[41] Sin and grace should not be conceived as alternative possibilities with their own rights and properties, for the grace of Christ's gospel "is a shattering disturbance, an assault which brings everything into question." Barth argued that it is precisely the shattering, overwhelming power of grace that makes the gospel something categorically different from religion. To make a religion out of the gospel is to turn Christian faith into one idolatrous possibility among others, he contended: "Since Schleiermacher, this attempt has been undertaken more consciously than ever before in Protestant theology—and it is the betrayal of Christ."[42]

The whole enterprise of rationalizing or psychologizing the experience of grace is pointless, Barth contended. This includes the enterprise of systematic theology. "If I have a system, it is limited to a recognition of what Kierkegaard called the 'infinite qualitative distinction' between time and eternity, and to my regarding this as possessing negative as well as positive significance: 'God is in heaven, and thou on earth,'" he declared.[43] Within time, human beings experience eternity in the absolute moment of revelation and anticipate the complete overcoming of time by eternity. The "No" of the prophet is the sign of the prophet's faithfulness to God the Holy One, the Wholly Other. "It is the faith of men which we meet in the awe of those who affirm the 'No' and are ready to accept the void and to move and tarry in negation," Barth pronounced.

"Where the faithfulness of God encounters the fidelity of men, there is manifested His righteousness. There shall the righteous man live."[44] This was the theme of Paul's epistle to the Romans, which speaks from the first century directly to modern hearers of the Word.

Barth's hyper-Expressionist rhetoric was appalling to his liberal teachers. His tendency to play words against each other, his use of hyperbole and irony, his paradoxical pairings of antithetical ideas, and his overwrought and sometimes overwritten language of crisis were deeply alienating to liberal theologians. His notion that he could move directly from Paul's epistle to the crisis of modern civilization made them incredulous. His apparent identification with Paul's supernaturalism was inexplicable. How could Barth expound Paul's skewed interpretation of the Old Testament, his deprecation of the historical Jesus, his theory of blood redemption, and his theology of predestination as though Paul were above criticism? How could he fail to distinguish between Paul's mythological prescientific worldview and modern critical consciousness? After reading Barth's first edition *Romans,* Harnack predicted that Barth would find a sect and receive inspirations. Upon reading the second edition, Harnack compared his "biblicism" to the apocalyptic radicalism of Thomas Munzer. Closer to the mark, Adolf Jülicher compared Barth to Marcion.[45]

It happened that Barth had just read Harnack's book on Marcion. He conceded that his spiritual interpretation of scripture contained "remarkable parallels" to Marcion's theology, but protested that these parallels broke down at crucial points.[46] Barth was not especially disturbed that the guardians of theological liberalism were tying him to heretics, however; what was more instructive to him was that their books on Paul were so tame by comparison. "Paulinism has stood always on the brink of heresy," he admonished his former teachers, but their writings drained the life and strangeness out of Paul.[47] Conventional biblical criticism dissected the forms, context, and language of scripture without bothering to explain why scripture is worth studying, he complained. It offered profuse scholarly commentary on the literary forms and history of the Bible without even trying to address the heart of the biblical witness. It evaded the true subject matter of scripture, the Spirit of Christ, while consigning Paul's religious claims to the worldview of mythical consciousness.

Liberal scholars derided his approach as "biblicist," "spiritualist," and even gnostic, Barth observed, but at least his approach sought to understand what the Bible was saying before he dismissed it. "Is there any way of penetrating the heart of a document—of any document!—except on the assumption that its spirit will speak to our spirit through the actual written words?," he asked.[48] In the prefaces to the book's later editions, he increasingly acknowledged the contextual character of his interpretation of Paul. He questioned whether he had merely put into words the feeling of crisis that prevailed in Germany after the war. He mused that the recent emergence of a "Barthian" school was perhaps a just punishment for expressing the spirit of the age. But Barth held firm to "that which gave so serious and so severe offence."[49] Religion is always idolatrous, he lectured; liberal theology is a betrayal of Christ; and the fallible, always-deficient effort to perceive the world of God in scripture must be attempted. No amount of historical knowledge can replace the necessity of paying heed to the Spirit of scripture if one is serious about seeking to understand the Bible.

This did not mean for Barth that scripture attests exclusively to the Spirit of Christ. In a critically probing review of Barth's second edition, Rudolf Bultmann pressed the point that Barth's indifference to historical criticism diverted his attention from the Bible's other spirits. Bultmann had been critical of Barth's first edition, arguing that it "completely reinterprets history as myth," but his assessment of the second edition was more favorable.[50] He praised Barth's recovery of the Pauline "existentialist" view of faith; with some misgivings, he also appreciated Barth's understanding of the Christ of faith as the symbol of a living, present power. He affirmed, with Barth, that "the Word speaks and is heard, and is therefore a living, present reality in connection with which it is completely unimportant how the historical Jesus of Nazareth is to be included in the context of psychic historical occurrences."[51]

The problem with the second edition was that Barth was still preoccupied with the Word-disclosing character of scripture. He therefore continued to interpret history as myth. By treating scripture exclusively as the unique medium and witness to the Spirit of Christ, Bultmann contended, Barth distorted the heterogeneous historical character of scripture. He interpreted Paul's letter to the Romans as though the only spirit within it was the Spirit of Christ. But this is plainly false, Bultmann objected. Biblical criticism examines not only the heights, depths, tensions, and contradictions within Paul's letter, but also the history of the Pauline Christ myth, the influences of Jewish theology and Hellenistic sacramental beliefs, and the possible influence of gnostic redeemer myths on Paul. Genuinely critical scholarship cannot ignore these lines of inquiry, Bultmann admonished. When he carried out his own biblical criticism, Bultmann proceeded "from the point of view of showing where and how the subject matter is expressed, in order to grasp the subject matter." In the case of the Pauline letters, this field of inquiry transcended Paul himself.[52]

The upshot was that Barth's either/or was unrealistic. The choice was not between historical criticism and attending to the Word within the words. No writer can always speak only from the subject matter itself, Bultmann cautioned. Even Paul listened to other spirits besides the Spirit of Christ. Biblical criticism must therefore approach the text not only as a witness to Christ, but also as a heterogeneous historical construction.

Barth countered that this seemingly reasonable approach produced its own distortions. It is not credible to think of the Spirit of Christ as competing within scripture alongside other spirits, he contended. To take this approach is to fall back into liberalism, where the critic identifies favorite passages with the Spirit of Christ and writes off the rest as myth or conjecture. Barth argued that biblical theology should rather perceive and elucidate "that the whole is placed under the crisis of the Spirit of Christ." He acknowledged that the text as a whole

comprises the voices of other spirits. The point at issue was not whether the
Bible contains many spirits, but how the whole should be understood in relation to its true subject matter, the Spirit of Christ. As Barth explained, "The Spirit
of Christ is not a vantage-point from which a ceaseless correction of Paul—or
of anyone else—may be exercised schoolmaster-wise. We must be content if,
despite other spirits, we are not wholly bereft of the Spirit; content if, standing
by Paul's side, we are able to learn and to teach; content with a readiness to
discern in spiritual fashion what is spiritually intended; and satisfied also to recognize that the voice with which we proclaim what we have received is primarily nothing but the voice of those other spirits."[53]

The closing phrase was typical. Barth unfailingly emphasized that his comprehension of the Word was fallible, relative, and riddled with cultural blind-
ers. He did not claim to possess God's truth, but only claimed that with "a
desperate earnestness" he was seeking to penetrate the world of God in the
Bible. In his perception, the theological establishment subordinated this concern to its concern for respectability. The theologies it produced reduced God
to a manageable cipher of the whole. The theological systems in which it took
pride were monuments to educated liberal hubris. The Word of God can be
expounded "only in weighty negations, preached only in paradoxes, understood only as that absurdum which is, as such, incredible," Barth countered.
"The Word of God is the transformation of everything that we know as
Humanity, Nature, and History, and must therefore be apprehended as the
negation of the starting-point of every system which we are capable of conceiving."[54] Because human beings live under the dominion of sin, every human answer to the human problem is an illusion except the righteousness of
God.

Debating Liberalism Between Two Eras

Did Barth really believe that the meaning of scripture could be understood
without critical historical knowledge? If the basis of faith is a radical either/or,
what is the relation of religious experience to faith? If God and the world are
radically dissociated, how can people be nurtured into the life of faith? If God
and the world are so radically separate from each other, how should the biblical analogy between love of God and love of one's neighbor be understood?
Did Barth really believe that the tradition of Goethe, Kant, and Beethoven was
worthless from a Christian standpoint? What about the biblical affirmation (Phil.
4:8) that God is knowable through the apprehension of the good, true, and
beautiful? If Jesus Christ is the center of the gospel, but we disparage the use
of scientific historical method, how can we be sure that we are relating to the
true Christ, and not a Christ of our imagination?

These questions were pressed upon "those among the theologians who are
contemptuous of the scientific theology" by Harnack in 1923. Though he believed that the "dialectical theology" movement had no chance of succeeding,

Harnack feared that it was capable of causing immense damage to theology. In 1920, he had heard Barth speak at the Aarau conference and was appalled. "The effect of Barth's lecture was just staggering," he confessed to a friend. "Not one word, not one sentence could I have said or thought. I saw the sincerity of Barth's speech, but its theology frightened me." He compared Barth's theology to a meteor "rushing toward its disintegration" and judged that "this sort of religion is incapable of being translated into real life."[55] By 1923, however, Barth's group already possessed a theological journal and an ambitious agenda. The most promising theologians of the postwar generation were either associated with the "crisis" movement or sympathetic to key aspects of it. They included Rudolf Bultmann, Eduard Thurneysen, Friedrich Gogarten, Emil Brunner, and Paul Tillich. Barth was not above partisan cunning in his efforts to promote crisis theology, but he maintained a more modest attitude toward its movement-character than some of his comrades. When Gogarten proposed to call their journal *The Word,* Barth replied that it would be better to call it *The Ship of Fools.* He and Thurneysen eventually sold Gogarten and Georg Merz on the title of a recent article by Gogarten, *Zwischen den Zeiten (Between the Times).*[56]

This name for the journal carried its own large presumption, however. It implied that crisis theology was developing in the aftermath of the death of theological liberalism. It was precisely this presumption that Harnack directly challenged. In the age of modern science and historical criticism, he asked, could there really be such a thing as a serious theology that does not have a "blood relationship to science?" Is there really such a thing as a genuine theological alternative to theological liberalism? "And if there be such a one, what power to convince and what value does it have?"[57]

Barth replied that he had nothing against historical criticism and was not "contemptuous" toward "scientific" theology. His objection was that this theology had strayed too far from its Reformation roots. Liberal theology taught that the meaning of scripture is knowable through a combination of inner openness, experience, historical knowledge, and critical reflection, Barth observed, but the Reformers understood that none of these factors is necessarily helpful (or harmful) to one's comprehension of the Bible. Luther and Calvin taught the crucial corrective to the historicism of modern theology. The meaning of scripture is knowable only in faith through the power of the Holy Spirit, which is the Spirit of the Bible. The Word of God in the words of scripture is knowable only to believers through the operative power of the Spirit. For this reason, Barth instructed, the purpose of theology is identical to the purpose of preaching, which is to take up and pass on the Word of Christ. True theology is not concerned with validating people's religious experiences, but with bringing them to faith in Christ. It does not strategize about how to bring people to God, but confesses with Jesus that "no one can come to me unless the Father who sent me draws him" (John 6:44).

Barth acknowledged that there is a connection between the peace of God which passes all understanding and the human experience of the good, true, and beautiful, but the connection is the Wholly Other Spirit of God, "the divine *crisis,* which is the only basis on which it is possible to speak seriously of the good, true, and beautiful." The connection between experience of God and experience of the good is not a human possession or an aspect of "religious experience." It followed for Barth that Harnack's concern to make modern Christianity stand with Goethe and Kant had nothing to do with the gospel. "'True statements about God can only be made at all where one knows he is placed not on some height of culture or of religion, but before revelation and thereby under judgment," he contended. The theologian stands with Goethe and Kant only in the sense that all human beings stand under judgment. Harnack wanted to enlist Christianity in the struggle of modern liberal culture against "barbarism," but the gospel takes no interest in this contest, Barth declared: "The gospel has as much and as little to do with 'barbarism' as it has to do with culture."[58]

And how did crisis theology validate its language about Christ? If it gave so little credence to historical criticism, how could this theological movement be sure that its Jesus was not a construct of Barth's imagination? Barth replied that historical criticism actually had a role to play in this area, especially for those who do not understand that we no longer know Christ according to the flesh (2 Cor. 5:16). Historical criticism confirms this truism for those who need to hear it from historians, Barth observed. At the same time, historical criticism also confirms that historical knowledge cannot be the basis of faith. "The reliability and common nature of the knowledge of the person of Jesus Christ as the midpoint of the gospel can be no other than that of a *faith* awakened by God," he asserted.[59] He exhorted theologians to regain "the courage to be objective." If theologians regained the courage to become witnesses of the revealed Spirit of Christ, they would have less to fear from science and less reason to sacralize whatever it is that scientists currently believe. Barth was only beginning to think with Luther and Calvin, but it was symptomatic for him of the problem with liberal theology that Luther, Calvin, and Paul were excluded from its idea of "scientific theology."[60]

Liberal theology called itself "scientific" but was actually highly subjective. Barth's writings hammered on this theme. His own theology had similar problems, however. His insistence on the priority and sovereignty of the divine Object of faith was undercut by his insistence on the absolute otherness of God and his apparent disinterest in the historicity of the gospel narrative. Harnack pressed both points in his rejoinder to Barth. It is not true to the spirit of the gospel to "sever every link between faith and what is human," he remarked, but Barth's emphasis on divine otherness and his complete disregard for Christian education opened a chasm between faith and humanity. Moreover, his disinterest in the historicity of the gospel was also alien to the gospel witness. Harnack warned that a triumphant Barthianism would unwittingly bring about the dissolution of theology itself. If Barth's method of spiritual interpretation should gain the ascendency, he predicted, "it will not be taught any more at all, but exclusively handed over to revival preachers, who freely create their understanding of the Bible and who set up their own dominance."[61] As theology, Barthianism was self-negating.

Barth countered that the historical reality of the revealed Christ proclaimed by the gospel is not the so-called historical Jesus, but the risen Christ. We do not know the historical Jesus, but through God's revelation we do know the risen Christ of faith.[62] As he explained elsewhere, the way to Christ is the same for us as it was for the early church: "It is the way of revelation and faith alone."[63] Faith is not an experience of dependence or even a will to righteousness, he argued, but the acceptance of God's saving Word in all of its offense to human reason, culture, and pride. It followed for Barth that the various struggles of liberal theology to overcome the mythical aspects of Christianity were all misguided. Liberal theology sought to make Christianity credible by separating its mythical forms from a domesticated religious worldview that could be believed. It took the offense out of revelation and sought to gain control over the religious content of Christianity by putting aside those aspects of revelation that were no longer believable.

But this strategy of gutting the Christian revelation is "worse than the bitterest and worst refusal to believe," Barth charged. At least atheists took Christianity seriously. Barth's sympathy for what he called "the most radical biblical science" was explicable in this context. From David Friedrich Strauss onward, he observed, biblical critics had shown that in the Bible "we are dealing with testimonies, and always *only* with testimonies."[64] The most radical forms of biblical criticism emphasized the evangelical character of the gospel narratives. What was needed in theology was not another strategy to salvage a credible piece of history or religion from the gospel, Barth argued, but a recovery of the Reformers' openness to God's world-transforming Word: "By the Spirit scripture bears witness that it is God's Word. It needs no other arguments, and there is no possibility of doubting it, because *in* it as the witness of the prophets and apostles, and also *over against* it (and therefore in us), God the Spirit bears witness to himself."[65]

So-called crisis theology was an explosion of culture-sundering dialectics. Much of its rhetorical and spiritual power was attributable to Barth's aggressive, uncompromised assertion of the cleavages between God and the world, existence and essence, and faith and reason. Against liberal theology, he asserted the priority of the Word of God for theology; but unlike Protestant orthodoxy, he took to heart the truism that theology can never gain control over the Word. Because revelation is divine *self*-disclosure and not the disclosure of propositional truths about Godself, Barth insisted that the content of revelation cannot be abstracted into univocal propositions. Revelation is God's pure act of self-communication, which is not analogous to any other act in the temporal world. As the science of faith, theology is required to interpret God's self-disclosure, but it can do so only "as through a glass darkly," (1 Cor. 13:12). Theological understanding of revelation is limited not only by the incomprehensible otherness of God, but also by the impossibility of extricating oneself from the revelatory act. It followed for Barth that theology can make progress only as a dialectical process of question and answer, answer and question, in faithful anticipation of the Spirit's movement, through which an always fallible discernment of the ineffable divine mystery takes place.

The Demands of Dogmatics

But is this enough? Was the life and faith of the Christian church adequately accounted for in the negations and faith of dialectical theology? Barth began to feel the weight of this question in the early 1920s after he began his academic teaching career at Göttingen. The notoriety of his first edition *Romans* had earned him an academic position for which he felt grossly unqualified. He was no longer a radical pastor railing against the theological establishment from outside. Though he vowed at first not to change his approach to theology, the responsibility of teaching the church's next generation of leaders was chastening to him. He realized that he knew little about the history of dogmatic theology and had no idea how to go about teaching it. He was supposed to teach Reformed confessional doctrine and theology, but he didn't own any of the Reformed confessional writings and had never read any of them, "quite apart from other horrendous gaps in my knowledge." Even his knowledge of Calvin was mediated through the lens of Herrmann's liberalism. "The movement stopped," he later recalled. "Work began. Now it was no longer a question of attacking all kinds of errors and abuses. All at once we were in the front rank. We had to take on responsibilities which we had not known about while we were simply in opposition."[66]

He immersed himself in the history of Christian dogmatics and found unlikely allies. "All day long I am reading pell-mell hundreds and hundreds of pages: Heim, Thomas Aquinas, Fr. Strauss, Alex Schweitzer, Herrmann," he told Thurneysen.[67] He studied Calvin and found him "a waterfall, a primitive forest, a demonic power, something straight down from the Himalayas, absolutely Chinese, strange, mythological; I just don't have the organs, the suction cups, even to assimilate this phenomenon, let alone to describe it properly."[68] He opened Heinrich Heppe's collection of Reformed dogmatic texts with weary resignation and found, as he expected, that the Reformed Scholastics were "out of date, dusty, unattractive, almost like a table of logarithms, dreary to read, stiff and eccentric on almost every page I opened."[69] Heinrich Schmid's compendium of orthodox Lutheran texts left the same impression.[70]

Yet Barth was deeply impressed by the rigor and seriousness of the old dogmatists, as well as moved by their devotion to the church. His researches in Reformed and Lutheran orthodoxy proved to be formative. He told Thurneysen that "after much head shaking and astonishment," he agreed with orthodoxy on almost every point and heard himself saying things in class that he could never have dreamed of teaching during his pastoral career.[71] His theology and rhetoric became more chastened and realistic as a result. Barth's arsenal of

Expressivist metaphors, word plays, and experimental techniques gradually disappeared from his writing in the later 1920s and early 1930s as he increasingly identified with the role of dogmatic theologian. His language became more representational and mimetic as a function of his effort to reinterpret the church's dogmatic inheritance. As he later recalled, during this period he gradually learned "along with a great centralization of what was material, to move and express myself again in simple thoughts and words."[72] Like the realist novels that he preferred, he increasingly wrote in a descriptive, objective style that had little use for rhetorical tropes of any kind, save an occasional resort to irony.[73]

This adoption of a realist style served Barth's equally gradual decision to serve the *church* as a dogmatic theologian. For all of his words about restoring the primacy of the divine revealer to theology ("let God be God!"), Barth's early theology provided little basis on which to say anything about God. His dialectic rested in its negations. Its emphasis on human limitations, depravity, the infinite chasm between God and the world, and the ineffable mystery of God seemed to provide little basis for dogmatic thinking about God. Hans Urs von Balthasar later remarked that in crisis theology, the world looked "so hopeless and forlorn that one might well wish it did not exist." He characterized Barth's dialectical method as a "dynamic theopanism" in which God stands at the beginning and end of an almost unreal temporal order.[74] In his influential reading, Barth's early attempts to develop a more appropriate method for dogmatic theology foundered on the limitations of this exaggerated dialectic. Though Barth warned against the tendency to give inordinate control over the subject matter of theology to any philosophical system, von Balthasar explained, his own writings in the 1920s were inordinately controlled by existentialist dialectics. In von Balthasar's reading, which Barth later confirmed on various occasions, Barth discovered the key to his mature theology only in 1931 as a byproduct of his teaching and writing on Anselm's theological method.[75] The key was his adoption of the "analogy of faith" implicitly expounded in Anselm's conception of theology as "faith seeking understanding."

Liberal theology had nearly erased the difference between God and the world in its efforts to appease scientific criticism. In its protest against theological liberalism, crisis theology emphasized the dissimilarity between God and the world so vehemently that it seemed to negate its own efforts to speak about God. Nothing can be known about God if human beings are totally dissimilar from God. Barth recognized in the 1920s that he needed to find a way to mediate between the theologies of exaggerated immanence and transcendence. In the course of his gradual transition from the almost pure dialecticism of the second edition *Romans* to the second volume of his later *Church Dogmatics,* he relied increasingly upon the concept of analogy to ground his dogmatic statements. Von Balthasar argued that it was Anselm's theory of "faith seeking understanding" that led him to replace a reliance on dialectic with a reliance on analogical reasoning. The fact that Barth scrapped his plans to complete a three-volume dogmatics in the later 1920s and then produced, instead, a study of Anselm's method gave ballast to this reading of his development.

Barth observed that for Anselm the search for religious understanding was immanent in faith itself. The miracle of faith spontaneously and necessarily gives birth to a desire for understanding, which cannot question its own basis. Theological reason is based upon and seeks to understand the gift of faith. "It is the presupposition of all theological inquiry that faith as such remains undisturbed by the vagaries of the theological 'yes' and 'no,'" Barth maintained. Theological reason can never exactly describe its object. But if theological understanding falls short of comprehending its object, he reasoned, "then in place of the joy of knowing there remains reverence before Truth itself, which is no less Truth because this is so."[76] Faith inherently desires knowledge that is never entirely available to understanding, but which brings us in obedience before God.

Though Christian theology is inevitably limited in its understanding, it proceeds with the assurance that it is grounded in truth, because it is based on God's self-revelation known through faith. "Strictly speaking, it is only God himself who has a conception of God," Barth explained. "All that we have are conceptions of objects, none of which is identical with God. Even the most worthy descriptions are only relatively worthy of him."[77] So how does one know that one's faith has been inspired by God's Spirit and not another spirit? Barth the dogmatic theologian replied that true faith is related always to the creed and practices of the church: "The knowledge that is sought cannot be anything but an extension and explication of that acceptance of the *Credo* of the Church, which faith itself already implied."[78] It is the church, that woefully inadequate and idolatrous vessel pummeled in Barth's *Romans,* that must maintain and pass on right teaching about the object of faith. Having already published the first volume of a projected three volume *Christliche Dogmatik,* Barth resolved to make a fresh beginning. He explained in the opening pages of *Church Dogmatics* that he was now determined to eliminate even "the slightest appearance" of existential philosophical support or justification for his theology. He vowed to end various scholarly debates about whether his thinking was ultimately a theology of the Word or of existence. He was also determined to establish more clearly that dogmatics is not a free science of inquiry, "but one bound to the sphere of the Church, where and where alone it is possible and sensible."[79]

The notion that Barth's thinking made a sharp turn in 1931 is belied by the battery of "mature Barthian" elements that were already present in his Göttingen lectures of the mid-1920s, however. His strictures against theological dependence on philosophy, his insistence that dogmatics is strictly a discipline of the church, and his distinctive doctrine of the threefold forms of the Word of God were already present in his first lectures on dogmatics. Though he generally followed the order of the orthodox scholastic systems in developing his first account of Reformed dogmatic teaching, he described the orthodox doctrine of biblical inerrancy as "an exhibit from the darkest corner of the orthodox chamber of horrors."[80] With less humor he decried the "incalculable damage" that the orthodox doctrine of revelation had caused to the church. To

reduce scripture to a book of inspired propositions was to deny the hiddenness of revelation in scripture and thus deny revelation itself, he argued. In this
way, Protestant orthodoxy began the process of subjecting revelation to human
control more than a century before the Enlightenment.[81] Barth's first lectures
on dogmatics proposed his alternative doctrine of the dynamic Word disclosed
through revelation, scripture, and Christian proclamation.[82]

He also relied upon and developed the concept of analogy far more extensively than von Balthasar's later description of his early theology suggested.
Von Balthasar never read Barth's Göttingen lectures and thus apparently did
not realize that even the early "hyper-dialectical" Barth employed various negative and positive analogical models in his explication of Reformed teaching.
The Göttingen lectures already spoke of human limit-experiences and the inevitability of death as analogies of the mystery, inaccessibility, and hiddenness
of God. More positively, Barth spoke of human action as analogous to divine
action, and he occasionally drew analogies between the relationships of the
threefold Word and the communion of persons in the divine Trinity. In recent
years these aspects of Barth's early "dialectical" theology have been explored
by numerous Barth scholars, notably Ingrid Spieckermann, Michael Beintker,
and Bruce McCormack. McCormack makes a case for fundamental continuity
in Barth's thinking from approximately 1924 onward, arguing that all of Barth's
postliberal theology was a form of dialectical realism.[83]

Though Barth maintained that his decision not to finish the *Christliche Dogmatik* marked a crucial change in direction, McCormack notes that it was characteristic of him throughout his life to exaggerate all of his various shifts in
position. The theological differences between the unfinished *Christliche Dogmatik* and the first volume of *Church Dogmatics* were too slight to require a
new beginning, he observes. The real reason that Barth started over in 1931
was not that Anselm gave him a new method for dogmatic argument, but because in that perilous historical moment, against the background of a disintegrating Weimar Republic, he was looking for a way to publicly dissociate
himself from his circle of supposed theological comrades. To his deep and
frankly expressed regret, nearly all of Barth's ostensible comrades were developing theological systems that made use of apologetics or natural theology, or
that blended theology with philosophy, or that politicized the gospel. In 1931,
McCormack explains, Barth's deepest personal need as a prominent theological figure was to dispel the impression that he belonged to a circle of "dialectical" theologians that included Gogarten, Bultmann, Brunner, and Tillich. This
explains his later tendency to exaggerate the extent to which his mature theology relinquished dialectical thinking in favor of analogical reasoning. In truth,
McCormack notes, the idea that Barth replaced dialectic with analogical method
misunderstands the critical role that the dialectic of "veiling and unveiling"
played in all of his later theology. No concept is more crucial to the *Church
Dogmatics* than the dialectical notion that God unveils himself in history by
veiling himself in human language.[84]

McCormack argues that Heppe's *Reformed Dogmatics* had a more transformative impact on Barth's thinking than Anselm. It was Barth's early cram sessions with Heppe that turned him into a dogmatic theologian, if not a "scholastic of a higher order." Other recent interpreters are less extreme than McCormack in arguing for a fundamental continuity in Barth's thinking from 1924 onward. Spieckermann and Beintker play up the continuities in Barth's development without calling for a wholesale rejection of von Balthasar's interpretive schematism. The finer points of this debate will surely preoccupy Barth scholarship for the next generation. One of McCormack's chief contributions to this debate is his emphasis on Barth's partisan consciousness and sense of intellectual isolation. Though Barth always claimed not to want followers, he was bitterly disappointed when his most prominent comrades all proved unwilling to take his theological path. Much of his work took a polemical form as a consequence, as in the opening pages of the *Church Dogmatics*.

Analogia Entis, Analogia Fides

Barth declared at the outset of his prolegomenonal volume that a new dogmatics was needed precisely to fight against the corruption of Christian teaching in both modern Protestantism and Catholicism. Between the paganized Christianity of the Catholic Church and the "constantly increasing barbarism, tedium and insignificance of modern Protestantism" he found little hope for a renewal of biblical faith. Modern Protestantism has lost not only the Trinity and the virgin birth, he protested, but also "an entire third dimension," the dimension of mystery that grounds all serious theology. Having refused to trust in the efficacy and power of God's uncontrollable Word, modern Protestant thinkers could thus be found whoring after "every possible worthless substitute" to the gospel. These included the various sectories of high church aestheticism, so-called German Christianity, religious socialism, "and similar miserable cliques and sects."

His reading of the Catholic situation was respectful by comparison. In the late 1920s, as the outline of his own dogmatic position took shape, Barth increasingly realized that his main rival was not Harnack or even Schleiermacher, but Thomas Aquinas. Roman Catholicism presented the most serious alternative to Barth's developing theological system. His contacts with Erich Przywara and other Catholic thinkers convinced him that at least they were serious; Catholic theology had not dispensed with the entire dimension of mystery that makes theology worth pursuing. In Barth's perception, the key to the Catholic idea of how theology should proceed was the Catholic doctrine of the *analogia entis* (the analogy of being), which posits that there is something in the being of human beings that has its analogue in the being of God. This idea provided sanction for the Catholic desire to argue from humanity to God without reference to revelation, Barth observed. It provided the basis for the possibility of natural theology. He therefore attacked it ferociously at the outset of the *Church Dogmatics*.

"I regard the *analogia entis* as the invention of Antichrist, and think that because of it one can not become Catholic," he declared. At the same time, he asserted that this was the only serious reason not to become Catholic. Catholicism preserved the doctrines and essential mystery of the faith, but in paganized form. The Catholic commitment to the analogy of being proved that the paganizing impulse in Catholicism was not peripheral, but central to its identity. The new expression of the old faith that was needed would break free from the shackles of both Catholicism and modern Protestantism. Neither tradition was willing to trust God's free Word. Neither tradition was willing to lay itself open to the judgment and will of God's Spirit, which blows where it will. Catholicism sought to make common ground with unbelievers on the basis of a philosophy of being, while Protestantism reduced the gospel to "every possible worthless" product of modern culture. Barth's alternative was a Word-centered church that derived its defining theological analogies not from psychology, philosophy, or science, but from revelation.[85]

His analogy of faith was a characteristic of action, not being. Unlike the Catholic attribution of a similarity between creature and Creator, which derives from reason, Barth understood the analogy of faith as an event fashioned by God from above. He insisted that the likeness of humanity to God confessed by faith is known only through God's action. Through faith, God's Word is disclosed in human words. Just as Anselm defined theology as faith seeking understanding, modern theology properly begins with the Word disclosed through faith. Theology does not begin its quest for knowledge of God apart from faith, but begins with faith in the Word of God revealed, disclosed through scripture, and communicated through preaching. Barth insisted that the question of theology's starting point is all-determinative. Whereas Schleiermacher began with the self's prereflective feeling, he began with the concrete self-disclosure of God in human affairs. Faith is the self's decision to accept the gift of God's ever gracious Word. "Faith is not the sort of determination of human action that man can apply to his action at will, or that, once received, he can maintain at will," Barth explained. "It is rather itself the gracious approach of God to man, the free personal presence of Jesus Christ in man's action."[86] It followed that the analogical relation between human and divine being is known only through the action of God upon creation apprehended in faith, which is the gift of God's freedom.

This insistence on the freedom and sovereign reality of God's grace was a defining theme of Barth's theology.[87] With unrelenting descriptive rhetorical force, his massive dogmatics showed what it means to accept that revelation is God's business. Barth acknowledged that most of the time, neither the Bible nor the church's preaching is the Word of God. To confess that the Bible is God's Word is to make a confession of faith, "a statement made by the faith that hears God Himself speak in the human word of the Bible." But the Bible itself is God's Word only "so far as God lets it be His Word, so far as God speaks through it," he contended. The Bible does not become God's Word because we accord it faith, but because by an act of divine freedom "it becomes revelation for us."[88]

Yet even revelation must not be turned into a theological principle, for revelation is the freedom of God's grace, the event in which God, as pure act, be-
stows grace without constraint. "We must think of every state of revelation as
a process of revelation, that is, as conditioned by the very act of revelation; of
every happening in which revelation takes place as connected with what in this
act happens once for all; of all fulfilled time as fulfilled by the fullness of this
time," Barth explained. "But revelation itself is connected with nothing different or higher or earlier than itself." Faith in Christ thus has no ground or possibility outside itself, but consists of "knowledge of God proceeding from God,
as free undeserved grace."[89]

Barth's theology of the Word thus blew away the problems of apologetics
and natural theology. The work of dogmatics is to bear witness to the truth of
the free, revealed, ever gracious Word of God, he instructed. Though his
polemics against the Catholic analogy of being were later softened as a consequence of his friendships with von Balthasar, Przywara, and other Catholic
scholars, Barth maintained throughout the *Church Dogmatics* that theology is
a work of Christian proclamation. It does not defend the reasonableness of
Christianity to outsiders, nor does it look for a common ground on which the
superiority of Christianity over other perspectives might be defended. Theology cannot move to neutral apologetic ground without forsaking its basis in
the circle of Word-inspired faith. Neither can it prove the truth of God's Word
"either directly or indirectly," Barth argued. "It can only trust in the Word's
demonstration of itself."[90]

That is, the possibility of human knowledge of God cannot be discussed
apart from the concrete actuality of our knowledge of God in faith. Theology
does not build up to a belief in Christ's incarnation by means of historical research or religious argument, but listens in faith for the Word disclosed in revelation, scripture, and preaching. Whether the gospel narrative contains myth
or faulty history is thus irrelevant to the question of the truth of Christianity, for
"true knowledge of God is not and cannot be attacked."[91] Christian truth is
known only from the inside.

Barth denied that his revelationism should be interpreted as an immunization strategy. His purpose was to listen to the Word, he explained; he had no
particular interest in protecting Christian theology from outside historical,
philosophical, and religious criticism. Many of his critics based their rejection
of his position, however, on the illegitimacy of his apparent attempt to evade
outside criticism.[92] From his Nazi prison cell in 1944, less than a year before
his execution, Barth's former student Dietrich Bonhoeffer gave famous expression to this critique. "Barth was the first theologian to begin the criticism
of religion, and that remains his really great merit," Bonhoeffer observed; "but
he put in its place a positivist doctrine of revelation which says, in effect, 'Like
it or lump it': virgin birth, Trinity, or anything else; each is an equally significant and necessary part of the whole, which must simply be swallowed as a
whole or not at all."[93] From this standpoint, Barth's revelational positivism was
simply too conservative and fideistic to be credible.

To read Barth merely as a conservative dogmatist is to obscure his radicalism, however. Barth's theology was a rhetoric of freedom that asserted the independence of theology from the accommodating pressures of all other disciplines and cultural values. It was precisely his refusal to commit Christian teaching to any independent philosophy or historical judgment that made him distinctively open to various mythical, Marxist, and radical humanist critiques of Christian belief. With one qualification, he strongly endorsed Ludwig Feuerbach's argument that all religious beliefs are projected wish-beings of human desire and anxiety. He commended Feuerbach's analysis on numerous occasions and urged his theological students to read Feuerbach.[94] His qualification was: unless God's Word is true. If God's Word is truth, then the truth can be known only in faith through God's self-disclosure. But if God's Word is not true, Barth argued, than Feuerbach is right. It is useless to speak of Christianity as a true religion or the highest religion if it is, in fact, merely a religion. Religion is a human search for God or ultimacy, but the Word of God is God's creative and convicting relation to humanity. Christianity is either a revealed faith or a mere human myth.[95] For Barth, Christian theology deserved to be taken seriously only if it took the risk of its truth claims this seriously.

By the end of the 1930s, Barth, Brunner, and Bultmann towered over the field of theology. Barth's third volume of dogmatics was completed, and theologians were already comparing him to Aquinas and Schleiermacher. His passionate opposition to the pro-Nazi "German Christian" movement and his authorship of the 1934 Barmen Declaration had made him a major figure in the life and witness of the dissident Confessing Church movement.[96] After Hitler's seizure of power in 1933, the state church blended "Christianity" with the Nazi ideology of nationalism, racism, and militarism. It welded together the swastika and the cross, placing *Mein Kampf* and the Bible on the same altar. Barth condemned this fascist perversion of the gospel as "the last, fullest and worst monstrosity of neo-Protestantism." His condemnation of German Christian idolatry provided the Confessing Church movement with its theological rationale for Christian resistance to the co-opted state church. His refusal to take the (unamended) oath of loyalty to Hitler led to his dismissal from his teaching position at Bonn in 1935. Barth remained in close collaboration with the Confessing Church movement after he left Germany and resumed his teaching career at Basel.[97]

For all of his fame and influence, however, Barth aptly noted in 1938 that his lifework seemed "to be wanting in a certain accumulative power." Though he struggled to accommodate a constant stream of students and theological followers who made demands on his time, it was chastening to him that his circle of close friends and colleagues was smaller in 1938 than it had been during his crisis theology years. The fallout over German Christianity accounted for part of the difference. Barth had always felt that Gogarten's character was seriously flawed, but in the mid-1930s he was stunned nonetheless that Gogarten developed "into a sinister-looking new German state theologian." He was less surprised that his former sparring partner at Göttingen, Emanuel Hirsch, became a full-fledged Nazi apologist. He lamented that Georg Merz was working out his salvation "in a half-patriarchal half-pastoral combination, with a bit of Luther, a bit of Hitler, and a bit of Blumhardt." And it saddened him deeply that Brunner was developing a new form of apologetics that he called "eristics."[98]

Brunner's theological position was actually closely related to Barth's, but in the early 1930s he argued that it was legitimate for a theology of the Word to make use of a limited form of natural theology, through an appeal to the category of general revelation, for apologetic purposes. He contended that Barth was wrong to reject all forms of natural theology, because a person who had no consciousness of God at all would not be able to hear the Word of God. Some conception of God's general revelation through nature is a necessary presupposition for preaching and theology. "What the natural man knows of God, of the law and of his own dependence upon God, may be very confused and distorted," Brunner conceded. "But even so it is the necessary, indispensable point of contact for divine grace."[99]

Barth's blistering response expressed his incredulity and fury that Brunner could even think of refurbishing natural theology at the moment when German church leaders were wedding "Christianity" to Nazi paganism. The gospel needs no point of contact other than that created by the Holy Spirit, he thundered. If a man is saved from drowning by a competent swimmer, he has no business claiming that his manhood gave him a "capacity for being saved." In the very year that the Confessing Church had been forced to draw lines against German Christianity by issuing the Barmen Declaration, Brunner was giving aid to a paganizing "theology of compromise." Barth further accused Brunner of implicitly denying the doctrine of salvation by grace through faith alone. The implication of a "point of contact," he insisted, was that salvation requires cooperation between grace and human effort. "Brunner has been unable to adhere to *sola fide–sola gratia*," Barth charged. "He has entered upon the downward path." This path led to Catholic paganism, or worse, to neo-Protestantism, which was now offering the world the spectacle of "German Christianity." Barth offended Brunner by pronouncing that after reading *Nature and Grace,* he could no longer distinguish Brunner from a Catholic or neo-Protestant.[100]

This polemical assault deeply wounded Brunner, whose writings cited the exchange for many years afterward as evidence of Barth's extremism and one-sidedness. Though his general position was quite close to Barth's, Brunner repeatedly emphasized his differences with Barth and defended his own position on natural revelation. In the first volume of his *Dogmatics,* he charged that Barth's extremism "injured the legitimate claims of Biblical theology" and thus hurt the cause of neoorthodoxy. Meanwhile, Barth complained that virtually all of his early followers were either stuck in the catch phrases of crisis theology or wandering after idols. His self-perception was that he, nearly alone, was continuing to move down the same path on which he started.[101]

Barth's conflict with Brunner captured the most attention in theological circles and the mass media, but the "follower" who most significantly challenged his theology, his self-perception, and ultimately, his theological pre-eminence, was Bultmann. It was Bultmann who retained a commitment to existential philosophy after Barth left philosophy, especially existentialism, behind. It was Bultmann who practiced radical biblical criticism and continued to discount the historical basis of the gospel long after Barth's theology adopted objectivist elements. And it was Bultmann who forced Barth to address directly the problem of the mythical character of Christianity and the related problems of hermeneutical understanding.

Theology and
Philosophical Understanding

Bultmann and Barth first met during Barth's student days at Marburg in 1908—both studied under Jülicher at Marburg—but their period of close friendship and collaboration began only after Bultmann's review of the second edition *Romans* appeared. Though Bultmann objected that the new edition's constructive argument still made a rather arbitrary appeal to the Pauline Christ myth, this did not strike Barth at the time as a decisive difference between them. Bultmann shared his opposition to liberal theology, his attraction to existentialism, and his commitment to a theology of the Word. Like Barth, he dismissed the Ritschlian claim that history (as known through critical research) has a positive value for faith.[102] Bultmann's colossal work of this period, *The History of the Synoptic Tradition* (1921), developed form-critical techniques that established the probable community origins of the sayings and narrative units that comprise the Synoptic Gospels. This book immediately eclipsed all of the critical literature on the Synoptic Gospels and established Bultmann as a major figure in biblical scholarship. It also established that the synoptic narratives provide relatively little historical information about Jesus.[103] It was published in the same year that Bultmann began his teaching career at Marburg; the following year, Martin Heidegger arrived at Marburg.

For the next six years, Barth and Bultmann maintained a strong friendship while Barth warily observed the increasing influence of Heidegger over Bultmann's thinking. In 1927, when Bultmann heard that Barth was critical of his book *Jesus and the Word,* Barth dodged his query by stating that he wasn't ready "to advance my stupid questions or objections." Each of them needed to feel free to pursue his own course, he assured.[104] But the following year, the publication of Barth's *Christliche Dogmatik* brought out one of the two fateful differences between them. Barth's resolve to become a dogmatic theologian of the Word was moving him to purge his theology of its dependence on Kierkegaard, Dostoevsky, and the rest. At best, he reasoned, philosophy gets in the way of allowing the Word to express itself; at worst, it becomes an idolatrous substitute for the Word. Barth's methodological argument in *Christliche Dogmatik* made a vigorous case for this position while retaining some existentialist elements.[105]

Bultmann replied to him outright that this position was mistaken and self-defeating. "You have a sovereign scorn for modern work in philosophy, especially phenomenology," he observed. Barth was trying to emancipate theology from philosophy by ignoring philosophy. The problem with this strategy was that it left him in the clutches of an unacknowledged and outdated ontology, Bultmann argued. The choice was not between using philosophy or not, since every theology is guided by implicit philosophical assumptions about the knower and the known. The theologian will either use philosophy intelligently as a helper of theology or allow an assumed philosophy to control theological thinking. Bultmann used Heideggerian phenomenology as an aid to his constructive theological reasoning, but Barth's disinterest in philosophy deprived him of the tools that he needed to break free from the discredited ontology of Protestant scholasticism.[106]

Barth's initial response was irenic; though he did not share Bultmann's enthusiasm for Heidegger, Bultmann's description of the choice at issue made enough sense to him that he wasn't prepared to defend in principle his lack of a philosophical orientation. He used philosophical concepts in an eclectic fashion whenever they helped him explicate his theological meaning; otherwise he was leery of commiting himself to a philosophical system. "I have come to abhor profoundly the spectacle of theology constantly trying above all to adjust to the philosophy of its age, thereby neglecting its own theme," Barth declared. Theology needed to have its own work to do. At the same time, he recognized that his haphazard use of philosophy exposed him to the charge of "a terrible dilettantism." In 1928, Barth was willing to live with the charge, while stopping short of the judgment that his friends, especially Bultmann, were accommodating the gospel to alien philosophies.[107]

But by 1930 this judgment seemed no longer deniable to him. Gogarten, Brunner, Tillich, Bultmann, and a host of lesser figures were all looking for ways to accommodate Christianity to modern philosophy and culture. From his standpoint, Barth reported to Bultmann, all of them represented "a large scale return to the fleshpots of Egypt." All of them were recommitting the liberal mistake of understanding faith as a human possibility, and were thus surrendering theology to philosophy. "Where people play around with a natural theology and are so eager to pursue theology within the framework of a preunderstanding that has not been attained theologically, the inevitable result is that they end up in rigidities and reactionary corners which are no better than the liberalisms of others," Barth contended.[108] He preferred old-fashioned Religious Socialism to Gogarten's new "states of life" theophilosophy and Brunner's theology of natural revelation and Bultmann's existential phenomenology.[109]

Several months later, Barth offended Bultmann by backing out of a conference speaking engagement at Marburg that Bultmann had arranged, mainly because he dreaded the prospect of being interrogated by Bultmann's students.[110] The testy exchanges that followed produced a sharp judgment from Barth that Bultmann was in danger of paganizing the gospel. By casting his theology in the concepts of Heideggerian philosophy, "you have done something that one ought not to do as an evangelical theologian," Barth scolded. If Bultmann asked, why not? Barth could only reply "not with an argument, but with a recitation of the creed."[111] As it was, he complained, Bultmann's subservience to the "shameless dictatorship of modern philosophy" was producing a purportedly kerygmatic theology that barely improved upon nineteenth-century liberalism.[112]

The spectacle of "German Christianity" after Hitler's ascension to power was disgusting to Barth; the eagerness of prominent German theologians to blend Christianity with German nationalist fascism confirmed his worst fears about the evils of paganized theology. Barth was not surprised when Hirsch and Heidegger became outright Nazi apologists. What did surprise him was that Bultmann joined the Confessing Church. He had assumed that Bultmann's culture-accommodating infatuation with Heideggerian philosophy would lead him straight into German Christianity. In November 1933 Barth confessed to Bultmann that he had somehow misjudged him. Bultmann was stunned to learn that Barth had expected him to join the German Christians; he observed that this proved that Barth had never really understood him.

Barth conceded the obvious, while noting that in most cases his suspicions were sadly being confirmed.[113] He vowed to reassess his understanding of Bultmann's position, and for several years they resumed their earlier disagreements. Bultmann chided Barth that his biblical exegesis never allowed the text to speak in its own voice, but rather forced the text to fit into his dogmatic scheme. "After a few sentences one knows all that will be said and simply asks occasionally how it will be produced out of the words of the text that follow," he complained. In his perception, the lid of dogmatics was placed so tightly over Barth's exegesis that the Word could not be heard through it. Barth countered that Bultmann's sermons were tedious and that his theology circled around the existence of believers. Christ is not truly proclaimed in all of this talk about human anxiety and possibility, Barth lectured. He also expressed his discomfort over the fact that Bultmann quietly took the Hitler loyalty oath in 1934.[114]

Mythology and the New Testament

But the deeper disagreement between Barth and Bultmann was yet to come. For twenty years Barth puzzled over Bultmann's insistence on linking his theology to a philosophical system. Why could Bultmann not let the Word demonstrate its truth? If Bultmann really believed that Barth's dogmatic categories distorted his exegesis and thus distorted the Word, why were his own writings filled with Heideggerian discussions of being, preunderstanding, anxiety, and authenticity? Barth did not dispute Bultmann's warning that every theology presupposes some philosophical account of the world, either implicitly or explicitly. But to him the appropriate evangelical response to this problem was to limit, as far as possible, the amount of influence that any philosophy might have over theology. Instead of keeping philosophy in its place, Bultmann committed

Christian theology to Heidegger's existential phenomenology. If Bultmann was not a paganizing German Christian, why was it necessary for him to sacralize Heidegger's pagan antimetaphysics? Why did he have so little confidence in the transforming power of the unaltered biblical Word? The answer was scattered throughout Bultmann's writings, but Barth grasped it, like many others, only when Bultmann published his sensational 1941 essay on the problem of New Testament mythology.

Bultmann's training as a critical scholar was in the Marburg history of religions school, which shaped his thinking about the formation of the Christ cult in early Christianity. His *Doktorvater,* Johannes Weiss, taught him to understand early Christianity in its context among the religions of the eastern Mediterranean during the Hellenistic age. Bultmann's early writings distinguished strongly between the noncultic Jesus of Palestinian Christianity and the mythical Christ of cultic Hellenistic Christianity; against liberal theology, however, he argued that the mythology of Christ as heavenly Lord was too deeply constitutive in the consciousness of the church that produced the New Testament to permit a reliable reconstruction of the historical figure behind it.[115] Though he believed that some historically reliable information about Jesus' life could be gleaned critically from the gospel narratives, he emphasized that the lack of first-person reflective accounts, the lack of information about the causal connections between biblical events, and the evangelical character of the gospels themselves seriously limit any attempt to lay hold of the historical Jesus. As he famously remarked in *Jesus and the Word,* "I do indeed think that we can now know almost nothing concerning the life and personality of Jesus, since the early Christian sources show no interest in either, are moreover fragmentary and often legendary; and other sources about Jesus do not exist."[116]

Was Christian theology therefore stuck with a mythical core? If liberal theology was discredited and Barthian neoorthodoxy evaded the issue, was there any way to preach the gospel of early Christianity without recycling early Christianity's outmoded mythological religion? Was Christianity mythical without remainder? The seeds of Bultmann's answer were scattered throughout his early writings, but "New Testament and Mythology" sought to set the matter straight, in plain language.[117] It owed some of its electrifying impact to its bluntness. In his opening paragraph Bultmann depicted the world picture of the New Testament as thoroughly mythical:

> The world picture of the New Testament is a mythical world picture. The world is a three-story structure, with earth in the middle, heaven above it, and hell below it. Heaven is the dwelling place of God and of heavenly figures, the angels; the world below is hell, the place of torment. But even the earth is not simply the scene of natural day-to-day occurrences, of foresight and work that reckon with order and regularity; rather, it, too, is a theater for the working of supernatural powers, God and his angels, Satan and his demons. These supernatural powers intervene in natural occurrences and in

the thinking, willing, and acting of human beings; wonders are
nothing unusual. Human beings are not their own masters; demons
can possess them, and Satan can put bad ideas into their heads. But
God, too, can direct their thinking and willing, send them heavenly
visions, allow them to hear his commanding or comforting word,
give them the supernatural power of his Spirit.[118]

It followed for the biblical writers that history is guided by supernatural powers, that these powers are drawing the world toward a cosmic catastrophe, and
that the immanent apocalypse will end with a final judgment to salvation or
damnation. Moreover, the New Testament picture of salvation corresponds to
this mythical world picture, Bultmann observed. The Son of God, a pre-
existent divine being, appears on earth as a man, atones for the sin of the world
with his death, abolishes through his resurrection the sentence of death caused
by Adam's sin, vanquishes the powers of Satan, ascends to heaven at the right
hand of God as Lord and King, and is due to return on the clouds at any moment to bring an end to history. Paul and the apostles expected to see the world
end in their lifetime.

"All of this is mythological talk, and the individual motifs may be easily
traced to the contemporary mythology of Jewish apocalypticism and of the
Gnostic myth of redemption," Bultmann observed. To modern people it is incredible talk, because the mythical world picture of biblical times is utterly prescientific. Bultmann argued that it would be incredible for the church to urge
modern people to accept this world picture. There is nothing specifically Christian about the world picture that happened to prevail at the time of Christianity's birth, he argued, echoing the theme of his former teacher, Wilhelm
Herrmann. Herrmann taught that we cannot repristinate a premodern world
picture now that our worldview is formed by science, nor should we want to
repristinate early Christian thinking. To make the acceptance of an outdated
mythology a demand of faith, he observed, would be to reduce faith to a work.
Bultmann embraced this thesis of his teacher without accepting Herrmann's
kerygma-negating liberalism. Though Bultmann's fundamental critique of liberal theology applied less directly to Herrmann than to Ritschl and Harnack,
Herrmann's appeal to the "inner life of Jesus" still reproduced in its own way
the fatal problem of theological liberalism: by eliminating mythology from
Christianity, his strategy also eliminated the Christian kerygma.[119]

The "kerygma" is the original religious core of Christian teaching. For Bultmann, this core was the message of God's saving act in Christ. Because his appeal to a "gospel core" was similar to Harnack's "kernel and husk" strategy, it
was crucially important to Bultmann to emphasize the difference between his
interpretive strategy and Harnack's. In his reading, Harnack's "kernel" reduced
the gospel kerygma to "an idealistic ethic that is religiously motivated."[120] Like
most liberals, Bultmann explained, Harnack reduced the defining core of Christianity to his own favorite religious and moral ideas. He fashioned a liberal
"gospel" that lived off its moralism and religious feeling, but the Christian

gospel is not about morality or feeling. The gospel is about the invasion of the eternal into time in the moment. For Bultmann, the saving message of the gospel was about the reality of an eschatological event that is open only to faith. This event is not open to historical criticism, but depends entirely on the self-authenticating effect of existential Christian experience. As he explained in his early career, "the meaning of religion is the being, the life, of the individual."[121] Bultmann's entire career as a theologian was devoted to the task of demythologizing the world picture of early Christianity without giving up the saving message of the gospel kerygma.

His program combined a history of religions approach to early Christian myth with an existentialist approach to faith. Like his mentors in the history of religions school, especially Weiss, he believed that early Christianity and probably the historical Jesus were suffused with the expectation of a soon arriving kingdom.[122] Like Johannes Weiss and Wilhelm Wrede, he understood "myth" as the use of imagery to express the otherworldly in terms of this world and the divine in terms of human life. In his words, "that mode of representation is mythology in which what is unworldly and divine appears as what is worldly and human or what is transcendent appears as what is immanent." His chief example was the biblical tendency to conceive God's transcendence as spatial distance: "Mythology is a mode of representation in consequence of which cult is understood as action in which nonmaterial forces are mediated by material means."[123]

Though he was repeatedly accused of taking a purely negative approach to myth, Bultmann insisted that his method did not seek to eliminate myth from Christianity. The proper aim of theological hermeneutics is not to get rid of the mythical aspects of Christianity, he contended, but to interpret and translate their theological meaning.[124] Demythologizing has a positive reconstructive dimension. It seeks to disclose the deepest religious truths that inhere within Christian myth. As Bultmann explained, "The real point in myth is not to give an objective world picture; what is expressed in it, rather, is how we human beings understand ourselves in our world."[125] This was the crucial point. The deepest purpose of myth is not to convey information about history or the world. To repudiate myth on the basis of its factual claims is to miss the point. For Bultmann, the subject of myth was always rather the human situation in the world.

"Myth does not want to be interpreted in cosmological terms but in anthropological terms—or better, in existentialist terms," he wrote.[126] Myth talks about the powers that human beings experience as the ground and limit of this world. It talks about these powers in a way that brings them into a familiar world of structures, emotions, and possibilities. It attributes an immanent objectivity to that which is transcendent.[127] For Bultmann, myth was thus an expression of human self-understanding in which the divine is described in terms of this world, the nonobjective as objective. It describes the gods as human and expresses the faith "that the familiar and disposable world in which we live does not have its ground and aim in itself." It is through myth that we recognize that we are dependent, not only within our familiar world, but especially on the powers that rule over the world that we indwell. Through myth we learn that it is through dependence on these transcendent powers that we can be liberated from the bondage of familiar limits and evils.

Bultmann argued that myth itself is therefore demythologizing insofar as it seeks to speak about a transcendent power that relativizes and subverts the authority of familiar powers. These familiar powers include the objectifying representations that obscure the truths that myths contain. It followed for Bultmann that the objectifying representations of New Testament mythology should hold little interest for modern Christians. If the most pertinent and deeply truthful aspect of gospel mythology is the understanding of existence that is expressed within it, the mythical forms should be disposable, he reasoned: "What is at issue is the truth of this understanding, and the faith that affirms its truth is not to be bound to the New Testament's world of representations."[128] As he explained elsewhere, "We must ask whether the eschatological preaching and the mythological sayings as a whole contain a still deeper meaning which is concealed under the cover of mythology."[129]

Bultmann conceded that the difficulty of demythologizing Christianity is compounded by the peculiar literary character of the gospels. The New Testament Christ differs from the cult myths of Hellenistic religion by virtue of its historical basis. The problem is that Christianity contains a peculiar mixture of history and myth, he observed. The parents of Jesus are well known (John 6:42), but Jesus is also presented as the pre-existent Son of God *and* as the son of a virgin; he is portrayed as one who emptied himself of divine power (Phil. 2:7), but he is also omniscient and a miracle worker. His crucifixion and resurrection are placed alongside each other in the gospel narratives with no acknowledgment that one is historical and the other mythical.

Bultmann reasoned that most of the mythical statements about Jesus in the gospels are meant to express the significance of his person for faith. His significance is not dependent upon or disclosed through historical observation. "We are not to ask about his historical origin, because his real meaning becomes evident only when this way of asking questions is set aside," he asserted. "We are not to ask for the historical reasons for his story, his cross; the significance of his story lies in what God wants to say to us through it."[130] In the mythological language of the New Testament, Jesus comes from eternity, and his origin is not human or natural because his significance as a figure cannot be known on the plane of innerworldly history.

And the cross? Does the historical aspect of the gospel salvation event make the cross more than a mythical event? Bultmann replied that all objectivist representations of the cross turn Calvary into a purely mythical event: The crucified Jesus is conceptualized as the pre-existent Son of God who vicariously atones for the sin of the world through his sinlessness and suffering. "We can no longer accept this mythological interpretation in which notions of sacrifice are mixed together with a juristic theory of satisfaction," he asserted. Though the New Testament is less precise and juridical in its references to the atonement than subsequent Christian tradition, the gospel tendency to represent historical events as cosmic events is undeniable. The New Testament raises the significance of the historical crucifixion of Jesus to cosmic dimensions in which Calvary is viewed as the divine judgment on the world. Paul declares that through this judgment the rulers of this age are brought to nothing (1 Cor. 2:6). Since we are among those who have fallen under the powers of the world, Bultmann observed, the cross is God's judgment against us.

This was the key to its demythologized meaning. "To believe in the cross of Christ does not mean to look to some mythical process that has taken place outside of us and our world or at an objectively visible event that God has somehow reckoned to our credit," Bultmann instructed. To believe in the cross of Christ is rather to accept it as one's own. The event of faith depends entirely on the self-authenticating effect of Christian experience. That is, the meaning of the cross depends entirely on our experience of being crucified with Christ. "As the salvation occurrence the cross is not an isolated event that has happened to Christ as some mythical person but rather in its significance this event has 'cosmic' dimensions," he explained. Moreover, the cross has a history-transforming meaning that is expressed by representing Calvary as an eschatological event. From this perspective, the cross is not an event of the past to which one looks back; rather "it is the eschatological event in time and beyond time insofar as it is constantly present wherever it is understood in its significance, that is, for faith." In faith the eschatological meaning of the cross is made present through the sacraments of Baptism and Communion as well as the daily experience of following the way of Christ.[131]

And what about the resurrection of Christ? Is it anything more than a mythical expression of the significance of the cross? Bultmann acknowledged that the problem of the resurrection is not analogous to that of the cross. With the resurrection, he explained, it is not a matter of discerning the religious significance of an historical event, for the resurrection is not historical. Modern science does not believe that the course of nature can be interrupted by a supernatural power, nor does modern history give any credence to reports about divine or demonic interventions in history. "Instead, the course of history is considered to be an unbroken whole, complete in itself, though differing from the course of nature because there are in history spiritual powers which influence the will of persons," Bultmann observed. "Modern men take it for granted that the course of nature and of history, like their own inner life and their practical life, is nowhere interrupted by the intervention of supernatural powers."[132]

But the resurrection of Christ is more than a mythical event, he asserted. Through its unity with the cross as a cosmic event, the resurrection is an eschatological event that attests to Christ's abolition of the power of death. It is not the basis of faith in the saving meaning of the cross, but is rather constitutive within the faith that gives meaning to the cross. Faith in the cross of Christ cannot be secured through faith in the resurrection, Bultmann argued, for in this case Christianity would be reduced to the establishment of one faith by another faith. Put differently, the resurrection of Christ is not the basis of Christian faith, but an object of faith that proclaims much more "than that a dead person has returned to life in this world." Christianity proclaims, rather, that Christ has broken the power of death universally. To believe in the meaning of the cross is to believe in the resurrection, Bultmann explained: "In fact, faith in the resurrection is nothing other than faith in the cross as the salvation event, as the cross of Christ." And on what basis may we believe in the redeeming effect of Christ's death? "Here there seems to me to be only one answer: because it is proclaimed as such, because it is proclaimed together with the resurrection," he replied. "Christ the crucified and risen one encounters us in the word of proclamation, and nowhere else. And faith in this word is the true faith of Easter."[133]

Is it enough to say that faith is nothing but simple hearing? Is it enough to say that faith grows out of the listener's encounter with the Word of God? Bultmann answered emphatically that this must be enough. "But this answer is valid only if the Scriptures are understood neither as a manual of doctrine nor as a record of witnesses to a faith which I interpret by sympathy and empathy," he cautioned. "On the contrary, to hear the Scriptures as the Word of God means to hear them as a word which is addressed to me, as *kerygma,* as a proclamation." Faith is not a piece of objective information or an historical conclusion, but a personal response to the Word. "The fact that the word of the Scriptures is God's Word cannot be demonstrated objectively; it is an event which happens here and now," Bultmann explained. "God's Word is hidden in the Scriptures as each action of God is hidden everywhere."[134]

Bultmann regarded demythologizing as analogous to the Pauline/Lutheran doctrine of justification by faith alone. More precisely, he sometimes argued that demythologization should be understood as an application of the doctrine of justification by faith alone to the sphere of religious thought. Just as the doctrine of justification by faith destroys the illusion of control and security in the sphere of salvation, he explained, so does the method of demythologization destroy every false security based on objective knowledge: "There is no difference between security based on good works and security built on objectifying knowledge. The man who desires to believe in God must know that he has nothing at his own disposal on which to build this faith, that he is, so to speak, in a vacuum. He who abandons every form of security shall find the true security. Man before God has always empty hands. He who gives up, he who loses every security shall find security."[135]

The Demythologizing Controversy

By mid-century these arguments about the mythical character and meaning of Christian faith dominated the agenda of modern theology. "New Testament and Mythology" alone set off an explosion of fundamentalist and conservative denunciations, hundreds of articles and books on demythologizing, and five volumes of collected responsive essays by liberal, Barthian, Anglican, Catholic, and Bultmannian theologians.[136] Conservatives generally regarded Bultmann's work as an outright attack on Christian faith and responded accordingly. The bishops of the United Evangelical-Lutheran Church of Germany were more restrained, but in 1953 they issued a statement read from every German Lutheran pulpit that censured Bultmann's movement for "leading to a denial of the facts to which Scripture bears witness."[137] Catholic theologians frequently made the same charge, while warning that the logic of Protestantism probably does lead to a demythologized kerygma, just as Bultmann claimed.[138]

Various theologians closer to Bultmann's position raised questions about the objectivity of the redemptive biblical events, the legitimacy of Bultmann's existentialist hermeneutic, and the problem of the relation between history and kerygma. Julius Schniewind questioned whether the human mind can ever dispense with myth and criticized Bultmann for reducing the meaning of the cross to the realm of personal experience. "Everything Bultmann says about the cross is located not at Calvary but in our human experience," he objected.[139] Helmut Thielicke similarly objected that in Bultmann's approach, the saving acts of God recorded in biblical history are turned into a mere prolegomenon to the actual event of redemption that occurs in present experience.[140] Austin Farrer rejected Bultmann's assumption that beliefs about the historicity of past events can be established only on historical-critical grounds.[141] Friedrich Schumann argued that existentialist analysis, which concerns itself with the being of the human subject as it is, cannot be identical with the Christian understanding of existence, which views the human subject always in relation to God.[142] John Macquarrie argued that Bultmann overestimated the problem of myth as a stumbling block to modern belief.[143] Gerhard Gloege observed that Bultmann's hermeneutical method left no room for divine action or being outside the realm of individual human experience. Like Schleiermacher, Bultmann's existentialism relegated the divine Trinity (in effect) to an appendix, since God's triune inner-relation cannot be read off directly from human experience.[144] From the theological left, Fritz Buri argued that Bultmann's method arbitrarily stopped short of demythologizing the kerygma itself.[145] From a position outside Christianity, philosopher Karl Jaspers countered that the true task for theology is not to demythologize Christian teaching, but to recover and appropriate the truth in Christian myth. Theology is never convincing or true when it hides behind the authority of science, Jaspers lectured. But instead of grounding his theological program in the reality and movement of the Spirit, Bultmann hid behind a mistaken understanding of science and myth.[146]

Bultmann responded to most such criticisms of his position by restating his conception of the kerygmatic center of Christianity. Against the German bishops and numerous others, he maintained that the kerygma does not contain any "facts" on which Christian teaching might be "founded." The New Testament does not bear witness to a collection of facts that are accessible to knowledge and prior to faith; rather, the New Testament bears witness to the eschatological phenomenon of the saving Christ. "In the kerygma Jesus encounters us as the Christ—that is, as the eschatological phenomenon *par excellence*," he explained. Not even the historical Jesus is part of the kerygma, for it is only as the Savior through whom God judges and redeems the world that Jesus becomes the object of faith. "I still deny that historical research can ever encounter any traces of the epiphany of God in Christ," he declared. "All it can do is to confront us with the Jesus of history. Only the Church's proclamation can bring us face to face with Kyrios Christos."[147]

Bultmann clarified elsewhere that this was not a purely existential claim. The meaning or truth of the Christ event as a thing of the past does not depend *entirely* upon the hearer's existential decision, he asserted. To accept Christ in faith is to open oneself to a claim that is latent in the Christ event of the past.[148] Bultmann argued that this historically grounded faith event is not mythical and therefore does not require demythologization. For some of his critics, this conception of the kerygmatic Word was too much to swallow; for many others it was not enough to base Christianity upon. Bultmann replied to both groups of critics that he would take his stand on the authority of the kerygma, which he described, in unabashedly circular terms, as "that which gives meaning to an occurrence to whose historicity it testifies."[149]

Kerygma and Saving History

This conception of the kerygma as the elusive but irreducible core of true Christianity, like Bultmann's distinction between *Historie* and *Geschichte,* was rooted in the nineteenth-century mediating theology of Martin Kähler, but Bultmann's commitment to an existentialist hermeneutic stripped Kähler's approach of its objectivist elements. In the 1890s, Kähler sought to establish a third way between orthodoxy and theological liberalism by showing that both approaches obscured the saving gospel message. Orthodoxy obscured the biblical picture of Christ by making belief in Christ dependent upon belief in the doctrine of biblical inspiration. In its effort to protect Christian truth, Protestant orthodoxy reversed the true relation of Christ to scripture and thus imprisoned the gospel message. On the other hand, liberal theology committed an equal disservice to the gospel by seeking to penetrate beyond the biblical picture of Christ to recover the Jesus of history.

More than a decade before Schweitzer's attack on the liberal life of Jesus movement, Kähler declared that the entire movement was "a blind alley." The various historical Jesuses uncovered by liberal theology were no closer to the real Christ than the "notorious dogmatic Christ" of Byzantine theology, he insisted.[150] Liberal Protestantism turned Jesus into a hero; its piety was thus a case of hero worship.[151] "In going behind Jesus Christ as he is portrayed in the church's tradition—and this means also behind the New Testament picture of Christ—it wants to get at the *real* Jesus," he observed, but in every case the critics produced a Jesus of their own imagination and desire. Kähler sympathized with the liberal-historicist desire to get to the "real Jesus" behind the gospel sources. "A blind alley usually has something alluring about it, or no one would enter it in the first place," he conceded.[152] But the futility of the quest for the historical Jesus was amply confirmed by the results of the life of Jesus movement. There is no "real Jesus" apart from faith that historical criticism can dig out of the gospels, he argued, for the gospels are testimonies of faith without remainder. The only "real Jesus" to be found or known is the historic Christ confessed by faith in the gospels.

The concept of the "historic Christ" was Kähler's invention, which he presented as a counterconcept to the liberal distinction between the Jesus of history and the Christ of faith. Herrmann's dichotomy between the basis of faith (the historical Jesus) and the content of faith (the biblical Christ) exemplified the kind of apologetic that Kähler sought to refute. Herrmann argued that the seeker's vision of the "inner life of Jesus" forms the basis of Christian faith, which then produces in the believer "thoughts of faith" pertaining to the nature of Christ, the resurrection, and the Trinity.[153] Kähler appreciated that Herrmann's appeal to the inner life of Jesus made his theology less dependent than other liberal theologies on the latest conclusions of historical criticism. It also made his theology less vulnerable to historical refutation.

But this advantage was only a matter of degree, he argued. Herrmann's idea of the "inner life of Jesus" assumed that the historical Jesus possessed a messianic self-consciousness, but this assumption was strongly disputed by many scholars. Moreover, Herrmann's characterization of the resurrection of Christ as a derivative "thought of faith" (Glaubensgedanke) epitomized the problem with liberal historiography. The resurrection of Jesus is not a derivative or secondary product of faith, Kähler argued, but the basis of faith. By separating the so-called historical Jesus from the Christ of faith, liberal theologians were trying to make Christianity believable to modern readers who found the New Testament Christ unbelievable.[154]

But the New Testament Christ is the only Christ we have, Kähler objected. We have no knowledge of a Christ who is not the Christ proclaimed by Easter faith. Kähler distinguished between history as the objective dead past (Historie) and history as the significant or "historic" past (Geschichte) to elucidate his thesis that the only possible basis of Christian faith is the historic biblical Christ and not the so-called historical Jesus. By "historic" he meant the discernible personal effect that a great figure leaves behind and which influences later generations. The decisive influence that Jesus had upon posterity "consisted in nothing else but the faith of his disciples, their conviction that in Jesus they had found the conqueror of guilt, sin, temptation, and death," he observed.[155] From this single influence everything else in Christianity has emanated. It was not history that gave Christ to the world—the historians of his time ignored him—but rather his historic influence upon the disciples.

And what was it that these early Christian evangelists proclaimed to the world? Kähler could have called it the gospel "message" (Botschaft) or "proclamation" (Verkündigung), but these terms already had fixed connotations in German theology, so he appropriated the ancient Greek word kerygma. "It is as kerygma, as a deliverance of the divine commission to his heralds and messengers, that the ancient word of Scripture acquires its significance in the church," he declared.[156] It is as kerygma that the meaning of the historic Christ event is brought forward in each historical present. The kerygma is directly related to *Geschichte,* but only indirectly to *Historie.* Christian believers should have no fear of historical criticism, Kähler assured, because mere *historical* criticism cannot get its hands on the kerygma, the faith of early Christian proclamation in which Christ dwells. The historical foundation of the kerygma is the preaching that created Christianity, Kähler argued. This is the irreducible core of Christian teaching. Every attempt to get behind it distorts the past and present reality of the true Christ:

> The real Christ, that is, the Christ who has exercised an influence in history, with whom millions have communed in childlike faith, and with whom the great witnesses of faith have been in communion—while striving, apprehending, triumphing, and proclaiming—*this real Christ is the Christ who is preached.* The Christ who is preached, however, is precisely the Christ of faith. He is the Jesus whom the eyes of faith behold at every step he takes and through every syllable he utters—the Jesus whose image we impress upon our minds because we both would and do commune with him, our risen, living Lord.[157]

Neoorthodoxy claimed these ideas for itself in the generation following Kähler's death. Barth declared that Kähler's critique of the life of Jesus movement "cannot be over-praised."[158] Brunner, Tillich, Gogarten, and many others adopted his concepts and much of his argument. Bultmann's kerygmatic positivism adhered closely to the spirit and content of Kähler's theology. In his hands, the concept of *Geschichte* translated readily into "existential significance." This translation opened up an important difference between Kähler and Bultmann, however. Bultmann and his followers tended to read their own existentialist individualism into Kähler, but this reading overlooked Kähler's emphasis on the total picture of the historic Christ and the holistic character of Christian faith, as well as his assumption that Easter faith has an objective referent. For Kähler, the reality of the "real Christ" always included the ever-expanding circle of his influence within the life, teaching, and preaching of the church. Kähler never reduced the meaning of Christianity to privatized I-and-Thou encounters, but always emphasized that the real Christ is not known to personal faith apart from the influence of the historic Christ in the Christian community.

Moreover, just as he rejected Herrmann's characterization of the resurrection of Christ as a derivative "thought of faith," it made no sense to Kähler to characterize the church's Easter faith as entirely a product of the disciples' experience. He took for granted that Easter was about something that happened first to Jesus and then to the disciples. To negate either side of the Easter event is to lose the biblical Christ, for as Carl Braaten has remarked, the history of Christ "includes the event of his resurrection."[159] That is, to negate the object of the Easter event is to lose the basis of kerygmatic preaching, and thus the gospel.

It is one thing to argue that the objective Easter event behind the church's proclamation is not open to historical science. It is another matter entirely to claim that the Easter event lacks any objective facticity. When Bultmann maintained that the kerygma contains no facts, he certainly appeared to deny that the resurrection has an objective dimension. Many of his followers made this claim without equivocation. In their defense, they pointed to numerous statements from Bultmann that denied any factual basis to the Easter faith. They also pointed to his claim that nothing can be known about the life and personality of Jesus, as well as his insistence that only the kerygmatic Christ is the Lord, and not the Jesus of history.[160] Bultmann's flippant assurance that no corpse has ever come back to life or risen from the grave added fuel to this reading of his argument.[161]

Yet Bultmann also occasionally made statements that included the historical Jesus and the Easter appearances in the content of the kerygma. In 1959, with no acknowledgment that he had changed his mind or that this statement contradicted many of his previous statements, he wrote that the content of the kerygma is "an event, a historical fact: the appearance of Jesus of Nazareth, his birth, but at the same time his work, his death and his resurrection." Does this mean that Christian preaching deals with historical facts? "Yes and no!" Bultmann asserted. "It is the communication of a historical fact which is at the same time more than a historical fact, so that its communication is something more than mere communication."[162]

Barth and Bultmann
on Kerygma and Existence

Bultmann's ambiguity about the relation of history to the kerygma thus contributed directly to much of the controversy over his theological position. It also moved Barth to complain that for all his concern about understanding, Bultmann was often impossible to understand. Barth understood enough about Bultmann's theology to conclude that it was too subjective and anthropocentric to justify its claim to biblical truth, however. In Bultmann's hermeneutic, we experience ourselves as we are—and as we should be—as hearers of the kerygma. Through faith in the gospel message, we then experience ourselves in transition from one state to another, which leads to the experience of ourselves as objects of God's redemptive act. But this is not the pattern of the New Testament message, Barth objected. "Does the New Testament begin with man's subjective experiences, with man as the recipient of its message?" he asked. "Is not this reversing the New Testament?"[163]

A host of related distortions flowed from Bultmann's commitment to existentialism. Rather than present Christ as the kerygma, he presented the Christ event as something that is known in and through the kerygma. This translation drives Christ to the margin, Barth observed. It presents not a doctrine of Christ, but a doctrine about the dynamics of existential transformation. "Is the kerygma, thus conceived, a *gospel*—a kerygma in which nothing is said of that in which or of him in whom its recipients are to believe?" Barth asked.[164] What happened to the religious object? Without an outside redeeming referent, what is this existential gospel but a new law? In an earlier reply to Barth, Bultmann had confirmed that "I *am* trying to substitute anthropology for theology, for I am interpreting theological affirmations as assertions about human life."[165] In this case, Barth responded, what has happened to the insistence on the priority of the divine act? The New Testament describes the cross of Christ as "an event with an inherent significance of its own," he observed, but in Bultmann's hermeneutic it only acquired any significance by being taken up into the kerygma and evoking the response of faith. In Bultmann's words, "The saving efficacy of the cross is not derived from the fact that it is the cross of Christ: it is the cross of Christ because it has this saving efficacy."[166] Barth rubbed his eyes. This statement is clear only in its determination to reverse the sequence of all New Testament statements about salvation, he judged.

Bultmann's strategy culminated in his reworking of the Easter event. Barth suggested that one might have hoped that, at least with the resurrection, Bultmann would have recognized that some objective referent is necessary to establish a basis for Christian faith and proclamation. But even here, Bultmann's Christ could not break out of his kerygmatic prison. "Even here, nothing can be said about its being an act of God on its own right quite apart from its happening in the kerygma and in faith," Barth complained. "Nothing can be said about it as the foundation and content both of faith and of the kerygma." Barth drove the implication home. In Bultmann's program, he observed, "nothing can be said about the risen Christ as such. He is not allowed any life of his own after he rose from the dead."[167] Under Bultmann's rules, nothing could be said about Jesus' encounters with the women and the disciples before they were charged with the kerygma and inaugurated the church.

Though Bultmann spoke of Christ's resurrection as an act of God, Barth observed, "this does not mean that men beheld the glory of God in the Word made flesh and put to death in the flesh, or that they beheld him raised from the dead in space and time as the outcome of his previous earthly life." In Bultmann's doctrine, the disciples beheld the glory of the resurrected Christ only in the kerygma, after his Lordship was proclaimed. Thus the resurrection of Christ was no longer for Bultmann "the basic fact of Christianity," Barth noted, "but only an explanation of the kerygma and of faith, and one which could be dispensed with if necessary." It has the status of Herrmann's thought of faith. Bultmann's Christ has no reality apart from the kerygma and faith. "I can only hear distant echoes of the New Testament," Barth complained, with evident sadness. "He seems to think that in the kerygma Jesus Christ is on his way to rising in us. And that is just why I cannot understand him . . . I am sorry to have to say this."[168]

Bultmann justified this project of reinterpretation on account of the imperative to demythologize Christianity. Barth would have saved him the trouble. "Not only is it a barbarism, but it is unnecessarily provoking," he remarked of demythologizing. Bultmann proposed that the biblical message can only be made intelligible by translating its mythical expressions into the nonmythical language of existential encounter. Barth countered that no text can be understood if it is approached with preconceived notions about its meaning, intelligibility, or credibility. "Is it not preferable to come to it with an open mind, and patiently follow what it has to say?" he asked. "Surely, if we want to understand any given text, the provisional clue to its understanding must be sought from the text itself, and moreover from its spirit, content and aim."[169] It is one thing to recognize that there is an element of philosophy in all theological language, Barth argued; it is something else when a particular philosophy is allowed to control theological concepts. Barth admitted elsewhere that he leaned toward Hegel, but Bultmann submitted entirely to a philosophy "that recognizes the existence only of the human subject."[170]

Barth recalled that the whole point of crisis theology had been to liberate theology from the Egyptian bondage of philosophy. The "neoorthodox" alternative rested upon the possibility of the human subject being known by the object of his or her knowledge through the movement of the Word. "As I see it, Bultmann has forsaken our road and gone back to the old one again," he concluded. "He has gone back to the old idea of understanding which we had abandoned."[171]

Truth as Encounter:
Barth, Bultmann, and Brunner

This debate between Barth and Bultmann consumed most of the energies of modern theology in the middle years of this century. Bultmann's closest followers repeated his strictures against biblical (and Barthian) mythology and insisted that myth is falsifying mainly because it objectifies religious experience. These theologians included Friedrich Gogarten, Hans-Werner Bartsch, the team of Christian Hartlich and Walter Sachs, and Schubert Ogden.[172] Though his dogmatics rarely discussed his disagreements with an ascending demythologization movement, Barth admitted that he found himself in an intensive ongoing debate with Bultmann.[173] "His subject is always present, even in those places where with his methods and results before me I have consciously ignored him," Barth reported.[174] Though he respected Bultmann and also those who sought to build bridges between his theology and Bultmann's, he insisted that the two theologies are incompatible; one must choose between them.

This did not stop theologians such as Helmut Thielicke, Heinrich Ott, and Hermann Diem from seeking to mediate the differences between Barth and Bultmann.[175] In his own way, the considerable popularity of Brunner's version of neoorthodoxy owed something (besides Brunner's superior clarity) to his mediating position.[176] Though his substantive theological discussions of divine reality, Christology, and the priority of the Word were generally close to Barth's perspective, Brunner's apologetic interest led him to develop a theology of natural revelation. Moreover, in his religious epistemology Brunner continued to expound a theory of existential encounter long after Barth's theology took an objectivist turn. Brunner never "outgrew" the Kierkegaardian thesis that human beings cannot find the truth about ourselves because the truth is not in us and we are not in it.[177] For him, the Kierkegaardian language of truth as encounter uniquely expressed the I-Thou relation of the saving gospel message. "Truth as encounter is not truth about something, not even truth about something mental, about ideas," Brunner explained. "Rather is it that truth which breaks in pieces the impersonal concept of truth and mind, truth that can be adequately expressed *only* in the I-Thou form. All use of impersonal terms to describe it, the divine, the transcendent, the absolute, is indeed the inadequate way invented by the thinking of the solitary self to speak of it—or, more correctly, of Him." It followed for Brunner that the truth about human beings "is founded in the divine humanity of Christ, which we apprehend in faith in Christ, the Word of God. This is truth as encounter."[178]

In Christ, truth *happens;* we find ourselves through faith and grace *in* the truth, which is not in us but comes to us. The truth of Christ sets us free by restoring our true being to us, Brunner asserted, "our being in the Thou, and our being for the Thou." In this experience of new being, the transformation that restores us to true form, having and being are united. That is, the experiences of having and being are brought together in the experience of new being. Brunner insisted throughout his career that this is not merely a Kierkegaardian way of speaking about truth, but that it is in fact "the only New Testament way of speaking." The New Testament speaks always of being in the truth, being in the Word, dwelling in love, being in Christ. In the New Testament, he repeatedly observed, being is of the essence of faith; the truth of Christ cannot be held or possessed, but rather takes hold of us.[179]

This was the language of crisis theology. It was this recognition of the existential and dynamic character of apostolic faith that the Barthian revolution recovered for the church, Brunner recalled many years later. The early Barth hoped above all for a new outpouring of God's Spirit and the consummation of God's rule. He believed that God always has more light to break forth from the Word. In Brunner's view, however, Barth's later work retained "hardly a trace" of the radical view of faith or the critique of Christendom that filled his early writings. Barth the dogmatist often spoke about something called "theological existence," Brunner observed. In his view, this ridiculous phrase was symptomatic of Barth's loss of nerve: "Nothing indicates more clearly his loss of his earlier insight—learned from Kierkegaard—that *faith* is an existence than this absurd connection of existence with *theology.*" There is such a thing as believing existence, or Christian existence, but there is no such thing as theological existence, Brunner rasped. Theology is not the life of faith, but merely reflection about faith. In Brunner's perception, Barth's increasing objectivism in the *Church Dogmatics* made him oblivious to the difference. His early sense of the radical Pauline understanding of truth as encounter was crushed by his turn to scholasticism and the sheer weight of his massive dogmatic enterprise.[180]

At the same time Brunner had little regard for Bultmann's existentialism and no sympathy at all for demythologization. He argued that Bultmann's "extreme subjectivism" cut his theology off from historical revelation; because Bultmann could speak only of subjective faith, his theology lost any capacity to speak of God's self-communication in act and Word.[181] It lost Jesus Christ in all but name. "What resulted from Bultmann's connection with Heidegger was a mutilation, not an interpretation, of the New Testament witness to Jesus Christ," Brunner judged. His alternative was a page from Kähler. Truth as encounter points to the God who speaks to us above all in the history of Christ, Brunner argued: "This Christ is neither the Christ of orthodoxy, nor the 'historical [*historische*] Jesus of liberalism, but the historic [*geschichtliche*] Jesus, the Christ and Savior of the Biblical message." Though it is true that much of the New Testament record concerning Jesus cannot withstand the tests of historical criticism, Brunner conceded, this fact does not diminish Christ's capacity to speak to us through the biblical tradition. The Spirit of Christ is as powerful today as before the dawn of biblical criticism. The revelatory truth of God encounters us whenever the Spirit of Christ moves our reading or hearing of the Word in faith.[182]

And what about the problem of the mythical forms and worldview of the biblical tradition? Brunner denied that there was any problem here to solve. The theological task of reflecting on the truth of God's revealed Word does not require any program of demythologization, he argued, because there is no such thing as Christian myth. He explained that if we remove from Christian teaching the "myth" of God's saving act in Christ's incarnation, cross, and resurrection, we will not salvage any "eternal truth" from Christianity. For the Christian faith "is faith in that which actually took place in Jesus Christ, or it is nothing at all." Tillich's definition of myth as "the history of the gods" contained the crucial clue for Brunner as to why "mythology" is not an issue in Christianity. Genuine myth is always polytheistic, Brunner argued; myths are always polymorphous, colorful, and irrational. Myth requires a plurality of acting divine subjects; without gods, there are no myths. But Christianity has nothing to do with gods or tales of the gods, he observed: "It is faith in the one revealed story of the one God." Therefore it is simply a misunderstanding to speak of Christian myth.[183]

Christianity represents the abolition of myth by virtue of its historical character. Through Christ's incarnation the myth has been abolished—"the myth of gods who become men and yet are not real human beings, the myth of the dying and rising Savior-God who yet never really died, and never really rose again, because he never really lived at all." It would be absurd to ask where Rama or Krishna died, Brunner remarked, but Christianity is quite specific about the circumstances of Jesus' death. "Myths are products of the religious imagination; their characters with their acts are not written in any book of world history: they are dissolved into nothingness by historical criticism," he observed. "They are dreams—the fruit of wishful thinking and of men's fears." But the life, passion, and death of Jesus are events in world history. The small piece of world history that they comprise is, for faith, divine history. Through Christ's victory over death "the whole pantheon of divine powers with a limited authority dissolves into nothingness, and the dream world of nonhuman and nondivine mythology disappears," Brunner concluded. The problem of myth is not a Christian problem because the meaning of our existence has been determined by God's act in Christ.[184]

The "neoorthodox" movement thus produced highly developed theological systems that claimed that Christianity contains no myth, other theologies that claimed that Christianity is unfortunately loaded with mythical teaching, and various mediating theologies that sought to minimize the problem of myth in Christianity.[185] Even this extreme continuum of positions did not exhaust the range of major neoorthodox perspectives on the problem of myth, however. The crucial problem with Bultmann's position pointed implicitly to the possibility of an approach that affirmed the existence and necessity of Christian myth. Though he insisted that he was not seeking to abolish myth, Bultmann's attitude toward it was decisively negative. He assumed with theological liberalism that myth is a primitive worldview that must be overcome. The task of the biblical theologian was to translate the truths about human existence that myth contains into a language that makes sense to modern people. Bultmann believed that the method of existential interpretation, using the early Heidegger's analysis of authentic and inauthentic existence, provided the nonmythical modern language that theology needs. Demythologizing was a program of nonmythical existential retrieval.[186]

But Bultmann defined myth in a way that excluded the possibility of nonmythical translation. In his usage, myth was the use of imagery to express the otherworldly in terms of human life. Myth described "the other side in terms of this side." This definition was self-negating, however. It categorized not only all prescientific pictorial religious language as mythical, but all symbolic and analogical religious language as well. By this definition, much of Bultmann's existential God-language was mythical, as well as the definition itself. In *Jesus Christ and Mythology*, Bultmann addressed this problem by distinguishing analogical language from myth. He argued that to use analogical expressions about the love or fatherhood of God "does not necessarily mean to speak in symbols or images. Such speech must be able to convey its full, direct meaning."[187] But analogical language is never full or direct; analogical language can claim only that one thing is like something else. A direct or univocal claim that God is a father would be anthropomorphic; analogical alternatives are indirect and partial by definition. In his attempt to identify (and thereby justify) some kind of God-language as nonmythical, Bultmann put forward a characterization of analogy that was simply wrong. Though he sought to rid Christianity of its mythical elements by translating them into a modern existential language, Bultmann's sweeping conception of myth applied to his own assurances about the reality of a "loving Father" who "acts" in human decisions.[188]

A tighter understanding of myth could have made his program of de-mythologization more coherent in its aims and more modest in scope. To an-other group of theologians, however, the crucial problem with Bultmann's theology was not that he executed this program with insufficient precision, but that his basic approach to myth was misguided. The limitations of his existen-tialist hermeneutic made his program seem reductionist. His failure to present a satisfactory nonmythical alternative to myth was instructive. In the light of these problems with Bultmann's approach, many theologians in the 1940s and 1950s made sense of the problem of myth by turning to Paul Tillich and Rein-hold Niebuhr.

True Myth and Ultimate Concern:
Paul Tillich

Tillich's basic approach to the problem was formulated in the 1920s, only a few years after he barely survived four years of bayonet charges, gunfire, ex-plosions, and the trauma of battle fatigue and mass graves as a German chap-lain in the Great War. The colossal brutality and evil of the war drove him to two nervous breakdowns and destroyed his religious and political innocence. He later wrote that the only kind of theology that deserved to be written after the war was the kind that addressed the "abyss in human existence" that the war exposed.[189] In the early days of the crisis theology movement, Barth wel-comed Tillich's opposition to liberal theology while recognizing that Tillich was not a kindred spirit.[190] From the beginning of their competitive relationship, he criticized Tillich's philosophical bent, his disregard for scripture, and his "hide-and-seek with the frosty monster, the Unconditioned."[191] Over the next several years, Tillich responded with increasing sharpness that Barth's appeal to the sovereignty of the Word was not a step beyond liberalism, but a return to a so-phisticated form of otherworldliness.[192]

The elements of Tillich's alternative were developed with extraordinary in-tellectual power through the course of his long theological career in Germany and the United States.[193] Tillich maintained that myth is not an inferior or dis-posable form of religious expression, but an essential component of human life and thought. Myth is much more than a prescientific explanation of events in the world, he explained; it is rather "a whole set of symbols, expressing man's relation to that which concerns him ultimately, the ground and meaning of his life."[194] Myth is the essential mode of encounter with the sacred. As the lan-guage of faith, the "universal category of the religious as such," it cannot be eliminated without negating faith.[195]

Liberal theology sought to displace mythical symbolism with a supposedly nonmythical religious symbolism, but Tillich countered that this strategy was misguided. "If mythology is in its essence a cultural creation like science, art, law, it is difficult to understand why it should be destroyed," he wrote. In fact, it is wholly misguided to seek to remove myth from theology, for myth "has its own proper and necessary place in the meaningful structure of cultural life."[196] Building upon Ernst Cassirer's theory of mythical symbolism, Tillich rejected the liberal/idealist classification of myth as an independent type of symbol-creation.[197] "In both science and religion mythology is an element that cannot be eliminated, even though it may be broken," he argued. Myth is an essential element in all intellectual and cultural endeavor. Though science is antimythical in its study of objects, even science is myth-creative in its conceptual theorizing, Tillich observed. Science can make sense of its world of things only by making use of concepts (such as "evolution") that are transcendent to things. By its nature, myth (like science) seeks to unify creation—or at least make it intelligible—under a single conceptuality.

This is a religious impulse, Tillich noted, but myth is not merely religious. In its "unbroken" form, myth links together the religious, the scientific, and what he called the "truly mythical" elements: "the religious element as related-ness to the unconditioned transcendent, the scientific as relatedness to objec-tive reality, the truly mythical as an objectification of the transcendent through the medium of intuitions and conceptions of reality."[198] The unity of unbroken myth is sustainable as long as the unconditioned character of the religious tran-scendent and the rationality of the natural world remain unknown. To the mythical consciousness, the religious transcendent is perfectly knowable, and the workings of the natural world are readily explainable. Pure unbroken myth is always a history of the gods. With the rise of Hebrew monotheism, the myth-ical unity of religion and science begins to break apart, Tillich observed. God is transcendent; his name is not spoken; he lives even if his nation dies.[199] With the rise of rationalist scientific consciousness, the realms of science and reli-gion break apart irrevocably. Human consciousness of the relativity of knowl-edge in both spheres makes each realm more independent.

But this does not negate the necessity or function of the truly mythical. The breaking of mythical consciousness allows the true character of myth to come forth, Tillich argued, "as a necessary element in the construction of a mean-ingful reality." Even in its broken state, the mythical imagination still seeks to find the hidden wholeness of reality. It is in this meaning-seeking drive to re-unify the world that broken myth has its primary value for theology. "Wher-ever the objective world is recognized in its relatedness to the unconditioned transcendent, and wherever the unconditioned transcendent is interpreted from the point of view of the objective world, the unity of religion with the desire to understand the world is restored in the mythical symbol," Tillich argued.[200] Thus science becomes myth-creative out of its need to theorize that which transcends the world of things, and theology accepts the authority of science regarding knowledge of the natural world, while relating all such knowledge to the religious transcendent. In its inherent drive to unify these fields of experience, myth participates in and points to the unconditioned: "The thing referred to in the mythical symbol is the unconditioned transcendent, the source of both existence and meaning, which transcends being-in-itself as well as being-for-us."[201]

Because symbolism is the language of faith, myth is inevitably present in every act of faith. It is not for that reason beyond criticism, Tillich cautioned. Though the religious ultimate transcends space and time, myth puts its stories of the divine into the framework of space and time. It even divides the divine into numerous figures, thus negating their ultimacy. For this reason, as numerous Christian apologists have asserted, prophetic biblical faith is inherently myth-critical in its insistence on the unconditioned sovereignty of God. Contrary to Brunner, however, Tillich noted that Jewish and Christian monotheism routinely make God an object of mythological language; scripture pictures God as an actor in the fall of Adam, the flood, the exodus from Egypt, and so on. It was in this sense that Tillich endorsed Bultmann's program of demythologization. Though the term is "negative and artificial," he complained, demythologizing is a necessary endeavor "if it points to the necessity of recognizing a symbol as a symbol and a myth as a myth."[202] Put differently, myth plays a constructive role in theology only if it is recognized as mythical, that is, only if it is broken. So-called demythologizing is valuable as a program that breaks Christian myth and deliteralizes it.

But as a program of myth-negation, Tillich argued, demythologizing is terribly wrong. It silences the experience of the Holy and deprives religion of its language.[203] It fails to understand that myth and symbol are ever-present forms of human consciousness. "One can replace one myth by another, but one cannot remove the myth from man's spiritual life," Tillich declared.[204] Christian symbols and myths should not be criticized because they are symbols and myths; rather they are subject to criticism only on the basis of their power to express the reality of Christ.[205] Religious symbols participate in the reality to which they point; they radiate the power of being and meaning of that for which they stand.[206]

And what makes any religious symbol true? Tillich argued that the only non-idolatrous answer to this question is the inner necessity that the symbol carries for the symbol-creating consciousness. Its truth is the degree to which it reaches the "Unconditioned" referent of all religious symbols.[207] When doubts arise about the truth of a symbol, consciousness about transcendence also changes. "The only criterion that is at all relevant is this: that the Unconditioned is clearly grasped in its unconditionedness," Tillich insisted. "A symbol that does not meet this requirement and that elevates a conditioned thing to the dignity of the Unconditioned, even if it should not be false, is demonic."[208] The demonic is precisely every action, idea, or doctrine that absolutizes anything that is relative or temporal. To worship anything less than the Unconditioned transcendent is to commit idolatry.[209] Unfortunately, Tillich observed, this is precisely what happens to most religious symbols in practice.

This is where demythologizing comes in. Tillich asserted that there would be no reason for Christian theology to take literalism seriously except for the fact that the church has misguidedly promulgated literalistic understandings of Christian teaching through much of its history. Christian teaching about the fall of humankind, for example, has represented this religious truth as a literal historical event. In order to explicate his own understanding of the Fall as a symbol of the universal human situation of estrangement, Tillich spoke of it as "the transition from essence to existence." This translation of the biblical story to the language of a modern existentialist/ontological system amounted, as he acknowledged, to "a 'half-way demythologization' of the myth of the Fall."[210]

No less than Bultmann, Tillich found it necessary to translate biblical myths into the language of his own philosophically driven myth-creative theology. The decisive difference was that he recognized that his demythologized theology was still mythical. Tillich contended that the work of modern theology is to translate the religious truth in biblical and early Christian myth into a form of myth that is true for modern people. Merely to repeat the biblical myths, even in a deliteralized metaphorical form, would not be spiritually or intellectually credible. Because *all* thinking has mythical elements, demythologizing can go only halfway. Because religion is always deeply, centrally, inherently mythical, theology must respect the mythical imagination, for "complete demythologization is not possible when speaking about the divine." Even if the Fall is reinterpreted as a transition from an essential human nature into existence, the language is still mythical because it retains a temporal element. "And if we speak in temporal terms about the divine, we still speak in mythical terms, even if such abstract concepts as 'essence' and 'existence' replace mythological states and figures," Tillich acknowledged.[211]

This critique of idolatry and Tillich's identification of the religious realm with the ultimate "depth dimension" of life provided the determinative elements of his theology of "ultimate concern." He observed that theology since the Enlightenment has sought to find a home for religion that is safe from the acids of modern scientific, philosophical, and historical criticism. Schleiermacher grounded religion in religious feeling; Kant proposed moral reason; Spinoza, Hegel, and the mystics variously regarded religion as a special mode of knowledge; the Romanticists appealed to the aesthetic function of religion. The problem with all of these strategies is that they reduce religion to a special function of the human spirit, Tillich argued. All of them resort to some form of reductionism because all of them assume that religion needs to have a home.[212]

Tillich countered that the only appropriate home for religion is everywhere. Religion is the dimension of depth in all of the functions of humanity's spiritual life, he contended; religion is "the aspect of depth in the totality of the human spirit." In biblical religion, there are no temples in the kingdom, for in the fulfillment of the kingdom God shall be all in all. To speak of religion as the dimension of depth in life is to point to that which is ultimate, infinite, and unconditioned in the spiritual life of humankind. "Religion, in the largest and most basic sense of the word, is ultimate concern," Tillich explained. "And ultimate concern is manifest in all creative functions of the human spirit." In the moral sphere it appears as the unconditional seriousness of the moral imperative; in the realm of knowledge it appears as the passionate desire to comprehend reality; in the aesthetic function of the human spirit it appears as the unquenchable desire to express meaning. "You cannot reject religion with ultimate

seriousness, because ultimate seriousness, or the state of being ultimately concerned, is itself religion," Tillich claimed. As the religious aspect of the human
spirit, religion is the ground and depth of humanity's spiritual life.[213]

Theology as True Myth:
Reinhold Niebuhr

Shortly after Tillich arrived at Union Theological Seminary in 1933 as a
refugee from Nazi Germany, the influence of his perspective on Reinhold
Niebuhr became evident in Niebuhr's writing. It was Niebuhr who arranged
Tillich's move to Union Seminary. Two years later, Niebuhr's major work on
the interpretation of Christian ethics adopted Tillich's already well-developed
analysis of religious symbolism and myth, without incorporating Tillich's ontological apparatus. "The distinctive contribution of religion to morality lies in its
comprehension of the dimension of depth in life," he declared at the outset.
Because it is grounded in its sense of the dimension of depth in life, religious
morality is concerned "not only with immediate values and disvalues, but with
the problem of good and evil, not only with immediate objectives, but with ultimate hopes," Niebuhr wrote.[214]

He argued that the key to the weakness of modern Christianity was its mistaken understandings of Christian myth. Both of the dominant forms of modern Christianity misconstrued the nature and necessity of religious myth.
Conservative orthodoxy refused to recognize Christian myth as mythical and
thus persisted in waging a futile and pathetic struggle against modern science.
If the conservative churches had not fossilized such dogmas as the inerrancy
of scripture and the historicity of the Genesis creation stories into literal objects
of faith, Niebuhr argued, such articles "would otherwise have long since fallen
prey to the beneficent dissolutions of the processes of nature and history."[215]
As it was, the "orthodox" churches made Christianity look ridiculous to educated people by insisting on viewing the Bible as a repository of inerrant propositions. Theological conservatism was defined fundamentally by its insistence
on taking mythical teaching literally.

Liberal Christianity made the opposite mistake, in Niebuhr's view. It sought
to adapt Christian faith to the modern mind by divesting Christianity of its mythical substance. In its eagerness to accommodate modern culture and science,
it gave up the religious substance of the great Christian myths of creation, the
Fall, the incarnation, and the cross. Liberal theology typically traded its religious
heritage for a rhetoric of moral progress and idealism more pleasing to the
modern mind. "It has discovered rather belatedly that this same modern mind,
which only yesterday seemed to be the final arbiter of truth, beauty, and goodness, is in a sad state of confusion today, admidst the debris of the shattered
temple of its dreams and hopes," Niebuhr wrote.[216] He meant that bourgeois
civilization was disintegrating in lockstep with the (presumed) dissolution of
capitalism, and liberal Christianity was going down with it. As a theological

strategy, the problem with liberal Christianity was that out of deference to modern culture, it did not take its mythical religious heritage seriously enough. Having shown that Christian myth is mythical, liberal theology gave no respect to it.

Niebuhr's alternative was that Christian myth should be taken seriously but not literally. Like Tillich, he argued that myth is the natural language of religion and the key to its truth. "It is the genius of true myth to suggest the dimension of depth in reality and to point to a realm of essence which transcends the surface of history, on which the cause-effect sequences, discovered and analyzed by science, occur," he asserted.[217] Science deals with the surfaces of nature and history. It breaks isolated objects of inquiry into their smallest possible costitutive parts in order to gain maximum control over them. In its effort to bring coherence to its radically subdivided and pluriform world, Niebuhr observed, science is always strongly disposed to propound an overly mechanistic view of reality. It excludes and demeans religious forms of understanding.

Niebuhr argued that religious myth belongs to a different realm of existence, however, than the realm of empirical causality on which scientific explanation operates. It does not challenge a properly chastened science that eschews scientism; it does not conflict with any science that sticks to its own realm and recognizes its own unprovable assumptions. Religion points to a deeper realm, Niebuhr argued, "the ultimate ground of existence and its ultimate fulfilment." With Tillich and Nicolas Berdyaev, Niebuhr viewed myth as a product of human spirituality that symbolically expresses human experiences of supernatural power or presence in the natural realm.[218] Because religious myths point to the ultimate ground of experience, they typically present transhistorical accounts of creation and redemption. "But since myth cannot speak of the transhistorical without using symbols and events in history as its form of expression, it invariably falsifies the facts of history, as seen by science, to state its truth," he observed.[219] Niebuhr gave particular emphasis to the Christian doctrines of creation, the Fall, and the cross as examples of myths that need to be taken seriously but not literally.

"It is only through the myth of creation that it is possible to assert both the meaningfulness of life and the fact of evil," he asserted. "To say that God created the world is to assert its meaningfulness; and to distinguish between the creator and his creation is to make a place for the reality of evil in the inevitable relativities of time and history."[220] The myth of God as creator is not a scientific postulate but a religious image that portrays God's organic relation to the world and God's distinction from it. In the Judeo-Christian myth of creation, God's being is conceived as constitutive of all reality while not being exhausted by it. If taken literally, Niebuhr observed, this teaching is irrational; but if taken seriously as true myth, it is religiously deep in meaning.[221] "The myth of creation not only expresses dynamic and organic qualities in reality which cannot be stated in rational terms, but paradoxical qualities which elude the canons of logic," he explained. The very concept of a religious "ground" or "dimension of depth" in life contains such a paradox. "All life and existence in its concrete forms suggests not only sources but possibilities beyond itself. These possibilities must be implied in the source or they would not be true possibilities," Niebuhr reasoned.[222] Christian myth therefore speaks of God as both the ultimate ground of reality and its ultimate good.

This interpretation of the Christian myth of creation illustrated Niebuhr's fundamental distinction between primitive myths and permanent myths. As a literally interpreted story about God creating the natural world in six days, the biblical account is an example of primitive myth, he observed. As a form of scientific explanation, the Christian myth is a form of bad science that needs to be demythologized. But as a religious symbol that relates the source of life to the natural world in terms that transcend scientific rationality, the myth of creation is permanently rich in meaning and truth. Fundamentalism distorts the religious truth of the myth of creation by treating it as a factual description; liberal theology misses the same truth by divesting the myth of its religious meaning. Theological liberalism yields the idea of creation to the modern idea of evolution. "The myth of creation, in which God is neither identified with the historical world nor separated from it, offers the basis upon which all theologies are built in which God is conceived as both the ground and the ultimate fulfillment of a meaningful world, as both the creator and the judge of historical existence," Niebuhr wrote. In his view, it was the only possible ground of a true and effective ethic, because it uniquely holds together the universal reality of evil and the promise of an evil-conquering good.[223]

Niebuhr applied the same dialectic to the theology of the cross, arguing that the mythic truth of Christ's sacrifice on Calvary was equally distorted by the atonement literalism of orthodox theologies and the moralistic reductionism of liberal theology. As true myth, the cross symbolized for him the Christian law of love. "The message of the Son of God who dies upon the cross, of a God who transcends history and is yet in history, who condemns and judges sin and yet suffers with and for the sinner, this message is the truth about life," he wrote.[224] The cross reveals the deepest mythic truth of Christianity, that Christ took on the suffering of the world in order to redeem it through his fellow-suffering love. The Christian myth of the cross is the ultimate symbol of sacrificial love, Niebuhr explained; Christ redeemed suffering not by abolishing it, but by sharing the condition of those who suffer. The law of love that Christ taught to his followers is the orienting reality that directs Christian behavior toward this other-regarding moral ideal.

But the example of true myth to which Niebuhr gave his most persistent attention was the myth of the Fall. Here again, "orthodoxy" and liberal theology both missed the point. Conservative Christianity took the biblical doctrine of sin with admirable seriousness, but based this doctrine on a literalistic interpretation of Genesis mythology. Under the pressure of the doctrine of biblical inerrancy, conservative theologians conceptualized the Fall as a literal historical event. By contrast, liberal Christianity did not take the myth of the Fall seriously enough, Niebuhr argued. Having dispensed with a literalistic understanding of the biblical creation narratives, liberal Christianity quickly degenerated into a culture religion that failed to take the religious meaning of the Fall with any seriousness at all. In the biblical story of the Fall, Adam and Eve brought sin into a sinless world by defying the command of a jealous God not to eat the fruit of the tree of knowledge. In liberal Christianity, Niebuhr observed, the effort to overcome literalism, anthropomorphism, and supernaturalism produced a theology that reduced the meaning of this story to an expression of the fears of primitive people toward higher powers. The Enlightenment myth of progress replaced a primitive myth about the jealousy of a divine tribal monarch.

Niebuhr countered that it was precisely the biblical myth of the Fall that expressed what was lacking in liberal Christianity. The biblical image of a jealous creator is not a primitive anthropomorphism, but a mythical depiction of the human situation. The root of human evil, he explained, is the pretension of being God. As creatures made in the image of God, human beings possess capacities for self-transcendence that enable us to become aware of our finite existence in distinction from God's infinite existence. But this same awareness tempts us to try to overcome our finiteness by becoming infinite, Niebuhr observed. This was Adam's sin. In its most fundamental forms, evil is always a good that imagines itself to be better than it is. Egotism is the source and driving force of evil. The biblical myth of the Fall is therefore not a dispensable relic of primitive fear and superstitition, Niebuhr argued, "but a revelation of a tragic reality of life." The truth of the Fall myth is attested by every page of human history. The Enlightenment myth of progress and human perfectibility embraced by liberal Christianity is a pitiful substitute for it.[225]

"The real situation is that man's very self-consciousness and capacity for self-transcendence is not only the prerequisite of his morality but the fateful and inevitable cause of his sin," Niebuhr remarked.[226] He cautioned that this is not to say that the story of the Fall is an account of the historical origin of evil. Neither is it an affirmation of Augustine's theory of the transmission of original sin through procreation. Niebuhr found this theory not only morally grotesque, but self-defeating to its moral purpose. The Augustinian doctrine of original sin destroys the basis for moral responsibility that Christian morality requires, he argued. If original sin is an inherited corruption, then human beings lack the freedom to choose not to sin; in this case we cannot be held morally responsible for being in sin.

But the doctrine of original sin is nonetheless a true myth, Niebuhr contended. It is a permanently valid symbol of a profound existential (not biological) truth. The reality of original sin is attested by history, but it is not itself historical. Just as the myth of the Fall is a description of the nature of evil rather than an account of the origin of evil, the reality of original sin is an inevitable fact of human existence but not an inherited corruption of existence. The human capacity for self-transcendence makes original sin inevitable. Original sin is a reality "in every moment of existence," Niebuhr explained, but it has no history. His major work *The Nature and Destiny of Man* built a massive theological edifice on the implications of this paradoxical truism, that sin is an inevitable existential corruption for which human beings are morally responsible.[227]

Niebuhr's brand of neoorthodoxy proposed to recover the truth in Christian myth. Though Bultmann claimed to protect the truth in the kerygma from demythologizing, Niebuhr countered that he failed to uphold the truth of Christian myth, partly because Bultmann failed to distinguish between primitive and permanent myth.[228] As for the Barthian approach, Niebuhr conceded only that it was an improvement on "the older dogmatisms of orthodox religion." At least Barth did not treat Christian myth as science or history. But the Barthians proclaimed the total truth of Christian myth on dogmatic grounds "with no effort to validate Christianity in experience against competition with other religions," Niebuhr objected.[229]

This was not credible. The choice of Christianity over other faith traditions must be defended, Niebuhr insisted. The mythical character of Christian myth and the religious claims of rival traditions have to be faced. Sophisticated dogmatism is still dogmatism. "How is it possible to escape this dogmatism?" Niebuhr asked. "It is possible only if it be realized that though human knowledge and experience always point to a source of meaning in life which transcends knowledge and experience, there are nevertheless suggestions of the character of this transcendence in experience." The truth in Christian myth is recoverable to knowledge only through experience: "Great myths have actually been born out of profound experience and are constantly subject to verification by experience."[230]

Though he blasted liberal theology with unsparing ridicule for the next twenty years, near the end of his career Niebuhr acknowledged the kinship of this argument with theological liberalism. He regretted that he spent so much of his career attacking the moral idealism of liberal Christianity. Though his appeal to mythical truth set him apart from the liberal tradition, his appeal to the authority of religious experience drew him closer to this tradition than to Barth's dogmatic objectivism. "When I find neoorthodoxy turning into sterile orthodoxy or a new Scholasticism, I find that I am a liberal at heart, and that many of my broadsides against liberalism were indiscriminate," he wrote in 1960. "On the whole I regret the polemical animus of my theological and political activities and am now inclined to become much more empirical, judging each situation and movement in terms of its actual fruits."[231]

The Twilight of Neoorthodoxy

By then the era of neoorthodox hegemony was drawing to a close. Neoorthodoxy was always a mishmash of theologies that were united more by generational experience than by precise theological agreement. Its major figures never embraced the term "neoorthodoxy," and Barth vigorously denied that there was such a thing as "Barthian" theology. Though he blasted everyone who disagreed with him, he claimed not to want followers. Bultmann, Brunner, Tillich, and Niebuhr made similar disavowals throughout the 1950s, while keeping careful watch over the legacies of their work. Having dominated

Christian theology for the past forty years, the giants of theological "neoorthodoxy" left it to their disciples in the early 1960s to work out the disagreements. Theologians such as Langdon Gilkey, Hermann Diem, Jürgen Moltmann, John Macquarrie, William Hordern, Schubert Ogden, David Tracy, and Frederick Herzog saw themselves at first as interpreters and refiners of the great theological systems of the past generation. Gilkey was to carry on the work of his teachers, Tillich and Niebuhr; Moltmann's early impression was that Barth had already said everything worth saying; Macquarrie and Ogden sharpened the issues at stake in Bultmann's program; Tracy interpreted the great neoorthodox Catholic theologies of Karl Rahner and especially Bernard Lonergan; Hordern and Herzog translated the insights of a blended European neoorthodoxy to American audiences.[232]

"We saw ourselves a generation of 'scholastics' whose function would be to work out in greater detail the firm theological principles already forged for us," Gilkey explained at the turning point. "We knew from our teachers what theology was, what its principles and starting point were, how to go about it."[233] Theology in the last third of the century would presumably synthesize and refine the Barth-to-Niebuhr theologies.

But this is not what happened. The neoorthodox/Christian realist continuum that Gilkey took for granted in his early career was blown apart in the 1960s by an explosion of repressed voices and critiques. In certain respects, Gilkey was a major contributor to the downfall of the dominant theological paradigm that he expected to refine; afterward his work addressed with exemplary seriousness the problems faced by theology in a postmodern situation. The story of the transition in theology from a modern to a postmodern context is perhaps best illustrated through his theological career and the development of his mature position, in which the contours of a post-neoorthodox liberalism are discernible. Perhaps more than any theologian of the past generation, Gilkey has addressed the distinctive problems and issues of contemporary theology while drawing upon the religious inheritance of modern theology. The theological perspective that emerges is a form of Schleiermacher's liberalism that reconsiders the value of the mythic imagination.

3

Beyond Neoorthodoxy: The Sacred Dimension

Though none of the chief architects of neoorthodox theology liked the term, by 1950 there were tens of thousands of self-described "neoorthodox" theologians and pastors. Many of the students of Barth, Brunner, Bultmann, and Niebuhr did not share their teachers' qualms about identifying with a movement label, even one with faintly Attic overtones. Under Brunner's influence especially, American theologians embraced the idea of neoorthodoxy. Brunner's clarity, his mediating position within neoorthodoxy, and his sharp attacks on both fundamentalism and theological liberalism were perfectly suited to the mood and interests of postwar American theologians. The central role that Brunner and Barth gave to scripture convinced a new generation of American biblical scholars that a merger between theological and biblical scholarship was possible. Brevard Childs later recalled that for the first time in many generations "the exciting possibility emerged that the new Biblical scholarship could join ranks with the new 'neoorthodox' theology to wage a common battle."[1]

The Biblical Theology Movement

The battle against an entrenched liberal establishment in biblical studies was led by American and British scholars, especially G. Ernest Wright, Bernhard Anderson, H. H. Rowley, Alan Richardson, Archibald M. Hunter, Floyd Filson, Otto Piper, Paul Minear, James Muilenburg, and later, Brevard Childs.[2] In common cause with theologians such as James D. Smart, Joseph Haroutunian, John A. Mackay, and Paul Lehmann, these scholars created the self-named Biblical Theology movement, which dominated American and British biblical studies in the generation following World War II.[3] The movement's neoorthodox character was exemplified in the scholarship it produced on the Hebrew scriptures. Wright, Rowley, Muilenburg, and Anderson emphasized the function of the Old Testament within Christianity as a bulwark against paganism. They accentuated the differences between monotheistic Israel and its polytheistic, myth-creating Near Eastern neighbors. They especially emphasized the distinctiveness of the Old Testament understanding of history, in which, they argued, history is the form of God's self-revelation through God's mighty acts. "The most enduring things that Israel attained were not the things she had in common with others, but the differentiae," Rowley declared.[4] For the Biblical Theology movement, Christian theology was based fundamentally on the recital of God's "mighty acts" in history. This recital was not merely a function or product of faith, for the historical character and uniqueness of Judeo-Christian monotheism were confirmed by objective critical scholarship. "It is the Old Testament which initially broke radically with pagan religion and which thus forms the basis on which the New rests," Wright asserted. "Christ came in the fulness of time, not time in general, but God's special time which began with Abraham."[5]

The Biblical Theology movement thus asserted with equal confidence that the Old Testament establishes the preconditions for Christian uniqueness and that Christ is the key to the religious meaning of the Old Testament. It called for and provided a renewal of biblical thinking in modern Christian theology and devotion; more important and controversially, it called for a renewal of theological thinking in modern scripture scholarship. For both reasons it gave short shrift to Bultmannian demythologizing. Wright explained that if he were forced to choose between Bultmann's demythologizing program and Niebuhr's understanding of Christianity as true myth, he would emphatically choose the latter. He further suggested that Niebuhr's distinction between permanent and primitive myth might be useful to the task of renewing biblical faith and thinking in the modern church. He recognized that the premodern, prescientific character of biblical cosmology posed interpretive problems for modern hearers of the Word.

But neither Bultmann nor Niebuhr offered a viable Christian solution to the problem of so-called Christian myth, he contended. What was needed was a third approach within neoorthodoxy that retained a *biblical* approach to the problem of myth. Most of the Biblical Theology movement's leaders sided with Brunner in their search for this alternative. Wright observed that the Bultmannian and Niebuhrian schools disagreed about whether myth is dispensable for theology, but both groups presupposed an expansive definition of mythology that made the problem of myth all-devouring. Both groups employed a way of talking about myth that was overreaching and ultimately destructive. "What has happened, it seems to me, is the same thing that has happened to a number of other words in theology," Wright explained. "Conceptions which originally in their own right had a certain definite and concrete meaning are taken from their proper context, given an extended meaning until their content is so watered [down] that they can no longer be used in serious theological discussion."[6]

"Mysticism" was a notable example. In *The Challenge of Israel's Faith*, Wright used the term in its traditional sense as a form of religious expression associated with eastern religions and Christian Neoplatonism. In this sense of the term, he argued, the Bible is strongly antimystical.[7] But in recent years, he later observed, the term had begun to acquire a vastly expanded meaning: many theologians were now using "mysticism" as a synonym for any kind of religious experience. The same thing was happening to "myth," partly because Tillich, Niebuhr, and Bultmann used the term so indiscriminately. Wright called for a theological grammar that restored the traditional meanings of these terms. He argued that part of the work of Biblical Theology was to reestablish the truism that biblical faith is neither mystical nor mythical. It was not mystical because "it insists on an objectivity of faith which is not centered in internal, self-conscious and self-propelled experience."[8]

Moreover, biblical faith is not mythical because it was based on the history-oriented Hebrew monotheism that opposed mythical religion. The Biblical Theology movement followed Wright in emphasizing that Hebrew religion was forged "against its environment" as a judgment on all idolatry and nature mysticism.[9] Israel opposed all mythical pagan traditions that knew no Lord of history. Wright observed that in world religious history, "mythology" properly refers to the literature of religions that saw the lives of the gods in the life of nature. Nature is alive to the mythical consciousness; mythical religion seeks to integrate human existence into the living powers that fill the natural world. It seeks to unite the human subject to a living natural world by telling stories about the gods, but these stories are never set in history nor primarily concerned about history. As Ernst Cassirer explained, the mythical consciousness is always fueled by the deep conviction of "a fundamental and indelible solidarity of life that bridges over the multiplicity and variety of its single forms."[10]

Mythical religion has no interest in history as such, but seeks always to bring humanity and nature into a unitive true order. Humankind is part of nature but has no special significance within or apart from it. This is the context in which it makes sense to speak of myth, Wright contended: "Yet modern theologians, with scarcely more than the most cursory regard for the word's proper meaning and with the most scanty attention to the theology of polytheism, now cheerfully 'steal' the word and say to the modern world: 'Christianity is mythology and to understand it we must demythologize it for you.' Or, they say, 'Christianity is mythology, but it is a true mythology, for you can only comprehend ultimate meaning in the world in terms of mythology.'" He countered that both options mark a retreat from the myth-negating faith of biblical religion. Biblical faith is not based on any intuition of the solidarity between nature, human society, and the divine. It rests instead "on the attempt to take historical events seriously in the understanding that they are not self-explanatory but point to the active God behind them."[11]

This God is the transcendent Lord of history whose special regard for humankind is known through God's "mighty acts" recorded in scripture. In biblical faith, Wright asserted, everything depends upon whether the central acts of God recorded in scripture actually occurred. Various aspects of scriptural narrative are surely open to historical doubt and correction, but there is no doubt "that there was an Exodus, that the nation was established at Mount Sinai, that it did obtain the land, that it did lose it subsequently, that Jesus did live, that he did die on a cross, and that he did appear subsequently to a large number of independent witnesses." These are the faith-founding, myth-negating facts of biblical religion, he explained: "To assume that it makes no difference whether they are facts or not is simply to destroy the whole basis of the faith." Moreover, to infer that these facts are irrelevant to the mythic truth of Christianity "would to the Biblical mind be a form of faithlessness or harlotry."[12] Christian faith has nothing to fear from historical criticism because Christianity is securely founded on historical events.

This claim was a staple of Biblical Theology rhetoric. If earlier generations of theologians had feared that historical criticism might demolish every shred of the Bible's historical accounts, this fear was now put to rest. The archaeological researches of William F. Albright and his students over the past generation repeatedly confirmed the historical accuracy of biblical accounts that liberal criticism had previously doubted or rejected.[13] By the early 1940s, the impact of the history of religions school was greatly diminished, partly because its founders had overzealously applied the concept of evolution to history. The discrediting of much of the *Religionsgeschichtliche Schule* theorizing about the evolution of Jewish monotheism emboldened a new generation of biblical scholars to emphasize the distinctiveness and historicity of Hebrew religion. "Even when we have noted all the similarities, the borrowing, and the syncretism, the differences between the literature of Israel and that of Canaan are far more remarkable and significant than the affinities," Wright declared.[14]

This development had implications for how theology should be done. For too long, the church's theologians had been scared off by the threat of historical refutation. An overblown fear of historical criticism had driven them to concoct various alternatives to the church's historically founded structure of belief. The Biblical Theology movement called this process of retreat to a halt. "The so-called destructive nature of Biblical criticism has been exaggerated and misrepresented," Wright asserted. "On the contrary, we today possess a greater confidence in the basic reliability of Biblical history, despite all the problems it has presented, than was possible before the historical criticism and archaeological research of the past century, and especially of the past three decades."[15]

The movement was not theologically monolithic; Wright was a neo-Calvinist, Rowley was a philosophical idealist, Richardson was an Anglican moderate, Smart and Childs were Barthians, Minear and numerous others identified with Brunner's existentialist/crisis theology approach. Most of its leaders followed Wright in emphasizing the uniqueness of Hebrew religion, but even here, Anderson argued that the uniqueness of Hebrew religion was perceptible only as viewed from the perspective of Hebrew prophetism.[16] Similar disagreements reflected the movement's dependence on competing strands of neoorthodox theology. As a generational movement of movement-oriented scholars, however, the Biblical Theologians spoke with one voice in criticizing the liberal biblical scholarship of the past half-century. Their voice was aggressive, confident, empirical, and religiously assuring. It denounced the overspecialization of recent scripture scholarship and the deep wedge that liberal scholars drove between the Old and New Testaments.[17] It defended the historicity of the central biblical events and called for a renewal of faithful theological interpretation of scripture. It gained impressive support for its agenda when Walther Eichrodt's epochal new work, *Theology of the Old Testament*, emphasized the unique covenantal and historical character of Hebrew faith.[18] Though it never routed liberal Bible scholars from the field in the way that neoorthodoxy routed liberal theology, the Biblical Theology movement dominated American scripture scholarship for nearly twenty years. It controlled the field's premier institutions and journals; the advisory board and publication list for SCM Press's prestigious "Studies in Biblical Theology" series read like a movement membership list.

As a young theologian and divinity school professor in the early 1950s, Langdon Gilkey shared the religious assumptions and confidence of this movement. His identification with theological neoorthodoxy was strengthened by the hegemony of neoorthodox biblical scholarship. He expected that his own work would relate the theological insights of Niebuhr, Tillich, and Brunner to the results of contemporary biblical scholarship. At the outset of his theological career, neoorthodox theology and neoorthodox biblical scholarship combined to form a structure that seemed not only dominant, but impregnable. Ten years later, Gilkey's searching critique of Biblical Theology exposed the literal weakness of its religious claims and raised the question whether neoorthodoxy really possessed an alternative to the methodology of theological liberalism. With astonishing swiftness, an imposing intellectual and institutional structure collapsed; by 1965, the Biblical Theology movement was referred to only in the past tense.[19] Perhaps more than any theologian of the past generation, Gilkey has interrogated and refurbished the modern theological traditions examined thus far.

Gilkey's Background and Early Career

Gilkey's background was well-suited for this intellectual role. Gilkey's father, Charles, was a prominent liberal pastor and the first Dean of the Chapel at the University of Chicago; his mother Geraldine was a feminist and national leader of the YWCA. Gilkey later recalled that in their liberal Protestant home, to be Christian meant "the critical spirit and the social gospel." His parents were "vastly concerned about social and racial justice and peace—above all peace" and their home featured a constant stream of visiting academics, preachers, and activists. Like many children of social gospel progressivism, Gilkey relinquished the religious part of his idealism upon entering college at Harvard in 1936, but his interest in religion was rekindled during his senior year by Reinhold Niebuhr's preaching. He had little sense of neoorthodoxy as a theological movement; Karl Barth had never been mentioned at home, and he had never heard of Kierkegaard, either. Gilkey thought of Niebuhr simply as one of his father's friends, but in the spring of 1940, at his father's urging, he heard Niebuhr speak three times at Harvard and promptly relinquished his acquired college humanism. Niebuhr's brilliance and passion for justice were intoxicating to Gilkey. He vividly described the terrors of a sinful, warring world without descending into any kind of cynicism. Niebuhr's spiritually grounded realism tore apart not only the illusions of liberal Christianity, but also the pretensions of Gilkey's ethical humanism. "As the torrent of insight poured from the pulpit, my world in disarray spun completely around, steadied, and then settled into a new and quite firm and intelligible structure," he later recalled.[20]

Niebuhr insisted that the moral perspective of biblical religion is grounded in an unflinching realism about the inevitability of personal and collective egotism. Unlike the make-believe yearnings of liberal Christianity and ethical humanism, he explained, biblical religion invests no faith in the goodness of human nature or the socially redeeming effects of moral effort. In Niebuhr's telling, biblical faith presented a realistic account of the pervasive reality of personal and social evil while calling Christians to bring the light of Christ—through their own weakness and fallibility—to a fallen world. The possibility of this kind of Christianity was a revelation to Gilkey. Europe was at war; American democracy was battered by the ravages of the Great Depression and the threat of war; and Gilkey felt very deeply the inadequacy of his humanistic worldview to account for anything that was happening. Niebuhr convinced him that a realistic form of the faith in which he had been raised was more true and redemptive. This belated discovery helped Gilkey survive his own unexpected fate in the wartime years that followed.

In August 1940 he sailed to China to teach at Yenching University in Peking, an American/British university for Chinese students. He felt no particular anxiety about traveling to the Orient as an American; the British were holding on against Hitler, the Japanese occupation of eastern China was in its fourth year, and the American war with Japan was more than a year away. After Japan attacked Pearl Harbor, however, all "enemy nationals" in China were placed under house arrest and later sent to an internment camp in Shantung province by their Japanese occupiers. Gilkey spent the war years as a prisoner in a walled-off former Presbyterian mission station near Weihsien, North China, where he and 2,000 fellow detainees were left to organize and maintain a mini-civilization on their own. Under these conditions, he witnessed ample confirmation of Niebuhr's anthropology.

Gilkey had known many of his fellow detainees in Peking, but under the conditions of confinement and material scarcity, they turned out to be nothing like the nice people he thought he had known. Nearly all of them were less rational and more selfish than he expected. Except for a group of monks and a few Salvation Army missionaries who were accustomed to scarcity, the conditions of camp life made nearly everyone, including Gilkey, behave with little regard for the needs of others. With a minimum of available goods, every act of generosity was costly. "In such circumstances no one feigns virtue any longer, and few aspire to it, for it hurts rather than pays to be good," he later recalled. "The camp was an excellent place to observe the inner secrets of our own human selves."21

What he observed was that order and justice are impossible in the midst of moral decay. The camp's leaders struggled persistently and for the most part unsuccessfully to bring about a just distribution of material and social goods. Rationally and morally, it was obvious that the internees needed to share space, resources, and responsibilities to ensure their survival. Gilkey kept assuring himself that when things got bad enough, people would recognize this necessity and begin to cooperate. What he witnessed instead, even in himself, was that reason and morality are the servants of immediate interest. A remarkably shortsighted sense of interest drove many internees to steal food, hoard supplies, refuse to share living space, and refuse to work, even while giving lip service to the importance of cooperating with each other.

Gilkey's reflections on the camp's consuming pathology of selfishness drove him to a deeper understanding of Niebuhrian texts that he already knew line by line. The problem of human nature is not only that human beings are fundamentally selfish, he reasoned, but also that people are often confused and conflicted by the unnaturalness of their consuming self-regard. In the camp, many people compiled an arsenal of "moral" reasons for always making the most self-regarding choice. If human beings were *naturally* selfish, Gilkey thought, they would be less conflicted about their egotism and much less driven to cover it up. The fact that selfishness is so pervasive in human relations and yet so persistently denied provided the central clue, for him, to the superiority of Christian theology over humanistic and naturalistic accounts of the human condition. Following Niebuhr, he perceived that the root of injustice is inward idolatry; social evil is the consequence of each person's worship of one's self or group: "The moral problems of selfishness, the intellectual problems of prejudice, and the social problems of dishonesty, inordinate privilege, and aggression are all together the result of the deeper religious problem of finding in some partial creature the ultimate security and meaning which only the Creator can give," he concluded.22

The reality of this "deeper religious problem" moved Gilkey to become a theologian. His internment experience convinced him that every person's moral strivings and failures are rooted in a unifying spiritual center that is unique to each individual. This spiritual center or soul provides whatever sense of meaning, coherence, or direction that a person possesses. Tillich's theology of ultimate concern later gave Gilkey a language for this perception of an underlying spiritual locus of security and meaning. Still later, this notion provided the groundwork for Gilkey's theology after he rejected much of the fundamental conceptuality of neoorthodoxy. But in its earliest form, the notion of a conflicted, unifying spiritual center made sense of Gilkey's wartime experience. When the total meaning of a person's life depends upon one's personal welfare, he perceived—or the welfare of one's group—then the subject is not free to be moral or rational in the very moments when morality and rationality are most needed. The pressure to foresake otherwise binding moral interests becomes intolerable whenever the security of one's ultimate concern is threatened. Put differently, when a person's *self* is basically threatened such that *he* or *she* is involved in the crisis, "a new power enters the scene, a power seemingly stronger than either the moral consciousness or the objective mind."[23]

The crucial question for each individual is therefore not whether he or she possesses an ultimate concern, but whether one's ultimate concern is worthy of the ultimacy invested in it. Though Gilkey had only begun to think through the implications of this perception when the war ended in 1945, he recognized that his driving intellectual concern was religious. If the religious dimension of human existence is the source of humanity's greatest evil, what kind of religion might provide the ground for a worthy ultimate concern? What kind of religion might provide the ground for a redeeming hope? He took these questions to Union Theological Seminary, feeling "infinitely old and thoroughly experienced," and already deeply influenced by Niebuhr's theology. At Union Seminary he studied under Niebuhr and Tillich when both theologians were at the height of their creative energy and influence. All of his subsequent writings bore the marks of their considerable influence over his thinking. Gilkey emerged from graduate school as he had entered it, religiously defined by Niebuhr's understanding of Christian history and theology. He joined Niebuhr's crusade against an expiring liberal establishment, embracing, like many American theologians of his generation, a form of neoorthodox theology that was untouched by any direct acquaintance with its Barthian origins.

Gilkey as Neoorthodox Theologian

The forbidding size of Barth's volumes and their reputation (among Americans) as impossibly difficult to understand deterred him from reading Barth during his early career.[24] Niebuhrian neoorthodoxy had little taste for Barth's scholasticism, and Gilkey's approach to theology was firmly Niebuhrian. It took some instruction from Brunner and Tillich on the finer points of theology, but gave little regard to Barth's elaborate reformulations of Christian dogmatic teaching. American neoorthodoxy was more concerned to claim that its form of religious realism was consistent with biblical religion and that it distinctively made sense of the modern social crisis. This outlook was in fact a variant of liberal theology, but in the heat of Niebuhr's polemical assaults on the bankruptcy of theological liberalism, Niebuhr and his American followers took little notice of the liberal elements in their perspective.

One incident near the end of Gilkey's graduate school career brought this predisposition to light. Gilkey participated in an American Baptist conference at Green Lake, Wisconsin, that included several other young neoorthodox theologians, including Robert Handy, William Hamilton, Robert Spike, and Howard Moody. The American Baptist denomination was deeply split between its modernist and evangelical wings, both of which were strongly represented at the conference and both of which were astonished by the presentations of the younger theologians. One by one, the church's next generation of theologians denounced the liberal progressivism of the past generation and called for a theology of transcendence, revelation, sin, and grace. Gilkey told the group that the traditional eschatological symbols of Christianity, especially the divine judgment and the second coming, were crucial for any theology that sought to make sense of the present age. Afterward a kindly, elderly evangelical told Gilkey and Handy how thrilled he was to hear young theologians talking this way about the second coming. "It's going to come soon, isn't it?" he asked them. "And where do you think it will be? Just outside Jerusalem?"[25]

Gilkey was stunned into silence. Was this a plausible misunderstanding? Did he really sound so much like a fundamentalist? For the first time, he realized that much of the theology he had inherited from Niebuhr and Tillich simply assumed a liberal/symbolic understanding of such concepts as the last judgment and the second coming. He did not believe in a literal second coming or the infallibility of scripture any more than Schleiermacher or Harnack. His theology sounded evangelical until he was pressed to explain what he meant by it. Years later, he would press the leaders of the Biblical Theology movement to explain what they (and he) meant by referring to "the mighty acts of God" in history. In his early theological career, however, Gilkey brushed aside the more disturbing aspects of the question. He set out to elaborate the third way between liberal modernism and conservatism that neoorthodoxy supposedly represented, recognizing that his teacher offered little guidance in spelling out its operative presuppositions or methodology. Gilkey's early writings sought to amplify Niebuhr's implicit theological perspective. His first book, *Maker of Heaven and Earth,* paid tribute to the accomplishments of theological liberalism while denying any deep affinity with it.

William Adams Brown was Gilkey's liberal exemplar. Like most theological liberals, Brown claimed that nature and the supernatural are not two different kinds of reality, but two aspects of the same reality. Nature and supernature are related as law and telos in the same process, he argued. Brown did not think of God as separate from the universe, but rather conceived divine reality as the immanent law of all reality, "an ever-present spirit guiding all that happens to a wise and holy end."[26]

Gilkey conceded that this emphasis on divine immanence restored an important aspect of Christian teaching that had disappeared in Protestant orthodoxy. It was the liberal emphasis on God's creative activity in the ongoing life of nature and humanity that brought modern theology into contact with the problems of modern science and culture. The problem was that liberal theology purchased its cultural relevance at the price of other aspects of Christian truth. It sought to avoid conflicts with science by making divine reality totally immanent within the processes described by science. It sought to avoid conflicts with naturalistic moral philosophy by conceiving moral values as emergent from the ongoing processes of natural and cultural life. But liberal theologians ironically failed to recognize that their own deepest convictions about the sacredness of life and the rights of individuals derived from the dualistic theism that they eschewed, Gilkey observed. Theological liberalism cherishes Christian moral teachings about the value of human individuality, freedom, and history, but these notions are products of the classical Christian picture of a transcendent creator and a dependent creation. Gilkey urged that the moral purposes of liberalism would be served better by an intellectually so-phisticated form of classical theism.

The key to his position was that the Christian doctrine of creation is neither a particular kind of science nor any kind of philosophy, but a biblical response to an existential question. Conservative theologies turn the doctrine of creation into a form of bad science or philosophy; Christian orthodoxy thus compels believers to reject modern scientific accounts of the natural world in favor of the primitive science contained in biblical folklore. Liberal theologians take the opposite strat-egy, revising religious ideas to fit the picture of the world offered by modern sci-ence and Enlightenment philosophy. But both approaches are misguided, Gilkey argued (following Niebuhr), since both assume that the Christian idea of creation commits Christian theology to some kind of scientific or philosophical perspec-tive on the natural world. Conservative theologies commit Christianity to primi-tive science, while liberal theologies seek to avert any conflict with science by disavowing the idea of divine transcendence. Gilkey called his alternative "neo-orthodoxy," by which he meant a creative blend of Niebuhr, Brunner, and Tillich.

The Christian idea of creation is a religious response to a religious question, he argued, "a much more burning personal sort of question than the scientific or metaphysical ones."[27] The religious question is fundamentally existential, personal, and mysterious. It does not pursue problems that cannot be solved, but explores the ultimately uncontrollable mysteries of living and dying. It asks, "What is the meaning behind my personal being? Is there any security or ground for my existence?" In the religious quest for meaning, Gilkey explained, "it is our anxiety, our frustration, our futility, our guilt—not our curiosity—that must be assuaged and satisfied." People are not delivered from spiritual tor-ment by proofs of God's existence. What the religious seeker needs is there-fore not the best possible argument for God's existence, but an experience of God. Only in an experienced encounter with divine reality can a person find the conviction to embrace the mysteries of living and dying.

Christianity teaches in the doctrine of creation that we are creatures of God who are ultimately dependent on God's power and love. Through the experi-ence of God's sovereignty and love in the covenant with Israel and in Christ's incarnation, Christianity confesses its belief in God the Father Almighty, maker of heaven and earth. This is a derivative belief, Gilkey noted. The doctrine of creation is the product of a lengthy historical process of extrapolation through which Hebrew and Christian believers reflected on the implications of their ex-perience of God's creative love. On the basis of this collective experience, Christianity affirms in the doctrine of creation that God is the ultimate origin of life, that human life is meaningful by virtue of God's transcendent holiness and power, and that each person's life is ultimately claimed by and belongs to this transcendent creator.[28]

Gilkey cautioned that these are mythological claims. The doctrine of creation is not "about" the significance of any particular fact within the natural world, nor does it refer to any particular event. In formulating a response to the religious question about the source of meaning behind all facts, theologians use the language of myth to affirm that all facts have an eternal source and ground. In formulating a Christian response to the same question, theologians draw upon the biblical testimony to God's saving acts in history to affirm that the eternal ground of being is loving and sovereign. The meaning of the myth is not to make a statement about any fact, including an "original fact" or moment in prehistory. "The myth of creation does not tell us about a first moment in time, any more than the myth of the Fall tells us about a first human being," Gilkey explained, following Niebuhr. What it does affirm is that every moment of time and every contingent thing owes its existence to God's creative power. The question concerning the first moment of time is a question for astrophysics, not theology; the question concerning the first Homo sapiens is for physical anthropology, not biblical scholarship. The Christian doctrine of creation is thus a religious myth about the spiritual ground of reality rather than any kind of account about the workings of the created world. As Gilkey put it, "The myth of creation expresses the true and valid religious affirmation that all of temporal creation comes into being through God's creative will."[29]

The pertinent question about creation is therefore not whether one should adopt a mythical conception of the source or ground of existence, but whether one should accept the Christian myth instead of a naturalistic myth or some other mythical conception. In its proper form, the question is unavoidable, since every conscious person carries some notion about the nature or meaning of life. Since the question of life's meaning is a religious question, Gilkey noted, every attempt to account for the mystery of life is ultimately religious in character: "If men have any feelings at all about the fundamental goodness or the meaninglessness of life; if they seek at all to understand the nature and source of evil; if they try at all to penetrate the mystery of human sin; if they look for any sort of fulfillment; and if they seek any kind of significance—in all of these quests, men cannot fail to ask about that on which the being and meaning of their life depend."[30]

Every life embodies some interpretation of life's meaning and thus represents a living answer to the existential question: "Why do I exist?" To press the question is to be drawn into metaphysical thinking, through which various competing answers can be tested. But whether or not one embraces a Christian answer, Gilkey argued, to press the question is to be driven to some mythical notion of transcendent origin such as nature, process, substance, the Absolute, or God. In this way, human self-consciousness inevitably raises the religious question of the transcendent origin of life.

Gilkey warned that philosophy cannot provide a Christian answer to this question. He repeated the standard neoorthodox warning that philosophy and natural theology unaided by revelation cannot describe the true God. The god discovered purely through reason and experience is not the God of biblical faith, but a product of idolatry-breeding imagination and desire. [31] Without the instruction of God's self-revelation, philosophy either conceives divine reality through the world of human experience (and thus makes God part of the world) or conceives God as the negation of human experience (and thus makes God the changeless transcendent Absolute, unaffected by the world). In either case, Gilkey cautioned, a construct of human reason and experience is held up as the transcendent origin of life, whereas the Christian understanding of divine reality is primarily founded upon revelation, which he defined as "God's revealing and saving activity within history."[32]

Neoorthodoxy taught that scripture is not revelation, but the unique and authoritative witness to God's saving acts in history. Scripture can become God's Word only as it is heard in faith through the movement of God's Spirit. Barth explained that the Word is never perceptible as a thing, but can be believed only as a happening. We "have" the Word as event only because it gives itself.[33] In their concern to give this notion some historical concreteness, Biblical Theologians such as Wright, Anderson, and Rowley emphasized that God's self-revelation to Israel and the Christian church occurred in publicly witnessed historical events. The Biblical Theology movement read scripture as a realistic narrative driven by God's saving acts in the exodus, at Sinai, in the rise of prophetic religion, in the incarnation and resurrection of Christ, and at Pentecost. Gilkey adopted this interpretive strategy, asserting that God's revelation occurred in and through special events and that scripture "is the human telling of these events and the human witness to their meaning."[34] To base one's theology upon Christian revelation is to privilege the religious meaning of the history of salvation as attested by scripture.

This does not mean that creation must be regarded as part of revelation, he noted. Biblical revelation is historical, but creation is not an event in history. Put differently, creation is not a historical event, but rather the necessary presupposition of God's saving acts in history. Without a divine creation, there would be no history and no self-disclosing acts of God within history. The Christian doctrine of creation is thus an inference from the nature of God as disclosed in God's historical relationship to Israel and the Christian church. The Hebrews were brought to faith in God as the creator of the world from their experience of God as the sovereign Lord of Israel. The myth of creation is an inference from revelation rather than a part of it.

Niebuhr taught that genuine spiritual appreciation requires a taste for paradox. Gilkey added that the paradoxes of Christian creation mythology must be embraced against all religious and secular criticism. Christianity teaches that before all time, God created time out of nothing; that God is eternal, yet creates and rules time; that God is infinite, absolute, and unconditioned, yet becomes conditional and dependent in Christ; that God's being is immanent everywhere in the world, yet also transcendent beyond creation. Gilkey warned against the impulse to "resolve" any of these paradoxes. It is only through paradox that the Christian mind can express its faithful knowledge that an eternal creator is the source of a good world, he argued: "The idea of creation is inevitably a paradoxical idea, because it seeks to express in human language a mystery known in the personal encounter of faith, a mystery too deep for a precise intellectual formulation, but a mystery which undergirds and supports all the more obvious coherences and meanings of our ordinary existence, and which is continually validated by them."[35]

Against the rationalizing immanentalism of liberal theology and the precritical supernaturalism of conservative theology, he affirmed the paradoxical character of Christian truth and the necessity of employing mythological language in expressing it. Like Niebuhr, he blended a conventional neoorthodox approach to scripture and an emphasis on paradox with a Tillichian perspective on religious language. For Gilkey, as for Niebuhr and Tillich, myth was a form of religious language that unites the concepts of analogy, revelation, and paradox into a single mode of God-language. Mythical language uses the analogy of the human person acting in history to describe the acts of God in history; it speaks of God as Father, King, Lover, Judge, Lord, and Spirit while cautioning that none of these terms should be taken literally. It speaks of God as though God were a finite being in space and time, while affirming that God is infinite and eternal. "Myth, then, is a way of talking about the God who transcends history in the dramatic terms of an active agent within history," Gilkey wrote. [36]

Yet he was not content to claim that Christianity is true only as true myth. Gilkey felt that Tillich's ahistorical ontology was insufficiently rooted in biblical faith; more broadly, he worried that neoorthodoxy as a whole was too deeply committed to existentialism. Christian faith and theology must be based "on historical revelation through concrete events in history," he cautioned. Though every Christian truth-claim inevitably contains mythical elements, Christian theology must affirm the historical basis of its claims. The doctrine of the incarnation employs mythical language, for example, but it also requires a historical foundation. Without a historical Jesus, Christology would be pointless. As Gilkey explained, "The life of Jesus was a 'literal' fact; but the divine dimension is described and interpreted 'mythically'; and that description and interpretation, and its relation to the historical base, form the content of Christian doctrines about Jesus Christ."[37]

A Univocal Ground?

But even this cautionary argument claimed only that Christianity requires *some* undefined degree of historical fact; moreover, it suggested that all knowledge of God is indirect, analogical, and symbolic. For 290 pages, right up to its closing sentences, *Maker of Heaven and Earth* implied that all human ideas about divine reality, "like tiny finite beams, barely rise into the darkness of an infinite night." Using meager analogies and symbols drawn from finite conditioned experience, theologians seek to account for the qualities of an infinite, unconditioned reality whose being transcends time and space. But can theology rest with this acknowledgment that it has no direct knowledge of God's ultimate nature? If it is true that God is not a "person" as we are persons, or that God does not "exist" or "create" as human beings exist and create, how can theology claim to be intelligible when all it possesses are symbolic analogies about God's personality, freedom, existence, and creativity? Must theologians concede that they have no knowledge of God apart from analogies that paradoxically suggest something about the mystery of God's unfathomable being?

These questions lurked below the surface of Gilkey's reassuring prose. Though he was sensitive to the problems that Niebuhr's reliance on myth and symbol bequeathed to theology, most of his book artfully avoided any direct discussion of them. It was only in the book's closing three pages that he suddenly announced that theology does require more than a symbolic knowledge of its object, "for a knowledge that is *merely* analogical and paradoxical is no knowledge at all."[38] Without any direct knowledge of God that grounds the various analogical claims that theologians advance, he asserted, theology can make no claim to intelligibility. Only a univocal religious claim can save theology from the equivocal subjectivity and relativism of mythography. But where should theologians look for this foundational source of identity and unity?

Gilkey gave passing notice to the ontological option proposed variously by Augustine, Anselm, Tillich, and (purportedly) Aquinas. In his reading, Aquinas argued that human beings acquire direct knowledge of God from thinking of God as being itself or the unconditional source of being.[39] While rejecting Aquinas's attempt to prove that God is the first cause of being, Tillich similarly claimed a univocal starting point for theology on ontological grounds. The reality of divine transcendence is tacitly affirmed in the truism that all language about God is symbolic, he argued. The statement that everything we say about God is symbolic "is an assertion about God which itself is not symbolic."[40] Tillich thus derived the notion of God as being itself from God's transcendence to the finite, which is implied by the fact that all human language about God is analogical.

Gilkey made occasional appeals to this mode of theological reasoning in buttressing his own arguments, but he judged that ontological arguments do not really solve the problem of the lack of a univocal ground for analogical claims. The metaphysical language of ontological theology is itself analogical and symbolic in character, he noted: "It uses as its fundamental categories concepts derived from a philosophical analysis of natural finite existence and then referred analogically to God as the infinite ground of that existence." The direct knowledge claimed by ontological theology is therefore knowledge of finite being, since a transcendent God cannot be the direct object of metaphysical inquiry. In ontological theology, the concept of being is applied to God as an indirect symbol of the kind of being that can be directly known—that is, finite being. This explains the tendency of ontological theologians to refer to God as *pure* being, being *itself,* or the *ground* of being, Gilkey observed. The practice of qualifying the language of being applied to God confirms that something different from commonplace finite being is being described when theologians apply it to infinite divine reality. The ontological language of being is no less analogical and symbolic than other God-language. Moreover, he argued, theologians who rely upon ontological arguments tend to privilege the analogical knowledge of God as being itself over the scriptural witness to historical revelation and the encounter with God made known in personal faith, but this practice violates the Protestant devotion to biblical revelation.[41]

Gilkey countered that the univocal center of Christianity is not a metaphysical claim about the analogical relation between human and divine being, but the person of Jesus Christ made known in historical revelation. It is in Christ's historical incarnation that the image of the invisible God has been disclosed. Through Christ the ineffable unconditioned ground of being has been made directly known. Through Christ, the revelation of God's nature as holy love united with holy power is disclosed without analogical mediation. "Thus the personal recreative love of God in Christ, not the ontological power of God in general existence, is the one unsymbolic and direct idea of God that Christians possess," he urged. God is known first as love and only afterward as being, for in Christianity "we know God as the source of our existence only when we first know him to be the love that will not let us go."[42]

Christ is the unmediated ground of the church's life and identity. Because the unseen creator is revealed through Christ, Gilkey argued elsewhere, Christian truth is founded on a univocal claim that transcends relative human wisdom. Moreover, because Christian truth contains the Word of God, the bearer of this truth—the church—is not merely a social institution, but the body of Christ in which Christ's Spirit dwells.[43] As a theology professor at Vanderbilt Divinity School, Gilkey sought to help seminarians negotiate between the historic claims of Christianity and the unavoidable challenges of modern science and culture. His model of "how the church can minister to the world without losing itself" was the neoorthodox model of combining selected liberal and orthodox elements. With liberal theology he accepted the results of science and historical criticism in "the whole area of spatio-temporal fact and event" and downplayed the "factual manifestations and explanations" of traditional Christian doctrine. For neoorthodoxy, he explained, Christian doctrines are propositions that point to the religious dimensions of events rather than propositions that contain factual information about events. Neoorthodoxy affirms that all of Christianity's creeds, doctrines, and sacred texts are human constructions that fallibly witness to the reality of the living Word of God. Moreover, neoorthodoxy takes from its liberal heritage the view that the structures of society are "fit objects for Christian reformation." It rejects the dualistic conservatism of Protestant orthodoxy, which denies any Christian mandate for transforming the social order.

At the same time, he taught, neoorthodoxy rejects the liberal faith in humanity's inherent goodness. It reaffirms the religious meaning of the orthodox doctrine of original sin; it proclaims the priority of revelation over reason; and it speaks not of "building the kingdom" but of manifesting Christ's Lordship over all aspects of a sinful world. At its best, he maintained, the "unusual grace of neo-orthodox Christianity" is demonstrated by its capacity to emphasize the uniqueness of Christian truth without falling into intolerance or authoritarianism.[44] Neoorthodox Christianity uniquely calls modern Christians to be servants of Jesus Christ, the Word of God, in whose service is perfect freedom.[45]

What is Historical
about Salvation History?

Gilkey's early writings occasionally acknowledged that the intricate relationship between the historical foundation of Christianity and its mythical or symbolic interpretation was an unresolved problem for neoorthodoxy. His constructive formulations drew upon neoorthodox biblical scholarship without explaining exactly what it means to say that Christianity is founded upon the "mighty acts of God" recorded in scripture. He routinely invoked the normative claims of Biblical Theology about the "peculiarly Protestant continuity with Christ through the Word of Scripture."[46] But in the early 1960s he began to doubt that neoorthodoxy was coherent. For all of its influence and commanding style, he could never quite define what made neoorthodox Biblical Theology basically different from a biblically oriented liberalism.

The question of how theology relates to history was especially pertinent and perplexing to Gilkey. Liberal theologians argued that Biblical Theology was too quick to take refuge in salvation history (*Geschichte*), which uprooted theology from its proper basis in scientific history (*Historie*). In 1956, James Branton noted the irony of the Biblical Theology appeal to history. He observed that despite its ample rhetoric about historical revelation, the Biblical Theology movement had no "real rootage in history."[47] The following year, Winston King sharpened this critique by focusing on the confused relation between fact and interpretation in Biblical Theology. He noted that Biblical Theology emphasized the historical character of biblical religion, but it also threw history overboard whenever it dealt with biblical events that were historically questionable. Much of its "historical" grounding was theological, not historical in the scientific sense. Moreover, Biblical Theologians made much of the historical nature of certain events while recognizing at the same time that scriptural accounts of these events were metaphorical. Biblical Theology thus played up the historicity of the call of Moses while treating the burning bush as a figure of speech.[48]

Neither of these critiques of the Biblical Theology movement attracted much attention at the time, but when Gilkey amplified their main arguments in 1961, the effect was stunning. With the insight of an insider, he argued that Biblical Theology was torn fatally between its liberal and orthodox elements. The worldview of Biblical Theology was modern, he explained, but its theological language was premodern. Neoorthodoxy merged a modern scientific cosmology with an orthodox-sounding faith. Conservative theology was coherent but not credible; liberal theology was coherent but religiously dessicated. Neoorthodoxy sought to recover the fullness of the revelationist biblical faith in a way that did not bring theology into conflict with modern science, philosophy, and historical criticism. But was it coherent?

Gilkey strongly suggested that it was not. Focusing on the writings of Wright and Anderson, he argued that Biblical Theology was not the intelligible third way that its proponents claimed to represent. Though Biblical Theologians rejected the liberal emphasis on God's immanent universal presence in favor of the biblical appeal to God's objective activity in special events, they shared the liberal assumption of a causal continuum of space/time experience. They invested no religious, historical, or apologetic significance in the Bible's miracle claims. Like their liberal predecessors, they presupposed the existence of a causal order among phenomenal events and thus did not accept the biblical miracle stories either as forms of historical explanation or as apologetics. At most they appealed to faith as a form of special understanding of the miracle stories.[49] Though they emphasized the biblical idea of God as the transcendent source of historical revelation, they did not share the biblical understanding of God as an intervening, partisan, miracle-making divine agent. Though they emphasized the historical character of biblical religion, the Biblical Theologians were quick to write off the historicity of key biblical accounts.

These were negligible differences to Wright, Anderson, and the movement's other leaders, but Gilkey observed that the differences between modern Biblical Theology and biblical theology were enormous. In the Bible, God created the world in six days, the Fall occurred in a real space/time Eden, and the patriarchs received audible commands from God; later, God intervened directly in history to cause the plagues in Egypt, the pillar of fire, the parting of the sea, the deliverance of the Mosaic law, and various maneuvers that brought about the conquest and the formation of Israel; still later, the prophets were instructed by God's audible voice. In the Bible itself, these were the "mighty acts of God" that revealed God's existence and providential care, but in Biblical Theology it was assumed that none of these events was historical. The Genesis events were described as mythological and the "acts of God" reported throughout Hebrew scripture were presumed not to belong to the plane of historical reality. In Gilkey's words, neoorthodox scholarship assigned these events to "the never-never land of 'religious interpretation' by the Hebrew people."

This profound difference in worldview separates modern theologians not only from the world of the biblical writers, Gilkey noted, but equally from such premodern theologians as Luther and Calvin. The world of the Bible no longer exists for educated readers. It is not only that modern people refuse to believe that God would sanction anything so grossly immoral as the mass murder of the Amalekites; for modern people, all of the verbal divine commands, promises, and interventions reported in scripture are gone. "Whatever the Hebrews believed, we believe that the biblical people lived in the same causal continuum of space and time in which we live, and so one in which no divine wonders transpired and no divine voices were heard," he remarked. "The modern assumption of the world order has stripped bare our view of the biblical history of all the divine deeds observable on the surface of history, as our modern humanitarian ethical view has stripped the biblical God of most of his mystery and offensiveness."[50]

Biblical Theology sought to bridge the chasm between modern and premodern Christianity by using religious language analogically rather than univocally. When the biblical writers and church fathers referred to God "acting" or "speaking" in history, they meant that God performed an observable act in space and time or that God's audible voice was heard by a living person. That is, they used the words "act" and "speak" univocally, applying them to God in the same ways that they spoke of human beings acting and speaking. Biblical Theologians rejected this understanding of religious language, Gilkey noted, but they retained the orthodox language about God as revealer and divine agent. That is, neoorthodoxy used the same words as classical Christianity, but did not use them in the same way. In seeking to dislodge an enervated theological liberalism, neoorthodox thinkers failed to acknowledge the vast differences between univocal and analogical usage.

But the problem went deeper than this. Having adopted an analogical approach to religious language, Biblical Theology was retrieving the biblical language of revelation and divine agency without explaining what these analogies meant, or how they were being used, or exactly what they pointed to. Without some explanation of how God's "acts" are "like" human acts, Gilkey argued, the operative language of neoorthodoxy was actually not analogical, but equivocal.

Wright and Anderson exemplified the problem. Like most neoorthodox scholars, they based their readings of Hebrew scripture on the exodus-covenant narratives, arguing that the acts of God in forming and delivering the Hebrew people gave rise to the faith of Israel. Hebrew religion thus began not with religious experience, but with God's creative and redemptive self-disclosure in Hebrew history. The Bible's pre-exodus events were regarded not as historical narratives recounting God's early relationship to the Hebrews, but as parables that express the faith of the post-exodus Hebrew community. The biblical accounts of the codification of the law, the conquest, the reigns of the kings, and the prophetic movement were similarly understood as creative interpretations of the meaning of exodus faith in post-exodus Hebrew history. "In sum, therefore, we may say that for modern biblical theology the Bible is no longer so much a book containing a description of God's actual acts and words as it is a book containing Hebrew interpretations, 'creative interpretations' as we call them," Gilkey remarked.

Even for Biblical Theology, the Bible did not describe the acts of God, but the faith of Hebrew religion. In the biblical accounts, God is the subject of the verbs, but in Biblical Theology, Hebrew faith displaced God as the subject of the verbs. For classical Christianity, the Bible contained a direct narrative of God's actual words and deeds, whereas for modern theology, the Bible contained parabolic illustrations of Hebrew faith. Gilkey's summary was deflating: "For us, then, the Bible is a book of the acts Hebrews believed God might have done and the words he might have said had he done and said them—but of course we recognize he did not."[51]

The upshot was that neoorthodox Biblical Theology actually recapitulated the liberal approach to scripture. Scripture focuses on the acts of God in history, but Biblical Theology made faith the object of biblical religion. Because Biblical Theology emphasized so strongly the biblical understanding of God as transcendent revealer and agent, Gilkey observed, it sounded like a corrective to liberal theology until one recognized that "the whole is included within gigantic parentheses marked 'human religion.'" In its governing assumptions and method, Biblical Theology was a form of liberalism.

This is not how Biblical Theologians characterized their approach, of course. For Wright and Anderson, the center of Old Testament faith was the scriptural account of God's creative and saving interventions in Hebrew history from the exodus to Sinai. This narrative center carried not only a historical meaning, but a defining confessional importance. Historical statements can take an indirect form, such as "we believe that the Hebrews believed that God revealed the law to Moses at Sinai," but confessional claims are always direct. Confessional statements declare one's own belief or the belief of one's community. To Luther and Calvin, the confessional meaning of the exodus was unambiguous, since they never doubted that the verbs of scriptural narrative should be interpreted univocally. They assumed that God directly caused the plagues, the pillar of fire, and the parting of the sea and directly proclaimed the legal conditions of the covenant. But when one asks a modern Biblical Theologian what actually happened in the exodus-Sinai narrative, Gilkey observed, the answer "is not only vastly different from the scriptural and orthodox accounts, but, in fact, it is extremely elusive to discover."[52]

Biblical Theologians gave remarkably little attention to the question of what God actually did in the exodus or any other "saving act" of biblical history. As critical historians, they assumed that the Hebrews knew no miracles. Wright maintained that because the biblical event in question is always indistinguishable from other events, and because each biblical event can be accounted for on naturalistic grounds, the Hebrew understanding of "revelation" was and is always dependent on faith. To call the exodus a "mighty act of God" is not to imply that the exodus events were miraculous or otherwise unexplainable. Biblical Theologians routinely explained that the sign to Moses in Exodus 3:7–12 was a variation of Egyptian serpent magic; the pollution and seasonal overflowing of the Nile were natural phenomena, as were the third and fourth plagues of gnats and flies; the fifth and sixth plagues—perhaps anthrax—could have been caused by the conditions created by the former plagues, and so on. Anderson noted that the climactic rescue of the Hebrews described in Exodus 14 probably resulted from an East wind blowing over the Reed Sea (not the Red Sea, but a shallow body of water farther north).[53] Wright gave even shorter shrift to the question of what God actually did in the exodus, offering a single sentence about "certain experiences that took place on the Holy mountain . . . which formed the people into a nation."[54] But this event is the historical foundation of Biblical Theology, Gilkey objected. It stunned him that the movement's chief proponents could be so unconcerned "with the character of the one act that God is believed actually to have done."[55]

When Biblical Theologians spoke *theologically* about historical revelation, they focused on outer objective events and employed the orthodox language of divine agency and revelation. But when they functioned as historians, they spoke of these events in purely naturalistic terms. They stripped away all of the elements that made the biblical accounts unique, while retaining the biblical concept of God as agent and revealer. They continued to speak of God as "acting" and "speaking," but they dispensed with the biblical wonders and voices that gave univocal meaning to scriptural testimony. This procedure raises unavoidable questions, Gilkey observed. If the main words and categories of scripture are no longer to be used univocally to refer to observable actions and audible voices, do they retain any intelligible content? What does it mean to say that God "acts" or "speaks" if God does not act or speak as humans do?

In Biblical Theology, however, these questions went not only unanswered, but largely unasked. Even the "special understanding" provided by faith was never clearly explained. For all of their insistence on the importance of beginning with God's historical revelation rather than humanity's search for God, Biblical Theologians were unable to explain exactly what God did in any of the "mighty acts." Since Biblical Theology is unable to give specific content to its basic analogies, Gilkey argued, the neoorthodox rhetoric of revelation and mighty acts is literally meaningless, except for the sense in which it actually contradicts the fundamental claim of neoorthodoxy.

The contradiction was that Biblical Theologians condemned theological liberalism while practicing an inconsistent form of it. Biblical Theology did not consider God's "mighty acts" to be objective acts in history, but pointed only to God's inward evocation of a religious response to marvelous (but ontologically ordinary) events. "If this is what we mean," Gilkey remarked, "then clearly we have left the theological framework of 'mighty act with faith response' and returned to Schleiermacher's liberalism, in which God's general activity is consistent throughout the continuum of space-time events and in which special religious feeling apprehends the presence of God in and through ordinary finite events." For all of its talk about the priority of revelation over experience and the activity of God in history, the biblical foundation of "mighty acts" theology turned out to be a religious interpretation of natural phenomena.

Gilkey pressed the point that this kind of interpretation has a name. So-called neoorthodoxy was a form of theological liberalism. "And yet at the same time, having castigated the liberals, who at least knew what their fundamental theological principles were, we proclaim that our real categories are orthodox: God acts, God speaks, and God reveals."[56] On the strength of this appeal to revelation, neoorthodox thinkers typically claimed immunity from outside philosophical, religious, and cultural criticism. They played up the "uniqueness" of history-centered Hebrew faith and denigrated the more cosmopolitan

Wisdom literature of Hebrew religion. They treated the Old Testament as a Christian bulwark against paganism and sustained a righteous Christian polemic against pagan religions. They sought to protect Christianity from the relativizing outside critiques that reduced theological liberalism to religious subjectivity. But neoorthodoxy is not a different *kind* of theology from liberalism, Gilkey admonished. Having stripped the wonders and voices from scriptural narrative, Biblical Theologians were left with a language of divine agency and revelation that carried no univocal meaning. They sought to reclaim the religious worldview of scripture by interpreting its language as analogical, but without explaining how God's agency is truly analogous to human activity. Neoorthodoxy derived from scripture the abstract notion of a God who acts and speaks, but dismissed all of the Bible's accounts of specific acts of God. So-called Biblical Theology was thus even more abstract than medieval scholasticism, Gilkey judged, because its basic concepts had no demonstrated concreteness.

Modern theology needed to reestablish the basis of its God-language. "What we desperately need is a theological ontology that will put intelligible and credible meanings into our analogical categories of divine deeds and of divine self-manifestation through events," Gilkey declared. "For if there is any middle ground between the observable deed and the audible dialogue which we reject, and what the liberals used to call religious experience and religious insight, then it has not yet been spelled out."[57]

If a genuine third way was still desirable, it remained undiscovered; Gilkey no longer claimed to know how to find it. His initial critique of neoorthodoxy carefully avoided any discussion of Christology and thus did not address the question whether he still affirmed the Christocentric conclusion to *Maker of Heaven and Earth*. Did he still believe that Christology could provide the crucial point of contact that meaningful Christian language requires? Was it credible to argue that the divine self-disclosure in Christ establishes a univocal ground of intelligible Christian God-language? Gilkey's writings in the early and mid-1960s avoided the critical thrust of this question while tacitly assuming an affirmative answer to it. He continued to assert that Protestantism must remain faithful to a revelationist, Word-oriented theology that "enthroned" Jesus Christ and testified to his sovereign living presence. The spiritual identity and purpose of modern Protestantism can be sustained on no other basis, he contended. His book on Christian ministry urged church leaders to resist the secularizing and materialistic pressures of American culture by holding fast to the Christocentric faith preserved in Protestant neoorthodoxy. "The Word made flesh in Christ and preached as the Good News in and by the apostolic community is the source and origin of the church," he wrote. "For in the message about Jesus Christ, His life, death, and resurrection, we know in faith of God's establishment of this new humanity; we know the judgment of God on our sins; we know of His forgiving love, which accepts the repentant into new fellowship; and we know of His promise in the Spirit that in faith we may grow in Christian holiness."[58]

Neoorthodoxy as Christian Existentialism

These assurances rested on the ultimate refuge of neoorthodox proclamation. Though he worried earlier that neoorthodoxy invested too much significance in existential interpretation, by the early 1960s Gilkey's defense of neoorthodoxy as a distinctive position was based entirely on a Brunner-type theory of existential encounter. He argued that it was precisely in its religious epistemology that neoorthodoxy differed fundamentally from the objectivism of orthodox and natural theologies, as well as the subjectivism of liberal theology. For neoorthodoxy, theological knowledge was neither a form of objective spectator knowledge about objects, propositions, and facts, nor a form of religious subjectivism. Neoorthodox theology claimed that God is revealed and truly known in the self's encounter with God's Word in faith through the Spirit. In this perspective, he explained, knowledge of God is real, inward, and existential: "it is 'real' because it involves communication with a divine reality that is over against us; it is 'inward' because it is neither derived from nor determined by matters of fact; and it is 'existential' because it is always personal, transforming knowledge."[59] Neoorthodoxy recovered the religious realism of orthodoxy without bringing theology into conflict with science; it did not consider knowledge of God to be objective (as an object of thought unrelated to the known), but claimed that true knowledge of God comes only through an existential encounter with the personal ground of all objects.

This Kierkegaardian core of crisis theology remains the key to neoorthodoxy and the key to any truthful account of God's personal reality, Gilkey asserted: "For example, I surely know at once of my own sin and, correspondingly, that God is a holy judge and a loving father—for I experience his wrath at my sin and his forgiving mercy in Jesus Christ." Moreover, one can know that God's Spirit is disclosed through special events and speaks through Word and sacrament, "since it is in relation to these events through scripture and liturgy that this revealing and saving encounter occurs." In this way, true theology explicates our knowing *of* God rather than our knowledge *about* God.[60] Existential interpretation excludes any discussion of divine reality outside the sphere of encounter. It excludes any claim about God that objectifies God outside the matrix of revelation, which is the realm of existential encounter. In neoorthodoxy revelation *is* encounter, Gilkey remarked; the alternatives are philosophy and biblicism.

The theory of existential encounter therefore did heavy work for neoorthodoxy. Gilkey still claimed that it was crucial to any true theology. He acknowledged, however, that it carried a heavy cost. If the theory of existential encounter provided a compelling and nonobjectivist way of speaking about God, it also limited religious knowledge only to that which can be known through personal encounters. It privatized the total meaning of Christianity by equating theology with epistemology.[61] In Bultmann's case, it produced a theology that had little to say about the divine Trinity or the sociopolitical dimension of Christianity. Gilkey puzzled over these problems in the early 1960s without rejecting Christian

existentialism. He was unsettled by the inadequacies of an epistemology that reduced the field of divine action and Christian truth to the sphere of personal encounter. He acknowledged that much of the social, moral, and spiritual meaning
of Christianity is lost in a purely existential approach to religious truth. The loss
that disturbed him especially was the Christian doctrine of providence.

He allowed that there were serious reasons why current theology had so little to say about providence. The liberal notion of providence as progressive
development was no longer credible, but neither was it possible to return to a
premodern understanding. For Luther and Calvin, the doctrine of providence
implied that God wills the sin that God punishes as well as the damnation that
God seeks to save us from. Gilkey noted that modern theologians are too influenced by modern humanism, Enlightenment rationalism, romanticism, and
finally existentialism to adopt any form of this religious worldview. The modern ideal of the free, autonomous, creative individual is too deeply insinuated
into modern theology to permit any recourse to a notion of God as all-con-
trolling.

But these options hardly exhausted the range of possibilities for a Christian
doctrine of providence. Gilkey reasoned that some stronger factor must have
prevented theologians from exploring the meaning of divine providence over
the past half-century. He proposed that this factor was the dominating influence of existentialism over modern theology. The idea of providence is not
completely lacking in existential significance to modern people, he allowed,
but nonetheless, it *is* mainly concerned with God's relation to events outside
the faith relation. For this reason, modern theology has had little epistemological basis for thinking about divine providence. Gilkey noted that this problem
was one of the reasons that Barth moved away from existential interpretation.
Barth was the only major theologian in recent years to give sustained attention
to the doctrine of providence. His discussion mixed a stunningly powerful and
sophisticated theology of divine sovereignty with a theory of nothingness that
posited a nonontological "nothing" as the root of *real* evil in existence.[62] Gilkey
was skeptical toward much of Barth's highly paradoxical theology of providence, but he embraced Barth's contention that a new understanding of providence was needed. He greatly admired Barth's attempt to provide one. Much
of his subsequent work was marked by his deep concern to rethink the ontological groundwork of religious knowledge as well as the Christian idea of
providence. He began to read Barth seriously for the first time, during the very
period when he concluded that the kind of neoorthodoxy promoted by the
Biblical Theology movement was not credible.[63]

The Semantics of Biblical Theology

Gilkey's judgment was confirmed by James Barr's devastating critiques of
the conceptuality and semantics of Biblical Theology. Barr observed that the
concept of history employed by Biblical Theologians amounted to "a construct

which is supposed to be related to the biblical material but which is ambiguous in the degree in which it affirms the actual form of the biblical material."[64] Biblical Theologians interpreted the entire Bible through the lens of their peculiar understanding of faith-inspired history, he noted. This procedure caused them to systematically distort the vast portion of scripture that did not submit or relate to their interpretive abstraction. For all of their talk about recovering the Bible, they either ignored or distorted most of the Bible, especially the Wisdom literature, in order to carry out their programmatic theology of history.

Moreover, Barr observed, scripture has no linguistic term that corresponds to the modern concept of history. The narrative passages of scripture "are not constant but variable in their relation to what we, by any definition which has any honest contact with modern usage, can call 'history.'" The upshot was that Biblical Theology based its construction of biblical teaching on a concept that lies outside scripture and does not cohere with much of the biblical witness. The fact that the Biblical Theology movement was forced to exclude the Wisdom literature from its purview did not speak well for its claim to biblical thinking, Barr asserted: "A history-centered revelational theology is at fault if it means that the Wisdom literature is found to be separated by a wide gulf from the narrative texts."[65]

Wright, Rowley, and others disdained the Wisdom literature out of their concern to emphasize the uniqueness of Hebrew religion. With its extensive influences and borrowings from non-Hebrew sources, the Wisdom literature fit poorly into the outlook of Biblical Theology. Barr remarked that there was something strange about a "biblical theology" that excluded much of the Bible itself in order to affirm a unique biblical message that lies outside the Bible. He added elsewhere that the same concern to affirm the historical and religious uniqueness of Hebrew faith was fueling bad linguistic scholarship. In order to bolster their contrast between Hebrew and Greek thought patterns, the Biblical Theologians were developing a method of highly selective lexicography that failed to treat Hebrew and Greek as true, fluid, complex languages. A skewed approach to semantics produced differences in semantic range between Hebrew and Greek that were interpreted as reflective of differing thought patterns. Biblical Theologians then used these results to argue that Hebrew thinking was not only different from Greek thought, but superior to it. Barr conceded that on its own terms, a biblically based theology might insist "that its biblically based concepts of faith or righteousness should be comprised within its concept of truth." But the attempt to make a case for the religious superiority of "Hebrew thought" on semantic grounds was spurious, he warned: "The attempt to interweave theological and linguistic argument only produces an ignoring or a wrong assessment of linguistic facts."[66]

The combined assaults of Gilkey and Barr left Biblical Theology as a movement in ruins. Barr's *The Semantics of Biblical Language* became a monument to the end of a theological era. Brevard Childs later remarked that "seldom has one book brought down so much superstructure with such effectiveness."[67] The collapse of this theological and institutional structure drove Gilkey to rethink his religious beliefs. He had begun his career thinking that he knew what theology was about and how it should proceed. In his early career he never doubted, as he later put it, that neoorthodoxy contained "universal value and truth." But by the mid-1960s he doubted nearly everything. His structure of certainties had dissolved. He reported in *The Christian Century* that what he had earlier thought to be solid earth "has turned out to be shifting ice—and in recent years as the weather has grown steadily warmer some of us have in horror found ourselves staring down into rushing depths of dark water." The dissolution of his theological certainties had occurred so rapidly, he confessed, that he found it "immensely embarrassing" to be asked about the direction of his religious thinking. He later recalled that while he was certain that Niebuhr, in his prime, would have known how to respond to this new theological situation, "I could find no handle with which to begin."[68]

Beyond Neoorthodoxy

An accumulation of doubts had broken his confidence that he had anything to say to an increasingly secular culture. It was one thing for an earlier generation of theologians to reclaim the language of prophetic faith during the turmoil of the Great Depression and the struggle against fascism, he reasoned. It was another matter entirely for theologians to proclaim the same faith during a period of peace and prosperity, when the foundations of Christian belief were being subjected to closer scrutiny. What *was* the meaning of the Fall if it had no point of historical origin? What *was* revelation without univocal acts or voices from God? What *were* God's "mighty acts" if the biblical miracles were ruled out? What *was* providence without God's actual rule? Gilkey observed, "Instead of the desperate wartime cry for help: 'How can we be saved in this mess? How can we find meaning in this holocaust of evil?' we now ask, 'How can we understand in the light of modern science and modern views of causality and value the salvation we thought we had experienced?' "[69] Neoorthodoxy had begun as a theology of crisis. Implicit in all of Gilkey's questions was the troubling suggestion that for all of its intellectual power and eloquence, neoorthodoxy was plausible only as a reaction to the world-historical crisis of Barth and Niebuhr's generation.

Gilkey's generation was faced with a more daunting, elusive, and disillusioning historical situation. Beneath the various intellectual problems that contemporary theologians struggled with, he noted, a deeper and more pervasive cultural pressure threatened to delegitimize theology itself. This cultural force was the "increasingly potent mood of secularism in our age." What made "the secular mood" such a distinctively threatening challenge to theology was its prerational character. Gilkey suggested that secularism would be much less threatening if it proposed a philosophy that competed with Christianity as an account of history, the human condition, or the cosmos. Secularism was not an alternative philosophy, however, but a basic attitude toward life. It consisted essentially of an intuitive sense about the meaning of life. The secularist mood that Gilkey found increasingly pervasive in American society was rooted in "the visceral sense that reality lies nowhere but amidst the visible and the tangible, that all causes are physical or human causes, that all events begin and end here and all interests lie solely in this world."[70] As he later put it, the modern secular mood is a "radically this-worldly" mindset.[71] To dispute this mood with arguments for God's existence was to misunderstand the nature of the phenomenon of secularism. Theology could respond meaningfully to secularism only by entering and addressing the realm of reflective experience out of which it arose. More important, in Gilkey's view, theology could provide an alternative to the secularist sensibility only if it could point to positive experiences of ultimacy and transcendence on the same deep level of subjectivity out of which secularism arose.

The kind of theology that was needed would require a "drastic reconstruction" of modern theology's governing assumptions and methodology, he argued. To any theologian who took seriously the challenge of secularity, the pertinent question was "just how drastic that reconstruction must be, how sharp the break with the theology of the past." Gilkey urged that the break had to be sharp enough not to retain any metaphysical or religious presuppositions from the past. The chief work of contemporary theology was to sweep away the entire inheritance of theological assumptions from the past and make a new beginning, so that "the God who has almost disappeared may appear to us again in power and in truth."[72]

This project of theological reconstruction would have to begin with the human subject. Gilkey was finished with neoorthodox appeals to a revelationist starting point. "If we felt sure that the divine word in Scripture was the truth, then the Bible might be our starting point," he explained. "Or if we felt some assurance that existence as a whole was coherent, a metaphysical beginning might be possible. But in our situation these two certainties are lacking." To take secularism seriously was to relinquish these starting points and begin the work of theology by explicating the human experience of relationality to an ultimate beyond the self. "At every crucial moment—when his humanity becomes evident, when man becomes uniquely man—we find some relation to this dimension of the ultimate or the unconditioned as the determining and shaping factor," Gilkey asserted. This essential relation of the self to an ultimate ground and love was the starting point for the theology that was needed.[73]

Theology was thus obliged to return to Schleiermacher's starting point. It would focus on the religious dimension of human existence while emphasizing aspects of human spirituality other than the dynamics of dependency and feeling emphasized by Schleiermacher. The theology that was needed would explicate the religious sources of joy and hope and longing and anxiety and terror. It would show that secular accounts of human existence are too thin to account for humankind's most important experiences. "God-language is meaningful because it reflects answers—deep experiences of power, meaning, value, acceptance and love—to questions raised and experienced by any human life," Gilkey asserted. "At his core man is a religious being, and this truth provides the clue both to his humanity and to his relation to God—for God-language is the explication of the answers to the deepest questions about man's existence."[74]

At the core of his theological reconstruction, Gilkey appropriated the language and method of his other former teacher. He relied heavily upon Tillich's language of ultimate concern and his correlational method of seeking religious answers to existential questions. He also began with a longer list of formative convictions than his rhetoric about dissolved certainties and dark water implied. Gilkey never doubted that Niebuhr's critique of liberal optimism and moralism was right. He knew from his wartime experience that self-interested egotism is nearly always a stronger force in human relations than the power of other-regarding rationality or moral concern. The reason that sin is so powerfully demonic and destructive in human affairs is because it is a *religious* phenonenon, he argued. It is the religious dimension of life that generates not only humanity's only hope for a life that transcends self-concern, but also the possibility of humanity's most demonic perversions, hatred, and cruelty. The crucial question for every human being is therefore not whether one will be religious, but whether one will give one's self to an ultimate concern that is worthy of ultimate concern. To make an unworthy choice is to choose idolatry.[75]

Most of his remaining formative convictions derived from this analysis of the dynamics of ultimacy. Because human beings cannot escape the essentially religious character of their humanity, he contended, theologians are justified in assuming that religious language is meaningful. Moreover, because human beings often find—in the face of life's unavoidable religious questions—that they can affirm life in spite of its ambiguities and terrors, the claim that religious language has a referent is justifiable on the basis of ordinary experience. Religious language is not merely a function of human nature, "but a valid form of symbolic discourse about the mystery from which we come and to which we return."[76]

These convictions formed the heart of Gilkey's subsequent theology. Virtually everything that he wrote over the succeeding three decades was marked by his commitment to rework these Tillichian and Niebuhrian themes into a new liberal theology that took to heart the demise of Christendom. A final conviction appeared much less prominently in his major theological writings but remained crucial to his spiritual outlook. This was that the "strangely potent figure of Jesus" embodies the ideal of true religion. Gilkey observed that the freedom of Jesus from self-concern made Jesus free to care for others. Through his life of free self-giving love, Jesus embodied and disclosed the pattern of authentic humanity. "In all the mystery of existence, with its emptiness, its ambiguity and its evil, surely this is clear," he asserted. "We find ourselves when, as Jesus did, we can lose ourselves in love for others. In this sense he is our 'Lord,' who provides us with our ethical model or perspective."[77]

Building upon the certainties of a sacral dimension in life and the existence of a realized moral ideal, theology could recover the inner meaning of God-language for secular individuals who yearn, often without knowing it, for God and love. The theology that was needed would unite the sacred dimension of human life, which is universal, to the particular saving power of the figure of Jesus.

4

Renaming the Whirlwind:
God Beyond Being

In 1963 Langdon Gilkey announced that an important and certainly novel theological movement was emerging, which he called "God-is-Dead theology." Though the leaders of this purported movement had never heard of each other until Gilkey drew attention to them, their writings did represent something worth naming. Theologians such as Paul van Buren, William Hamilton, Thomas J. J. Altizer, Richard Rubenstein, and others were calling for a secular theology that rejected every existing form of Christian or Jewish theism. They argued that theologians were obliged to radically rethink the fundamental categories of Jewish and Christian faith in a "world come of age" that had outgrown its need for religion. Gilkey's announcement set off an explosion of position taking in the mass media as well as hundreds of sermons by defensive clerics. If theologians didn't believe in God, how could Christianity survive? Did the spectacle of atheist theologians prefigure the distintegration of American religion and culture?

At the height of a prolonged media controversy over the question of God's demise, the antitheologians began to realize that they had little in common. The differences between Hamilton's Feuerbachian humanism, van Buren's commitment to verificationist language analysis, Altizer's ecstatic Nietzschean romanticism, and Rubenstein's post-Holocaust Jewish paganism were too great to sustain Gilkey's claim that they were leaders of any kind of movement. Some of the polemics against them must have made some of them regret Gilkey's role in instigating their Warholian fifteen minutes. Long after the controversy over God-is-Dead theology subsided, however, Gilkey persisted in taking it seriously. In different ways, the radical theologians insisted that there is no credible basis for affirming the existence of the God of Judeo-Christian theism. Some of them drew inspiration from the later writings of Dietrich Bonhoeffer, who, from his Nazi prison cell in the closing years of World War II, proclaimed that only a "religionless" Christianity could have any meaning in a world come of age.[1] As Gilkey remarked, the challenge of the secular theologians was to call into question "the reality of God, and so the possibility of meaningful talk about him."[2] His major work of this period addressed the challenge of contemporary antitheistic theology and set the stage for Gilkey's theological alternative.

Naming the Whirlwind: The Renewal of God-Language was Gilkey's prolegomena to any future theology. It was not a work of constructive theology, but a prolegomenal work that sought to demonstrate the meaningfulness of religious language under the conditions of what he called the reigning "secular mood." In Gilkey's view, the secular mood was not a philosophy, but the prerational disposition and cultural background out of which all modern philosophies had arisen. It was characterized by distinctively modern ways of thinking about contingency, relativity, temporality, and autonomy. To the secularized consciousness, he observed, such religious notions as transcendence, providence, and divine order are simply unreal; secular "reality" is grounded in the immediate dictates of experience and the institutional social constructions produced by experience.

To take the triumph of secular consciousness seriously is to rule out the option of basing theology on any appeal to revelation or any metaphysical system, Gilkey asserted. The theology that is needed would take Schleiermacher's option of disclosing the meaning of religious language through an analysis of ordinary life experience, this time by developing a hermeneutical phenomenology of experience.[3] In the manner of the early Heidegger, he proposed that the hidden religious dimension of human existence can be uncovered by pursuing a phenomenological interpretation of ordinary (secular) experience. Unlike Husserl's phenomenology, it did not claim to uncover the eternal necessary forms apparent to consciousness, but only the latent meanings or implicit structures of ordinary experience. Unlike Heidegger, on the other hand, Gilkey's work was not concerned to uncover the ontological structures of human existence, but only to disclose experiences of ultimacy as aspects of ordinary existence.[4] Put differently, it conducted an "ontic" rather than an ontological analysis. Building on the distinction in analytical philosophy between meaning (meaning as use value) and validity (verification through experience), *Naming the Whirlwind* generally excluded the question of validity or truth in theology.[5] Gilkey's concern was to demonstrate that, whatever the status of its truth-claims may be, religious language is (or can be) meaningful. His opening section argued that the defining secular experiences of contingency, relativity, temporality, and autonomy cannot be adequately conceptualized or comprehended on purely secular grounds.

The point was to clear a space for theological reflection, but Gilkey cautioned that only a new kind of theology could meet the challenge of modern secularism. *Naming the Whirlwind* reviewed the past century of liberal and neoorthodox responses to the "secular thesis," arguing that the recent spate of death-of-God theologies was a product of the failure of modern theology to take the modern secular mood seriously enough. For all of their internal disagreements, he observed, theological liberalism and neoorthodoxy both assumed that human fulfillment is attainable only in relation to a total environment symbolized as "God." But the secular consciousness has no experience or conception of a divine ground. The only reality known to secular reason is that human life is left on its own to create whatever meaning it may find in a radically contingent cosmos. "The heart of modern secularity is that human experience, secular or religious, is devoid of relation beyond itself to any ground or order, and that there is no form of human thought that can by speculation come to know of such a ground or order," he remarked.[6] Having reached an apparently terminal stage in the process of secularization, the modernized consciousness is far more totalizing in its negation of the sacred than Schleiermacher imagined.

Liberal and neoorthodox theologies typically challenge the secular understanding of secular experience on either theological or metaphysical grounds, but Gilkey proposed to take secularity more seriously. He proposed to follow the lead of the death-of-God theologians without accepting their conclusions. Some of the radical theologians rejected God-language while trying to save Jesus as an object of religious discourse; others projected their personal experiences of nothingness onto the cosmos; all of them endorsed the secular understanding of secularity.[7] Gilkey countered that "Jesus without God" makes no sense as the basis for a credible theology and that most of the radical theologians overgeneralized their own experience. His alternative focused on the question of how secular experience should be understood.

The problem with the secular understanding of secular experience was that it could not provide the symbolic forms that are necessary to understand its actual character. The death-of-God theologians were right to take the modern secular mood seriously, but wrong to endorse the secular understanding of modernity. Gilkey observed that secularism has interpreted human life as though it should be understood solely in terms of biology, chemistry, social environment, and other measurable finite forces. It has emphasized the contingency of human existence and dismissed all symbolic religious language as unintelligible. But there is a generative dimension of secular existence that is explicable only through the use of symbolic or mythological religious language, he argued. This is the dimension of ultimacy, the presence of unconditionedness in human life through which a self faces mortality and embraces its relative meanings. Built into every person's self-experience and world is a human-making dimension that transcends both selfhood and environment.[8] Paul Ricoeur maintained that religious symbols reveal an otherwise hidden dimension of human existence. If this claim is true, Gilkey proposed, it should be possible for a hermeneutical phenomenology to disclose the latent sacral elements of experience.

This project would not be merely an elaboration of Ricoeur's hermeneutical analysis. For Ricoeur the work of hermeneutics was to uncover the meanings that religious symbols disclose about experience.[9] Gilkey, however, rejected Ricoeur's Wittgensteinian assumption that language precedes experience. He observed that language is impossible without being, process, relatedness, and experience. Because these ontological categories lie behind the possibility of language, he argued, a hermeneutic of "actual experience" is also possible.

Gilkey did not claim that a phenomenological analysis can prove the existence
of a dimension of ultimacy, because analysis can only disclose something and
point to it, "it cannot prove that it is there." The establishment of a dimension
of ultimacy by means of a phenomenology of experience thus "rests solely on
our 'seeing' for ourselves that we do experience this dimension, that it does in
fact appear in its strange way in the experience of all of us."

This dimension of ultimacy in human experience is the ground and limit of
human being, he argued; it is the presupposition of all relative human thinking and acting. It is not what is seen, "but the basis of seeing; not what is known
as an object so much as the basis of knowing; not an object of value, but the
ground of valuing; not the thing before us, but the source of things; not the
particular meanings that generate our life in the world, but the ultimate context within which these meanings necessarily subsist."[10] It is the reality of this
dimension of human life that makes religious language meaningful and necessary.

Restricting himself to an ontic phenomenological description of human experience rather than an ontological analysis of the structures of being, he argued that the dimension of ultimacy manifests itself as the source or ground of
being and as a recognition of fundamental human *limits*. As the ground or horizon of the given it appears as the source of being; negatively, as the limit of
the given it appears as the ultimate negation of being, the nihilating power of
the Void. The dimension of ultimacy is also disclosed in the activity of knowing and as the source and basis of values; without it we have nothing. Since
the loss of this dimension of unconditioned transcendence would eradicate all
value, meaning, and being, Gilkey observed, religious language appropriately
refers to it as the realm of the sacred. The essential element of mystery within
the sacred compels us to use religious language in talking about it. In every
moment human beings depend upon and are threatened by the dimension of
ultimacy within them. The experience of ultimacy is part of ordinary life, yet it
requires a different use of language than the discourse about measurable things
spoken by science. In this crucial way, he argued, the secular language of modern secularity is too spiritually impoverished to account for the realities of secular experience.[11]

Naming the Whirlwind compiled ample phenomenological evidence for this
thesis. Gilkey showed that some trace of ultimacy is perceptible in every experience of human creativity, thought, desire, and fear. It is disclosed in the experience of contingency as a nihilating unconditioned threat, as explicated in
existentialism, modern literature, and psychology. It is disclosed in the desperate drive for unconditioned power or status acted out by achievers who
want to guarantee their security. It is disclosed in the innumerable ways that
people seek to achieve immortality or divert their attention from their awareness of mortality. In every conscious and unconscious effort to find an unconditioned answer to the nihilating power of the Void, human beings disclose the
reality of ultimacy in their lives. "These experiences of an ultimate and sacral
ground of life, and of an ultimate Void that threatens life, are undeniable, and

the questions they raise about an ultimate security are, therefore, significant questions," he remarked.[12]

It followed that religion in some form is inevitable, even in a secular culture that thinks it has outgrown religion. "Modern secular culture, sure on the surface that it has come of age and has no remaining religious problems, spends a good deal of its resources to hide the reality of death from its awareness—all totally unsuccessful," Gilkey observed. Nothing is more pressing or intelligible than the human need to thematize this experience. But the mystery of the self in its will to freedom and immortality while bound to its mortal finitude can be explicated only in the language of religious myth and symbol.

Though Gilkey accepted much of the Feuerbachian/Nietzschean critique of religion as a devitalizing and dehumanizing cultural force, he argued that humanism does not come close to an adequate account of human experience. He conceded to Thomas J. J. Altizer and Norman O. Brown that religion often drains the powers of life from its followers, leaving them deprived of true feeling, authenticity, and the capacity to relate to others. But the critical value of this critique is nullified as soon as it proposes an alternative to religion, he observed. From Feuerbach to Nietzsche to Jean Paul Sartre to Norman O. Brown to William Hamilton, atheistic humanism seeks to free humanity by getting rid of God, and thus reveals its hopeless naiveté about the human situation.[13] Atheism does not deliver people from unreality, isolation, or meaninglessness, but only condemns them to it. The source of human brokenness is not the divine, but our own alienation from ourselves and each other. The picture of the human self propounded in the literature of atheistic humanism is thus deeply mistaken, Gilkey remarked, "picturing him as a good guy able to affirm himself in power and to love his neighbor in sacrifice were it not for the entry of the transcendent onto the scene." Nietzsche's children nearly always portray the godless self as creative, healthy, life-affirming, and other-regarding, but this defining conceit of modern humanism has no evidence in its favor. Gilkey observed that in fact, the evidence is entirely against the humanist creed, "not the least being the continuing reality of alienation, isolation, and guilt in an almost totally secularized culture."[14]

What the self needs is not to be "liberated" from the only possible source or ground of unconditional redemption, healing, and grace, but to be made whole through the experience of acceptance and love. The ultimate disclosure of the self's dimension of ultimacy appears in this need. Gilkey noted that the human need for love is unconditional. If our brokenness is to be healed, it can only be healed by true love, which is unconditional in character. Earned love is not love, but reward. Our attempts to overcome alienation and the terrors of nonbeing through achievement are therefore always self-defeating. We cannot give ourselves what we need nor earn it through our efforts. What we need must be given to us without condition. But for love to be real, Gilkey observed, it must be given to us in the knowledge of our condition, with an acceptance "that knows both our guilt and yet still loves us." The biblical affirmation that God is love expresses the Christian experience of such a forgiving acceptance and grace. Atheistic humanism derides Christian teaching as sentimental or ignorant, but it is humanism that clings to illusions about love. Without an unconditioned ground, love has no ground and thus no reality at all.

Gilkey argued that religious language is meaningful as a "thematizing answer" to the question of how one might find love, meaning, and courage in the face of an otherwise coldly indifferent universe. Religious language is not rooted in any special experience or realm of history, but in ordinary human experiences that are interpreted "religiously" by one's primary spiritual community. "The mythical language of a community discloses to us the structures of ultimacy in which our community lives, and through these symbols the face of ultimacy manifests itself to us," he wrote. "Thus particular symbolic forms, carried by a community and a tradition, are the essential media of each human apprehension of ultimacy and so of our creative answers to ultimate issues."[15] In each religious community or tradition, the manifestation of the community's experience of the sacred is symbolized in ways that distinctively define its identity. The way that each community or tradition interprets the appearance of the sacred is shaped by the character and structure of its symbols. But in each case, including Christianity, Gilkey cautioned, the *what* that is disclosed through the community's religious symbols is never the sacred by itself but always the manifestation of the sacred in and through the finite. The *what* is never an unmediated object but always relational to a given pattern of experiences and symbols.

Gilkey thus embraced the core assumption of theological liberalism. Schleiermacher argued that any attempt to speak truthfully about God or God's self-disclosure "can only express God in his relation to us." It followed for him that any attributes that theology may ascribe to God "are to be taken as denoting not something special in God, but only something special in the manner in which the feeling of absolute dependence is to be related to him."[16] Gilkey adopted this approach in every respect excepting its romanticism. Schleiermacher believed that religious symbols can be drawn out of feelings, but for Gilkey, even "feelings" or "experiences" were relational phenomena resulting from the interaction of symbols and life. Theological liberalism after Schleiermacher typically assumed that symbols are produced by experience, but Gilkey's perspective was informed by sociological and sociopsychological theories that view "experience" as being shaped by the language, customs, and symbols of a given community.[17] In his view, Christian experience combines the forms of awareness that derive from our existential situation with the symbolic patterns or myths through which this situation is apprehended.

Making Liberalism Rethink Myth

One of the key insights of *Religionsgeschichtliche* scholarship was crucial to this reformulation. In his influential work, *The Symbolism of Evil*, Ricoeur observed that the history of religions school (especially as exemplified by Mircea

Eliade) has uncovered the explanatory significance of myth through the process of dispensing with its explanatory pretensions. "For us, moderns, a myth is *only* a myth because we can no longer connect that time with the time of history as we write it, employing the critical method, nor can we connect mythical places with our geographical space," he observed. By getting rid of the expectation that myths should convey factual information, however, history of religions scholarship has unveiled the explanatory significance of myth, which Ricoeur called its "symbolic function." The function of myth is to disclose with emotive power the bond between human beings and the sacred. The irony of modern religious studies is that in the process of demythologizing myth, Ricoeur noted, modern historical consciousness has uncovered the truth of myth and thus made myth "a dimension of modern thought."[18]

This argument has informed all of Gilkey's work on the mythic dimensions of religious language from *Naming the Whirlwind* onward. He contends that the conventional modern understanding of myth as untrue fable makes the secular mind not only unable to understand religion, but also blind to its own mythic elements. For Gilkey, as for Ricoeur and Eliade, myth is a certain mode of language "whose elements are multivalent symbols, whose referent in some strange way is the transcendent or the sacred, and whose meanings concern the ultimate or existential issues of actual life and the questions of human and historical destiny." Understood in this way, religious language is essentially mythical, and the work of theology is to present "involved yet disciplined reflection" upon the mythical symbols of particular religious traditions.[19]

Theological liberalism customarily took a pejorative approach to myth; Niebuhr and Tillich wrote as critics of liberalism; the Bultmannians claimed that biblical myth prevents modern people from hearing the gospel.[20] Gilkey's novel blend of liberal and myth-affirming sources raised the possibility of a new kind of liberal theology. He conceded that the prescientific cosmology and neo-Aristotelian metaphysics of traditional Christian theism present serious problems for modern theology, but he argued that the liberal and Bultmannian strategies fail to address a deeper problem. The fundamental problem for modern theology is that the secular mind, while not recognizing its own mythical elements, is highly attuned to the mythic elements in *every form* of religious language and therefore rejects all religious beliefs as mythical. To the secular mind, Bultmann's kerygmatic existentialism sounds as strange and unreal as the Bible's prescientific cosmology. None of the various strategies to overcome or demythologize the mythic elements of Christianity makes Christianity credible to the modern secular mind addressed by modern theology. In this situation, Gilkey judged, theologians must present a keener and more sympathetic interpretation of the explanatory significance of myth.

Drawing upon Eliade's analysis of "primitive" and ancient forms of mythical language, he noted that the language of all premodern religious traditions expresses a particular mode of human self-understanding, "namely one achieved through an experienced relation to the fundamental sacral structures of man's cosmic environment."[21] Unbroken myth proposes that a special quality of intimacy with sacral structures of space, time, nature, and history can be found and continually reexperienced by opening one's self to the reality of the sacred as disclosed through sacred symbols. These mythical forms offer a guide to the mysteries of life and death and provide models for the follower's personal and social life.[22] Myths shape the horizon of human experience by providing a conceptual structure for formative natural and social experience; they legitimate a community's relation to nature and its social structures; they help community members deal with pain and tragedy and give them grounds for hope that evil will be overcome; and they provide sources for moral reflection and judgment.[23]

Central to Gilkey's conception of myth is its multivalence. Mythical symbols do not refer only to finite objects, but also to the transcendent, the unconditioned, and the manifestations of the sacred in and through sacred symbols. Most ancient mythical forms are cosmogonic: they connect the sacred to the originating divine powers that created the world, and thus offer to reconcile or restore human beings to their original creation. Most of them also posit some notion of eternal return: they seek salvation from damnation, alienation, dissolution, or chaos through ritual reenactment of the founding symbolic forms.[24] Ancient myth is therefore invariably backward-looking, he observed; it presupposes a cyclical view of time and assumes that freedom is not fulfilled through creativity, but through one's participation in the ritual reenactment of original forms given by the gods.[25]

Hebrew religion and Christianity embrace only parts of this ancient mythical structure. Gilkey noted that the Christian emphasis on linear history, historical revelation, the liberating power of the "new" in history, and the openness of the future to an eschatological end of history make Christianity very different from religions that sacralize a myth of eternal return. Early Christianity was strongly future-oriented and historical by comparison to backward-looking cosmogonic religions that presupposed a cyclical view of the structure of time.

But even in the forms that predated its later development of a sacramental cultus, early Christianity shared other mythical elements with ancient religion, especially the notion of divine reality as transcendent, creative, providential, and ordering. It is precisely these traditional mythic elements in Christianity that modern secular reason finds meaningless, Gilkey observed. The secular mind disbelieves in any transcendent or sacred reality within or beyond the physical world known to science. It has no sacral home in the cosmos, but "knows" that it has been thrown into a purposeless world in which human subjects are on their own to create their own meanings. It therefore celebrates the creative possibilities of human autonomy and disparages the repressive, communal, backward-looking spirit of the mythic imagination. The modern spirit is insistently antimythical, Gilkey explained: "It is of the essence of modernity to believe that myth is part of the infancy of man, to be outgrown in the scientific and autonomous age of modernity."[26]

The revealing contradiction in the secular mind's account of the world is that it invariably resorts to mythical language in expressing its "antimythical" world-view. The ideals of the self promoted by modern secular culture provide instructive examples. The rationalist image of the critical, scientific "man of reason" is a mythical construct, as is the "authentic" self of existential philosophy, the unrepressed and loving self of humanistic psychology, the liberal democratic self of civic humanism, and the pragmatic manager of business culture. These images of the ideal self are clearly different from each other, Gilkey noted, yet all of them are distinctively *modern* ideal-types with common mythical features. All of them assume that to understand something is to have power over it, since knowledge requires control over the objects of knowledge. Secular reason simply assumes that consciousness and knowledge should be used to transmute the (previously) blind determining force of consciousness into means by which human power over nature may be obtained.

Modern secularists further assume that the realization of freedom is always a moral good, however differently this "good" is pictured among the various images of the ideal self. Gilkey observed that the secular mind always conceives freedom as being freedom *from* evil, not freedom *for* evil. In every modern secular mythology, the ideal self finds emancipation from its particular form of bondage through some transformation of consciousness. It is increased *awareness* of the dynamics that determine the self against its will that liberate the self to find its "true" identity. Secular reason resolves the problem of evil in the self's behavior through its various mythologies of awareness, for which evil is always located "outside of freedom." To the extent that the modern self has been liberated to become truly rational or authentic or loving or democratic or pragmatic or whatever, it is liberated from its former evil. "Fate and sin arise from beyond the inward center of man: in ignorance, in repression, in the false objectification of things, in prejudice and false ideals," Gilkey explained. Secular reason therefore trusts in faith that greater knowledge and awareness will make the world a better place. Evil in the world will decrease as people become more rational and gain greater control over nature and history.[27]

This is precisely the myth that Niebuhr demolished in *Moral Man and Immoral Society*. Following Niebuhr, Gilkey observed that the prospect of increased human control over nature is just as likely to imperil human freedom as to advance it. The modern secular predisposition is to view evil as a "problem" to be solved; secular reason therefore typically adopts an engineering or medical model of analysis in which the putative "causes" of evil are identified, isolated, controlled, and extinguished. To understand the factors that cause evil is to be able to extinguish it. "We really believe that if we know or are aware of everything, if we understand all relevant causes and factors, we can control everything," Gilkey remarked.[28] As Niebuhr repeatedly cautioned, however, this faith in the redemptive power of rationality ignores the immense possibilities for evil that the attainment of knowledge and power always holds.[29]

Because it problematizes the mystery of evil, secular reason typically embraces a false myth. Gilkey countered that the phenomenon of evil is a mystery of existence that infects human freedom, including the efforts of all who strive to gain power to eliminate evil. This truth of human experience is explicable only in the language of myth and symbol. Secular existence raises ultimate questions that only mythical language can thematize. Even the pursuit of scientific truth discloses traces of ultimacy, he noted, "in the eros or passion that supports its individual and social embodiments, in the role of global visions and of the theoretical structures that follow from them, and finally in the self-affirmation of the rational consciousness as knowing veridically in proximate judgments." These *human* aspects of science disclose a dimension of ultimate concern, "a relation to an unconditioned value, order, certainty, and being beyond our own making."[30] But when science is turned into scientism or positivist philosophy, its mythic elements must be shunned. Having set out to eliminate mythical reasoning, the secular mind tries to rationalize the mysteries of life and creates poor myths in the process.

The mythical discourse that is needed would be temporal, multivalent, and cognizant of its limitations, Gilkey argued. Theologically, it should emphasize process, history, and the dynamic character of divine reality as a corrective to the backward-looking cosmogonic myths of ancient religion. In its language, it must be multivalent, referring to the finite and to that which transcends the finite. As a mode of language that explicates concrete human experience, myth must speak to both the mystery of existence and the concrete life forms of historical existence. Gilkey frequently invoked Ricoeur's argument that while mythical language may refer to factual propositions, it does not properly assert, entail, or contain information.[31] As a multivalent mode of language, myth refers to both the finite and the transcendent, but its references to the finite must be understood to have no normative meaning as historical or scientific information.

In other words, mythical language necessarily refers to the finite as its medium of transcendence, but it does not provide information about the nature or character of the finite. "Revelation tells us of the God who manifests himself in nature and in the events of history, but not of the character of nature and what must have happened and when in that history," Gilkey explained.[32] The language forms of myth are always phenomenal, historical, and personal, but mythical meaning always points beyond these forms to a realm of transcendence.

Gilkey did not believe that myth is the first or even the most important element of religious experience, since the desire to understand is not the deepest need in human life. The origins of religion lie "in deep prereflective levels of awareness, 'prehensions' of the sacral forces on which man depends." Religion is the product of the interaction between these "prehensions" and humankind's deepest subjective responses to the world, "responses both of joy, gratitude, celebration, and confidence or hope on the one hand, and of anxiety, terror, despair, and guilt or remorse on the other."[33] The purpose of myth is to organize the total "world" of one's desires, environment and social situation into a reflective form that makes sense of the world.

It follows that the purpose of theology is to reflectively explore the meaning and validity of mythical discourse. What makes modern theology distinctive in religious history is the fact that modern theologians know that their myths are myths. Theology no longer claims to be able to make indicative statements about matters of fact. It is only as broken myth that Christianity's mythical inheritance can be appropriated. More than any particular problem in theological method or interpretation, it was Gilkey's deepening awareness of the novelty of modern theology that moved him to rethink his theological perspective. His early writings sought to maintain continuity with the mainstream of traditional Christian theology through their appeal to the revealed Word of God. The neoorthodox vocabulary of Word, revelation, and "mighty acts" preserved the appearance of continuity with the tradition of classical Christian theism. *Maker of Heaven and Earth* argued that this structure of religious affirmation is univocally grounded in the person of Jesus Christ.

But in the 1960s Gilkey deconstructed the neoorthodox recital of God's "mighty acts" in history. His early writings on mythical language implied that neoorthodoxy could not maintain the kind of continuity with traditional Christianity that it claimed, even if it used the same words, because it understood Christian myths to be mythical. *Naming the Whirlwind* suggested that the central "mighty act" of God proclaimed by scripture has the same problematic character as any other biblical miracle story. Modern historians do not accept miracle stories as explanations of historical events, he observed. Moreover, modern biblical criticism is exposing the heavily layered, often contradictory process by which the gospel narratives were constructed. "If there were no miraculous removal of the body, no empty tomb, no later appearances in miraculous form—if in fact it was not an 'event' in the ordinary sense of an observable occurrence in the space-time nexus—what do the words 'event' or 'act' mean here?" Gilkey asked. "How does God act in history in this 'pseudo-event,' and what on earth does it mean to say God *acted* here if nothing happened more than the appearance of faith among the disciples?"[34]

Though he addressed other aspects of the new eschatological theologies of Wolfhart Pannenberg and Jürgen Moltmann, Gilkey did not assess their recent attempts to reestablish the historicity of the resurrection event.[35] Whatever the truth may be with regard to the historical status of the resurrection, he implied, it is no longer credible for theologians to treat the resurrection narratives as historical accounts about a miraculous event directly caused by God. "Events" of this kind are not "historical" in the ordinary senses of both terms. The act/event language of Easter faith is therefore meaningful only outside the framework of critical history and ordinary experience. Neoorthodoxy may be irrefutable as an appeal to faith, but Gilkey argued that theology must do better than appeal to faith in the historicity of the pseudo-acts of God. What is needed is a theology that bridges the gap between Easter faith and secular history, or between religious experience and secular experience.

This is what Tillich and Bultmann sought to do. Gilkey judged that their preeminent influence in the past half-generation was attributable to this feature of their work. Tillich, Bultmann, and Niebuhr all sought to bridge the gap between

Christian faith and modern secular experience. Gilkey sought to build on their mediating work. Like his teachers, especially Tillich, he asserted that if theological language is to be made intelligible to the modern secular mind, it must look for the basis of its discourse in secular experience. *Naming the Whirlwind* uncovered the dimensions of ultimacy in personal, existential experience; *Religion and the Scientific Future* and *Nature, Reality and the Sacred* looked for dimensions of ultimacy in cognitive experience, especially scientific inquiry; *Shantung Compound* and *Reaping the Whirlwind* found dimensions of ultimacy in social and historical existence; *Catholicism Confronts Modernity* and *Message and Existence* used the disclosure of ultimacy method to explicate Gilkey's constructive theology; and *Society and the Sacred* and *Through the Tempest* looked for sacral dimensions in various aspects of modern culture. As he explained in *Catholicism Confronts Modernity*, for Gilkey the burden of modern theology was to synthesize the myths, stories, and symbols of Christian experience with modern scientific and philosophical reason.[36] The influence of Niebuhr and Tillich over his pursuit of this project marked nearly every page of his work, but as Gilkey developed his constructive theology of history in the 1970s, he acquired a nearly equal debt to Whiteheadian process thought.

Metaphysical Structure
or Historical Process?

Gilkey's prolonged effort to rethink the Christian doctrine of providence was crucial to this theological turn. For many years, he reflected on the religious meaning of his wartime internment experience; for nearly as many years, he puzzled over the fact that modern theology has so little to say about providence. *Shantung Compound* offered an account of his imprisonment in China and, especially, the insights about human nature, consciousness, and evil that he drew from this experience. The impact of this experience upon his developing thought informed all of his theological work, especially his writing about the sacral dimensions of politics, destiny, and fate. In an early section of his dense, symphonic theology of history, *Reaping the Whirlwind*, he remarked that those who scorn the guardians of social order reveal that they have never been hungry or faced the prospect of anarchy. Because it is good to continue to be, the work of politics is good work, he admonished; human life cannot flourish in the absence of stable social structures. At the same time, the anxieties that human beings rightfully hold about their security can easily become demonic, "and this concern for our being generates the peculiar intensity of political and economic conflict, as well as the dominance of these areas over other values of life."[37] Gilkey's major work of constructive theology offered a religious interpretation of the human historical struggle for survival and freedom. *Reaping the Whirlwind* reinterpreted the Christian understanding of divine providence in the light of modern historical consciousness and the ambiguities of modern social existence.

One of the fundamental debates in modern theology centers on the question whether theologians should conceptualize history fundamentally in terms of its metaphysical structure or historical process. Should a Christian understanding of human existence give priority to a metaphysical account of the permanent structures of being or to a philosophy of history that emphasizes the dynamic movement of historical change? With the rise of historical consciousness in the nineteenth century, the renewed appreciation of the dynamic character of Hebrew thought in modern biblical theology, and the emergence of eschatological and liberation theologies in the 1960's, modern theology in several of its major forms has sought to dehellenize Christianity by privileging historical change, process, or the future over the static, structural categories of traditional theism. Much of the energy of modern theology has been invested in the attempt to overcome the static metaphysical dualism of traditional Catholic and Protestant theology. At the same time, the structural language of traditional theism has been reinterpreted and defended not only by numerous conservative theologians in this century, but also by existential theologians, Tillichians, and—in their distinctive way—process theologians.

Gilkey's turn to Whitehead took place against this background. Seeking to avoid the problems that inhere in any theology that one-sidedly emphasizes either structure or process, he tried to hold both approaches together by incorporating much of Whitehead's process metaphysics into a reconstructed liberal theology that remains continuous, in its key accents, with the theologies of Tillich and Niebuhr. Tillich's theology of providence began with an ontology of history that posited the polarity of self and world as the basic structure of existence. He interpreted the polarity of destiny and freedom as an element of the self/world structure.[38] Gilkey embraced his teacher's claim that an adequate theology of providence requires a grounding theory of historical being, but he believed that Tillich's categories of self and world were too static to account for the dynamism of history. The opening sentence of *Reaping the Whirlwind* declared that "change is basic in human experience and in the world that is experienced." Gilkey's theology of history sought to explicate the religious meaning of this truism by adopting the Whiteheadian dialectic of freedom and destiny. He proposed that the primary ontological structure of historical existence is not self and world, but actuality and possibility. History moves and is experienced in the interplay of freedom and destiny, bringing together the historical given with the actualization of new possibilities. The process dialectic of destiny/freedom not only provides a more dynamic understanding of the ontological structure of historical being, he explained, but also shows how this fundamental structure "entails its own deepest grounds."[39]

For Gilkey, as for Whitehead, destiny is that which is "given" in personal and social life from the past. It is an inheritance from the past that cannot be removed. Yet destiny is also a given on which human freedom can work and, to some variable degree, can bend or reshape to particular ends. Destiny becomes fate when its oppressive weight overwhelms our spirit and powers and thus destroys our freedom. Fate is the sigh of the lost or defeated soul that has stopped struggling for freedom from the given. Like sin and death, it negates human flourishing; it represents historical experience as demonic. In Gilkey's words, to be fated "is to be stripped of one's humanity, and so anxiety about being fated is a fundamental human anxiety—and central to all politics."

Because the human experience of history as fate is rooted in the fundamental anxiety for security that stalks every conscious human being, it is always religious. Gilkey observed that in the experience of fate, a person experiences history

> as an objective power over against his own enfeebled powers; as a power against which he, his group, and even the finite gods have no power, no freedom and so no security. For destiny and fate alike represent the historical sea out of which human beings and each group have arisen; it is by destiny that every human power is *constituted* and so it can be by fate, when destiny becomes fate, that every human power can be submerged.[40]

Social experience thus discloses a crucial dimension of ultimacy. To the secular mind, the very question of an ultimate sovereignty in history smacks of religious dogmatism or ignorance; but in the enacted life of every person and human group, Gilkey argued, the constitutively human fear of fate inevitably raises the question of whether we are immersed in a march of events that will support our being. The religious question of whether history will support us or march us into an annihilating unknown is "the most unavoidable of concerns" in social existence. "For there is a fundamental terror as well as an open possibility to historical being, to any finite being that has been 'thrown' into a situation that it did not create, that maintains its precarious being over time and so projects that contingent being into an unknown and uncontrollable future," Gilkey wrote. This is the clue to the unreality of naturalistic or other essentialist understandings of history. In secular social theory, historical change is pictured as determined by impersonal natural, social, or psychological laws—or alternately, as shaped by rational or moral judgments—but all of these accounts strip history "of its qualitative characteristics, its demonic character, its unnaturalness, its guilt." To be reflectively aware of the richness and terror of concrete human existence is to apprehend the existence and corruption of historical dimensions of ultimacy that secular reason screens out.[41]

Just as individuals typically face their fear of fate only in moments of great anxiety about it, so do nations typically acknowledge their fear of the future only in moments of national crisis. Gilkey observed that political existence becomes explicitly religious in these moments and therefore inevitably demonic. The ruling authorities assume sacred legitimations and powers; the language of religion is used to sacralize the nation's efforts to gain control over its threatening fates; rival nations or groups are demonized. "At such times even our 'scientific' modern political and historical ideologies, and even nonideological pragmatic liberalism, alike partake of explicit myth," he remarked. The work of politics is thus inevitably religious in its concern to rescue freedom and security from the powers of nonbeing. Moreover, it is not only in its concern with these fundamental questions of being that political existence discloses a dimension of ultimacy. Modern politics also raises questions of meaning and moral purpose, seeking to create communities and other social structures that affirm human achievements and that provide a sense of belonging, purpose, and moral direction. The crisis of meaning is especially acute for those who have no community to confer meaning on their achievements: "In a mobile society 'meaning' as achieved status disappears—a matter of telling and retelling how important we are to new faces who know and care little about these things; vital insignia of importance are always lost on strangers." In a society that specializes in the mass production of meaningless commodities and achievements, he observed, it becomes a question of survival whether one will find a meaning-bestowing community that is sustained by credible symbolic forms.[42]

The sacral dimension of political life is similarly disclosed in the ultimacy that human beings invest in their moral and political convictions. Most people do not regard their fundamental political norms as relative, Gilkey noted. Conservatives do not think of radicalism or big government as being relatively wrong. Even relativistic liberals do not think of racism or exploitation as being wrong only from their perspective. Virtually everyone who participates in political life ascribes an ultimacy to their core moral/political convictions that transcends cultural relativity.[43] Liberals do not say that it is merely "unwise" for their government to invade a small country or to ignore the needs of the poor; they declare that such actions are morally wrong, unacceptable, indefensible. To make such a declaration is to invoke an obligation on all parties that is not subject to circumstance and which therefore has, for the speaker, the character of ultimacy. The call of political conscience is a sacred disclosure that cannot be disregarded. Gilkey was content in *Reaping the Whirlwind* to observe that political life therefore bears a religious character even in highly secularized societies; his later writings took this observation a step further, noting that modern secular culture is *producing* unconventional forms of religious expression, including alienated political religions.[44]

His implicit thesis was that history cannot be interpreted adequately by secular reason alone. A theological interpretation of the ultimate dimensions of historical existence is possible and necessary. Moreover, because the inevitability of change raises deep existential and religious problems for human beings, this theological perspective must hold structure and process together, interpreting history through the dialectic of freedom and destiny. "It is in temporal man's movement into the new future, not in some frozen eternal moment, that the 'shock of non-being' largely occurs, and the questions of courage, wisdom and justice are posed," Gilkey observed. The religious dimension of each future-entering person causes her to experience history as ultimate threat or ultimate promise. It is because of the dimension of ultimacy in historical experience that political existence "is at once filled with deep violence, cruelty and destruction, that it searches for ultimate meanings, that it is directed by ultimate moral judgments and buoyed up with ultimate hopes."[45] To be human is to be immersed in temporal change, yet it is also at the same time to transcend passage so that we may be aware of our temporality, may know it, fear it, judge it, and shape its future.[46]

We make history by transcending the historical temporality in which we are immersed. This struggle for freedom and life has an inherently religious character. The crucial question for a theology of history is not whether the historical dialectic of destiny and freedom has a religious dimension, Gilkey argued, since this dimension of ultimacy is readily demonstrated. The crucial question is whether history has a unifying transcendent ground: "Is there such a principle or factor uniting past actuality and not-yet possibility, destiny and freedom in their widest scope, an ultimate creativity and sovereignty in history that makes intelligible the ultimate dimension or horizon of history and the quest for an ultimate order and a sacred norm?"[47]

History, Myth, and Modern Theology

Reaping the Whirlwind amplified Gilkey's theory of myth in laying the groundwork for his response to this question. Every theology or philosophy of history has a mythical character, he observed. Every interpretation of history as a whole tells a story about the relation of determining forces or destiny to freedom in a way that seeks to make sense of the known world. Moreover, every religious or philosophical attempt to account for the whole of history takes up questions about meaning, historical good and evil, and prospects for the future, as well as questions about the norms that should govern human existence. Orthodox Christianity, Enlightenment humanism, modern Progressivism, and Marxism are four prominent examples of myths that have provided the symbols that represent, in Tillichian terms, the "religious substance" of presently competing interpretations of history. "When we ask why the form of language we have called myths is not only appropriate to the interpretation of history but inevitably basic to all interpretations of history, cultural or theological, we encounter the dialectic of mystery and meaning in historical existence," Gilkey wrote, invoking a Niebuhrian theme.[48]

For Niebuhr, the fundamental task of a theology of history was to sort out and dialectically interrelate the ambiguous, paradoxical tangents of mystery and meaning that are constitutive of all historical experience. To regard meaning either as undialectically transcendent to historical passage or as totally immanent within it is to depart from what he called the "biblical approach to history." Meaning is always constitutive of historical experience without being identical with or exhausted by experience.[49] Following Niebuhr, Gilkey affirmed that the biblical understanding of history is "based on a theologically formulated myth: a cluster of religious symbols concerned with the evident mystery—both transcendent and immanent, both of God and of man's freedom—in historical life in relation to its elusive and yet real meanings."[50]

Unlike Niebuhr, however, Gilkey was sensitive to the fact that this kind of appropriation of biblical theology is distinctive to modern religious thought. *Reaping the Whirlwind* reviewed the Augustinian and Calvinist understandings of providence and the story of the discrediting of these religious worldviews by modern science and historical consciousness in order to emphasize the novelty of the religious situation faced by modern theologians. Modern theology in all of its major forms has been obliged to begin with the assumption that the classical understandings of providence are not credible. Augustine, Aquinas, and Calvin presupposed that historical structures such as "the order of creation" were created by God and are thus eternal, absolute, and sacred. They further presupposed that historical change is caused either by continuous divine action or by special divine intervention. In either case, traditional Christian theism simply assumed that God makes history.[51]

Modern theology is "modern" precisely in its break with the view that God directly causes all natural and historical events. For modern theology, as for modern secular historiography, the "structures" of history are relative and transient; a belief in the existence of natural laws available to rational inquiry has replaced the myth of supernatural causation; and the making of history is viewed as the work of finite naturalistic causality and human action. Gilkey observed that the combined inheritance of modern science, Enlightenment philosophy, and historical criticism forced theology in the nineteenth century to make "a fundamental reinterpretation of itself, a reinterpretation from the ground up."[52] Three main forms of modern theology have been offered since that time, he noted: each of them has emphasized some crucial aspect of the theology of history that is needed, but each has also limited or reduced the Christian understanding of history to its distinctive hermeneutical principle.

Liberal theology retained a strong conception of providence by virtue of its faith in cultural progress and its view of God as the causal ground of the developing process of nature and history. When the liberal belief in progress could no longer be sustained, liberal theology was routed from the field by a theology that typically reduced providence to the inward movement of God's Word of judgment and grace.[53] Whereas liberal theology sought to reconcile science and religion, neoorthodoxy dissolved the purported conflict between science and religion by removing the religious field from nature and history. The doctrine of revelation as existential encounter allowed theologians to recover the language of biblical theology without coming into conflict with modern science or historical criticism.

But the privatization of theology also left neoorthodoxy without much to say about the prophetic meaning of Christianity. This limitation was blasted in the theologies of hope and liberation that emerged in the 1960s. In Gilkey's reading, the primary theorists of the "new theological consciousness" were the post-Bultmannian German theologians Wolfhart Pannenberg and Jürgen Moltmann, whereas liberation theology was a derivative phenomenon. Liberationists such as Gustavo Gutiérrez and Ruben Alves were mentioned only in passing as Latin American proponents of the "new eschatological theology." Gilkey suggested that while the emergence of this religious movement made sense as a political phenomenon, its theology was an unlikely concoction of the social gospel and Albert Schweitzer's apocalypticism. It sharply rejected Bultmann's existentialism for turning a potentially revolutionary faith into a form of depoliticized, antihistorical pietism. Pannenberg and Moltmann both embraced Schweitzer's claim that Christianity is inherently and thoroughly eschatological, but they also reclaimed the historicism and social concern of the social gospel through their eschatological understanding of God as the power of the future.

Moltmann proclaimed that eschatology is not an element of Christianity, but "the medium of Christian faith as such, the key in which everything in it is set, the glow that suffuses everything here in the dawn of an unexpected new day." As the power of the future, God masters the present toward the future goal of history, the kingdom of God. In Pannenberg's words, "God in His powerful future separates something new from itself and affirms it as a separate entity; thus, at the same time, relating it forward to Himself." Because God comes to the present from the future, the eschatological theologians argued, God does not directly affect or replicate historical causes from the past. As the power of the future, God works *into* the present in the same way that the future is always in mastery of the present. Moreover, as the power of the absolute future, God's mastery of the present relativizes history and appears as the negation of the prevailing order. The kingdom reappears in Christian theology as a radicalizing and ultimate goal of history. "God is not the ground of this world and not the ground of existence, but the God of the coming Kingdom which transforms this world and our existence radically," Moltmann asserted. God is causally active in the present as the power of the future, bringing the present forward to its consummation in the kingdom.[54]

Moltmann and Pannenberg thus creatively reaffirmed the apocalyptical and liberal traditions by relating eschatology to the future of the world. Moltmann explained that the God of Christian faith "is not in us or over us but always before us." By conceiving God as the power of the future, the "hope theologians" sought to provide a basis of hope for the future without making God the author of present evil or a threat to human freedom. Their fundamental move amounted to a temporal revision of radical neoorthodoxy. Like Barth's early crisis theology, hope theology divested human experience of any present communion with God, though now on the basis of a temporal claim instead of a vertical, transcendent claim.[55]

But this move negates the source and basis of religious language, Gilkey objected. Religious language has no meaning without religious experience. If it cannot identify any situation in which the word "God" needs to be invoked, Christian language about God is unintelligible.[56] Put differently, religious language has "no experiential component to its meaning" if there is no human experience of ultimacy to which theology may refer.[57] To be told that God masters the present from the future does not make God any less responsible for evil; it only makes language about God unintelligible. Moreover, if God has no present relation to dimensions of human experience, the religious dimensions of social and political experience also become inexplicable. The unavailable God of the absolute future has little relevance to current social and political problems. Gilkey implied that hope theology was oblivious to the mythical—and especially the demonic—elements of politics. In its pursuit of innocence, it produced a utopian politics that lacked any wisdom about the struggle for practical solutions in a fallen world. It overlooked the ambiguity of actual freedom in its resolve to set a redemptive future against a sinful past.

Gilkey's account of the "new theological consciousess" was less discriminating and interested than his descriptions of liberalism and neoorthodoxy, but his point was not that it had no value. Ultimately the same point obtained for hope and liberation theology as for the liberal and neoorthodox movements. Each theological movement had something to contribute to the theology of history that was needed, but none of them adequately conceptualized the historical dialectic of freedom and destiny. Liberal theology proclaimed a doctrine of providence, but could not sustain it in the face of the apocalyptic evils of the twentieth century. Neoorthodoxy recovered the doctrine of the Word of God, but found little place for it in history. Hope theology recovered the doctrine of eschatology and the ethical concerns of the social gospel, but emptied the present and past of religious meaning. Each of these movements seized upon one theological symbol as the key to the meaning of history to the exclusion of other symbols, Gilkey argued. For liberal theology, it was providence; for neoorthodoxy, it was Christology; for hope theology, it was eschatology.

The new theology of history that is needed would synthesize the constructive elements of these theological movements, he urged. It would give equal emphasis to providence, redemption, and eschatology. It would speak of God's ordaining and sustaining work in history without compromising any aspect of the modern understanding of history as contingent, relative, transient, and autonomous. "Nothing in history is eternally ordained, direct choices of the divine will for history," Gilkey cautioned.[58] Thus, even a *theology* of history must understand all historical events "naturalistically" in terms of their relations to particular webs of contingent finite factors. At the same time, though no specific events can be directly attributed to God's action or intentionality, the world process does not proceed autonomously but in dependence on its divine ground. The spirit and elements of Gilkey's understanding of process were strongly Whiteheadian, especially in his reliance upon the modal distinction between achieved actuality and undetermined possibility, but Gilkey's theological appropriation of process thought presented a major revision of Whitehead's metaphysical scheme.

Being, Process, and Providence

Process thought begins with the fundamental metaphysical presupposition that becoming is more fundamental than being; for Whitehead, reality is a dynamic flux of events rather than a structure of continuous substances.[59] History is thus conceived as radically open; it is not predetermined by God, but constituted by genuinely open possibilities. At the same time, Whitehead argued that real possibility is possible only as it exists in creative relation to actuality. Pure openness would be nothing; possibility is real only in creative relation to historical forms. It followed for Gilkey (and Whitehead) that even the most creative and autonomous actions therefore require a universal order of possibilities, for possibility "must be related to an eternal, everlasting and encompassing actuality, some being that orders possibility for the whole process."[60] The very possibility of openness to the future requires a divine ground.

Whiteheadian philosophy distinguishes between the "primordial" and "consequent" natures of God. God's primordial nature is the total potentiality of all existing entities at all moments of their actualization; the life and freedom of each self-actualizing entity is made possible by its participation in God's primordial nature. At the same time, the freedom of each entity makes it possible for all subjective entities to choose evil; each self-actualizing self possesses the power to actualize or negate the life-enhancing aim of God's primordial nature. In process thought, God lures God's subjects to make other-regarding, life-enhancing choices, always creating new possibilities to choose life, but God never infringes the freedom of the moral agent to make choices.[61] The consequent nature of God is the accumulated actualization of whatever choices God's subjects make. That is, in Whiteheadian philosophy God's consequent being is shaped through its process of interrelation with self-actualizing subjects. As the ground in actuality of all possibility, God is the metaphysical reality that unites actuality and possibility.[62]

Gilkey's appropriation of this metaphysical perspective began with a Christian corrective to it. He observed that the idea of God as the principle of being through which becoming takes place over time is rooted in classical Christian theism, especially that of Augustine. Augustine argued that the freedom of each subject and the continuing being of every event are made possible by God's being. For Gilkey, this principle of the divine power of freedom to become event offered a better understanding of the relation of process to divine reality than did Whitehead's metaphysics. In Whiteheadian philosophy, God plays a secondary role in relation to creativity; the fundamental ontological reality is creativity—the process itself—in which God envisages and orders possibilities.[63]

Gilkey's alternative wedded the traditional Christian understanding of God as the source of all being to the process dialectic of destiny and freedom. He proposed that God should be understood as the source of being, but that God's being should be conceptualized in terms of the process dialectic of achieved actuality and future possibility. Whitehead conceived divine reality as distinct from the more basic reality of creativity, but Gilkey argued that creativity should be understood as constitutive in the power of being that is God's being. "It is God as the power of being that carries forward the total destiny of the past into the present where it is actualized by freedom," he explained. "Creativity, the flux or elan of existence out of which in process thought each new occasion arises becomes, in other words, the power of being of God, the providential creativity of God that originates and sustains our continuing existence."[64]

As the creative power of being and source of our total existence, the divine being influences, through secondary causes, all self-actualizations of the present as well as the causal efficacy of the past upon the present. God does not ordain the form or content of destiny; the inheritance from the past that appears in the present as "the given" is always the product of human freedom and natural causation. "But the efficacy and so the continuing being of that achieved actuality, its power after having actualized itself to continue in being in order to become the presented destiny (the 'data') effective within the next event, and so a living aspect of that present actuality, this is the work of a power that transcends contingency and passage," Gilkey wrote. God is the power that makes the process of becoming possible. As the dynamic power that transcends contingency and temporality, God is the ground of the possibility of process and is therefore also the ground of the possibility of causation, order, and cognition. Christian theology should take from process thought the notion that God is in dynamic process, he argued, but it must reject the Whiteheadian doctrine that God is therefore subject to process: "For process, if taken seriously, means the passing out of existence of what has been."[65] If the reality of the given world is to be affirmed, there must be a divine being whose power transcends the finite temporality of destiny and freedom. But if God is such a power, and thus the worthy object of Christian devotion, God must not be subject to passage.

The core of Gilkey's understanding of divine providence derived from this argument that God "acts" in and through the secondary causes of destiny and freedom. He observed that the ontological dialectic of destiny, self-actualization, and undetermined possibility yields (and requires) the notion of God as the source and ground of becoming, actuality, and possibility. As the ground of the movement from the actual into the possible, God is the limiting and ordering ground of future possibility. It followed that divine providence is "the sustaining and creating work of God within the ambiguity of historical life that leads to the divine eschatological fulfillment as the latter's presupposition and ground."[66]

In other words, Gilkey affirmed the liberal understanding of providence: God is the divine ground of all being that sustains the historical movement of being. But this conception of providence is not enough, he cautioned; the crucial error of theological liberalism has been its tendency to interpret history solely in terms of the movement of freedom. Liberal theology has typically conceived history as a movement of freedom in confrontation with various forms of nonfreedom, such as ignorance, inertia, and oppression. Rauschenbusch was an instructive example. For all of his emphasis on the organic, nihilating, collective reality of the "kingdom of evil" that opposes God's will and purposes, even Rauschenbusch assumed that the structure of historical process as freedom is good.[67] Liberal theology presupposes that in its confrontations with nonfreedom, freedom is always on the side of the good in opening creative new possibilities. The new theologies of hope and liberation were currently making the same mistake.

But freedom can also become sin, Gilkey noted. The possibilities open to freedom and made possible by God can be betrayed; destiny can become fate. The problem with liberal theology is not that it has paid no attention to evil; sometimes it has. The problem is that even when liberal theology has taken account of the immensity of personal and social evil in history, it has understood freedom to be inherently good and therefore untainted by evil. This essentialist understanding of history as creative and progressive was sustainable to a generation that found the world getting better, he recalled, but to a later generation that found the predatory powers of freedom being unleashed in displays of apocalyptic violence, only evil seemed free. Niebuhrian realism arose from this experience. Niebuhr's doctrine that evil is always constitutive in the good helped a chastened generation make sense of its experience of history as tragedy.[68] It is a truism not only for Niebuhr's time but ours, Gilkey insisted, that freedom can produce not only futility and illusion, but also forms of monstrous evil.

Theological liberalism rightly interprets God's providence in history as the work of sustaining created life over time, but the liberal tradition has not featured any conception of providence as a principle of judgment over against the evils created by freedom. It was only with the emergence of crisis theology that this aspect of the meaning of providence was recovered in modern theology. Barth described history as the footprint of God's wrath; Niebuhr remarked that the liberal failure to appreciate the biblical understanding of God as wrathful and jealous was a crucial clue to its religious inadequacy.[69] The hidden work of God includes the negation of the destructive works of freedom, Gilkey conceded, but it is precisely because the wrath of God against evil is part of God's providential nature that Christianity is able to sustain hope for new possibilities in the face of evil. Calvin taught that to believe in providence is to have faith that God's creative sovereignty is at work in every historical situation, including those that provoke the divine judgment.[70] Translating this doctrine into the idiom of modern theology, Gilkey explained that to believe in providence is to expect creative new possibilities to emerge from tragedy, oppression, and the divine judgment; it is to expect the arrival of a new age of creative possibilities.

But even if providence is understood as God's sustaining, judging, and liberating work in history, the tragic realities of human freedom and providential possibility ensure that providence will not be enough. With all of the creative and emancipating possibilities that exist within history, history remains deeply ambiguous. Niebuhr's thesis stands as a judgment on all theologies that overemphasize providence: because evil is inextricably bound up with every good act and intention, the possibilities of evil grow with the possibilities of good.[71] For this reason, Gilkey argued, providence needs to be supplemented by redemption and eschatology. The crucial weakness shared by most forms of liberal and process theology is that they have not recognized that the persistence and pervasiveness of evil in history create a need for something "more" than providence. Christianity depends as much upon the redeeming work of Christ and the kingdom hope of eschatology as upon its faith in divine providence. As Augustine argued against Pelagius, freedom cannot be the determining ground of redemption because freedom shares in the corruption of a fallen humanity. It followed for Gilkey that the same freedom that brings about the actualization of creative/divine possibilities in history must therefore *itself* be transformed by grace "if the possibilities of history are to be realized."[72] Without the redeeming work of Christ, freedom remains in estrangement, and the hope of a new age has no basis.

Gilkey's theology of providence thus retained the orthodox Protestant themes of preservation and concursus while rejecting the theme of governance. As a product (in part) of modern historical consciousness, he argued, modern theology requires an understanding of providence that eschews the sovereignty model of Protestant orthodoxy. God does not direct the wind or cause diseases to spread; neither does God direct our freedom or ordain us to will what we will:

> Rather, it is we who actualize our own being in each present out of the destiny given us from the past combined with the possibilities and their demands granted us from the providential future. It is God's creative and providential power of being that carries our destiny into the present, that thus continues in being the conditions of our freedom in the present, our power of self-actualization; and it is providence as the envisionment of future possibility that presents us, challenges us and calls us with relevant possibilities.[73]

God makes process intelligible as the union of actuality and possibility in the present event of freedom. But human freedom and the openness of future possibility are possible only by virtue of God's self-limitation. Without a divine ground, the polarity of destiny and freedom would have no sustaining power, telos, or new possibilities: history would be meaningless. Without a divine power that is self-limiting, however, there would be no history at all; neither freedom or new possibilities would exist. Gilkey argued that God therefore acts in history through human freedom and is limited by human freedom. The hope of the world is that providence and freedom will combine to create emancipating new possibilities in history, but because freedom is real, so is the possibility that freedom will be used to create even more evil forms of violence, exploitation, and oppression. As the power of being, God *preserves* the past by bringing it into the present as a factor that contributes to the continuity and order of life; but God's accompanying or *concurring* providence also "brings into being the present as self-determining in each present."[74] God is the creative power of being through which the reality of each occasion arises and comes to be. Put differently, God is not only the ground of our freedom and destiny, but also the ground of our relevant possibilities. Gilkey explained elsewhere that God's creative providence is the "power of the continuing being of 'destiny,' the ground of our freedom, and the locus of possibilities to come."[75]

Reaping the Whirlwind thus presented answers to the theological problems of secularity described in *Naming the Whirlwind*. The four defining experiences of the modern spirit do not negate the possibility of a divine ground, Gilkey argued, but require it. Possibility can be real only if it is related to actuality, but it cannot be *possibility* if it is solely related to that which is already actual; otherwise the future would merely repeat the past. Genuine possibility can only exist "in relation to an actuality of transcendent scope, an actuality that is capable of holding within its power of envisionment the entire and so open realm of possibility." Moreover, if the actualization of possibility is to reshape or transform the inheritance of destiny, new possibilities must be related to actuality according to a graded structure of relevant options. Relevance is the test of the creativity, worthiness, and sheer reality of possibility in human affairs; it is the necessary condition of all historical change. But "relevant possibility" is itself only possible if it is grounded by "some actuality that spans achieved actuality and infinite possibility alike, giving to infinite possibilities both their locus in actuality and also their relevance to that actuality—for every event arises out of given actuality in union with relevant possibility."[76]

For Gilkey, this description of transtemporal actuality was one important way of naming the whirlwind. As the creative power of being, God is transtemporal in the sense that God is transcendent over passage; God is the ground of all process without being subject to process. But as the ground of all process, God is also temporal in the sense that God is the condition of each moment and is present in each moment of the movement of actuality into new possibilities. As the continuing source of being actualized in time, God is the unifying ground of past actuality, present realization, and future possibilities.[77] "God" is thus a way of naming the necessary creative power that transcends the temporal while working within it to ensure its continuation. "The becoming of reality calls for being, temporal passage calls for eternity, freedom and novelty for an ordered range of possibility, if a self-creative process is to be possible," Gilkey explained. The defining modern experiences of contingency, relativity, temporality, and autonomy do not negate the possibility of a divine ground but are dependent upon God for their intelligibility and continuity. Just as we experience our contingent being as a self-actualizing process of uniting the past to future possibility, "so the infinite and absolute being of God unites past and future into those self-actualizing 'presences' which constitute process."[78]

Theology and Process Philosophy

The influence of process thought in modern theology has been limited by its totalizing character. Because it presents a distinctively self-contained metaphysical system, the language and insights of process thought have been appropriated only rarely by theologians who do not adopt process thought as a system.[79] The general tendency over the past half-century is that theologians have either adopted Whitehead's metaphysical vision and proceeded to work out some form of process theology, or they have paid little attention to the efforts of Whitehead and Charles Hartshorne to rehabilitate metaphysical reasoning.[80] Gilkey's theology of history presents the most significant exception to this pattern. Without adopting process thought as an alternative theological system, his theological perspective appropriates the process thesis that entities in process require a divine ground for their actualization. Without adopting Whitehead's doctrine of God, his account of the relationships between creativity and divine reality, or his interpretation of providence, Gilkey employs Whitehead's modal distinction between actuality and possibility and therefore reconceptualizes divine reality as the ground of all process. His claim that "providence is not enough" is crucial to his positioning as a Christian theologian who appropriates process thought, as distinguished from a process theologian who translates Christian teaching into the language and system of neoclassical metaphysics.

Like Tillich and Niebuhr, Gilkey is always dialectical; more than his teachers, he nearly always uses dialectic in a way that requires the middle member of a triad to do most of the work, especially in holding together disparate perspectives.[81] *Reaping the Whirlwind* featured the triads of liberalism, neoorthodoxy, and eschatological theology, which led to a brief excursus in the book's closing pages on God as being, logos, and love. In both cases, the middle position or subject clearly made the strongest claim on Gilkey's personal faith; for all of his criticisms of neoorthodoxy, it is still his appropriation of the Niebuhrian/Tillichian approach to myth and religious truth that holds his theological perspective together. At the same time, his major works give most of their attention to themes that amplify or correct this position—a procedure that has created curious imbalances in his work. Gilkey's elaborate discussion of providential ordering, for example, drew heavily upon process thought to construct a highly developed theory of God's preserving and concurring work in history. At the crucial turn in his argument, however, having declared that God's providential activity is not enough to redeem humanity or to sustain human hope for a new age to come, he simply asserted that God's redemptive activity in the saving Word is necessary and real. Though the doctrine of providence required an extensive regrounding in neoclassical metaphysics, the doctrine of Christ's redeeming work in history supposedly required no such reinterpretation.

Edward Farley suggests that perhaps Gilkey meant to imply that God's redemptive activity is analogous to God's providential ordering.[82] In this case, the same account would apply to both providence and redemption, since God acts in history by rearranging and reordering priorities. Process theologians such as Norman Pittenger, John B. Cobb, Jr., and Schubert Ogden have given considerable attention to the question of how Christology and redemption should be reconfigured to fit the dynamic worldview of Whiteheadian philosophy.[83] But Gilkey ignored the question as well as the efforts by process theologians to reinterpret Christology. Though he apparently meant to imply that God's redeeming activity in history is more than God's rearranging and reordering of historical possibilities, his account left an unresolved tension between a process theology of providence and a kerygmatic theology of redemption.

This implicit tension between the process and traditional elements of Gilkey's position was magnified in his discussion of eschatology. On the one hand, he asserted that the divine will shall be fulfilled (working through human freedom) in the eschatological end of history. He attributed not only proximate purposes to God, but ultimate purposes, speaking in quite traditional Christian language about "the ultimate goal God has for the world." On the other hand, he repeatedly asserted that modern theology must assume with modern science and historical consciousness that creaturely existence is permanently contingent, relative, temporal, and autonomous. *Reaping the Whirlwind* alternately maintained that history is going somewhere and that history has no telos; it both relied upon and negated teleological reasoning. Farley observed that Gilkey's statements about God's ultimate goal for the world could be supported only by restoring to Christian theism some notion of divine ordering or governance.[84] That is, some version of the sovereignty model of providence is needed if Christian theology is to sustain its faith that God is working to bring about a new age to come. Without any notion of divine reality as sovereign over history, the religious claim that the future belongs to God is unintelligible. Neither is it possible to ground or sustain the faith that God is actually making something new in the world out of our strivings for freedom, justice, and peace.

Theology of Culture
and Religious Pluralism

Gilkey briefly considered the possibility of writing a major systematic theology when he finished *Reaping the Whirlwind*. His system would have synthesized Niebuhr, Tillich, Whitehead, and Eliade, while also appropriating contemporary liberation theologies. He later remarked that any serious theologian today must address both the hermeneutical problem of the modern meaning of Christian symbols *and* the range of issues recently brought to the forefront of religious concern by liberation theology.[85] One concern that weighed upon him in contemplating the possibility of a theological system was the example that Tillich's immense, intricate system set for him. A related problem was the weight of Tillich's influence over him. On various occasions he noted that his readings of Tillich nearly always produced the unsettling experience of rediscovering some insight or argument that he had long thought to be original to himself. In 1964, at the turning point of his theological career, he had shown Tillich the unpublished paper that later became the basis of *Naming the Whirlwind*. Tillich's somewhat deflated response to the paper was, "But Langdon, I said all this years ago." Gilkey replied that with the recent eclipse of neoorthodoxy, it was only now that he comprehended the significance of

Tillich's work, "and I have, therefore, only now found myself saying it after you, but now in my own way."[86]

His work after *Naming the Whirlwind* outgrew some of Tillich's influence over his thinking. *Reaping the Whirlwind* appropriated process theology and eschatological theology, and as Gilkey became increasingly interested in comparative religion, he turned to Eliade for guidance.[87] Given the influence of Tillich's theology over him and the massive example that it set, however, Gilkey questioned whether he should devote himself to elaborating a new system. To commit himself to this project would prevent him from exploring various issues in the theology of culture, interreligious dialogue, and the dialogue between science and religion.[88] He finally decided that having a system wasn't worth the cost. "An unavoidable realism about the level of my own present learning and capacities, and the length of time remaining to improve either one, have together cautioned against such an ambitious and demanding project," he later explained.[89] His only systematic work, *Message and Existence,* was gauged as an introduction to theology for "interested beginners." It used the Tillichian method of phenomenological prolegomenon and existential correlation to articulate Christian answers (theological symbols) to the "religious" questions of ordinary experience.[90]

Thereafter his work turned almost exclusively to the essay form, addressing a wide variety of topics in the theology of culture, science, and world religions. Gilkey's later writings reflect his concern to relate Christian symbols to the problems of modern culture, science, politics, and religious pluralism, but his strongest continuous concern has been his desire to interpret the meaning of Christian faith in the context of what he calls "a time of troubles" and "a culture in decline." Through most of the 1980s the apparent intractability of the Cold War and America's support of oppressive dictatorships in the third world fueled Gilkey's deep pessimism about the future of American culture and civilization. He saw little hope for a culture that invested its faith in scientific rationalism and devoted most of its scientific energy and resources to military ends. His opening chapter in *Society and the Sacred* declared that the end of the modernizing Enlightenment era is at hand. The Enlightenment belief in the power of secular rationality to emancipate humanity from ignorance, poverty, violence, and alienation is no longer a credible faith, he observed. Modern industrialism and technology threaten to destroy the earth's ecology; capitalism has created a plethora of goods, but also terrible disparities and resentments; the beneficial products of modern technology are outweighed by its destructive effects; and the most esteemed segment of Enlightenment culture—the medical profession—is now widely despised for its ignorance and greed. It is an instructive phenomenon, he cautioned, that today people hate doctors the way that late medievalists despised the clergy.[91]

His account of the crisis of modern secular culture and the disintegration of its faith in instrumental reason makes no claim to originality; his point is that these are commonplace truisms barely in need of explication. Gilkey's more distinctive contribution to postmodern criticism has been his variation on the theme of the return of the repressed. He argues that to the extent that modern secular culture has delegitimized or repressed its yearnings for the sacred, it has created the conditions under which highly irrational, bizarre, and sometimes malevolent forms of religious expression are bound to erupt. The rise of politicized fundamentalism in the 1970s confirmed to him that the religious dimension of life is not only good and benevolent but often "terrifying, terrible, and demonic as well."[92] His touchstone is the Tillichian thesis that the substance of culture is always religious in some form, whether formulated in "religious" terms or not.[93] In Gilkey's usage, as in Tillich's, this doctrine contains a warning: "If the social world is bereft of all genuine, creative, and religious substance, new demons will rush in and take over, trampling under academic, philosopher of religion, and mediator together!" The culture that pushes religion to the sidelines or tries to wipe it out is likely to create a backlash of unassimilated religious forms. The closing decades of the modern age are witnessing this return of the repressed, he observes, "for as we have seen, society is religious, its politics are sacral, and left without religious criticism and concern, it can well become demonic."[94]

His related spiritual concern is to address the reality of religious pluralism that a decentered liberal Protestantism presently faces. Gilkey observes that the reality of religious pluralism has become the dominant problem for modern Christian consciousness as a direct result of the dethronement of Western culture. As long as Western civilization was able to maintain a "credible" claim to superiority over other world cultures, the liberal Christian successors to Schleiermacher, Ritschl, and Troeltsch were able to sustain their faith that Christianity is "the absolute religion."[95] Liberal Protestantism was generally liberal in its attitude toward other religions; it recognized that some measure of grace and truth can be found in the world's various religious traditions. But the measure of this grace and truth was liberal Protestantism. The guardians of liberal Protestant theology valorized other religious traditions to the extent that they found reflections of their own religion in them.

Gilkey does not disparage this approach to religious pluralism. He remarks that the liberal comparativism of Ritschl and Troeltsch remains "about as far as we can get at the moment."[96] It represents an estimable advance upon the traditional Christian belief that other religions are simply false or idolatrous. The spirit of liberal Protestantism is discernable in numerous recent attempts to deal with the problems of religious pluralism, including the typological religious theorizing of George Rupp and, in Catholic theology, Karl Rahner's influential theory of "anonymous Christianity."[97] In their own ways, many Hindu and Buddhist scholars employ the same method, looking for their own central symbols in other religious traditions. But Gilkey argues that this approach does not go nearly far enough in respecting the integrity and parity of diverse religious traditions. Instead of adopting a methodological imperialism that looks for its own image in the other, what is needed is a theology of religious pluralism that respects the diversity of truths in diverse traditions. The Christian dialogical theology that is needed would not interpret an "alien" tradition as an undeveloped form of its own religious consciousness, but would look for truth and grace in the other tradition that is *not* found in Christianity. To pursue interreligious dialogue in this way would begin to divest liberal Christianity of its inherited imperialism and would therefore re-open Christian theology to the possibility of being enriched by other traditions.

Gilkey recognizes the danger of a purely relativistic approach to religious pluralism. If theology has no absolute starting point rooted in revelation, tradition, experience, or even reason, on what basis can it presume to enter a dialogue with any other tradition? "In a situation of recognized parity, where each viewpoint shares truth and grace with others, the usual unconditional starting point for each tradition seems to have dissolved and constructive reflection of any sort appears to be frustrated," he acknowledges.[98] With a multiplicity of possible centers, on what basis can any constructive dialogical theology be formed? Gilkey notes that a few "brave would-be pilots" have sailed forth into this uncharted sea, seeking to find a post-Christian starting point that lies beyond every religious tradition, while including all of them.[99] In different ways, Frithjof Schuon, Raimundo Panikkar, Huston Smith, Wilfred Cantwell Smith, John Hick, and Paul Knitter have all offered some "perennial philosophy" or universal religious principle on which a theology of world religions might be built.[100]

Gilkey admires the spirit of these theological efforts while rejecting them as misguided. In their attempts to find a common essence, spirit, or principle in the world's religious traditions, these theologians inevitably recreate the imperialism of liberal Christianity—but now in the name of a religious worldview that exists only in the minds of a few scholars. The reflected essence of religion that these theologians base their comparative theologies upon is invariably parochial and relative, Gilkey observes: "It represents—try as it may to avoid it—a particular way of being religious and so a particular interpretation of religion." Just as liberal Protestant theologians looked for liberal Protestantism in other traditions, so do the post-Christian perennialists misinterpret other traditions in order to incorporate them into their own interpretive schemes. The result is a new form of the old religious colonialism, "the interpretation of an alien viewpoint in terms of one's own religious center."[101]

Gilkey's alternative is for each theologian to reinterpret her own tradition in the light of parity. For the Christian theologian, this would mean that the project of interpreting reality would remain "at home" in the language of Christian scripture and tradition. The center of a truly dialogical Christianity is not some imagined universal essence of religion, but neither should Christian theologians enter interreligious dialogue without a center. Without a Christian center, Christian-Buddhist or Christian-Islamic "dialogue" cannot take place, because Christianity is absent. Conversely, it is pointless for a Christian theologian to enter a Christian-Buddhist dialogue with a "Buddhist" who doesn't begin from a Buddhist center. Too often, Gilkey argues, what passes for interreligious dialogue is some comparison of academic typologies or categories that have no rootage in any tradition.[102]

To reinterpret Christianity in the light of parity, on the other hand, is to open Christian theology to the possibility of being enriched by the spiritual experiences and doctrines of other traditions. It is to relate to Christianity in a "relative-absolute" way, interpreting Christian faith as "a valid but particular representation of the ultimate reality" that all world religions seek to express.[103] In a postmodern age that recognizes not only the relativity of history, culture, and science but also the relativity of postmodern consciousness itself, each religious tradition is obliged to interpret itself in the light of pluralism: "that is, in the presence of genuinely alternative ways of looking at and responding to existence." But whenever a tradition relinquishes its center, it becomes worthless; it embodies no ultimate principles of faith, experience, moral concern, or transformation.[104] A totally relativized perspective has no Word to speak outside the circle of the already converted and brings nothing to the enterprise of interreligious dialogue.

Gilkey acknowledges that his alternative has little history and few examples. No theologian has shown on a large scale how to reinterpret Christianity from a standpoint that privileges Christian symbols while remaining open to the insights and truths of other religious traditions. Theologians such as John B. Cobb Jr., Hans Küng, and Kenneth Cragg have offered beginning level examples of this kind of interreligious thinking from very different theological perspectives.[105] The postmodern project of facing up to relativity while renewing one's commitment to an unconditional faith is a perilous undertaking, filled with paradox and precarious uncertainty. But, Gilkey remarks, "in a time of troubles, it is precisely this mixture of the relative and the absolute, of criticism and affirmation, of humility and courage that we are called to embody."[106]

His reflections on the Christian privileging of being over nonbeing provide an instructive example of the promise of this kind of theological thinking. Gilkey's encounters with Buddhist thought and practice in the 1970s prompted him to rethink his understanding of God as the power, or ground, of being. His acquaintance with Nietzschean philosophy and existentialism gave him some appreciation for the Buddhist argument that the God of sheer being extinguishes human spiritual freedom. Masao Abe's Zen Buddhist critique of Tillich helped Gilkey make the connection between the Nietzschean and Buddhist protests against the heteronomous God of being as an enemy of freedom.[107] But Buddhism goes beyond the Nietzschean cry for human freedom and authenticity, Gilkey observed; it protests as well "in the name of the sacrality of nothingness, another and quite different name for the divine."[108] It was this seemingly contradictory, counterintuitive Buddhist affirmation of nothingness over being that pushed Gilkey to recognize the crucial problem with even Tillich's theonomous understanding of God as the ground of being.

The problem is that the Western tradition of univocally predicating being or actuality to God actually limits divine reality to the human desire for survival and expansion of being. If God is the transcendent mystery of Christian faith, Gilkey reasons, then God must transcend the categories of being and nonbeing. God can be the divine ground of *all* process and reality only if

God is known through the dialectical union of self-affirmation and self-negation. The Buddhist sense of the sacrality of nothingness is a true insight. The reality of negation is too overwhelming to ignore or dispute, and *this* reality provides the symbolic clue to the essential character of divine reality. As Gilkey explains, the reality of nothingness opens up the character of divine ultimacy and thus "opens up the character of our own essential being as selves." To project the human desire for expansion of being onto God in an undialectical fashion is to violate the spirit and message of the gospel, which is the way of the cross. "Being itself" does not univocally represent or signify divine reality, he argues, but represents one of the polar symbols of religious experience. The symbol of being applies to the divine mystery only in dialectical correlation with the symbol of nonbeing, which is grounded in the experience of negation.[109]

Tillich and Whitehead recognized that if God is to be conceived as dynamically active in a changing world, God must be conceived not only in terms of being and actuality, but also of becoming and potentiality. The Buddhist affirmation of nothingness pushes Christian theology to deepen its understanding of the dialectic of actuality and possibility, Gilkey observes: "God as creative providence unites dialectically the power of being originative of each present, and the relative nothingness of possibility—lest the reality of the present as the locus of finite decision and so of finite selfhood be denied." A world that was "full of being" would have no possibility; it would extinguish not only the freedom but the being of finite spirit. "For finite being to be there, the nonbeing of potentiality must be there as well, and must, if the potentiality be real, be shared in by the divine as creative providence," Gilkey argues. "The divine in time, as in the original positing of free creatures or entities, manifests itself as sharing in becoming and thus as uniting dialectically being and nonbeing."[110]

He cautions that nothing in this understanding of divine reality negates the three central affirmations that he defended in *Maker of Heaven and Earth:* the doctrine of *creatio ex nihilo,* the naming of God as being or being itself, and the religious affirmation of the world as God's creation. What it does negate is the undialectical and therefore unqualified identification of God with being. In the history of Christian theism the mainstream tendency to conceptualize God's being in an undialectical fashion produced the transcendent God of absolute being. The God of classical theism was not a divine mystery that transcends being, but the transcendent power of absolute being—the God who represents the absolute degree of being. The difference was subtle, but crucial, Gilkey maintains, for God's nature thus became defined "by its unconditional and absolute character rather than by its mystery." The dialectical relation of the divine mystery to being was lost, and with it was lost any sense that God is intimately related to the world. God became the hypostatized, self-sufficient, necessary absolute being of Protestant orthodoxy. Put differently, the God of traditional theism came to represent "the transcendent glorification of being rather than the transcendence of being and thus the principle of being's transmutation."[111]

Gilkey's theology strongly dissociates Christian theism from this "over-affirmation of being," which represents, from his Christian perspective, "an expansion of power, interest and will untrue to the gospel and a nemesis for both self and world."[112] That is, the flattering name of "absolute being" was an idol representing force rather than the familial, intimate, self-giving "Father" addressed by and made known in Jesus Christ. Gilkey's post–neoorthodox work is notably reticent in its language about Christ, but the gospel theme of the self-giving Christ as the image of the invisible God informs all of his theology. "If the cross, as well as the incarnation and resurrection, is a true symbol of the nature of God, the omnipotent power and being of God manifested in creation and redemption must be qualified by and integrated with the nonbeing within God visible in Christ's death," he declares.[113] To absorb the Christian teaching that the incarnate Son of God died a humiliating, Godforsaken death by crucifixion is to approach the level of negation represented by Buddhism: "All existence is suffering." Bonhoeffer's maxim was a true insight: if God is revealed in the suffering of Christ then we must look for God primarily in God's grief in the world.[114]

The Christian myth thus affirms that God is disclosed primarily through finitude, weakness, vulnerability, suffering, and death. That is, God is revealed through nothingness and the negating force of nonbeing. Gilkey acknowledges that Christian theology has generally shied away from attributing these qualities of being to divine reality. Christian orthodoxy has insisted on locating the divine mystery in the wrong place, he argues, "namely, in the relation of God as absolute being to the weakness and death of the incarnate one." Gilkey suggests that a more truthful Christian theology would relate the vulnerable, suffering, contingent nothingness of nonbeing not only to the Son of God, but to divine reality itself: "nonbeing in all its terrors for us as a sacral nothingness."[115] The gospel proclaims that in all of the signs of nonbeing, including death, the God of Jesus Christ is disclosed: "In our experience precisely of negation, and in our suffering from it, we encounter there the divine and can thus have hope. Just as at his death the 'Godly' denial of self is manifested by the Christ, so there, too, the nonbeing within God and the divine participation in our own nonbeing reveal themselves."[116] The heart of the interreligious project on which theologians have only begun to work is to understand divine reality in relation to the dialectical mystery of being and nonbeing; to understand Christian revelation in relation to the revelations of other traditions; and to understand the redemptive, ever-gracious work of Christ in relation to other manifestations of salvation and grace.[117]

5

Return of the Repressed: Postmodernism and the Sacred

The search for the sacred is a recent phenomenon. For most of human history, the sacred was readily available and assumed. Every culture was organized around the sacred observances of a cult, which mythologized and ritualized its meanings of birth, life, identity, community, sexuality, work, salvation, and death. The real world was the meaning-conferring realm of the gods, whose history shaped and explained human history. People did not talk about their lives as journeys in search of the sacred, nor did they question how myth confers or discloses religious meaning in history. They understood history as myth and themselves as participants in sacred time and space.

But for modernized Western people the secular world of work defines the real world and religion is a private option for individuals. The sacred cosmos has been demythologized by science, and the sacred underpinnings of culture in cult have been deconstructed to expose its configurations of desire and power. Culture has no attachment to a sacred realm, but is real precisely as human work. For two centuries, modern philosophers and social scientists have described the logic of secularization within this social process as inexorable. The founder of modern sociology, Auguste Comte, explained that because the mythical consciousness belongs to an outmoded stage of human awareness, religion has no future.[1] A century later, Dietrich Bonhoeffer observed that modern theology had already surrendered all problems pertaining to nature and history; in a world "come of age," he predicted, people will stop turning to religion for help with the so-called ultimate questions as well.[2]

For most of its history, liberal Protestantism has struggled to ward off this fate while accepting the judgment of modern intellectual culture against the mythical consciousness. By adopting the thought forms of a triumphant secular culture, liberal theology sought to salvage some form of Christian God-language that could not be implicated in the modern critical repudiation of myth. Schleiermacher invented "religion" as a distinct dimension of experience; Harnack appealed to a liberal gospel kernel of faith; Shailer Mathews identified Christianity with the modern movement for social and intellectual progress; Douglas C. Macintosh tried to refashion theology as a form of empirical science. In each case, a rhetoric of progress and enlightenment sought to dissociate modern theology from the backward, ahistorical language of myth.

Demythologizing Reaffirmed:
Schubert Ogden on Myth and Truth

This remains a viable and, to some, compelling position within theology, especially among liberal theologians who argue for some form of Christian philosophy or process theology. The Bultmannian process theologian Schubert Ogden is a prominent example. Like many theological liberals before him, though in his case in dialogue with Bultmann's demythologizing program, Ogden argues that the truth in Christian myth must be translated into the language of a credible philosophy without remainder before it can be employed by theology. His early work, *Christ Without Myth,* allowed that Christian myth contains existential truth but argued that myth itself must not be given any normative function in theology. Rather, the truth that Christian myth contains, which is the understanding of existence contained in the Christian kerygma, can be appropriated for theology only through the work of philosophical translation. "Christian faith is to be interpreted exhaustively and without remainder as man's original possibility of authentic existence as this is clarified and conceptualized by an appropriate philosophical analysis," he maintained.[3] Because myth is always an inadequate mode of objectification, demythologizing must be pressed without limit.

With some allowances for Bultmann's occasionally unclear language, Ogden argued that this was also Bultmann's position. Bultmann's so-called "left-wing" critics misunderstood his conception of the scope of demythologizing, Ogden insisted, for Bultmann never sought to protect any aspect of the kerygma from myth-critique. His purpose was always to extricate the truth in Christian myth from symbolic forms that he viewed, without exception, as injurious to Christian belief. Ogden defended this position from various critics on both sides of the "scope of demythologizing" debate. He argued that the problem with Bultmann's approach was not that he overstated the problem of myth or that he imposed an arbitrary limit on demythologizing. To the contrary, Bultmann's program of demythologizing and existential interpretation is the only credible method that theologians have devised for dealing with the problem of Christian myth. Bultmannian demythologizing uniquely saves the gospel message from the thought forms of a primitive worldview.

But doesn't this program require the elimination of all symbolic and analogical language about divine reality? Especially if Bultmann is to be read as a thoroughgoing demythologizer, doesn't his expansive conception of myth undermine the possibility that theology might make credible or even intelligible claims about God? Ogden conceded that there was a problem with Bultmann's approach, but he insisted that it was only a problem of execution. Bultmann made a compelling case for the necessity of philosophical translation, but he did not provide a satisfactory example of it. His failure to distinguish adequately between analogy and myth undercut his capacity to use analogical or symbolic language about God. He never explained clearly how it might be possible to speak of God analogically without resorting to mythical language.

This deficiency in Bultmann's position was linked, in Ogden's reading, to his exaggerated subjectivism. A notorious example was Bultmann's claim that "the cross is not the salvation-event because it is the cross of Christ; it is the cross of Christ because it is the salvation-event."[4] A more typical example was his claim that, for Paul, "every assertion about God is simultaneously an assertion about man and vice versa," or his subsequent claim that Paul's theology "is most appropriately presented as the doctrine of man."[5] In all of these cases of subjectivizing exaggeration, Ogden observed, Bultmann overreacted to the problem of objectivization as such. His legitimate opposition to certain kinds of objectivization, especially mythology and German idealism, moved him to renounce all forms of theological objectivism.[6]

But this extreme aspect of Bultmann's position not only exaggerated the problem of objectivism as such, Ogden asserted; it also undermined the genuine substance of Bultmann's theology. It suggested that despite Bultmann's assurances that faith has an object in the Word of God, his theology was actually subjective without remainder. Ogden proposed that this problem was linked to the problem of Bultmann's deficient God-language. In both cases, his theology needed a more developed philosophical foundation for its program of myth-translation. Lacking a sufficient philosophical base, he was unable to refute the charge of subjectivism or justify his use of symbolic God-language.

Bultmann's philosophical interlocutor was the early Heidegger, whose distinction between *existential* and *existentiell* understanding actually provided part of the philosophical groundwork that was needed, in Ogden's view. *Existential* knowledge is philosophical understanding of existence in general; it is "knowledge-about." *Existentiell* knowledge is the understanding that an individual has of one's own unique situation; it is personal "knowledge-of." This distinction between two kinds of understanding was invoked frequently by Bultmann in his writings on hermeneutics and theological anthropology, but it disappeared whenever Bultmann talked about God. His discussions of God-language gave no sanction to the possibility of *existential* knowledge about God; with reference to God, he spoke only of *existentiell* understanding.

Ogden argued that this restriction of God-language to the realm of personal *existentiell* understanding weakened Bultmann's entire project. It restricted the scope of philosophical inquiry in theology to the realm of human existence. It offered no basis on which to analyze divine existence. The philosophical theology that is needed to carry out Bultmann's program of demythologization, Ogden urged, would provide an objectivizing metaphysic of existence in general that includes divine existence: "We must insist that what Bultmann himself means by 'existential interpretation' can be properly carried out only when

Heidegger's analysis of *human* existence is viewed in the perspective of the general ontology it seems to imply and in which *divine* existence also is appropriately analysed and conceptualized."[7]

Christ Without Myth proposed that a fusion of Heidegger's (early) existentialism and Whiteheadian process philosophy (especially as developed by Charles Hartshorne) might provide the myth-translating philosophical theology that is needed. Ogden's subsequent work has sought to build a bridge between Heidegger/Bultmann and Whitehead/Hartshorne. It is process philosophy that grounds his God-language and shapes his execution of the task of myth-translation. On the other hand, from his first work onward, the core of his Christology has derived principally from Bultmann. *Christ Without Myth* rested its constructive Christological argument on the difference between *existential* and *existentiell* understanding, which Ogden described as the "*conditio sine qua non* for a more adequate Christology."

He observed that Jesus spoke much less *about* humanity and God than *of* the relationship between them. "When Jesus speaks of the forgiveness of God, his intention is not to describe it to the theoretical intellect, but, as one who is 'sent' or authorized by God, actually to bestow it as an *existentiell* possibility," he explained. It followed that the gospel should not be understood as a body of timeless truths, but as a personal *existentiell* communication demanding decision. Jesus is the definitive re-presentation of the truth of humanity's existence before God. His truth is not a piece of information but personally transforming truth as encounter. "What confronts us in Jesus is not, in its first intention, a 'worldview' addressed to our intellects, but a possibility of self-understanding that requires of us a personal decision," Ogden argued.[8] Jesus is not primarily a teacher about God and the world, but a preacher of the kingdom of God.

Ogden sought to open up Bultmann's transactional individualist Christology by appealing to Frederick Denison Maurice's understanding of the kingdom of Christ. As a nineteenth-century Anglican interpreter of the logos-theology tradition, Maurice emphasized the cosmic incarnational dimension of Christian teaching. For him, as for the fourth gospel, Jesus was the eternal Word of the Father begotten without origin; Christ existed as the hidden power and inner meaning of human events before he took human flesh.[9] Maurice refused to reduce Christ to one historical event among others; his central theme was that the Christ event is a cosmic eschatological Word of unconditional light and love. This is the crucial note that Bultmann's nominalist Christology lacks, Ogden acknowledged. What is needed to correct Bultmann's existentialism is a theological vision that perceives the Christ event as the ground and end of all historical events, in which all people are addressed in all of the events of their lives. Such a theological vision would perform a demythologizing function by rejecting the traditional dichotomies between Old and New Testament, law and gospel, faith and reason, philosophy and theology, general revelation and special revelation, and nature and grace. Ogden explained that each of these dichotomies rests ultimately on a mythological understanding of revelation in which divine action is falsely objectified. All of them therefore misconstrue the nature of true faith.

His subsequent writings maintain that Bultmann's theory of myth was essentially right, though somewhat unclear. His reformulation of Bultmann's position defines myth as a particular form of language that re-presents some field of experience in a particular way. The field of experience that myth re-presents is our original internal awareness of ourselves and the world "as included in the circumambient reality within which all things come to be, are what they are, and pass away." Myth re-presents this awareness in categories that are "based in our derived external perception of reality as the object of our ordinary sense experience."[10] Drawing upon H. A. Hodges's philosophy of language, Ogden assumes that human experience contains different fields that are reflected in the logically different kinds of language that individuals speak. His definition focuses on the differences and relations between the existential and objective fields of experience. Existential experience is our nonsensuous inner perception of ourselves and the world as parts of an encompassing whole, he explains; objective experience is our sense-derived outer perception of the external world.

Like other forms of language, myth derives simultaneously from both of these fields of experience, but the distinctive feature of mythical thinking is that it misrepresents existential experience in the language of objective experience. Myth is inherently misrepresentative; it commits what Gilbert Ryle called a "category mistake," in which truths belonging to one category are presented in an idiom appropriate to another category.[11] "Although the 'facts' myth presents are our selves and the world as fragments of the totality of being, the 'idioms' in which it speaks are those appropriate to the world itself as disclosed to us through the particular perceptions of our senses," Ogden explains.[12]

He illustrates the point with Bultmann's favorite example, in which myth misrepresents divine transcendence as spatial distance. When myth represents divine reality as existing far away, its intention is to express an inner human awareness of human existence and the world as related to an all-encompassing reality of which human beings are part. "But this, its true intention, is in fact obscured by the linguistic terms in which it speaks; for the category of space that its terms presuppose is based not in this inner awareness of our existence in relation to totality, but in the very different perception through our senses whereby we objectify the world external to us," Ogden observes.[13] This misrepresentation of its intention is precisely what myth always does; because it always obscures its actual function, myth is never to be taken literally. At the same time, Ogden argues, following Niebuhr, myth must always be taken seriously "because it functions to express one basic dimension of our encounter with the real." He thus affirms that myth contains existential truths that are important for theology. What Ogden denies is that myth has any normative role in theology as such.

The reason derives from the problem of how to understand and assess the cognitive status of existential truth. Ogden observes that many philosophers still insist on a field-invariant concept of truth in which "truth" has a single meaning across the entire range of fields of experience. The logical positivist identification of truth with formal logic and the principle of verification/falsification is a prominent example.[14] By contrast, philosophical pluralists conclude from the radically diverse understandings of truth in different fields that "truth" has no common meaning from field to field.[15] Truth is field-dependent. Ogden notes that field-invariant approaches necessarily exclude numerous fields of experience from the realm of truth; in the case of logical positivism, for example, the truths of aesthetic and moral experience are simply defined out of existence. A singular concept of truth can be sustained only by denigrating the worthiness of other kinds of knowledge.

But Ogden cautions that the defenders of field-invariant positivism or rationalism are not entirely wrong in insisting that the word "truth" must have some common meaning. After all, the same word is vigorously employed and claimed from one field to another. Though it is clear that no *criterion* of truth is shared from field to field, the question of the *meaning* of truth is another matter. Stephen Toulmin's analysis of the meaning of truth provides the key to Ogden's understanding of truth claims. Toulmin observes in *The Uses of Argument* that the word "true" is used in ordinary language as "the most general adjective of commendation" that one can make pertaining to matters of belief. To call a statement "true" is to commend it to others as something that is worthy of being believed or accepted. Truth claims do not express mere subjective preferences, but rather seek to commend and persuade through argument. As Toulmin explains, they do not assert that one merely happens to believe something; rather, truth claims always commit their advocates to demonstrate the worthiness of whatever beliefs that are claimed.[16] For this reason, Ogden argues, the word "true" can be used properly only in connection with some specified criterion of credibility.

Because the question of the meaning of truth is always connected closely to the question of the criterion of truth, the two questions are often blended together, even by analytic philosophers. But the difference between these questions is crucial, Ogden notes, for in ordinary language usage, the meaning of the word "true" is constant from one field of experience to another, but the standards that regulate the proper use of the word are widely variable. In Toulmin's words, the *force* of the word "true" is field-invariant, but the *criteria* that are implied in using the word are field-dependent.[17] Ogden argues that the value of this distinction for theology is that it helps theologians assess the question of truth in myth. Myths can be true in a sense of the word that has a constant meaning, but the nature or degree of this truth is assessible only on the basis of contextual criteria. "In testing the merits of a claim, we must always take pains to determine the specific 'criteria' whereby the credibility of the relevant assertion can be judged," he observes. "Thus, we should never ask whether the assertion conforms to canons for assessing judgments of some other logical type, but only whether it meets *its own* appropriate standards of achievement."[18] One does not ask whether a moral judgment is true on the basis of empirical verification or whether an aesthetic judgment is true on the basis of formal logic. Each field of experience generates its own criteria for the judgment of truth-claims according to the kind of question that is asked within each field.

In Ogden's view, the question asked and answered by religious myth is the question of faith, in which some kind of assurance is given that life as such is worth living. Religion addresses the question of how to understand the whole to which human subjects belong, so that even in the face of suffering, guilt, and death, the faith that life is worth living may be affirmed. This is what all religions are fundamentally about. Religious myth is always fundamentally about the human need for assurance that life is worthwhile. Since the criterion for truth assessment in any field is always generated by the question it addresses, Ogden reasons that mythical assertions are true "insofar as they explicate our unforfeitable assurance that life is worthwhile that the understanding of faith they represent cannot be falsified by the essential conditions of life itself."[19]

Like the principle of scientific verification, this criterion specifies that no belief is worthy of being believed if it is falsified by the facts of human experience. But in the case of mythical truth claims, Ogden cautions, the "facts" are not the variable elements or events of human experience, but the constant structure of human experience. "The reality with which mythical assertions must come to terms is not the ever-changing world disclosed by our senses, but our own existence as selves, as those who, whatever their external perceptions, always experience themselves and the world as finite-free parts of an infinite whole," he explains. Mythical truth is therefore radically field-specific. It is not only that true myths express an understanding of faith that is not falsified by experience; the deeper trusim is that true myths *cannot* be falsified by experience. "To object that this disqualifies mythical utterances from even being true at all is simply to invoke a criterion of truth that has no jurisdiction over this kind of utterance," Ogden declares.[20] Mythical truth is *sui generis*.

Then how is mythical truth to be understood or appropriated for theology? How is the credibility of the mythical answer to the question of faith to be assessed? Ogden gives Hegel's answer: The truth of mythical assertions can be assessed only if its meaning is first translated into nonmythical language. Since myth misrepresents itself, it cannot be taken literally. On the other hand, Ogden asserts, if one judges myth in terms of its field-specific criterion, the claims that it presents can be taken only as symbols whose meaning must be translated into nonmythical terms before their truth can be judged. "In other words, one can actually verify mythical assertions only by following the twofold hermeneutical procedure that Bultmann has called 'demythologizing,'" he explains. Because mythical assertions always misrepresent themselves, the "facts" they present must always be reallocated to the language of an appropriate idiom.[21]

In other words, mythical assertions can be shown to have cognitive significance only if they are translated adequately into the language of a cognitive philosophical discourse. The reason is not only because myth always misrepresents its true intention, but because neither myth nor science can provide the language that is required to express whatever cognitive assertions that myth might contain. In approaching mythical texts, therefore, the theologian must interpret the statements contained in these texts to attain their answer to the question of faith and then translate this answer into the most useful and credible nonmythical discourse that can be found. This discourse must be a philosophy. Ogden argues, for only philosophy can make cognitive assertions within a discourse framework that is broad and rich enough to interpret the various cosmological, anthropological, moral, and metaphysical assertions contained in myth. Philosophical reason makes it possible to express the meaning of mythical assertions in nonmythical language. Without this interpretive capacity of philosophy, Ogden claims, it would not be possible to maintain that any particular mythical assertion is true.[22]

Ogden is careful to emphasize the Bultmannian lineage of this argument, but his position takes an important step beyond Bultmann in its deferral to philosophy. Bultmann argued that mythical truth must be identified and translated by philosophy before it can attain the status of a cognitive claim within theology. But Ogden maintains that philosophy must not only identify and translate mythical truth, but must also evaluate its claims. It is philosophy that provides the cognitive norms by which the metaphysical assertions contained in myth can be assessed. Theology is therefore dependent upon the capacity of philosophy to evaluate the metaphysical assertions contained in myth. At the same time, theology is dependent upon the unique capacity of philosophy to confer cognitive status on its mythical truth claims. In Ogden's reinterpretation of the case for demythologization, the deep connection between Bultmann's program and the liberal approach of the Hegel/Strauss/Baur tradition is thus implicitly affirmed. With the aid of a mediating philosophy, theology seeks to transcend myth altogether.

The Desacralized Universe:
John Cobb's Process Theology

The eminent process theologian John B. Cobb, Jr. presents a similar verdict on the role of myth in theology. Like his liberal forebearers, Cobb regards the mythical consciousness as a prerational form of thinking that was outstripped by the growth of reflective consciousness during the first millennium before Christ. His foundational work, *The Structure of Christian Existence,* appropriates the stage theory of Karl Jaspers in tracing the historical shift from mythical to rational reflective consciousness. Though Cobb argues that this shift was more fluid than Jaspers's rather schematic account implies, he accepts Jaspers's basic description of the eclipse of mythical consciousness during the so-called axial period of 800 B.C. to 200 B.C.[23] In mythical thinking, the reflective consciousness supercedes the purely receptive awareness that characterized premythical existence, but its mode of symbolization is governed by the kind of creative and associative thinking that characterizes the unconscious. In mythical thinking, the center of consciousness is the unconscious; its reflective consciousness has no autonomy; its symbolic ordering of experience is mainly unconscious; and it does not submit to empirical correction. It is therefore a mistake to think of myth as an attempt to explain the external world, Cobb observes, for mythical awareness lacks the consciousness of subject/object duality that is requisite for reflective explanation.[24]

Preaxial people were unable to distinguish between their own unconscious symbolizations and the external world that they inhabited. They had little sense of the difference between inner and outer, subject and object, or past and present: "There was a single meaningful whole," Cobb explains. "The meaning of the whole was primarily determined by symbols arising out of the unconscious aspects of experience. There was no second-level critical reflection about these meanings. Hence, they were absolute."[25]

Because the mythical consciousness lacks any critical reflective capacity beyond the elementary supersession of reflective consciousness over purely receptive awareness, the world that myth creates is absolute. Because the world that myth creates is absolute, it is sacred. The power of the sacred is bound up with the perdurance of an undifferentiated consciousness. It is precisely this consuming sense of the sacred that was broken by the rise of a more autonomous and self-unified reflective consciousness in the axial period, Cobb observes. The problem of desacralization is not new; Christianity was born into a world in which the force of the mythical world-picture was already greatly diminished. In the prophetic Hebrew faith that Christianity inherited, God was still known in his sovereign holiness, but the world was profane. Cobb notes that Christian theologians have sought ever since to save the remnants of the mythical consciousness. Whenever theologians conceptualize Christianity as a religion—that is, as a special mode of apprehending sacred reality—they commit themselves to the classical project of saving some fragment of a bygone mode of consciousness.

But with the utter triumph of the profane rationalist unconsciousness since the Enlightenment, Cobb contends, this strategy has become not only futile, but unreal. Modernity is precisely the utter negation of sacrality. It makes no sense to appeal to any residual sense of the sacred in a culture that views reality as a profane unity. In 1970, Cobb made a programmatic case for a secular, myth-negating, philosophical theology. "We cannot reaffirm God on the basis of any fading and distorted apprehension of the sacred," he insisted. This strategy has no power beyond its capacity to manipulate the guilt feelings of guilt-driven people who know that they have no experience of God as sacred reality. Gilkey's "dimensions of ultimacy" strategy is a dead end. The alternative for theology, Cobb argued, is to affirm divine reality "within the very context of the profane consciousness."[26]

Christianity has always contained a bias against the mythical consciousness—especially in its attitude toward time and history—though not without certain inner contradictions. The prophetic biblical polemic against idolatry has always contained or at least implied a critique of all religion. Cobb proposed that liberal theology should appropriate the prophetic attitude toward religion within the thought forms of modern critical consciousness. This approach would give a stronger philosophical basis to the modern tradition of secularization theology represented by Friedrich Gogarten and recently popularized by Harvey Cox.[27] It would follow Whitehead in affirming divine reality without any appeal to concepts or norms outside the modern profane consciousness. It would develop an understanding of God as the ground of creative process that is compatible with Christianity but derived from rationalist premises.

For Cobb, as for Ogden, speculative neoclassical theism is the answer to the crisis of belief, though Cobb concedes that the God of process theology does not solve the modern problem of meaning. This is because, within a profane context, there is no solution to the essentially religious problem of meaning. "Human meaning refers essentially to the sacred," he explained in 1970. "Hence, the elimination of the sacred initiates a quest that, in principle, cannot be fulfilled." He reasoned that if Christian theology could rescue a credible basis for believing in God, however, this belief could be made to serve "as a principle of openness to the sacred and a focus for those flickering apprehensions that still occur and will recur."[28] If we find our way to belief in God, it is possible that we may come to know God again as the Holy One, but this knowledge will have to come from the profane consciousness, which always requires rational reasons.

"This means that for our time we must do without myth," Cobb declared. "Where God is not known as sacred reality, the *sui generis* language of religion has no place." With the triumph of the rationalist consciousness, myth has no place at all, even in theology. Cobb cautioned that this does not mean that myth and the sacred have no future. Every form of consciousness has a history; every mode of consciousness known to history thus far, except modern scientific consciousness, has been superceded by a new way of thinking and being. He did not rule out the possibility that the language of myth and the sacred might become intelligible again in a postmodern cultural epoch that lived out of a different kind of consciousness. But this was a faint hope at best. "If they do come to know him again as the Holy One, let them use myth," he concluded. "But in our time this knowledge is not possible."[29]

This verdict was written in the closing hour of the modern theological epoch. For Cobb, "in our time" referred to a contemporary sociocultural period that began with the Enlightenment. Apart from his later pioneering work in ecotheology, most of his writings tried to solve problems bequeathed to theology by modern rationalist and historical criticism.[30] All of his efforts to restore the credibility of theology gave the seat of judgment to modern critical consciousness. Through his early commitment to process philosophy, he sought to revise and renew theological liberalism at a time when neoorthodoxy dominated the field.

Liberation Theology and
The Postmodern Turn

But by 1970 neoorthodoxy was dethroned, and a profusion of new voices and movements took its place, many of which had no interest in reconciling

Christianity to modern consciousness. Latin American and African American liberationists proclaimed the necessity of doing theology from the standpoints of
oppressed Latin American and black people.[31] Rather than begin with the skeptical questions of privileged academics, liberation theology begins with the experiences of suffering and faith in the lives of oppressed people. It does not
concern itself with the challenges to belief posed by nonbelieving intellectuals, but seeks to explicate the experiences of oppressed, faithfully Christian
people in their struggles for freedom.

The prospect of a postmodern turn in twentieth-century theology was first
signaled by the emergence of these theologies. Thinkers such as Gustavo
Gutiérrez, Juan Luis Segundo, and James Cone did not make universalist claims
for their ideas; they did not claim that liberation theology is a new orthodoxy,
or that it solves the problems of theological liberalism, or that it offers a new
foundation for modern theology. The first generation of liberation theologians
eschewed foundationalist claims of all kinds. They proposed to make theology
address other kinds of problems, especially the concrete struggles for person-
hood and survival faced by millions of oppressed people who, in their own
ways, seek to know what it means to follow Christ in their time. With the simultaneous emergence of Latin American and African American liberation theologies, the universalizing foundationalism of most bourgeois theologies was
called into question. The modernist theological project of accommodating
Christianity to the modern consciousness was strongly challenged by movements that had little reason to admire the achievements of modern theology,
philosophy, or liberal democracy.

An explosion of new, decentering, post-Enlightenment theologies made similar moves in their efforts to make theology speak to other interests. Feminist
theologians such as Rosemary Radford Ruether and Mary Daly blasted the deep
and pervasive androcentric bias of all existing forms of Christian theism. The
revolutionary implications of feminist criticism quickly became evident in the
early 1970s, as Daly in particular pressed the question whether radical feminism is compatible with any kind of Christianity. A host of related liberationist
and postcolonialist currents produced new environmentalist, narrativist, political and Christian socialist, gay and lesbian, deconstructionist, and poststructuralist theologies and other perspectives that sought to subvert traditional
relations of power pertaining especially to race, gender, and class privilege.
With the partial exception of feminist theology, none of these movements gave
much attention at first to the problems of interpreting myth and the sacred.
Gutiérrez and Segundo both related liberation theology to current socialist
movements, while Cone related black liberation theology to Black Power politics. The political character of most liberation theology militated against any
constructive interest in myth interpretation. In 1978, when Ogden introduced
a new edition of *Christ Without Myth*, he acknowledged with an apologetic
tone that his book belonged to a bygone era of theological reflection. The most
urgent theological problem today is not the modernist problem of myth interpretation, he allowed, but the fact that most people in the world "still do not

share in the benefits of modernity." This was still a modernist way of framing the issue, but it signaled nonetheless his recognition of a profound change in religious consciousness. Liberation theology outstripped the liberal and neoorthodox traditions not only because it privileges the question of social justice, but because it understands that the universalizing discourse of modern theology is no longer a theological possibility. As Ogden remarked, "Perhaps nothing dates—and severely limits—the argument of my book quite so much as the global way in which I there spoke of "modern man" and of "*the* theological problem," without taking sufficient account of the vast differences between the rich nations and the poor nations, and all the other differences—racial and sexual as well as economic and cultural—by which persons even in our own society remain divided."[33]

Cobb recognized, as well, that the turn in theology away from the standpoint of the universalizing bourgeois male academic presented a strong judgment on his early work. He later explained that he could not continue to write systematic theology from a detached, purportedly objective subject position after he was exposed to the decentering critiques of liberation theology.[34] From liberationist criticism he absorbed the truism that theological reason is always a situated servant of interest. His conversion to environmentalism in 1969 drove him to rethink the relation of Christian truth to concrete sociohistorical practices.[35] His commitment to Whiteheadian process metaphysics actually strengthened with his resolve to correct the nature-harming anthropocentrism of most classical and modern Christianity. As his writings on myth and the sacred attest, however, Cobb was less prepared for the challenge to his thinking on issues pertaining to spirituality that the "return of the repressed" in postmodern culture has brought forward.

The notion that Christian myth must be translated into the language of a Christianized philosophy has always foundered on the problem that this procedure inevitably distorts mythical meaning. Neither the impersonal Absolute of Greek metaphysics nor the Absolute Spirit of Hegelian philosophy constitute an adequate substitute for the personal God of biblical faith. Whenever Christian theology has turned to philosophy to provide a rational cognitive language for its mythical claims, it has sacrificed some important aspect of the religious character of biblical faith. For all of his commitment to the process theism of Whitehead and Hartshorne, even Cobb concedes that Whitehead's "power of dynamic being" is significantly different from the personal God portrayed in scripture. The debates between proponents and opponents of demythologizing in the 1950s and 1960s centered mainly on the question whether such differences are the necessary price for saving any Christian message at all.

Even among those who most strenuously disputed that demythologizing is necessary, some form of secularization theory was taken for granted. Cobb's pronouncement that the sacred is dead was a longstanding theme of American neoorthodoxy, a fact that surely explains why most of the death-of-God theologians of the mid-1960s were former Barthians. Though Tillich steadfastly maintained that human beings are naturally religious and that the desacralizing impact of modernity has been at least as destructive as it is liberating, many theologians agreed with Bonhoeffer's verdict that a world come of age has no need of Tillich's religiose assurances. Tillich set out to interpret the world—against its will—through religion, Bonhoeffer explained, "but the world unseated him and went on by itself." Tillich sought to understand the world better than it understood itself, "but it felt that it was completely misunderstood, and rejected the imputation."[36] The age of sacred meaning is over. A generation of American Barthians and other theologians accepted this religious preunderstanding, which, in the United States, found its apotheosis in death-of-God theology.

The Persistence of the Sacred

Meanwhile tens of millions of Americans continued to practice their faith and/or search intently for spiritual meaning. Most of those who heard about death-of-God theology could not fathom what the media were talking about. It is one thing, after all, to recognize that the crisis of modern theology is a crisis of belief; it is something else to claim that the crisis of belief negates the possibility of faithful living. The death-of-God episode signaled for many observers not so much the end of Christianity, but the self-destruction of academic theology. Finding little spiritual wisdom in theology, many people turned to conservative churches or alternative religious traditions. Many looked for guidance in the writings of popular religious writers such as C. S. Lewis, Morton Kelsey, John Sanford, Joseph Campbell, Matthew Fox, and M. Scott Peck, who were less inhibited than most academic theologians in speaking about the spiritual life.

Though the point is rarely acknowledged by academic theologians, the popularizers typically write about sacred reality in a bolder, more direct, and spiritually serious manner than is true of most academic theology. Moreover, except for Lewis, all of the spiritual writers listed above draw upon the psychological theorizing of C. J. Jung in arguing for the objective reality and power of the sacred. Kelsey and Sanford are Jungian theologians; Campbell's best-selling works on mythography draw heavily upon Jung's theory of the archetypes of the unconscious; and Peck's all-time best-selling *The Road Less Traveled* bases its spiritual argument on a Jungian understanding of God as the collective unconscious.[37] Aspects of Jungian theory have also been adopted by numerous academic specialists in psychology and religion, especially Robert Moore, Wallace Clift, Ann Ulanov, John Heaney, Eugene Bianchi, Don Browning, and Robert Doran.[38] To his numerous theological followers, Jung's doctrine that human beings are connected to each other through deep structures of the psyche provides a uniquely fruitful and objective foundation for the apprehension of Christian truth.

The notion that mind or consciousness contains identifiable universal structures is hardly unique to Jung; his theory of the archetypes of the unconscious has analogues in Plato's theory of the forms and Kant's theory of the categories of mind. More recently, the argument that the mind contains specific universal structures has been propounded in linguistics by Noam Chomsky, in anthropology by Robin Fox, and in ethology by Niko Tinbergen.[39] Jung's positive view of myth as integrative and world-constructing also has analogues in Ernst Cassirer's philosophy of symbolic forms, the structural anthropology of Claude Levi-Strauss, and the history of religions comparativism of Mircea Eliade.[40] Jungian theory thus contains numerous points of connection to a wide range of disciplines and is subject to partial verification or falsification through them. In his important book, *Archetypes: A Natural History of the Self,* for example, psychiatrist Anthony Stevens argues that recent developments in neurobiology and ethology provide confirming evidence for the existence of Jungian-type archetypes that have evolved through natural selection.[41] Whether Jung was a "Darwin of the mind," as Stevens contends, or a theorist with less claim to scientific achievement, is a question that dominates much of the literature about Jungian psychology.[42]

This debate is not without significance for Jung's theological followers, since the key to the appeal of Jungian theory for theologians is its claim to offer a real, accessible, universal basis for language about the sacred. Theologians who adopt Jungian theory are obliged to consider whether the kinds of arguments advanced by Stevens are scientifically credible. As many of them are quick to observe, however, Jung's demonstration of an existing objective soul or psychic ground of spirituality was put forward in a process that was unavoidably subjective. Jung explained at the outset of his autobiography that his life was a story of the unconscious coming into self-realization: "Everything in the unconscious seeks outward manifestations, and the personality too desires to evolve out of its unconscious conditions and to experience itself as a whole. I cannot employ the language of science to trace this process of growth in myself, for I cannot experience myself as a scientific problem." It is only through myth that the reality of what we are to our inward vision can be expressed, he argued: "Myth is more individual and expresses life more precisely than does science. Science works with concepts of averages which are far too general to do justice to the subjective variety of an individual life."[43] With distinctive intellectual courage, Jung acknowledged that his own experience was a crucial source of his psychological theorizing, and in both cases it was myth that provided the vehicle for his understanding.

His introduction to the reality of the unconscious and the disclosive role of myth as a vehicle of psychic expression both came directly from Sigmund Freud, his early mentor, but Jung's reflections on the extrasexual nature of the unconscious caused him to break from Freud.[44] For Freud, the unconscious was a kind of psychic reservoir of past individual and communal experiences that included, especially, repressed memories of early childhood sexual conflicts and the primal drives or urges of the libido. He urged his followers that his theory of psychosexual stage development must be taught "as a dogma." Jung's introspective analysis of his own psychic experience, his studies of world art and literature, and his encounters with patients convinced him that Freud's strongly sexual account of the unconscious was inadequate, however. As Jung later explained, "the conceptual framework into which he fitted the psychic phenomenon seemed to me unendurably narrow."[45] Freud persisted in his devotion to scientific rationalism even after his discovery of the unconscious undermined its assumed materialism. Jung countered that this attempt to fit the unconscious into the framework of an obsolete rationalism failed to take seriously the disruptive, chaotic, spiritual nature of the unconscious. His own work proposed to take more seriously the spiritual character and generative role of the unconscious in human existence.

Consciousness as Spirit:
Jungian Theory

An experience with a schizophrenic patient in 1906 first prompted Jung to think about the possibility of a collective unconscious. The patient was an adult male who had suffered from paranoid schizophrenia since his youth and was incurable. Most of his life had been spent in mental hospitals. One day he pointed to the sun and vividly described a series of images that he was seeing in it. Jung couldn't see anything besides the sun, but the incident disturbed him for several years because he sensed that it represented something more than pathological delusion. Then in 1910 he came upon a book by the philologist Albrecht Dieterich that contained the text of an ancient Mithraic ritual in which the same vision of a wind-producing tube hanging from the disc of the sun was described. How could his long-institutionalized patient possibly have come into exact possession of this obscure image? The question launched Jung far beyond Freud's narrowly sexual conception of the unconscious. It produced a cluster of questions that he spent the rest of his career seeking to understand and answer.[46]

Jung's basic answer distinguished between the forgotten or repressed memories of individual personal experience that he called the "personal unconscious" and the extrapersonal psychic reality of the "collective unconscious." In his formulation, the collective unconscious was an inexhaustible reservoir of psychic reality that impinges upon and influences every individual human psyche. Whereas the experiences deposited in the personal unconscious are all products of each individual's personal experience, the collective unconscious contains experiences that cross space and time. "The collective unconscious contains the whole spiritual heritage of mankind's evolution, born anew in the brain structure of every individual," he asserted.[47]

His major work, *The Archetypes and the Collective Unconscious*, explained that the personal unconscious rests upon this "deeper layer" of experience, "which does not derive from personal experience and is not a personal acquisition but is inborn." He called it the *collective* unconscious because "this part of the unconscious is not individual but universal; in contrast to the personal psyche, it has contents and modes of behavior that are more or less the same everywhere and in all individuals." In other words, he wrote, the collective unconscious is identical in all people "and thus constitutes a common psychic substrate of a suprapersonal nature which is present in every one of us."[48]

Paul Tillich once remarked that Jung did not think of the collective unconscious as derivative, but rather, as "the source of the instinctual forces of the psyche and of the forms or categories that regulate them, namely the archetypes."[49] That is, for Jung the collective conscious consists of archetypes that he conceived as psychic analogues to the instincts of the body. Jung invested great significance in the fact that certain specific patterns and themes recur in the mythology and folklore of human groups throughout the world. In one of his lectures on psychology and religion he noted that these motifs constantly appear in nearly identical form: "I have called those motives archetypes and by them I understand forms or images of a collective nature which occur practically all over the earth as constituents of myths and at the same time as autochthonous, individual products of unconscious origin."[50]

Jung's sprawling corpus of writings analyzed numerous examples of this apparently innate human predisposition to produce certain common images. They included all of the standard motifs of mythology: the great mother, the divine child, the wise old man, the hero, the hidden treasure, the passage from darkness to light, and so on. He discovered that there are also archetypes for the structural components of the personality, such as the ego, shadow, anima/animus, persona, and self. In each case, according to Jungian theory, these archetypes represent psychic realities that must be mobilized or developed if mature self-integration is to occur in any person. For example, the shadow is the undeveloped side of one's personality, and the anima/animus is the personification of female qualities in the male or vice versa. The object of Jungian therapy is always to effect a balanced wholeness among these aspects of the individual's psychic reality.

Jung borrowed the concept of an archetype from Augustine; as patterns of mind that impinge upon and shape human experience, the archetypes are a priori powers of representation analogous to Plato's forms and Kant's a priori categories of the mind. As Don Browning observes, however, Jung's categories differ from these Platonic and Kantian analogues in their biological nature.[51] Jung assumed with much of modern philosophy that mind is an instrument of the body; as analogues to the instincts of the body, he therefore conceptualized the archetypes as common embodied psychobiological tendencies and needs by which human beings across all known cultures organize their experience. Perhaps most important, this meant that for Jung, the archetypes are the source of all religion.

Philip Rieff observes that Jung was one of the first modern intellectuals to champion a "meliorative sense of myth" as the privileged source of wisdom and regeneration.[52] In Jung's case, this appreciative attitude was connected to the unique role that myth and symbol play in decoding the archetypes of the unconscious. Myths give distinctive historical and cultural form to the hidden archetypes that unify all human conventions and religions, he argued. Unlike philosophy, science, or religious doctrine, myths affect the whole person at once. They appeal to the mind while transcending the power of reason; they affect not only our thinking, but also our feelings, will, and intuition. It is through myth and symbol, the primal creations of myth-creative beings, that human beings come into contact with the "deeper layer" of our unconscious.

For this reason Jung regarded Bultmann's demythologizing program as profoundly misguided. It is wrong to think of myth as outmoded science, he argued; myth is rather something that *happens* to us in continually repeated events. Myth expresses the human experience of relation to something greater than ourselves. In the early 1950s Jung observed that Protestantism was already so rationalized and devoid of symbolism that it stood on the verge of spiritual bankruptcy. If Bultmann's demythologizing program is embraced by the church's theologians, he warned, "Protestantism will become even more boring and penurious than it already is."[53] Jung's protest against demythologizing did not imply that theologians should simply recycle the mythical forms of the past; he argued that what is needed is new mythical language that keeps alive the religious content of Christian myth. A religion that can no longer assimilate the mythical imagination "is forgetting its proper function," he warned. The spiritual vitality of any faith tradition depends "on the continuity of myth, and this can be preserved only if each age translates the myth into its own language and makes it an essential content of its view of the world."[54] Put differently, Jung believed that the crucial task of the theologian is not to negate or overcome the church's mythical inheritance, but to remythologize it as the discourse of a living tradition.

Only the image gives life. Jung regarded the symbolic images that his patients presented in their dreams and fantasies as expressions of the unconscious in consciousness. Myths and dreams represent projections from both the personal and collective unconscious. This is the clue to the distinctive disclosive power of myth and symbol, he argued, for in these vehicles consciousness and the unconscious are brought together. The reason that the same mythical motifs arise independently throughout the world is that "they are fashioned out of the same worldwide human unconscious, whose contents are infinitely less variable than are races and individuals."[55] Jung's belief in the reality of the collective unconscious functioned as a kind of premodern god-concept or Platonic heaven. He suggested that if all of the world's traditions were suddenly destroyed, all of the world's mythology and religion would promptly start over again in forms of energy producing recurrent images. History neither creates nor saves.

So what is gained by bringing the conscious self into contact with the wellspring of its life and history? Jung assumed that what is gained is salvation, the surrender of the ego to a process of relation to the true self, which is the central archetype of the collective unconscious. The self is the transcendent center of every human life that guides all psychic functions. It is the unknown, ineffable power of the unconscious to whom the ego must submit in order to obtain wholeness. In Jungian theory, an increasingly ego-transcending self attains wholeness through its gradual reconciliation of opposites, which Jung called the process of individuation. A self becomes individuated as the various one-sided aspects of one's personality are brought together to create a new unified personality. Jungian therapy seeks to enable a person to freely choose the life of wholeness that one's inner self is always calling us to choose. The call is answered whenever one makes a choice that leads to greater inner freedom and wholeness. The achievement of psychic wholeness always takes place at the meeting point between consciousness and the unconscious, Jung taught, "where the centre of the total personality no longer coincides with the ego, but with a point midway between the conscious and the unconscious. This would be the point of a new equilibrium, a new centering of the total personality."[56]

Jung was not shy in affirming the analogues between his concept of the self and the Christian idea of the indwelling Spirit of God. Though he cautioned that his idea of the self did not imply "a deification of man or a dethronement of God," he observed that it could nonetheless be called the "God within us." When pressed on the point, he always explained that he was "simply formulating a definite psychological fact."[57] He was not a theologian, but a psychologist who demonstrated empirically "the existence of a totality supraordinate to consciousness."[58] It was not his business to theorize the relation between the self and the transcendent metaphysical deity of Christianity, he insisted. As a psychologist it was not his concern to distinguish the God-like experience of encounter from that which is experienced. In fact, Jung's writings crossed the line into theological speculation on numerous occasions, especially with regard to the Christian doctrine of the Trinity and to what he called the "dark side" of divine reality.[59] He sought to innoculate his thought from theological criticism while indulging his impulse to make theological arguments.

This impulse occasionally prompted him to make tantalizing remarks about the relation between God and the archetypal God-image of the self. Near the end of his life, when he was asked by a television interviewer whether he believed in God, Jung replied: "Difficult to answer—I don't need to believe; I know." He explained that he could never simply *believe* anything; as an empiricist he either knew something or did not.[60] The plain implication was that he knew God without having to "believe" anything.[61] But elsewhere he maintained that the notion of the God-image "has nothing whatever to do with the question of God's existence." Human reason can never prove that the metaphysical God of Christian faith exists, he observed; moreover, the very idea of such a proof is superfluous, "for the idea of an all-powerful divine Being is present everywhere, unconsciously if not consciously, because it is an archetype."[62]

To Jung this concept included every idea of the ultimate regardless of name.[63] The God-image is never anyone's possession, nor is it subject to definite knowledge claims. It is always beyond realization, for the process of individuation never finds perfect integration between the conscious self and the divine. Does this mean that there is no escape from religious relativism? Jung's deep concern for the spiritual vitality of the world's great religious traditions made the question unavoidable. He replied that the refusal to view any single religion as the only true faith does not necessarily imply that religious truth claims cannot be made legitimately. Could it not be thinkable, he asked, that God "has expressed himself in many languages and appeared in diverse forms and that all these statements are true?"[64]

Jung's various writings on Jesus Christ sought to finesse the most critical aspects of this question for Christians. He viewed Christ as an ideal exemplification of the archetypal character of the God-image. What made Jesus the Christ, he argued, was that Jesus apparently participated deeply in the archetypal life of the collective unconscious. Christ therefore symbolizes the possibility of the completion of the process of individuation, in which the conscious self and the God-image of the collective unconscious are united. The figure of Christ represents "a totality which surpasses and includes the ordinary man, and which corresponds to the total personality that transcends consciousness."[65] This total personality is the self. The idea of Christ's incarnation thus exemplified for Jung the ideal of holistic self-realization, while the passion of Christ exemplified the reality of individuated redemption through suffering. At Gethsemane, Jesus submitted his ego to the saving power of the inner God-image and thus saved his life by losing it. Jung remarked, "The drama of the archetypal life of Christ describes in symbolic images the events in the conscious life—as well as in the life that transcends consciousness—of a man who has been transformed by his higher destiny."[66]

With the possible exception of the Buddha, Jung regarded the Christ symbol as the most highly developed and differentiated example of the saving process of individuation.[67] In Jungian theory Christ is a symbol of the self, the unknown redeeming power who wills integrated wholeness for every person through sacrifice of the ego. Without claiming that Christ is the only possible means to salvation, Jung argued that in the West, nothing else remotely compares to the transforming power of the Christ symbol, "the still living myth of our culture."[68] In the West, the idea of the incarnation is the defining symbol of the process of individuation, just as the figure of Jesus Christ symbolizes the possibility of achieved unity between the conscious self and the God-image. Jung observed that in the East, on the other hand, the possibility of true salvation is mediated effectively by various living symbols of the self: "In the West the archetype is filled out with the dogmatic figure of Christ; in the East, with Purusha, the Atman, Hiranyagarbha, the Buddha, and so on."[69] Jung noted elsewhere that Eastern religions as a whole have a richer history of engagement with the reality of the unconscious than is true in the West.[70]

Though he exhorted Christian theologians to initiate dialogues with Eastern traditions to foster deeper religious understanding on both sides, he cautioned that dialogue is no substitute for inner work. "We must get at the Eastern values from within and not from without, seeking them in ourselves, in the unconscious," he urged.[71] With singular persistence Jung maintained that the answer to the predicament of every individual is spiritual. Modern people go to psychotherapists because they have lost contact with their souls. Near the end of his life he reported that among all of his patients in the second half of their lives "there has not been one whose problem in the last resort was not that of finding a religious outlook on life. It is safe to say that every one of them fell ill because he had lost that which the living religions of every age had given to their followers, and none of them has really been healed who did not regain his religious outlook."[72]

For many of his theological followers, the attraction of Jung's theory of the collective unconscious is that it gives theology an empirical, liberal, universal foundation. It appeals to a realm of objective nonphysical reality that is accessible through myth, dream, and symbol. Barth's Word of God seems like a ghostly abstraction by comparison. Jungian theory warns ego-driven people that they will never find wholeness or inner peace if they remain cut off from the transpersonal spiritual source of their own being. Moreover, the Jungian approach valorizes the very mythical aspects of Christianity that the past two centuries of modernist criticism have problematized as primitive or unbelievable. Jung equated demythologizing with spiritual suicide. He warned that the spiritual truth of the gospel is violated whenever the gospel myth is replaced with a modern philosophy. He judged that a theologian would only resort to demythologizing after "he is no longer impressed by the revelation of holiness and has fallen back on his own mental activity."[73]

Jung countered that the solitary ego makes a pathetic starting point for theology. It tries to assess the truth of something of which it has no knowledge. It treats Christian truth as a deposit of rational information external to experience, without comprehending that the truth of Christian myth is unknowable to the self-centered ego. Whenever the historical elements of the gospel narrative are separated from the archetypal characterization of Jesus presented in the gospels, he contended, the gospels "immediately lose their character of wholeness."[74] Similarly, whenever theologians seek to replace or transcend Christian myth with their own philosophy, they produce ego-driven monuments of intellection that do not bring healing or salvation to anyone.

True myth comes to us as a Word of God, Jung taught. We cannot devise the myth that will bring us to wholeness; rather, saving myth always comes to us within the process of our individuating search for the God-image. "Myth is the revelation of a divine life in man," he explained. "It is not we who invent myth, rather it speaks to us as a Word of God. The Word of God comes to us, and we have no way of distinguishing whether and to what extent it is different from God." The Word as myth is not a product of our will, but comes upon us spontaneously and places obligations upon us. "Our chief feeling about it is that it is not the result of our own ratiocinations, but that it came to us from elsewhere," he wrote.[75]

Christ or Self as Symbol?

Jung's theological followers generally embrace his theory of the collective unconscious and his understanding of myth as a representation of spiritual reality without adopting his speculations on the "evil side" of God, or his anti-church individualism, or his denigration of Judaism. Theologians such as Kelsey, Sanford, and Clift defend Jung from the common charge that he reduced God to the self or made an idol of the indwelling God-image.[76] They repeat his explanation that he sought only to understand what could be learned about the sacred mysteries of Christian faith from the standpoint of empirical psychology. Without denying the possibility of a perceptible referent in psychic experience, they explain, Jung did not distinguish the experience of encounter with the God-image from that which is experienced.

Jung was emphatic that he wanted theologians to transgress the disciplinary boundary that he set for himself (and often failed to observe). He wanted theologians to make use of his work in developing new theologies that blend psychology, religion, and philosophy. The Jungian theologians thus have a strong warrant for their claim that believing in the realm of spirit that Jung called the collective unconscious does not necessarily limit or distort one's understanding of divine reality from a Christian standpoint. The doctrine of divine indwelling is foundational to Christianity, and Jung's demonstration of the existence of a transpersonal realm of spirit gives many Christian thinkers greater confidence in the meaningfulness of religious language. Speaking from a quite traditional theological perspective, Kelsey and Sanford are especially insistent that Jungian psychology provides the sense and language of spiritual realism that contemporary Christian theology needs to overcome its modern history of spiritual impoverishment.[77]

The notion that Jung's psychology of spirit can be readily Christianized for religious and theological purposes runs into serious difficulties in the area of Christology, however. The problem obtains implicitly everywhere in Jung's thought, but the question of Christology exposes it fully. In one of his numerous visions, Jung was told that a woman named Salome was worshiping him because, as she said, "you are Christ." Jung rejected the message from his unconscious that he was the Christ, but this vision raises the key problem with his conception of spiritual transformation. In the Jungian understanding of the self's conversion of the ego to true form, Christ is valorized as a symbol of the self; the symbol of Christ represents one exemplary way of knowing one's self.

Jung acknowledged that his psychology of the Christ-image sought merely to show how this image has acquired the characteristics of an archetype, specifically the archetype of the self. His aim and method were analogous to art history, he explained, in which the historian traces the various influences that contributed to the formation of a particular Christ-image. He noted that the key difference between the psychological archetype and its parallels in art history, philology, and other fields is that the psychological archetype "refers to a living and ubiquitous psychic fact, and this naturally shows the whole situation in a rather different light." The upshot of the difference is that greater importance is "naturally" subscribed to "the living presence of the archetype than to the idea of the historical Christ."[78] What is at stake here is not merely a question of methodological consistency, Jung explained, but the problem of ascertaining the *real* agent of change. His writings on the archetypes of the collective unconscious made it clear that for him, the archetype of the self was the actual agent of change in history and consciousness. While claiming to steer clear of theological terrain, Jung made a decisive normative judgment on psychological grounds that the self is not a symbol of Christ, but rather Christ is a symbol of the self.

The difference is crucial, for Christianity proclaims that Christ is the revelation of being itself, not merely an example or even the best example of an inner God-image. James Loder observes that the Jungian approach confuses the order of being and knowing. Jungian theory privileges an account about the structure of knowing spiritual truth over the truth of being-itself. By making Christ a symbol of the self, it gives ultimacy to the self rather than to Christ. But if ultimacy is ascribed to a myth-creative, individuating self rather than to Christ, there is nothing to prevent an individual from seeing one's self as the answer or, for that matter, from worshiping Jung as Christ. As Loder remarks, the Jungian mistake is to confuse the spiritual truth of Christ's redemption with a structure for knowing it.[79] If the Christ of Christian faith is to be known at all, Jung's order of being and knowing must be reversed so that the ultimacy of Christ with respect to the predicament and experiences of the self may be known.

The difference is crucial not merely for the sake of theological orthodoxy, but because it impinges on the character and effect of spiritual transformation. Here again, Jung's theological followers tend to obscure the differences between salvation in Christ and the achievement of an archetypal structure of personal wholeness. The gospel is not concerned so much with the attainment of a balanced personality as it is with knowing the truth that sets us free. If Christ is a symbol of the self, then the structures of the self will define the meaning of Christ; but if the self is a symbol of Christ, then Christ defines the self and makes possible a spiritual conversion to true form that the self could not achieve. Loder observes that if the latter kind of transformation pertains, "it will be marked not by anything resembling a static balance, but by sacrificial love, the form that transformation takes in Christ."[80] The Jungian model arrests the process of transformation in Christ by making an idol out of its goal of balanced wholeness.

Jung's writings are loaded with powerful spiritual imagery and his interpretation of Christianity as true myth has provided for many people a credible way of speaking about and seeking spiritual meaning. For some thinkers, this theoretical construct represents the only remaining credible form of belief in a transpersonal eternal being. Among its numerous adherents, Jungian theory has inspired some feminist theologians to use the anima/animus archetypes as mediating concepts in the project of relating feminist criticism to Christianity. Jung's highly suggestive writings on gender support a sizable literature of feminist psychology that critiques—while appropriating—his theories of gender complementarity and androgynous being. Here as elsewhere, Jungian theory represents the last form of essentialism that many postmodern theorists take seriously.[81]

Postmodernism as Myth Deconstruction

As a project that continues to posit a deposit of meaning in a realm of Spirit that underlies all existence, however, Jung's essentialism is subject to the same critiques that deconstructionists level against other theisms and philosophies of being. As William Doty observes, the kind of linguistic a priori that Jung posits is inconceivable "without the corrective recognition that an archetypal representation must be in itself already a movement within language—expressed metaphorically, in a limit-aware context but yet open-endedly symbolic."[82] Jacques Derrida's "difference" principle expresses more clearly this point of deconstructionist and poststructuralist criticism. According to Derrida, language does not describe any essence or presence that exists or is expressed outside a system of relationships; rather, language describes what is *not* present. We speak at all because some void needs to be expressed.[83]

Doty concedes that Jung's language of the archetypes might be retainable if it is regrounded in a wider semiotics and semantics of myth and discourse. For example, Eric Gould proposes that the archetypes could be reconceptualized as signs that signify that language cannot be spoken fully or ultimately. In this considerable retreat from Jung's meaning, archetypes would be understood as significances shared by speaker and listener who share the same discourse tradition and who seek, however fallibly, to employ metonyms to bridge the gap between event and meaning. Gould explains, "The archetype carries a necessary exteriority whose interpretive challenge must be met—as metonymy becomes metaphor—or else we lapse into a superstitious worship of the hidden side of its meaning."[84] That is, if the archetypes are not understood as signs for the necessary exteriority of speech, we inevitably lapse into some myth-breeding essentialism like Jung's. To Gould and Doty, the remaining significance of the archetype does not depend on any notion of a realm of spirit or nonphysical sacred reality, but consists merely in its signification of meaningful patterns. In Gould's words, the archetype should thus be understood as "a representation of experience resulting itself from the quite distinct intent to make an interpretation of the world."[85] Archetypes are master signs that ground the telling of one's own fictive myth.

As a movement that rejects any kind of epistemological foundationalism, so-called postmodernism defies precise definition. Jean-Francois Lyotard claims in *The Postmodern Condition* that the hallmark of postmodern thought is its "incredulity toward metanarrative,"[86] but, of course, postmodernists are forced to employ metanarratives of their own when they seek to justify their disbelief in *grande histoire*. Postmodernism is more a style of discourse than a defense of any particular position or argument.[87] Not all forms of postmodern theology are linked to the deconstructionist and poststructuralist movements that Doty embraces. Process theologian David Ray Griffin, for example, calls his work "postmodern theology" because it affirms "that humanity can and must go beyond the modern" in its approach to science, the natural world, and the sacred. He dissociates his reconstructive postmodernism from the "eliminative" or nihilistic spirit of Derrida-style criticism. French deconstructionism is not really an option for postmodern theologians, he implies, for deconstructionism is precisely the negation of *all* affirmations of being, presence, and sacred meaning.[88]

Though they agree on little else, the latter suggestion is vigorously confirmed in the writings of several religious thinkers who do embrace deconstructionism, including William Doty, Carl Raschke, Mark C. Taylor, Thomas J. J. Altizer, Max Myers, and Charles Winquist.[89] In *Twilight of the Idols,* Nietzsche declared that "the true world" is a refuted idea that must be abolished.[90] Deconstructionism is the offspring of Nietzsche's pronouncement of the death of God/presence/being. It is not a development in modern Western theology, Raschke explains, but a movement in Western culture as a whole that reveals "the inner vacuity of the much touted 'modern outlook.'"[91] Deconstructionism repeats Nietzsche's claim in *The Gay Science* that consciousness is a mere web of signs, "only a net of communication between human beings."[92] If the world that "consciousness" apprehends is a world of mere surfaces and signs, as Nietzsche insisted, it follows for deconstructionists that all appeals to a referent outside language are illegitimate, if not deceitful.[93]

Deconstructionism takes from modern discourse theory and semiotics the lesson that the "meaning" of a word is a function of its location in a cluster of significations. "The 'object' to which an expression 'refers' is simply another set of sign-relations," Raschke asserts. What is called "consciousness" is merely the act of interpreting or mediating between different sets of sign-relations. Deconstructionists apply this (modernist) discovery of the relativity of consciousness to the social scientific and philosophical discourses that have produced it, however. They criticize the tendency of modernist intellectuals to reify their own theories about relativity or the limits of understanding; modernist theories are not more "factual" merely by virtue of their awareness of relativity. Deconstructionists repeat Richard Rorty's maxim that the relativization of consciousness goes all the way down.[94] Because modernist thinking has replaced classical realism with various forms of self-referring metaphysics, Raschke explains, it "remains yoked to the fantasy of what Derrida dubs 'the transcendental signified.'"[95]

This is the notion that all signs are somehow directed toward a unifying ground or object of reference. In Derrida's characterization, the "transcendental signified" is a semantic analogue for the God of Western theism, which grounds the Western myth of an eternal logos that pervades all reality. Deconstructionism forcefully demythologizes the Greco-Christian rhetoric of "presence." It makes "logocentrism" an epithet and delegitimizes all language of presence and being. Derrida observes that there is no point in the sign process at which it can be said that the "meaning" of a text has been established; signification is open-ended at both ends. So-called meaning is merely the unending *displacement* of one sign by another, for "from the moment there is meaning there are nothing but signs."[96] As Raschke remarks, deconstruction "is the internal and self-propelled dismantling (as well as the equable reshaping) of the structures of understanding and meaning like the chick that shatters the egg, or the moth that bursts the chrysalis."[97] New "meanings" are generated not by addition, but by disruption and differentiation. Derrida's difference principle (misspelled *differance*) thus emphasizes that it is through displacement that significance is continually produced.[98]

The deconstructionist thesis of the instability of meaning subverts not only traditional understandings of authorial intent and authority, but the very notions of author/ity. Taylor remarks that from a deconstructionist standpoint, language is neither grounded in nor does it point toward an extralinguistic referent. The deconstructionist thematization of the total contextuality of meaning is a variation on death-of-God theology. "The death of God paves the way for the birth of the sign, the sign whose distinctive traits are its conventionality and its external relation to and thus arbitrary association with the signified," Taylor explains.[99] In Raschke's words, deconstruction "is in the final analysis *the death of God put into writing,* the subsumption of the 'Word' by the 'flesh,' the deluge of immanence."[100] Deconstructionism shows that all "-ologies" are futile defenses against the Void; it marks not only the end of religious myth, but the end of theology.

Deconstructionist criticism typically seeks to show how a given discourse covers up a disruptive truth, or undermines its own thesis, or masks its desire for power, or rationalizes its complicity in oppression or deceit. It employs close readings of texts to identify the rhetorical maneuvers that function to secure agreement or submission through the establishment of key premises, arguments, and stable meanings.[101] Raschke argues that in Christianity, a posture of pious submission to the divine ghost of Being has covered up the subversive implications of the gospel passion narrative, which ends not in glory, but forsakenness. Christian theologians have long spoken of the *theologia crucis* in the manner of intellectual voyeurs, but with the arrival of the deconstructionist movement, he declares, it is time for theologians to accept the fact of Godforsakenness symbolized by the cross. With the death of God, theologians must give up the ghost of Being and the enterprise of theology itself: "A 'death of God theology' is, and always was, an oxymoron, a tasteless jape, a *tour de farce.* The revelation of the farce is writing; and theology must write itself into the grave."[102]

Raschke cautions that the death of God is not necessarily to be celebrated. Too many of Nietzsche's children have already oversold the promise of a brave new world or a new liberated humanity without God. Deconstruction does not promise emancipation, fulfillment, or an end to oppression. It represents rather a venture "into the underworld of limitless writing, the dismembering of all names and concepts, the dance of Dionysus." Following James Hillman, Raschke recalls that Hades and Dionysus are the same in the dance of death; deconstructionism is the dance of death upon God's tomb.[103]

If God is ruled out and theology is finished, does Christian myth have any useful future? That it has some kind of future can be taken for granted, since the mythic struggle against the Void is amply displayed in human behavior everywhere. But is it possible from the standpoint of a deconstructionist sensibility to valorize the mythical impulse or any mythical language about the sacred?[104] Doty replies that an affirmative response is possible if the sacred is conceived in terms of its fictiveness or "mythicity." To deconstruct a mythical text is to expose the structures by which it works and the cultural contexts that ground its forms of expression and worldview. Doty observes that deconstructive criticism also has the capacity to explicate the possible alternative futures to which the fictive gestures of a myth might lead, however. In the latter case, the value that deconstructive criticism might find in religious myth is not in the mythical attempt to replace empirical explanations with a unifying worldview, but to see myths as radically symbolic, fictive *additions* to empirical explanation.

Empirical and mythological forms of thought are reflective, but myths are "privileged metonymic explanations" that make the world come alive. Doty observes that literature has become more imaginatively fictive in recent years after its move away from reflective realism; following Gould, he proposes that myth should be understood similarly as a refusal to accept the world's reality. Just as fiction is always in some way a protest against a world that is not sufficient, the meaning of a fiction is always potentially mythic. Because we tend to forget that myth is no less provisional than fiction, however, the demythologizing function of deconstructive criticism is always needed. Deconstructive criticism corrects the authoritarian impulse that closely attends every outbreak of the mythic imagination, no matter how subversive it may seem.

With modern Sausserian linguistics, deconstructionists caution that meanings are made possible only by *systems of differences* and through choices that *displace* alternative meanings. Meanings are not made possible by revelations from a transcendent author/ity. With poststructuralist hermeneutical theory, deconstructionists conclude, as Gould asserts, that "there is in writing no lost origin to be sought after, no inherent monomyth to celebrate, but only the enigmatic myth of interpretation as play, dependent on concealed lack."[105]

Western philosophy from Plato to Whitehead has used God-language to cipher the incapacity of language to bridge the chasm between event and meaning. Doty observes that postmodernism is the condition under which this strategy is given up. "We live within a world where symbolic meanings may help—do help—yet are never fully able to bridge the ontological gap; fictions and religious myths both aspire to do the bridging work, yet both remain incomplete, insufficient," he observes. Building on Gould's suggestion that myth is "discourse resisting mere ideology," he proposes that myths should be understood as symbolic fictions that expose the inability of language to signify ultimately. Myths disclose the patterns of relationships between things *within* the stories told by language. There is nothing else. "The most sacred expressions are those that most fully express the absence of a meaning-present, the absence of God, the nonpresence of the Totally Other," he concludes.[106] Myths disclose, often inadvertently, the absence of the Word.

Deconstructionism and the
Feminist Myth Critique

Deconstructionist and poststructuralist critiques expose the structures and ideologies through which dominant groups maintain their power over subjugated peoples, cultures, and knowledges.[107] They expose the will to power that fuels and is variously concealed by virtually all rhetorical strategies. Within the tradition of discourse theory pioneered by Michel Foucault, in particular, postmodern criticism seeks to demonstrate that the rhetoric of universality is always a discourse of the privileged.[108] Deconstructionism is not necessarily feminist or politically radical; Derrida's writings on women verge on being insulting to feminism, and much of the French feminist literature inspired by deconstructionism spurns political engagement.[109] Notwithstanding the various debates concerning the politics of French postmodernism, however, it is at least fair to say that the decolonializing, multiculturalist spirit of most deconstructionist criticism makes it amenable to feminist appropriation. Much of the work in contemporary transatlantic feminist theory makes use of deconstructionist and poststructuralist tools of criticism, and in North American theology a poststructuralist feminist movement is emerging. Feminist theologians such as Rebecca Chopp, Sharon Welch, Serene Jones, Mary McClintock Fulkerson, and (mixed with hermeneutical philosophy) Sallie McFague use deconstructionist and poststructuralist critiques as aids to their refiguration of Christian myth, usually without accepting as a totalizing truth the deconstructionist denial of divine presence.

Feminist theology as an enterprise is inherently deconstructionist in its concern to critique or negate the patriarchal character of traditional Christianity. Even in its milder forms, feminist theology breaks apart the traditional Christian rhetoric of divine kingship, fatherhood, and sovereignty to retrieve emancipatory aspects of Christianity that have been subjugated by the dominant tradition. Liberal feminists such as Letty Russell, Patricia Wilson-Kastner, Anne Carr, and Catherine Mowry La Cugna are strongly critical of the dominance-reproducing androgyny of Christian myth while identifying themselves unequivocally as *Christian* theologians.[110] A more radical current of feminist theology represented by Rosemary Radford Ruether, Elisabeth Schüssler Fiorenza, and Carter Heyward displaces the authority of scripture and Christian tradition with a stronger appeal to the authority of women's experience, especially the experiences of modern feminists.[111] The new poststructuralist movement rejects this appeal to women's experience on account of its essentialist and universalist assumptions, however. Thinkers such as Chopp, Fulkerson, and McFague begin instead with the poststructuralist belief in language as the site of transformation.

Should feminist theology ascribe fundamental normative significance to experience or to language? One major feminist perspective rejects the question. In her epochal early work, *Beyond God the Father*, Mary Daly famously observed that the historical evil inadvertently portrayed in the Genesis myth of creation is that "women have had the power of *naming* stolen from us." In the Genesis story, Adam named the animals and the woman; throughout history, it is men who have named the world and claimed sovereignty over it. "We have not been free to use our own power to name ourselves, the world, or God," Daly remarked. "Women are now realizing that the universal imposing of names by men has been false because partial. That is, inadequate words have been taken as adequate."[112] Language is the site of transformation because those who name the world own it.

At the same time Daly's work routinely invoked the lessons of "women's experience" in unabashedly universalistic terms. Her early writings argued that Christian myth has been harmful to women; she later claimed that patriarchy "is itself the prevailing religion of the entire planet, and its essential message is necrophilia." So-called cultural pluralism is a self-serving male myth, she insisted, for the entire world lives in fact under the tyranny of a single woman-hating culture. "All of the so-called religions legitimating patriarchy are mere sects subsumed under its vast umbrella/canopy," she wrote. "They are essentially similar, despite the variations. All—from buddhism and hinduism to islam, judaism, christianity, to secular derivatives such as freudianism, jungianism, marxism, and maoism—are infrastructures of the edifice of patriarchy." All of the world's myths function primarily to shield men from their dreaded enemy. To be a woman is to be the object of this terror, she argued; women everywhere are "the projected personifications of 'The Enemy,' the real objects under attack in all the wars of patriarchy."[113]

Daly read biblical myth as a prototypical example of this world-embracing assault against women. The Bible portrays God as King and Father; it portrays man as the center of creation and subordinates women to men; it blames the first woman for the Fall of humankind and nature; it sacralizes the social mores and institutions of patriarchy; and it makes a male redeemer the focus and hope of new being. For thousands of years, theologians managed not to notice the absurdity of portraying men as the givers of life while blaming women for the world's evil. When the mythical nature of biblical myth finally became too obvious for the church to ignore, Daly observed, modern theologians demythologized the explanatory aspects of myth while seeking to retain its existential meaning. She noted that from the way that theologians such as Bultmann and Tillich reinterpreted the myth of the Fall into an abstract story about universal alienation and existential estrangement, "one could get the impression that the vision of the man-woman relationship portrayed is unimportant for modern consciousness, religious or secular."[114] Modern theology has proceeded as though the biblical account of gender relations is no more important or pertinent than its stabs at plant biology.

But the harm done to women by biblical myth belongs to a different category entirely, Daly urged, for the malignant image of women contained in scripture "is still deeply embedded in the modern psyche." Modern literature and the mass media recycle the "temptress Eve" motif with mind-numbing monotony, while discriminatory attitudes toward women pervade every sector of modern society. "In view of the fact that the destructive image of women that was reflected in and perpetuated by the myth of the Fall retains its hold over the modern psyche—even though in a disguised and residual manner—it is not adequate for theologians simply to intellectualize and generalize the alleged content of the myth as an expression of a universal state of alienation," Daly argued. "Indeed this approach is intellectually bankrupt and demonic. It amounts merely to abandoning the use of explicitly sexist theological imagery while failing to acknowledge its still persistent impact upon society."[115] When theology is silent about the harm that Judeo-Christian myth has done to women, it not only conveys the message that women's oppression is a nonproblem, but also becomes an instrument of it.

To Tillich and Niebuhr, the myth of the Fall was a crucial corrective to the utopianism and cultural optimism of liberal Protestantism. To Daly, it was a "prototypic case of false naming." The myth of the Fall misnames the mystery of evil and is thus a source of evil to women. It cultivates a woman-harming, backward-looking consciousness in which women are typed as the primordial scapegoats. "In a real sense the projection of guilt upon women *is* patriarchy's Fall, the primordial lie," she remarked. "Together with its offspring—the theology of original sin—the myth reveals the 'Fall' of religion into the role of patriarchy's prostitute."[116] In this crucial sense, the medium of the myth is itself the message, for the biblical myth of the Fall is an instrument of patriarchal evil.

Daly's subsequent work has sought to rename the self, the world, and ultimate reality in movement-language that reflects her voyage into what she calls "the Realm of Wild Reality."[117] She declares that really moving beyond God the father "means Living the process of participation in Powers of Be-ing. Elementally Metaphoric words and the actions they encourage and reflect are signals of these Powers. They are Metamorphic, shifting the shapes of space and time, rearranging energy patterns, breaking through and relocating boundaries."[118] Daly spins new "Be-witching" words to free women in revolt from patriarchal space and consciousness: "Wicked Websters declare that women and words have served the fathers' sentences long enough. We ride the rhythms of Racing Rage, freeing words. Like birds uncaged, these soundings rush and soar, seeking sister-vibrations. Wicked women, when heard, sound the signal that Tidal Time has come." Wording thus becomes a kind of "Witches' Hammer" that "Revolting Hags" use to smash patriarchy: "We do not use words; we Muse words. Metapatterning women and words have magical powers, opening doorways of memories, transforming spaces and times. Rhymes, alliterations, alteration of senses—all aid in the breaking of fatherland's fences."[119]

A more exalted view of language as the site of transformation would be hard to find. In the name of her passionate warning that "assimilation is deadly," Daly insists that female Spirit cannot be liberated from its bondage to patriarchy without a new "Wicked Grammar" that sparks and reflects the "e-motional" potency and Unfolding spiritual ecstasy of Lusty Wymyn. "Powerful old words whose Metaphoric force has been faded under the phallocratic rule include *Spinster, Webster, Weird, Hag, Witch, Sibyl, Muse,* and many Others, as well as

Goddess," she remarks. "The waning of such words' powers is part of the program of elimination of female powers."[120] Daly's separatist ideology assumes not only that "women and men inhabit different worlds," but that most women are "degraded caricatures of women" who need to be liberated from the self-loathing and fear instilled by patriarchy.[121] This imperative rules out "Christian feminism" even as a theoretical possibility. Since Christianity is inherently a conspiracy to freeze and imprison female Spirit, she reasons, so-called feminist priests are accomplices in the patriarchal enslavement of women, serving up dead symbols "to starving congregations of bamboozled believers."[122]

The deeply gnostic character of Daly's spiritual vision has often been noted. Ruether observes that in Daly's account, "the history of women becomes a trail of crucifixions, with males as the evil archons of an anticosmos where women are entrapped." Her project of remythologizing seeks to establish for radical feminists "an alternative land within their inner selves" that replicates the spiritual dualism of ancient gnosticism. The difference in this case is that feminist gnosticism is built "on the dualism of a transcendent spirit world of femaleness over against the deceitful anticosmos of masculinity," Ruether remarks.[123] Daly's further explorations and imaginative leaps into uncharted Cronespace have taken her deeply into the world of the occult. Her autobiographical *Outercourse: The Be-Dazzling Voyage* describes her voyage through the "four spiral Galaxies" and cites occult literature for support.[124]

In light of her prominence in feminist theology, Daly's journey from liberal feminism to radical feminism to postfeminist occultism presents a cautionary tale. At what point did a crucially important, emancipatory critique of Christian myth veer into a project of anti-intellectualism and witchcraft? Ruether points to Daly's stigmatizing separatism, which treats only feminist women as normative humanity and dehumanizes men as a class. This enemy-making of men and nonfeminist women makes Daly's feminism an example of the bigotry it claims to hate, Ruether implies: "One duplicates evil-making in the very effort to escape from it once and for all, by projecting it on the 'alien' group."[125] Other feminist critics, notably Audre Lord, have observed that Daly writes about women in a way that reduces all non-Western women of color to victims and predators.[126] Sheila Devaney notes that for all of her rhetoric about smashing Western culture, Daly's image of the emancipated woman is the autonomous, whole, self-defining being lionized by Western post-Enlightenment discourse.[127] Ellen Armour adds that this strategy binds the privileged Western liberated woman "to herself and others like her."[128] In her insistence on the essential sameness of women's condition and experience, Daly binds religious feminism to a reverse-image of the social evil she opposes.

Though there is some evidence that Daly has taken parts of Lord's critique to heart, she otherwise gives short shrift to her multiculturalist and poststructuralist critics. Her autobiography tells them to please shut up, adding: "You bore me, you gore me. You are killing me with your academented stupidity."[129] To her, the postmodern emphasis on cultural difference and the sociocultural construction of the self obscure the universal sameness and evil of patriarchy.

Feminism is about the liberation of the female subject from a singular evil world culture. From this standpoint, the postmodern emphasis on the instability of meaning and the eclipse of the subject appear to threaten the personal and social gains of modern feminism. With a more discriminating perspective than Daly's, but a similar concern over the loss of a generic female subject, Nancy Hartsock inquires, "Why is it that just at the moment when so many of us who have been silenced begin to demand the right to name ourselves, to act as subjects rather than objects of history, that just then the concept of subjecthood becomes problematic?"[130]

Poststructuralist Feminism

Fulkerson, Chopp, and other poststructuralists reply that the subject must be challenged on feminist grounds precisely because the generic pretensions of conventional feminist theory demean and exclude most women. By universalizing its own subject position, white academic feminism has tended to repeat the errors of patriarchy. Fulkerson explains, "By making available other portraits of women, their oppression, and their faith practices, womanist, Asian, African, *mujerista,* and lesbian feminist theologians display the partiality and specificity of feminist theology's subject—as white, Euro-American, heterosexual, middle class, and privileged." Moreover, there is no reason why feminist theology should thematize only the experiences of different kinds of academic feminists. Fulkerson proposes that feminist theology should be centered by its liberating commitment to the *other,* "a commitment that emerges out of a particular liberationist recognition of the fracture of gender oppression."[131] It is not possible to grasp the truth about "women's experience" or "oppression" outside the semiotic processes by which these realities have attained meaning, she cautions. All realities, including those most precious to feminism and Christianity, are socially signified, not natural. "Historical practices of attaching 'natural' meanings to women's bodies, white and African American alike, have allowed them to be subjected to uses perceived as natural to female reproductive organs or to 'racial' characteristics," she observes. "Challenging ostensibly natural [uncoded] entities also confronts ideological effects or imbalances in power that are supported by categories not subject to question."[132]

This does not necessarily mean that testimonials to experience are ruled out in poststructuralist feminist theology. Welch observes that a feminist appeal to experience—even one that excludes women who are different—can have the effect of freeing up the voices of previously silenced women, especially women of color.[133] Feminist recountings of experience often inspire others to reflect upon and express their own experiences. She argues that what is needed is an "ethic of conflict" that values and sustains ongoing discussions among various, often conflicting perspectives.[134] Chopp proposes that the appeal to women's experience should be valorized as one aspect or moment of feminist theologizing, so long as this appeal is understood in pragmatic (not ontological) terms. Building on Julia Kristeva's interrogation of the speaking subject, she contends that feminist invocations of experience can be generative and emancipating if they are understood to be historically particular, intimately bound up with historical communities, and marked by ambiguity, "expressing desires and wants she may not consciously recognize."[135]

This movement to privilege language over experience as the site of transformation is only in its beginning stage in feminist theology. Though they make considerable use of deconstructionist and poststructuralist criticism in laying out their approaches to myth, culture, and theology, poststructuralist feminists have given little attention to the implications of deconstructionist criticism for religious belief. They typically evade the question whether any kind of religious belief is possible without a metaphysics of presence. Welch repudiates the notion of divine transcendence altogether and implies that she takes no interest in the question of unbelief. She maintains without any acknowledgment of exceptions that the concept of a transcendent deity "serves to subvert rebellion and remove the imperative of responsibility for social change." Her commitment to liberation theology is not centered on the "God" of the liberationist movement, she explains, but on the movement's practices of resistance and solidarity. "I find an openness to many different understandings of truth in the women's movement and in some segments of the peace movement," she reports. "In sisterhood there is freedom from a self-securing that requires absolutizing one's perspective. In the Christian tradition, however, I find a pathological obsession with security, an obsession that impels the denial of difference (thus concern with heresy and essences), an obsession that leads to a blinding Christian triumphalism, an obsession that receives symbolic expression in the concept of the sovereignty of God."[136]

Fulkerson is not as politicized or as absolutely negative toward transcendence as Welch, but she also gives a liberationist reason for not justifying the faith claims that she invokes. "As a nonfoundationalist, I do not find the project of proving or defending the existence of God to be an interesting one, particularly for liberation theologies," she observes. "While I do not want to argue that poststructuralism is simply a principle of finitude or fallibility (it is not), I do think a poststructuralist account of discourse rules out the possibility of claims that can be validated somehow outside of communities and their languages." It follows for her that as the discourse of a particular kind of liberating community, feminist theology must dissociate its interests from the kinds of communities that question the existence of God or the intelligibility of Christian language. Fulkerson explains that she continues "to use theological commitments out of the conviction that the sign 'God,' like any other, is always invoked in a web of significations and embodied practices, such as academic criticism, worship, and social activism."[137] The sign "God" has meaning only within a particular web of other signifying practices. In feminist theology it acquires meaning only within a complex of practices lived out by liberating communities of resistance and solidarity. For these communities, the pertinent practices of solidarity, resistance, faithfulness, and hope assume God's existence. Like Latin American and African

American liberation theologies, feminist theology rightly understood therefore does not problematize the question of unbelief, but rather problematizes the pressing realities of dependence and oppression.[138]

Welch and Fulkerson present two ways by which feminist theology might appropriate deconstructionist and poststructuralist criticism without allowing these critical perspectives to invalidate the enterprise of theology itself. In the spirit of Foucault, Fulkerson asserts that "we have no access to the real outside of our power-laden constructions."[139] But the force of this epistemological ni-hilist principle applies also to secular poststructuralists who presume to judge the validity of Christian God-language. "Tradition-based belief in God already shapes human communities, including mine, and does so redemptively," Fulk-erson observes. "Just as the deconstructionist move is always deployed within existing structures, so a theological position only emerges within a discourse of belief; whatever destabilizing occurs can never produce the positive claim that there is no God."[140] To problematize knowledge in the manner of episte-mological nihilism is not necessarily to assert that there is no truth. As Fulker-son suggests, it is one thing for theologians to affirm that reality only becomes intelligible as discourse; it is another matter for theologians to adopt the post-structuralist dogma that there is no reality outside language. By giving up every essentializing definition of religious truth, the former affirmation opens up new possibilities for theology as a liberating discourse.[141] The latter claim negates theology nearly without remainder.

"I find that the truth of faith is like the resistance of the world: instances of this resistance as gracious and transforming are utterly inconsistent and un-predictable," Fulkerson remarks. She argues that if the kind of clear, linear, pro-gressive resistance imagined in the metanarratives of social gospel theology is no longer credible, at least the kind of fragmented, gracious resistance prac-ticed in today's liberation movements is a possibility. It is worth looking for. Borrowing David Toole's image, she proposes that the truth of faith is like the flash of a fish on a fisher's line. Religious truth is not something that one makes progress toward and attains, but something that occasionally surfaces from the depths of the world and then recedes. Toole remarks that "because we glimpse the flash of its passing and, at times, experience the power of its pull, the ac-tivity of living remains meaningful." This kind of experience is a form of gra-cious resistance, Fulkerson observes; it is real and unexpected, and constituted by silence, anxiety, and waiting. "The compulsion to say more in academics, to find another arena, that of an extracommunal subject position, violates this kind of truth," she contends.[142]

Remythologizing the World:
Sallie McFague

But is this enough? Does theology deserve to be taken seriously if it signi-fies nothing more than the evocation of a momentary flash of well-being?

Putting aside the ethical and socioeconomic aspects of the question, can theology even claim to be a discourse of religious truth and liberation if it makes no cognitive claims? The most prominent feminist advocate of a mythopoetic/metaphorical approach to theology argues that an affirmative answer is possible if theologians change the dominant metaphors through which they think theologically. Sallie McFague observes that in recent theology "much *deconstruction* of the traditional imagery has taken place, but little *construction*." This is a serious failing, she suggests, for if metaphor and concept are intimately bound up with each other in theology, it is imperative that theologians replace the outmoded and oppressive metaphors with which they work. Language is the site of transformation in theology, but only if it is reconstructed as liberating mythicity.

The alternatives to a reconfigured mythical theology are conservative retreat and thoroughgoing abstraction. The first approach commits Christianity to anachronistic models and therefore ghettoizes theology, she observes; the second approach negates all pictorial thinking and thus makes theology sterile. The reconstructed fictive theology that is needed would remythologize the relationship between God and the world. It would affirm that theology is a mostly fictional enterprise that elaborates key metaphors and models. Moreover, it would keep in mind that all theological concepts derive from metaphors and that all metaphors are ambiguous.[143]

Every metaphor contains an "is not" that denies any claim to identity in its assertions. McFague cautions that whenever it treats its grounding metaphors as immediate or immutable principles, theology degenerates into idolatry. "We will not relinquish our idolatry in religious language unless we are freed from the myth that in order for images to be true they must be literal," she warns.[144] At the same time, to say that good theology is a project of fictive remythologizing is not to say that "anything goes" in theology. "Some fictions are better than others, both for human habitation and as expressions of the gospel of Christian faith at a particular time," she explains. Today the great need in theology is to rename the relation of God to the world in a way that promotes life and flourishing.[145]

Though her theology is deeply feminist in its spirit and sensibility, McFague affirms that her religious purpose transcends the liberation of women to include concern with the condition of all humanity and the natural world. "Metaphorical theology is a postmodern, highly skeptical, heuristic enterprise, which claims that in order to be faithful to the God of its tradition—the God on the side of life and its fulfillment—we must try out new pictures that will bring the reality of God's love into the imaginations of the women and men of today," she asserts. Just as liberation theology has insisted that redemption includes social and political emancipation in the world, McFague urges that the purview of liberation theology must be further deprivatized "to include the well-being of all life."[146] As an example of the kind of life-affirming remythologizing that theology today requires, her work elaborates the models of God as mother, lover, and friend in the context of an image of the world as God's body.

She begins by delineating her relation to Derrida-style deconstruction. The deconstructionist emphasis on absence calls attention to the idolatrous tendency of religion to seek security through human constructions, she observes. Most religion is fueled by a childish nostalgia for presence. Religion typically offers dogmatic idols to "believers" as protection from their otherwise devouring inner emptiness and fear. McFague asserts, "The desire for full presence, whether in the form of nostalgia for the garden of Eden, or the quest for the historical Jesus, or the myth of God incarnate, is a denial of what we know as adults to be the case in human existence: such innocence, certainty, and absoluteness are not possible."[147] Deconstructionism names the sense or fear of absence that most of us actually feel most of the time. It points to the deep emptiness and uncertainty that all metaphors evoke, for according to deconstructive criticism, every metaphor is a sign that stands for another sign in a repetitive spiral of words with no beginning or end. McFague observes that if there is truly nothing outside the text, including neither author nor referent, then all words are inappropriate in an unending process of metaphoricity that has no canons of appropriateness.

She accepts most of the deconstructionist critique of the myth of real presence without accepting its nihilistic dogma, borrowed from Heidegger, that language is the prisonhouse of being without remainder.[148] Deconstructionism offers no help in judging which constructions are better than others; it acutely describes the uncertainty and emptiness of metaphor, but never deals with the *is* of metaphor. "I agree with the deconstructionists that all constructions are metaphorical and hence miss the mark," McFague observes. "I nevertheless disagree with them when they say that language (writing) is only about itself and that no construction is any better than any other. To claim that all constructions are metaphorical is to insist that one never experiences reality 'raw'; it does not follow from this, however, that there is nothing outside language. All that follows is that our access to reality is in every case mediated and hence partial and relative."[149]

The worthiness of any partial and relative theological position can be judged only by trying to live with it. Does it make sense? Does it speak with redemptive power to pressing current needs? "Theological constructions are 'houses' to live in for a while, with windows partly open and doors ajar; they become prisons when they no longer allow us to come and go, to add a room or take one away—or if necessary, to move out and build a new house," she remarks.[150]

Theological houses are built with models, which McFague describes as dominant metaphors that are both imagistic and conceptual. Models are metaphors with staying power which provide structures for ordering and understanding experience, systematizing one area in terms of another. It is through the construction of models that the images of primary religious discourse (especially myth) and the concepts of secondary theological abstraction are brought together, she observes.[151] Because models are closer than abstract theological and philosophical concepts to the pictorial language of myth that fuels

Christianity, McFague argues that they are less susceptible to absolutism and literalism than most abstract theological systems. For the same reason, they are less likely to fall into idolatry or irrelevance. This theme distinguishes McFague's position from other constructivist theologies, such as those of Paul Tillich and Gordon Kaufman, that are otherwise similar to hers.[152] Her emphasis on fictive metaphoricity makes her theology distinctively experimental, image-oriented, myth-creative, and pluralistic. Metaphorical theology is heuristic, she explains; it plays freely with various possibilities and is always open to others. It welcomes many models of God and does not seek the appearance of a finished system.

She proposes that one promising way to remythologize the gospel for our time is to think of the world as God's body: "If we experiment with this metaphor, it becomes obvious that royalist, triumphalist images for God— God as king, lord, ruler, patriarch—will be inappropriate. Other metaphors, suggesting mutuality, interdependence, caring, and responsiveness, will be needed." McFague cautions that this is a project of theological imagination. To imagine the world as God's body is not necessarily to claim that the world *is* God's body or even that God is present to human experience in the world. "Those things we do not know; all that resurrection faith can do is imagine the most significant ways to speak of God's presence in one's own time," she contends. "And the metaphor of the world as God's body presents itself as a promising candidate."[153]

If the world is imagined as the sacramental self-expression of divine reality, certain metaphors that express experiences of nurture, cooperation, support, and mutuality become more appropriate for Christian theism than the royalist imagery of God as king and sovereign lord. When God is no longer imagined as a power ruling over the world, the seemingly novel images of God as mother, lover, and friend lose their strangeness. McFague acknowledges her kinship to earlier theological traditions of Christian mysticism, panentheism, and process theology, and she reports that Catholics and Anglicans tend to find her sacramental vision more compelling than do Word-oriented Protestants.[154] The purpose of her work is not merely to feminize earlier traditions of sacramental panentheism or process metaphysics, however, but to remythologize the gospel faith "as a destabilizing, inclusive, nonhierarchical vision of fulfillment for all of creation."[155]

The primary metaphors for most classical and modern Christian theologies have been drawn from the political arena. Accordingly, most forms of Christian ethics have been preoccupied with the question of how human life should be governed. McFague proposes that a postmodern Christian ecotheology should be more concerned with the question of how human beings are able to sustain life through love. Her images for divine and human love are drawn from the loving relationships of parent to child, lover to beloved, and friend to friend. Like the panentheist and process traditions that she draws upon, she emphasizes God's indwelling immanence in the world without claiming that God's body is limited to the world. "God is not a solitary deity distant from and unrelated to the world, nor a God submerged into the world and undifferentiated from it," she explains. "Rather, God as mother, lover and friend of the world as God's body is both transcendent to the world (even as we are transcendent to our bodies) and profoundly immanent in the world (even as we are at one with our bodies)."[156]

Not all of her pieces fit together even as heuristic metaphors; the notion of God as the mother of her own body makes little sense of any kind. Through the play of her most compelling metaphors, however, McFague opens up new ways of understanding the world as "our meeting place with God." Her metaphors seek to conceive God's transcendence in an immanental or "worldly" mode. If we see the world as God's body, she urges, we might begin to apprehend the world again as sacred space and movement: "God's immanence, then, being universal, undergirds a sensibility that is open to the world, both to other people and to other forms of life, as the way one meets God."[157]

McFague's later work elaborates what it means to perceive and confess that the world is our meeting place with God. She rejects all of the God/world, self/world, nature/history, and male/female dualisms on which traditional Christian theism has based its denigration of the natural world and the female sex.[158] She argues for an organic model of embodiment in which Christian theology thinks and acts "as if bodies matter." Her remythologization of the God-world relation suggests "that God is closer to us than we are to ourselves, for God is the breath or spirit that gives life to the billions of different bodies that make up God's body."[159] But God is also the power and goal of life on whom creation depends, she affirms. As indwelling immanence, God is the breath of each and every creature; as transcendent power, God is the energy that empowers creation.

Like Teilhard de Chardin, McFague thus presents a remythologization of Christianity that resacralizes the natural order.[160] Her fictive theology of nature functions ultimately as a new myth in which God is imagined to be affected by *whatever* happens in the world. "The body of God, shaped by the Christic paradigm, is also the cosmic Christ—the loving, compassionate God on the side of those who suffer, especially the vulnerable and excluded," she remarks. "All are included, not only in their liberation and healing, but also in their defeat and despair." As the life-giving lover whose presence extends to all life forms in the world, God is not only liberating and healing, but fellow-suffering. Christ is the image of the invisible God as fellow-suffering love and transcendent life. In McFague's words, "The resurrected Christ is the cosmic Christ, the Christ freed from the body of Jesus of Nazareth, to be present in and to all bodies."[161]

Having declared in her earlier writings that she cannot accept the doctrine of the incarnation of Christ, McFague has thus been moved by the remythologizing spirit of her project to reinterpret Christ as the paradigmatic sacrament of God.[162] She still believes that the incarnation must be minimized in relation to Jesus of Nazareth, but her theology of embodiment maximizes the incarnation in relation to the cosmos. Strauss was wrong only in limiting the incarnation to humanity. The power of God is incarnate throughout the world in all of our efforts to heal the world and let the oppressed go free. We are not alone when we struggle for the healing and liberation of oppressed bodies, she argues: "And the excluded and outcast bodies for which we fought belong in and are comforted by the cosmic Christ, the body of God in the Christic paradigm."[163]

Just as liberal theology sought to reconcile Christianity to the reductionistic, atomistic determinism of modern science, McFague's metaphorical theology seeks to relate a new understanding of Christianity to the relational, interdependent, organismic worldview of postmodern science.[164] Where liberal theology sought to give religious meaning to a forward-moving, teleological understanding of the world, her ecofeminism seeks to celebrate and care for a world that is "complex, diverse [and] intricate beyond our wildest imaginations." It eschews the liberal preoccupation with purpose and conceptual synthesis in favor of a postmodern mode of destabilizing, highly metaphorical, pluralistic discourse. It thinks of creation not as a machine, but as an unpredictable, ongoing work of art. It rejects the modern "layer-cake" view of science in favor of the postmodern view that all observation is theory-laden.[165]

McFague's theology seeks not to negate or transcend Christian myth, but to transform it into a life-affirming vision of "sympathetic inclusiveness" and flourishing. It asserts that the real problem of Christian myth is not that Christianity is mythical, but that much of its mythical content has proven harmful to women and the natural world. "Remythologizing involves both appreciation and understanding; it is a form of embodied thought combining image and concept that calls forth both a feeling and a thinking response," she remarks.[166] If Christian theology is to have a worthy future, it must offer a new myth of healing, relationality and embodiment that counters the bad myth of sovereignty and domination sustained by the perpetrators of the worldwide ecological crisis—ourselves.

Postmodernism is often viewed as the advent of Nietzsche's dystopia, the cultural moment when the death of God is not only generally suspected, but taken for granted. The deconstructionist polemic against the myth of presence takes for granted that religious language has no referent. It assumes that religious appeals to spiritual experience are forms of false naming that cover the abyss in human existence with bad faith. But despite the biases and presumptions of its most heralded proponents, postmodernism is a disruptive, decentering cultural force that creates a more congenial intellectual climate for theology than ever existed under modernity. The postmodern critique of Enlightenment foundationalism and universalism opens a space for religious discourse that modern rationalism excluded. If all observation is theory-laden and there are no raw data on which empirical disciplines might base their discourses, the positivist claim of superiority over other ways of knowing is discredited. If all knowledge is socially constructed, partial, and open to unending interpretation, theological claims are hardly disadvantaged by their mythical character. Many academic disciplines today are only beginning to acknowledge that their knowledge is constructed and perspectival. The fact that theologians have struggled for the past two centuries to deal with the relativity of their discipline makes theology better prepared than some disciplines to function in a postmodern environment.

A Normative Role for Myth?

But how should theologians view the normative role of myth in theology? Even in a postmodern situation, this issue is too fundamental to leave unsettled. If Tillich, Niebuhr, Gilkey, McFague, and the Jungians are right that myth is intrinsic to theology, it follows that theologians should use mythical language normatively in as creative and compelling a manner as possible. If, on the other hand, theological liberalism and its spiritual descendants are right that theology can and must transcend myth if it wants to make credible cognitive claims, then a thoroughgoing program of demythologizing is necessary for theology and for faith. This is not to suggest that the question plays out as a choice between remythologizing and demythologizing. Most remythologizers assume a fair amount of demythologizing in laying out their constructive positions; Tillich, Niebuhr, Gilkey, and McFague take for granted that much of the biblical narrative must be demythologized before it is usable for theology. The either/or is not between remythologizing and demythologizing, but between those who assign a normative role to myth in theology and those who reject such a role for it. Is there a way to mediate this disagreement?

Though she never directly addresses the question, McFague's theology presents the best candidate for a middle ground in the dispute over myth, because her project seeks to mediate the deeper disagreement over transcendence that drives much (though not all) of the modern theological debate about myth. The categorical difference between Tillich/Gilkey and Cobb/Ogden over myth is a function of their fundamental perceptions of divine transcendence. Neither position thinks of divine transcendence as God's remoteness or spatial distance from the world. For Tillich/Gilkey, transcendence refers to God's creative power to overcome the threat of nonbeing. God is transcendent not as an hypostatized being outside of being or becoming, but as the ground or power of being. For Cobb/Ogden, however, transcendence refers to God's inexhaustibility, not to God's personal power over nonbeing. For process theology God is not an exception to becoming, but is rather the inexhaustible society of events within becoming that lures its subjects to make healthy, other-regarding choices.

The God of process theology inexhaustably creates new possibilities to choose life, but always in a way that does not coerce whatever choice is made. The actualizations of all of the particular choices that are made are taken into the being of God, into what Whitehead called God's "consequent" nature, which is shaped through interrelation with self-actualizing entities.[167] Whiteheadian metaphysics thus conceives divine transcendence as one of the categories of immanence on the model of human immanence. Just as human beings are immanent in our bodies, yet also transcend our bodies through the power of self-consciousness, so also God is thought to be immanent in the universe while somehow becoming more than the universe through the power of God's self-conscious focus upon it.[168]

Wilbur Urban explains the upshot of the difference between these conflicting religious perceptions. The crucial question is whether there is more in becoming than in that which becomes. This is an either/or question, he observes. If there is really more in becoming than in that which becomes, then process is the last word. But if there is more in that which becomes, "then this 'more' must come from participation in that which does not become—something that is there 'from the foundation of the world.'"[169] The lack of a logical middle ground between these possibilities presents theology with a fundamental choice. Should divine transcendence be conceived as God's unfailing inexhaustibility or as God's power over nonbeing? Put differently, should God's transcendence be interpreted as an ultimate exemplification of the categories of immanence, or should it be understood as the ultimate ground of all categories? Most important, should theology base its conceptualization of divine transcendence upon some experience of transcendent ultimacy or upon the judgment that no experience of the sacred is real?

If divine transcendence is understood as God's creative power to overcome nonbeing, and if this conception is supported by some appeal to an experience of God as the power or ultimate ground of being, then myth becomes indispensable to theology. Gilkey's theology is paradigmatic of this option. If transcendence is reduced to an exhaustively immanent meaning and the lack of sacred presence is affirmed as a normative principle, however, then theology has no need of myth. Christianity can make sense only as a form of speculative philosophy.

This fundamental difference in religious perception has created an impasse in theology for most of the past century. Tyron Inbody argues that the crucial differences between these positions cannot be resolved because they rest upon contrasting absolute presuppositions that cannot be questioned. In his book, *An Essay on Metaphysics,* R. G. Collingwood defined metaphysics as the science of absolute presuppositions, or alternately, as the attempt "to find out what absolute presuppositions have been made by this or that person or group of persons, on this or that occasion or group of occasions, in the course of this or that piece of thinking." A relative presupposition is subject to judgment and correction, he explained; it stands relatively "to one question as its presupposition and relatively to another question as its answer." But an absolute presupposition is a fundamental nonpropositional assumption that is not subject to judgment, verification, or correction. Relative to all questions to which it is related, it stands as a presupposition and never as an answer. Absolute presuppositions are the nonpropositional intuitions about reality that we bring to any discussion of contestable claims or views.[170]

These are the kinds of differences that drive the theological debate over myth. For most of the past century theological perspectives on the normative role of myth in theology have been shaped by the absolute presuppositions of theologians regarding the nature of divine transcendence. Among those who practice normative theology, the debate over the normative role of myth in theology has been driven by differences in fundamental religious perception that do not submit to critical analysis. As Inbody observes, the myth question has reached an impasse that no methodological innovation can touch.

What could mediate this disagreement is an alternative set of absolute and relative presuppositions. Gilkey's perspective speaks the language of myth and the sacred while appropriating much of the conceptuality of process theology, but his theological blend maintains the classical notion of transcendence as power over nonbeing. Though she never directly addresses the issue, it is McFague who mixes the metaphorical and panentheist perspectives in a way that remythologizes divine transcendence. Her position comes the closest to mediating the split between the two dominant theological orientations. "When we begin to think of ourselves—and of God—in an ecological context, everything changes," she observes. "To think of ourselves, our nature, and our role in the scheme of things from a cosmic, planetary perspective and to think of God as the One who is in, with, and under the entire process of the universe removes us from a narrow psychological or broader political viewpoint."[171]

McFague recognizes that there is nothing novel about the cosmological perspective, which has a distinguished history in Western theology and, more prominently, in Eastern Orthodoxy. Her proposal is that the ancient Christian vision of the universe as God's domain might help to reawaken a myth-creative sense of the sacred among people who reject or are left cold by the language of blood atonement and power-over theism. By thinking of God as the empowering, ongoing breath of life within all creation, contemporary people might recover the intuition expressed by Gerard Manley Hopkins that "the world is charged with the grandeur of God." Immanence and presence go together; process theology is true not as a religious philosophy that compensates for the lack of sacred presence, but as a religious view of the universe that looks for God in the differences, variety, and complexity of all that is known and unknown. "Divine transcendence need not mean God's external sovereignty over the world," McFague remarks. "A procreative-emanationist model of creation focuses our attention on a transcendent immanence, or an immanental transcendence. That is, it keeps our eyes on what we can see and touch and know: the universe as God's body with God's spirit as its enlivening breath is the place that we turn to learn of *both* transcendence and immanence."[172]

In Western Christianity transcendence has mainly meant external sovereignty, but it can also refer to that which is surpassing, excelling, or extraordinary. McFague urges that if we imagine the universe as God's body, we should look for divine transcendence not apart from the material universe, but in all that is surpassing, excelling, or extraordinary. The universe itself thus offers an embodied way to mythologize divine transcendence. McFague's idea of im-

Doctrien
+

manental transcendence will not satisfy anyone—including the present author—for whom the fundamental religious question is whether God has power
over being and nonbeing. She does not claim that there is more in becoming
than that which becomes. Her remythologization of Christianity, however,
comes closer than any other theology to mediating the disagreement over absolute presuppositions that has divided modern theology. The spirit of postmodernism is notoriously fragmenting, subversive, secular, and destabilizing,
but in the hands of its religious visionaries, it yields new myths of wholeness
and sacred presence.

6

Dialectics of Word and Spirit: Christ as True Myth

Perhaps the most significant realization to come upon me while writing this book was that nearly all of the theologies I was describing appealed to me in some way as plausible religious perspectives. This realization was a bit unsettling as I worked with and felt the evocative appeal of process theology, Jungian spirituality, and McFague's immanental ecofeminism. I believe that the chief theorists of these perspectives are wrong to give up the notion of God as transcendent holy mystery. If God is not free from us in some way that makes God's power transcend the world, God cannot be free for us in our suffering and mortality. God cannot sustain life beyond death if God's transcendence does not include power over nonbeing. I believe that the theorists of modern immanental theologies are wrong, therefore, to speak of God as something less than the triune mystery who has power over the void.

The immanentalist move, however, is made in the name of ethical and spiritual concerns that I share. Even in the face of fundamental religious disagreement, I greatly respect and feel attracted to the process, Jungian, and ecofeminist theologies, just as I admire various other perspectives (such as Bultmann's myth-negating existentialism) with which I disagree. All of the major theological perspectives discussed in this study contain some distinctive strength that should not be lost to Christianity. Modern immanental theologies offer new ways to recover and reconfigure a sense of sacred relation to the whole. In different ways they evoke an awareness of the cosmic context that makes much of mainstream Protestantism seem provincial by comparison. In different ways they express powerful moral critiques of the self-preoccupied spiritualities that mainstream traditions have engendered. Process theology, Jungianism, and ecofeminism all express and develop important religious themes that are missing or skewed in conservative, liberal, and neoorthodox theologies.

It is because I cherish the open, dialogical spirit of modern theology at its best that this study gives special attention to Langdon Gilkey's theologizing. More than any Christian thinker of the past half-century, he appropriates and builds upon most of the major movements of modern theology. Gilkey identifies with and reinterprets the liberal and neoorthodox traditions; he appropriates process thought and eschatological theology without wholly adopting these perspectives; he rethinks the relation of theological reasoning to science in the light of postmodern critiques of all forms of epistemological foundationalism; he pursues the postmodern project of interreligious dialogue without giving up his Christian center. As an interpreter of the language and meaning of Christian myth, he has pioneered a post–neoorthodox liberalism that brings the Niebuhr/Tillich approach to myth into a theological tradition that has generally sought to "overcome" or transcend mythical reason.

Gilkey's work teaches the value of addressing current moral, religious, and political problems by thinking through the traditions of classical—and especially modern—Christian theology. To a postmodern theological generation that prizes novelty and thrives on fads, he has offered theological rethinking that is always on the cutting edge of religious and intellectual concern but that also persistently relates itself to the major traditions of modern Christian thought. He shows that Christian theology can and must keep its religious center while seeking truth from other religious traditions. His work is thus particularly instructive to those who recognize not only their hunger for myth, but also their desire for religious truth in a world of many gods.

But even Gilkey has failed to listen to certain voices that could have enriched his own. His Niebuhrian sense of paradox and tragedy made him quick to write off most liberation theology as utopian. His early fixation on Jürgen Moltmann's futurism caused him to read Moltmann as a political utopian and pure eschatologist long after Moltmann corrected these misreadings. His appropriation of feminist theology was slight at best. Ironically, after giving up the hope that neoorthodoxy could become a genuine third way in theology, he also overlooked some of the creative possibilities that this tradition bears for theology in a postmodern context. Though Gilkey read a fair amount of Barth's theology after committing himself to a novel form of theological liberalism, he routinely categorized Barth as the apostle of an untenable "neoorthodox revelationism." Though armed with ample evidence of Barth's narrowness, this fundamental judgment missed the relevance of his theology to a postmodern theological consciousness.

Barth's narrowness was often prodigious. He was spiritually tone deaf to any manifestation of the Spirit outside the witness of preaching and scripture. With regard to gender, though he assured that men are not superior to women in any way, he claimed that men are "first in sequence" in the divine order and thus bear a "primacy of service" before God.[1] Moreover, his later dogmatic work stifled the rhetorical dialectics and the polemic against religion that gave his early work its spiritual power. For all of his warnings about the narrowness and hubris of theological systems, his own dogmatic theology took on the appearance of a massive new Scholasticism. He claimed not to want followers, but blasted even close followers when they dissented from any of his positions. He took little interest in other disciplines and no interest at all in other religions.

Though he claimed to accept the legitimacy and necessity of critical biblical scholarship, he made practically no use of it.[2] Though he emphasized the freedom of the Word in explicating his methodology, Barth's insistence on correct doctrine often appeared even to his followers to militate against any positive regard for theological freedom, difference, or diversity.

It is on the latter score, however—his supposedly weakest point—that Barth's theology actually speaks most pertinently to a postmodern consciousness.[3] Long after he relinquished the expressionist tropes of his "crisis theology" period, his theology remained a rhetoric of freedom. Barth refused to reduce God to one element of a system, he rejected every kind of philosophical foundationalism, and his theology blended too many themes to be reducible to any single theme. Though he unfortunately retained some of the sexist "orders of creation" conceptuality of classical Protestantism, his religious vision was nonetheless distinctively pluralistic and discursively open-ended. He insisted that Christian theology can be healthy and free only if it remains open to a multiplicity of philosophies, worldviews, and forms of language. Neither is there any hierarchy among theological topics, he argued; there is no reason why a dogmatics should not begin with the Holy Spirit or salvation or eschatology: "There is only one truth, one reality, but different views, different aspects: just like the sun shines on different places."[4]

Barth's arguments against the colonization of theology by philosophy or any other cultural discourse prefigured the critique of totalizing discourse presented in contemporary poststructuralist criticism without the nihilist presumption that there is no ground of truth. Feminist poststructuralists such as Luce Iragaray and Julia Kristeva argue that the colonizing effect of any philosophical system preempts even the possibility that true difference might be recognized.[5] Barth's polemic against theological modernism anticipated the postmodern critique of philosophical foundationalism in this respect. He emphatically rejected the foundationalist claim that philosophy or social science can provide secure universal knowledge. By insisting so strenuously upon the transcendence and integrity of the divine object, he tried to liberate theology from its bondage to philosophy, bourgeois culture, and church tradition. He perceived the bankruptcy of modernism while most theologians were seeking to accommodate theology to it. Though his "crisis theology" writings made the point with greater spiritual force, he perceived the importance of remaining mindful that the God of Christian faith negates and transcends Christian theism. By refusing to defend God with arguments that reduced God to the logic of a system, he lifted up to modern Christianity the ineffable mystery, hiddenness, ever-graciousness, and glory of the divine source of revelation.

My case for a postmodern dialectic of Word and Spirit that develops theological moves initiated by Barth, postliberal narrative theology, and other sources must be reserved for a later work, but the defining features of this perspective can be noted briefly. Modern theology has been nearly united in its resolve to determine the meaningfulness of Christianity on rational or other grounds that are independent of the narrated Word of Christ. Put differently, as Hans Frei often observed, theological modernism has been defined by its fundamental assumption that theologians are obliged to adapt Christianity to the regnant or best available worldview. This is exactly the assumption that Barth sought to overturn in his debates with Harnack, Bultmann, and other modernizers. He countered that theology should not be in the business of endorsing worldviews or any independent theory of existence. Rather than commit itself to any particular worldview, he argued, Christian theology should use or appropriate as many worldviews and forms of language as are necessary to explicate the truth of God's Word. Just as theology should not privilege literal meaning over the language of narrative, paradox, irony, and dialectic, neither should theology commit itself to the enervating task of adopting and then discarding one worldview after another. A healthy pluralism in philosophy and rhetorical forms is needed if theology is to be free to do its work, which is to locate the event of correspondence between human word and divine truth.[6]

Barth did not deny that there are myths and even outright fairy tales in the materials out of which some of the biblical narratives were constructed. Though he preferred to speak of biblical "saga" rather than "myth" in order to distinguish biblical myth from the monist mythologies of other religions and philosophies, he urged that by either name, the "mythical" aspects of scripture should not be regarded as dispensable for contemporary theology.[7] The demythologizers unfairly demeaned the biblical worldview in their attempts to adapt Christianity to a modern worldview, he contended: "We ought not to overlook the fact that this particular world-view contained a number of features which the primitive community used cautiously but quite rightly in its witness to Jesus Christ." Moreover, these "mythical" features remain indispensable to Christian proclamation. "We have every reason to make use of 'mythical' language in certain connexions," Barth insisted. "And there is no need for us to have a guilty conscience about it, for if we went to extremes in demythologising, it would be quite impossible to bear witness to Jesus Christ at all."[8]

This response to Bultmann marked the crucial difference between Barth and the demythologizers. It also marked the crucial difference between Barth and his Biblical Theology followers. Barth's call for a new kind of critical biblical scholarship helped to inspire the Biblical Theology movement, which called a halt to the deconstructive tendency in biblical criticism to tear apart the biblical text without any recognition of its character as sacred scripture. The movement answered Barth's call for a kind of biblical scholarship that respected the canonical integrity of the biblical text.[9] It also heightened his insistence on the history-oriented distinctiveness and antimythical character of biblical faith. Biblical Theology became a powerful movement on the strength of the latter themes especially, but its emphasis on these themes exposed the movement to devastating criticism. At the height of its influence in the mid-1950s, the movement exaggerated the distinctiveness of Hebrew religion and failed to justify its defining claims about the "mighty acts of God" in biblical history. It relied heavily upon a notion of "biblical history" that was foreign to scripture itself. Gilkey's pointed questions about what God had actually done in the exodus events were remarkably deflating for a movement that had dominated biblical studies for more than a decade. Biblical Theology was weakened by its hubris in claiming a historical foundation that it neither possessed nor should have desired. It would have done better to invest its faith in the Spirit-illuminated Word that subverts and transcends all historical categories and theological themes, including the domesticated theme of "theology as recital." Put differently, Biblical Theology would have done better to embrace the implications of Barth's argument that "we have every reason to make use of 'mythical' language in certain connexions."

Biblical Theology created a form of neoorthodoxy that proposed to base Christian claims on a purportedly secure historical record. Against all such forms of neoorthodox, liberal, and history of religions foundationalism, Barth insisted that to hear scriptural narrative as God's Word has nothing necessarily to do with defending its historical character or some putative historical element within it. The notion that biblical narratives must be historical in some sense in order to convey God's truth is a disastrous inheritance of both theological liberalism and orthodoxy, he contended: "Both Liberalism and orthodoxy are children of the same insipid spirit, and it is useless to follow them." There is no good reason "why the Bible as the true witness of the Word of God should always have to speak 'historically' and not be allowed also to speak in the form of saga."[10]

Barth read the biblical creation stories as pure sagas because they are "intuitive and poetic pictures" of reality that are nonhistorical and prehistorical in a distinctively pure sense. Scripture otherwise contains few examples of either pure saga or pure (historical) history, he judged. Most of the Bible mixes saga and history so thoroughly together that it is impossible to definitely distinguish one from another. As the true witness of God's Word, scripture is obliged to speak in the form of saga "precisely because its object and origin are what they are, i.e., not just 'historical' but also frankly 'non-historical.'" Just as the Word is never contained or exhausted by history, he explained, the medium of God's Word is never merely historical, either. The Bible would not be scripture if it did not absorb the nonhistorical element into its witness, "and if it did not usually do it by mingling the two elements." One does not look for revelation only in the historical element that may or may not be possible to disentangle from a particular narrative.[11]

Barth distinguished pagan myth from biblical saga by identifying "genuine myth" with monist pictures of the One and All. Pagan myth knows only the single reality of a sacred cosmos that includes humanity, he explained. It may speak of God or gods, but it always understands the divine as a mere agent or agents within the economy of a single consuming reality. In the biblical witness, however, God is a sovereign creator who is distinct from the creature and who acts in history. Scripture repudiates the pagan view of humanity and its cosmos as self-moved and self-resting. Scripture does not only *use* narrative, as pagan mythology does, but is *itself* narrative through and through. It does not teach a philosophical worldview, like philosophy or myth, for what it says can be said only as narrative.[12] In his amplification of Barth's case for a narrativist understanding of Christian claims, Hans Frei explained that the narratives of scripture are not secondary illustrations of fundamental biblical doctrines or mythic truths or anything else. The gospel story is itself the basis and means by which doctrines are formulated. The gospel affirmation that "the Word became flesh" is not an independent or logically prior proposition, but the center of the gospel *story* through which Christ is made present to the story-shaped Christian community.[13]

Barth's insistence that scriptural narrative is myth-negating was not altogether convincing. By restricting myth to monist pictures of the One and All, he sought to establish that biblical faith is not "mythical" in the precise sense of the term even when it incorporates plainly mythical elements. In the service of his commitment to maintaining the priority of the narrated Word of Christ, he reduced all religious myth to only one kind of myth, taking no account of exceptions to his schematism nor to the problems posed by dying-god mythologies such as Mithraism that resemble Christianity. Some of his followers made similar moves for "Barthian" reasons. Frei acknowledged that on the historical level Christianity appears to be quite similar to several dying-god mythologies that were prevalent in the ancient Mediterranean world during the birth of Christianity, but for this very reason, he declared, "I shall not attempt to evaluate the *historical* reliability of the Gospel story of Jesus or argue the unique truth of the story on grounds of a true, factual 'kerygma' in it." It is only in its character as a story that theologians should seek to discern the meaning of Christianity, he argued. Mythology sacralizes religious symbols, but in the gospel story Jesus insists on the unreplaceable uniqueness of his person and mission. He does not symbolize any mythical type or theme, but is presented as self-focused and unsubstitutable. The gospel narrative as a genre is therefore antimythical, Frei contended, whatever similarities Christianity as a historical phenomenon may bear to any mythical tradition.[14]

This argument shares with Barth a certain evasiveness with regard to the relationship of Christianity to critical history. It defines myth by a single exclusive factor and simply brackets off the problem of the historical parallels between Christianity and other ancient Mediterranean religions. It rules out the very question of how to account for these parallels as a concern of Christian theology. I believe that this is not the only possible option for the kind of new neoorthodoxy that Frei pioneered. Frei assumed that the gospel story should be read either as an illustration of myth or as a narrative refutation of mythical speech. In taking from Barth the principle that theology should hold fast to the priority of Christ's narrated presence in the Word, he made a compelling case against every form of the strategy that makes the gospel an illustration of mythic truth or process metaphysics or any other independent criterion. Christian theology uses, but must never be subservient to, any form of philosophy, myth, or critical methodology, including historical criticism.[15]

Barth's assertion of this theme broke apart the modern preoccupation with ascertaining the methodological limits of truth. If truth is grace, it cannot be known through any method except grace. The force of this truism in Barth's thinking moved him (and many of his followers) to promote a rather contrived and reductionist definition of myth, but it also moved him to liberate theology from its dependence on philosophy and its vulnerability to demythologizing criticism. His entire dogmatic project anticipated the thesis of Gadamerian hermeneutical theory that modern philosophy has truncated the limits of truth in its subservience to method.[16] With powerful religious force he protested against the totalizing implications of all claims to methodological neutrality, epistemological foundationalism, and philosophical preunderstanding. The interpreter has no chance of hearing a new word if she brings her own preunderstanding to the text as a final norm, he cautioned. The Word does not seek to be mastered by us in order to be understood by us. It seeks rather to lay hold of us in our openness to its voice: "It wants to be evaluated in its relation to what is said in it when this has been spoken to us and made itself intelligible to us." Our understanding of the Spirit-illuminated Word cannot arise from our preunderstanding of it, but only from the "mystery of the sovereign freedom of the substance," the subject matter, which invites us through human words and the movement of the Spirit to "investigate the humanity of the word by which it is told."[17]

Barth's alternative implied a methodological pluralism, not an impossible blank slate. He did not dispute the need for theology to use philosophy or hermeneutical theory; he disputed only that theology should sanction or presuppose any "fixed canon of possibility, truth and importance."[18] A priori commitments are not open to revision or relinquishment. It was therefore for the sake of saving theology from the bondage of a closed system that Barth opted for a pluralistic and eclectic approach to philosophy. His theological method in this regard was a form of ad hoc minimalism. "If we do not commit ourselves to any specific philosophy we will not need totally or finally to fear any philosophy," he remarked.[19] His primary rule of interpretation was that "a text can be read and expounded only with reference to and in light of its theme."[20] Sacra Scriptura sui ipsius interpres. For him this meant that the authority claimed by the text (or by the person of whom it speaks) must ultimately be self-authenticating. To appeal to any further authority to distinguish between text and theme is to set aside the priority of the Spirit-illuminated Word.

Moreover, this process of authentication does not come upon individuals in isolation or abstraction from the church, for the Word discloses itself through the church's canonical scripture and in its proclamation. Barth's doctrine of the threefold Word implied simultaneously the indissoluble unity of the Word with the texts, tradition, and present life of the church, but also the necessity of always distinguishing between the Word and the text, the text and the community, and the present creeds and future possibilities. Because human beings are immersed in that which is transient, relative, and passing, it is always a mistake to identify the promise of the church's message with the questionable possibilities emerging out of the historical process. The gospel conveys the radically new possibilities of God, which are fallibly understood in the present, which stand on the borderline of human achievements, and which become evident precisely in the negation of these achievements.

Christianity is forward-looking in its faithfulness to an eschatological Word that relativizes all historical possibilities and achievements. Though his later theology expressed the point more gently, and less one-sidedly, Barth never retracted his early theme that only an eschatological Christianity can be faithful to Christ. The Spirit of Christ is the power of the future and ground of all redemptive possibility. It followed that "Spirit which does not at every moment point from death to the new life is not the Holy Spirit."[21] The eschatological Word is enough. It is never an object of perception or cognition, but can only be believed. The Word is different from all other objects because it gives itself. Christianity either lives faithfully by this life-renewing Spirit of Christ, or it resorts to sickly religious substitutes. Barth's list of poor substitutes included not only philosophy and myth, but every form of apologetics, natural theology, and ritual practice.[22]

The intricacies of his arguments on this score and the problems with them must be reserved for a later work. I believe that in the process of making a powerful and convincing case against the apologetic procedure of appealing to reasons prior to faith, Barth lurched to an extreme position that failed to do justice to the apologetic aspects of theology done as "faith seeking understanding." In the case of the theme of the present work, a similar tendency, though not as extreme, showed forth in his work and in Frei's. Barth's concern to refute the variable notion of Christianity as an illustration of mythic truth moved him to set Christianity against an artificial and reductionist conception of myth. Though he acknowledged that scripture contains mythical elements even in his sense of the term, he defined myth in essentially anti-Christian terms. It is doubtful that he ever would have used the term in a positive sense if Bultmann's demythologizing had not driven him to it. The seed of a more promising approach to Christian myth was contained in his rejoinder to Bultmann, however. There is no reason why the gospel cannot be mythical and true. There is no compelling reason for Christian theologians to oversell the distinctiveness or antimythical character of Christianity, for the gospel uses and is an example of mythical speech. As Barth told Bultmann, "there is no need for us to have a guilty conscience" about recognizing *and proclaiming* the gospel in all of its mythical character, for if all of the myth in the gospel were removed, it would be impossible to witness to Christ. Whether it is called myth or saga, mythical speech is intrinsic to Christianity. If Christianity is true, it is true as true myth.

One Christian thinker who grasped this point with particular insight was C. S. Lewis. Compared to Barth, Lewis's understanding of the history and problems of theology was slight, even simplistic. Despite his lack of theological training, however, his religious writings were marked by a keenly perceptive and realistic sense of the mythical character of Christianity that eluded Barth. His stature as an influential Christian apologist owes much to the fact that he approached the myth question with greater openness and discernment than most theologians. As a young Oxford classicist, Lewis moved from determined atheism, to Hegelian idealism, to a belief in a personal divine power before allowing himself to consider whether the Christian version of the myth of the dying god might be true.

He judged that as literature the gospels are too artless and historical to convey the taste and feel of genuine myth, but he recognized that the substance of the gospel narrative "was precisely the matter of the great myths."[23] The gospel core is a common mythical motif, he observed; it shows up in the myths of Balder, Adonis, Osiris, and Bacchus. Less than a century before Christianity, it appeared in Mithraism. What is the relation of these myths to Christian myth? Lewis could not address the question without confronting the fact that he liked the pagan myths, but was repulsed by Christianity. Something in him made him turn away from the story and images of the Christ myth. After a prolonged inner struggle to understand his visceral reaction, he realized that the Christ myth made a claim to truth that was both distinctive and personally threatening. The myth of the dying and rising god has always been true, he reasoned, but Christianity claims that in Christ the myth was concretely realized. If the Christ myth is true in the way that it claims to be true, it stands to other myths as the fulfillment of their promise and truth. It is not an illustration of mythic truth, but the ground of its possibility and the realization of its fragmentary glimpse of the Real. The question is not whether Christianity is fundamentally mythical, but whether Christ became and fulfilled the great myth.[24]

It occurred to Lewis while studying the gospels that if ever a myth was realized in historical time and space, "it would be just like this." He was struck in particular by the distinctive literary character of the gospels and their representations of Jesus. The gospels as literature are like the ancient myths in some ways and also like the ancient histories in other ways, he noted, but in their total character they are not like anything else. More importantly, no person in any literature is like the New Testament figure of Jesus: as real as Socrates, "yet also numinous, lit from a light from beyond the world, a god."[25] The force of this impression brought Lewis to Christianity. He found in Christ the source of the truth and delight he had known in pagan mythology.

He never tired of explaining the peculiar/ultimate way that myths are true. What myth communicates is not "truth" in the formal sense, he observed, but reality. Truth is always about something, "but reality is that *about which* truth is." Myth is not abstract, like truth; nor is it bound to the particular, like direct experience. Myth is more like the isthmus "which connects the peninsular world of thought with that vast continent we really belong to." Just as myth transcends thought, the Christian mystery of the incarnation transcends its mythical nature. "The heart of Christianity is a myth which is also a fact," Lewis explained. "The old myth of the Dying God, *without ceasing to be myth,* comes down from the heaven of legend and imagination to the earth of history." In the life, death, and resurrection of Jesus, myth *happens.* Christ is true myth because the Word became flesh in the man Jesus. "We pass from a Balder or an Osiris, dying nobody knows when or where, to a historical Person crucified (it is all in order) under Pontius Pilate." The miracle is that in Christ the myth of the dying God does not cease to be myth. The Christian accepts Christ as the fulfillment of myth with the same imaginative embrace that she rightly accords all myths.[26]

The historical and mythical elements are equally necessary. Lewis was not always clear that he understood these elements to be irreducibly intertwined, but the logic of his understanding of Christian myth leads to the kind of conclusion about myth/history that Barth took toward saga/history. What gives the Christian gospel its distinctive identity is precisely its irreducible conflation of truth-claiming myth and history. Christianity is myth that works on us in the same way that the dying god myths of Balder and Bacchus work upon us, except that in the case of Christianity, the myth becomes God's Word through God's saving historical action in Christ. "The story of Christ is simply a true myth: a myth working on us in the same way as the others, but with this tremendous difference that *it really happened,"* Lewis wrote. Christianity is true myth not in the sense of being a univocal description of divine reality, "but in the sense of being the way in which God chooses to (or can) appear to our faculties." Put differently, Christian myth works on us as a Word of God in forms that limited human understanding can appropriate. Though his own theology was conventionally orthodox, Lewis emphasized that "the doctrines we get *out of* the true myth are of course *less* true," for doctrines are translations of God's mythical Word into relative, fallible concepts.[27] All of our efforts to express the actuality behind the Christ event are less true than the actuality itself.

The upshot for theology is that God's language is the actual movement of God's Word in the incarnation, death, and resurrection of Christ. The Word is known as event. Pagan myths express certain truths about God through the images that mythmakers have found at their disposal, Lewis explained, but Christianity is God's myth expressed "through what we call 'real things.'"[28] Myths are proximate forms of transformation that must themselves be transformed by the Word in order for their truth to be realized. As James Loder remarks, "the Christ event resonates with the transformational potential in every personality."[29] The presence of Christ's Spirit calls for ongoing transformation in the form of life-giving works of love. The Word becomes true myth in order to redeem all history through ongoing transformations of the human spirit.

The danger that attends every project of mythmaking is that the new myth will create new forms of idolatry. Against every attempt to make God relevant or identify God with a cause or conceive God as a knowable object of thought, Barth insisted that God's actuality is prior to the logical form of contradiction. The true God is the unknown mystery of the world whose holiness is violated as soon as God acquires a name. God is beyond being and nonbeing, belief and unbelief, theism and atheism. God is hidden, holy, and mysterious, the ineffable source of revelation and grace. The God of biblical faith is not concerned about unbelief, but about the sin of giving one's heart and mind to idols.

Though he often claimed in his later career to have moved beyond the spirit and method of dialectical theology, Barth's mature theology continued to affirm the dialectical movement of God in self-revelation. In revelation, he persistently affirmed, God becomes objective without ceasing to be hidden. God enters our condition and makes Godself present to us in Christ, but in a way that eludes human control. The dialectic of presence and hiddenness is fundamentally constitutive to Christian existence.[30] To break the dialectic in either direction is to betray the living truth of revelation. That is, to move one-sidedly in the direction of presence is to falsely objectify the gospel; to emphasize absence or "wholly otherness" is to betray the living truth that God has disclosed to us in Christ.

For Barth it was axiomatic that true knowledge of God begins not with an act of imagination or creativity, but with the knowledge of God's hiddenness. God is incomprehensible, for God does not exist in the sphere of human power. "God is not a being whom we can spiritually appropriate," he explained. "The pictures in which we view God, the thoughts in which we think Him, the words with which we can define Him, are in themselves unfitted to this object and thus inappropriate to express and affirm the knowledge of Him."[31] No image from myth, doctrine, or even scripture can bring us to God or show God to us. But through the movement of God's Spirit-illuminated Word, the various images that scripture contains can become God's truth. The Word is made known as event through forms of language and action that include myth. The myth of the dying god becomes divine speech through God's action in Christ. None of the images that become God's truth acquire this status through any capacity or quality of their own, but only through grace. God thus remains hidden from us. "We do not encroach upon Him by knowing Him: we do not of ourselves become like Him; we do not of ourselves become master of Him; we do not of ourselves become one with Him," Barth explained. "And all this means—we cannot of ourselves apprehend Him."[32]

Only in one place is the hidden God apprehensible, and even there, the hidden source of revelation is apprehended only indirectly. In Christ the hidden God is apprehended "not to sight, but to faith. Not in His being, but in sign. Not, then, by the dissolution of His hiddenness—but apprehensibly."[33] The Word made flesh is the first and definitive sign of all signs, but the Word is made known to us only after the flesh, through the Spirit. For in Christ we see the human face of God no longer according to the flesh, but in and through the movement of the Spirit.

Notes

Notes to the Introduction

1. See Gustav Stahlin, "Muthos," in *Theological Dictionary of the New Testament,* vol. 4, ed. Gerhard Kittel and Gerhard Friedrich, trans. G. W. Bromiley (Grand Rapids: Wm. B. Eerdmans Publishing Co., 1973), 794.
2. Clark H. Pinnock, *The Scripture Principle* (San Francisco: Harper & Row, 1984), 122–23.
3. On the early mythical school tradition, see Christian Hartlich and Walter Sachs, *Der Ursprung des Mythosbegriffes in der modernen Bibelwissenschaft* (Tübingen: J.C.B. Mohr, 1952).
4. See Johannes Weiss, *Jesus' Proclamation of the Kingdom of God,* trans. D. Larrimore Holland and Richard H. Hiers (Philadelphia: Fortress Press, 1971); idem, *The History of Primitive Christianity,* 2 vols., trans. and ed. Frederick C. Grant (New York: Wilson-Erickson, 1937).
5. See Ernst Troeltsch, "The Dogmatics of the 'Religionsgeschichtliche Schule,'" *The American Journal of Theology,* 17 (January 1913):1–21; Helmut Koester, "Early Christianity from the Perspective of the History of Religions: Rudolf Bultmann's Contribution," in *Bultmann: Retrospect and Prospect,* ed. Edward C. Hobbs (Philadelphia: Fortress Press, 1985), 63–67; Joachim Wach, "Introduction: The Meaning and Task of the History of Religions (Religionswissenschaft)," in *The History of Religions: Essays on the Problem of Understanding,* ed. Joseph M. Kitagawa (Chicago: University of Chicago Press, 1967).
6. Mircea Eliade, *Myth and Reality,* trans. Willard R. Trask (1963; reprint, New York: Harper & Row, 1975), 5–6.
7. See Langdon Gilkey, "Modern Myth-Making and the Possibilities of Twentieth-Century Theology," in *Theology of Renewal,* vol. 1, ed. L. K. Shook (Montreal: Palm Publishers, 1968), 283; idem, *Religion and the Scientific Future* (New York: Harper & Row, 1970), 66–67.

Notes to Chapter 1.
Theology Beyond Myth: Liberal Christianity

1. See Allen W. Wood, *Kant's Moral Religion,* (Ithaca, N.Y.: Cornell University Press, 1970); Emil Fackenheim, *The Religious Dimension in Hegel's Thought* (Bloomington, Ind.: Indiana University Press, 1967); Richard B. Brandt, *The Philosophy of Schleiermacher: The Development of His Theory of Scientific and Religious Knowledge* (New York: Harper & Brothers, 1941).
2. See H. R. Mackintosh, *Types of Modern Theology: Schleiermacher to Barth* (London:

Nisbet and Company, 1937); B. M. G. Reardon, ed., *Religious Thought in the Nineteenth Century: Illustrated from Writers of the Period* (Cambridge, England: Cambridge University Press, 1966); Claude Welch, *Protestant Thought in the Nineteenth Century,* 2 vols. (New Haven, Conn.: Yale University Press, 1972, 1985).

3. Immanuel Kant, "An Answer to the Question: What Is Enlightenment?" in *Perpetual Peace and Other Essays On Politics, History, and Morals,* trans. Ted Humphrey (Indianapolis: Hackett Publishing Co., 1985), 41.

4. Immanuel Kant, *Critique of Pure Reason,* trans. Norman Kemp Smith (New York: Macmillan Publishing Co., 1973), 500–31; see idem, *Lectures on Philosophical Theology,* trans. Allen W. Wood and Gertrude M. Clark (Ithaca, N.Y.: Cornell University Press, 1978), 23–42.

5. Immanuel Kant, *Religion Within the Limits of Reason Alone,* trans. Theodore M. Greene and Hoyt H. Hudson (Chicago: Open Court, 1934), 123; see also pp. 95–96.

6. Friedrich Schleiermacher, *On Religion: Addresses in Response to Its Cultured Critics,* trans. Terrence N. Tice (Richmond: John Knox Press, 1969), 47–48.

7. Friedrich Schleiermacher, *The Life of Schleiermacher as Unfolded in His Autobiography and Letters,* 2 vols., trans. Frederica Rowan (London: Smith, Elder and Co., 1860), 2:56–58; closing quote in Schleiermacher, *On Religion,* 48.

8. Schleiermacher, *On Religion,* 77.

9. Robert R. Williams, *Schleiermacher the Theologian: The Construction of the Doctrine of God* (Philadelphia: Fortress Press, 1978), 25.

10. See Immanuel Kant, *Anthropology from a Pragmatic Point of View,* trans. Victor Lyle Dowdell, rev. and ed. Hans H. Rudnick (Carbondale, Ill.: Southern Illinois University Press, 1978), 9–129; idem, *The Critique of Judgement,* trans. James Creed Meredith (Oxford: Clarendon Press, 1973), 204–27; Karl Ameriks, *Kant's Theory of Mind: An Analysis of the Paralogisms of Pure Reason* (Oxford: Clarendon Press, 1982), 84–123.

11. See Friedrich Schleiermacher, *Soliloquies,* trans. Horace Leland Friess (Chicago: Open Court, 1957), 10–25; Brandt, *The Philosophy of Schleiermacher,* 105–44; Williams, *Schleiermacher the Theologian,* 4–7.

12. See Edmund Husserl, *Ideas: General Introduction to Pure Phenomenology,* trans. W. R. Boyce Gibson (New York: Humanities Press, 1976), 41–47.

13. Schleiermacher, *On Religion,* 79.

14. Ibid., 82.

15. Ibid., 79.

16. Ibid., 94; see Karl Barth, *The Theology of Schleiermacher,* trans. Geoffrey W. Bromiley (Grand Rapids: Wm. B. Eerdmans Publishing Co., 1982), 246–58.

17. Schleiermacher, *On Religion,* 94–95.

18. Ibid., 147.

19. Ibid., 162. This discussion of mythology is a supplementary note to the Second Address, which Schleiermacher added to the book's second edition (1806).

20. Ibid., 162.

21. Ibid., 162–63.

22. Ibid., 163.

23. Ibid., 49. In the third edition (1821), Schleiermacher added that "we should recall that this severe judgment on the English people came at a time when it could seem proper to protest against the prevailing Anglomania, using the excessive stress admissible in rhetorical discourse." He saw no reason "to retract much from my earlier judgment, however," and he retracted nothing regarding the French (63–64). Ironically, the religious work of Schleiermacher's generation that came closest to *On Religion* in its spirit, argument, and genius was written only four years later by an English poet—Samuel Taylor Coleridge's *Aids to Reflection.* Though Coleridge's life and thought lie outside the narrative line of the present study, his theology bears strong similarities to the German/American tradition of theological liberalism.

24. Ibid., 115.
25. Friedrich Schleiermacher, *The Christian Faith*, ed. H. R. Mackintosh and J. S. Stewart (1928; reprint, Edinburgh: T. & T. Clark, 1968), 374–475.
26. Schleiermacher, *The Life of Schleiermacher*, 2:201–11; for a thorough overview of Schleiermacher's life and work, see Martin Redeker, *Schleiermacher: Life and Thought*, trans. J. Wallhauser (Philadelphia: Fortress Press, 1973).
27. Friedrich Schleiermacher, *Brief Outline on the Study of Theology*, trans. Terrence N. Tice (Atlanta: John Knox Press, 1977), 19–114; see idem, *Introduction to Christian Ethics*, trans. John C. Shelley (Nashville: Abingdon Press, 1989).
28. Schleiermacher, *The Christian Faith*, 12, 14, 31–34.
29. Ibid., 16.
30. See Karl Barth, *Church Dogmatics, The Doctrine of God;* vol. 2, bk. 1, ed. G. W. Bromiley and T. F. Torrance (Edinburgh: T. & T. Clark, 1957), 338–39, 531–32; Schleiermacher, *The Christian Faith*, 738–51.
31. Schleiermacher, *The Christian Faith*, 17.
32. Ibid., 54–55.
33. Ibid., 57.
34. Friedrich Schleiermacher, "Christ Our Only Savior," in *Servant of the Word: Selected Sermons of Friedrich Schleiermacher*, trans. Dawn De Vries (Philadelphia: Fortress Press, 1987), 29–30.
35. Schleiermacher, "Christ the Liberator," in *Servant of the Word*, 55.
36. Ibid., 56.
37. Schleiermacher, *The Christian Faith*, 99.
38. Ibid., 262. This emphasis on the double character of Christian experience is slighted in Richard R. Niebuhr's otherwise discerning study of Schleiermacher, *Schleiermacher on Christ and Religion* (London: SCM Press, 1965). Niebuhr invents the term "Christo-morphic" to suggest that Schleiermacher's system as a whole is shaped by Christology.
39. Ibid., 261.
40. Schleiermacher, "Christ Our Only Savior," 33.
41. Ibid., 31.
42. Ibid., 34.
43. David Friedrich Strauss, *The Christ of Faith and the Jesus of History: A Critique of Schleiermacher's Life of Jesus*, trans. Leander E. Keck (Philadelphia: Fortress Press, 1977), 4.
44. See Hermann Samuel Reimarus, *Fragments* (Philadelphia: Fortress Press, 1979); Albert Schweitzer, *The Quest of the Historical Jesus: A Critical Study of Its Progress from Reimarus to Wrede*, trans. James M. Robinson (1906; reprint, New York: Macmillan Co., 1968), 13–26.
45. See Johann Gottfried Eichhorn, *Einleitung in das Neue Testament*, 2d ed., 3 vols. (Leipzig: Weidmannischen Buchhandlung, 1810–1820); Johann Carl Ludwig Gieseler, *Historisch-kritischer Versuch über die Entstehung und die frühesten Schicksale der schriftlichen Evangelien* (Leipzig: W. Engelmann, 1818). For an analysis of the early mythical school tradition, focusing on Eichhorn, Gabler, Herder, and Schelling, see Christian Hartlich and Walter Sachs, *Der Ursprung des Mythosbegriffes in der modernen Bibelwissenschaft* (Tübingen: J. C. B. Mohr, 1952).
46. Friedrich Schleiermacher, *The Life of Jesus*, trans. S. Maclean Gilmour, ed. Jack C. Verheyden (Philadelphia: Fortress Press, 1975), 36–42.
47. Schweitzer, *The Quest of the Historical Jesus*, 64–65.
48. Schleiermacher, *The Life of Jesus*, 455.
49. B. A. Gerrish, *A Prince of the Church: Schleiermacher and the Beginnings of Modern Theology* (Philadelphia: Fortress Press, 1984), 52–54; see idem, *Continuing the Reformation: Essays on Modern Religious Thought* (Chicago: University of Chicago Press, 1993), 176–77.
50. Schleiermacher, *Brief Outline on the Study of Theology*, 19.
51. Douglas Clyde Macintosh, *Theology as an Empirical Science* (New York: Macmillan Co., 1927), 16–17; for a similar comment, see Gerrish, *A Prince of the Church*, 45.

52. Strauss, *The Christ of Faith and the Jesus of History*, 4.
53. Ibid., 166.
54. Ibid., 167.
55. Ibid., 162.
56. G. E. Lessing, *Lessing's Theological Writings*, ed. Henry Chadwick (Stanford, Calif.: Stanford University Press, 1957), 12–13.
57. David Friedrich Strauss, *The Old Faith and the New*, trans. Mathilde Blind (New York: Henry Holt, 1873), 13–107, quote on 87.
58. See Peter C. Hodgson, "Editor's Introduction: Strauss's Theological Development from 1825 to 1850," in David Friedrich Strauss, *The Life of Jesus Critically Examined*, trans. George Eliot, ed. Peter C. Hodgson (Ramsey, N.J.: Sigler Press, 1994), xx.
59. Schweitzer, *The Quest of the Historical Jesus*, 68–69.
60. Strauss's letter to Christian Märklin quoted in Hodgson, "Editor's Introduction: Strauss's Theological Development," xxi.
61. Quoted in Leander E. Keck, "Editor's Introduction," in Strauss, *The Christ of Faith and the Jesus of History*, xxii.
62. Schweitzer, *The Quest of the Historical Jesus*, 70.
63. See Theobald Ziegler, *David Friedrich Strauss*, vol. 1 (Strassburg: K. J. Trubner, 1908), 94; William J. Brazill, *The Young Hegelians* (New Haven, Conn.: Yale University Press, 1970), 96–101.
64. For the most extensive discussion of Strauss's development, see Gotthold Müller, *Identität und Immanenz: Zur Genese der Theologie von David Friedrich Strauss* (Zürich: EVZ-Verlag, 1968).
65. See Ferdinand Christian Baur, *Symbolik und Mythologie, oder die Naturreligion des Alterthums*, 2 vols. (Stuttgart: J. B. Metzler, 1824–1825), 1:xi.
66. See F. W. J. Schelling, *Vorlesungen über die Methode des academischen Studium* (Stuttgart: J. G. Cotta, 1830); idem, *System of Transcendental Idealism*, trans. Peter Heath (Charlottesville, Va.: University Press of Virginia, 1993), 225–33; discussion in Keck, "Editor's Introduction," li.
67. For a discussion of Baur's early philosophical idealism and the influence of Schelling upon his thought, see Peter C. Hodgson, *The Formation of Historical Theology: A Study of Ferdinand Christian Baur* (New York: Harper & Row, 1966), 9–12.
68. See Philipp K. Marheineke, *Die Grundlehren der christlichen Dogmatik als Wissenschaft* (Berlin: Verlag von Duncker und Homblot, 1827); Karl Rosenkranz, *Encyklopädie der theologischen Wissenschaften* (Halle: C. A. Schwetschke und Sohn, 1831).
69. Kant, *Critique of Pure Reason*, 74–91.
70. G. W. F. Hegel, *The Phenomenology of Mind*, trans. J. B. Baillie (New York: Macmillan Co., 1931), 457.
71. G. W. F. Hegel, *Lectures on the Philosophy of Religion*, vol. 1, trans. from 2d ed. by E. B. Speirs and J. Burdon Sanderson (New York: Humanities Press, 1974), 25, 33; see idem, *Early Theological Writings*, trans. T. M. Knox (Chicago: University of Chicago Press, 1948). Hegel gave four series of lectures on the philosophy of religion (in 1821, 1824, 1827, and 1831). Marheineke's first and second editions (1832 and 1840) drew from all four of these series and were based mostly upon students' lecture notes. The Speirs/Sanderson translation is based upon the Marheineke/Bruno Bauer expanded second edition of 1840. For a new construction of the 1827 lecture series, see the one-volume edition edited by Peter C. Hodgson and translated by R. F. Brown, P. C. Hodgson, and J. M. Stewart (Berkeley, Calif.: University of California Press, 1988).
72. G. W. F. Hegel, review of Carl Friedrich Göschel, *Aphorismen über Nichtwissen und absolutes Wissen im Verhältnisse zur christlichen GlaubenserKenntnis* (Berlin: Verlag von Dunker und Humblot, 1829), reprinted in Hegel, *Sämtliche Werke*, vol. 20, ed. Herman Glockner (Stuttgart: Frommon, 1968), 276–77. See Göschel, *Von den Beweisen für die Unsterblichkeit der men-*

schlichen Selle im Lichte der spekulativen Philosophic (Berlin: Verlag von Duncker und Humblot, 1835); Carl Ludwig Michelet, *Vorlesungen über die Persöhnlichkeit Gottes und Unsterblichkeit der Seele oder die ewige Persöhnlichkeit des Geistes* (Berlin: Verlag von Ferdinand Dummler, 1841); Kasimir Conradi, *Unsterblichkeit und Ewiges Leben: Versuch einer Entwicklung des Unsterblichkeitsbegriffs der menschlichen Seele* (Mainz: F. Kupferberg, 1837). For Hegel's critique of Göschel's hypostatization of divine reality, see G. W. F. Hegel, *Berliner Schriften, 1818–1831,* ed. J. Hoffmeister (Hamburg: Verlag von Felix Meiner, 1956), 324–29.

73. Hodgson, "Editor's Introduction: Strauss's Theological Development," xxxvi.
74. Quoted in Keck, "Editor's Introduction," lv.
75. On Hegel's understanding of the relation of religious and philosophical truth, see Quentin Lauer, S.J., *Hegel's Concept of God* (Albany, N.Y.: State University of New York Press, 1982), 21–56; Fackenheim, *The Religious Dimension in Hegel's Thought;* and George Rupp, *Christologies and Cultures: Toward a Typology of Religious Worldviews* (The Hague: Mouton & Co., 1974), 105–58.
76. Quoted in Hodgson, "Editor's Introduction: Strauss's Theological Development," xxiii.
77. See Karl Daub, *Die dogmatische Theologie jetziger: Zeit oder die Selbstsucht in der Wissenschaft des Glaubens und ihrer Artikel* (Heidelberg: J. C. B. Mohr, 1833); Carl Friedrich Göschel, *Von den Beweisen für die Unsterblichkeit der menschlichen Seele;* Göschel, *Der Mensch nach Leib, Seele und Geist diesseits und jenseits* (Leipzig: Dorffling und Franke, 1856); Kasimir Conradi, *Selbstbewusstseyn und Offenbarung; oder die Entwickelung des religiösen Bewusstseyns* (Mainz: F. Kupferberg, 1831). For an especially pointed critique of Strauss from the right-Hegelian camp and a strong affirmation of God's hypostatized reality independent of the world, see Georg Andreas Gabler, *Die Hegelsche Philosophie: Beiträge zur ihrer richtigeren Beurtheilung und Würdigung* (Berlin: Verlag von Alexander Dunker, 1843), 89–167.
78. David Friedrich Strauss, *Charakteristiken und Kritiken: Eine Sammlung zerstreuter Aufsätze aus den Gebieten der Theologie, Anthropologie und Aesthetik* (Leipzig: O. Wigand, 1839), 224.
79. Quoted in Hodgson, "Editor's Introduction: Strauss's Theological Development," xxiii.
80. Strauss, *The Life of Jesus Critically Examined,* li.
81. See Heinrich Eberhard Gottlob Paulus, *Das Leben Jesu, als Grundlage einer reinen Geschichte des Urchristentums* (Heidelberg: C. F. Winter, 1828); idem, *Philologisch-kritischer Commentar über das Neue Testament,* 4 vols., (Leipzig: J. F. Bohn, 1804–1805); Schweitzer, *The Quest of the Historical Jesus,* 48–57.
82. Strauss, *The Life of Jesus Critically Examined,* li.
83. See Wilhelm Martin Leberecht de Wette, *Lehrbuch der historisch kritischen Einleitung in die Bibel Alten und Neuen Testaments,* 4th ed., 2 pts. (Berlin: G. Reimer, 1833–1834); de Wette, *Über Religion und Theologie: Erläuterung zu seinem Lehrbuche der Dogmatik* (Berlin: G. Reimer, 1821); F. C. Baur, *Die christliche Gnosis, oder die christliche Religions-Philosophie in ihrer geschichtlichen Entwicklung* (Tübingen: C. F. Osiander, 1835).
84. Strauss, *The Life of Jesus Critically Examined,* 60.
85. Ibid., 275–471.
86. Ibid., lii.
87. Ibid., 87–92.
88. Ibid., 739–43.
89. Ibid., 744.
90. Ibid., 57.
91. Ibid., 52–53.
92. Ibid., 53–54.
93. Ibid., 76.
94. Ibid., 80.
95. Quoted in ibid., 81.
96. Ibid.

97. Ibid.

98. Ibid., 87.

99. Ibid.

100. Ibid., 78, 757.

101. David Friedrich Strauss, *Streitschriften zur Verteidigung Meiner Schrift über das Leben Jesu und zur Charakteristik der gegenwärtigen Theologie,* vol. 3 (Tübingen: C. F. Osiander, 1841), 95.

102. Reprinted in David Friedrich Strauss, *Ausgewählte Briefe von David Friedrich Strauss,* ed. E. Zeller (Bonn: E. Strauss, 1895), 48; quoted in John Edward Toews, *Hegelianism: The Path Toward Dialectical Humanism, 1805–1841* (Cambridge, England: Cambridge University Press, 1985), 276.

103. Strauss, *The Life of Jesus Critically Examined,* "Preface to the Fourth German Edition," lviii.

104. Quoted in Toews, *Hegelianism,* 281.

105. David Friedrich Strauss, *Die christliche Glaubenslehre in ihrer geschichtlichen Entwicklung und im Kampfe mit der modernen Wissenschaft dargestellt,* 2 vols. (Tübingen: C. F. Osiander, 1840–1841), 1:71.

106. Strauss, "Preface to the Fourth German Edition," lviii.

107. Strauss, *Streitschriften,* 3:60–94. Strauss gave particular attention to the writings of Carl Friedrich Göschel, Georg Andreas Gabler, and Bruno Bauer in his attack on right-Hegelian theology. See Carl Friedrich Göschel, *Von den Beweisen für die Unsterblichkeit der menschlichen Seele;* Göschel, *Der Mensch nach Leib, Seele und Geist diesseits und jenseits;* and Gabler, *Die Hegelsche Philosophie.* Strauss placed Rosenkranz in the center of the Hegelian right/center/left continuum because, though he sought to uphold the idea of an individual historical incarnation through speculative philosophy, Rosenkranz gave up any claim to grounding speculative theology in the gospel history. See Strauss, *Streitschriften,* 3:94–126.

108. See Bruno Bauer, *Die Posaune des jüngsten Gerichts über Hegel den Atheisten und Antichristen: Ein Ultimatum* (Leipzig: O. Wigand, 1841); Ludwig Feuerbach, *The Essence of Christianity,* trans. George Eliot (New York: Harper & Row, 1957). For a recent theological interpretation of Hegel that is strongly critical of right-Hegelian theology and critically sympathetic to Strauss's position, see Rupp, *Christologies and Cultures,* 140–57.

109. Strauss, *Die christliche Glaubenslehre,* 1:1–2; 2:173–240; "pulling down a structure" conclusion, 2:624.

110. Strauss, *The Life of Jesus Critically Examined,* 88.

111. Schleiermacher's lecture manuscripts on hermeneutics are published in Friedrich Schleiermacher, *Hermeneutics: The Handwritten Manuscripts,* trans. James Duke and J. Forstman, ed. H. Kimmerle (Missoula, Mont.: Scholars Press, 1977); selections reprinted in Keith Clements, ed., *Friedrich Schleiermacher: Pioneer of Modern Theology* (Minneapolis: Fortress Press, 1991), 157–71; quote on 167.

112. Hans-Georg Gadamer, *Truth and Method,* 2d rev. ed., trans. Joel Weinsheimer and Donald G. Marshall (New York: Crossroad, 1989), 168–69; see Gadamer, *Hegel's Dialectic: Five Hermeneutical Studies,* trans. P. Christopher Smith (New Haven, Conn.: Yale University Press, 1976).

113. Strauss, *The Life of Jesus Critically Examined,* 461; F. C. Baur, *Kritische Untersuchungen über die kanonischen Evangelien* (Tübingen: L. F. Fues, 1847), 41–46, 71–74. For a critical account of Tübingen school positivism, see R. G. Collingwood, *The Idea of History* (1946; reprint, London: Oxford University Press, 1976), 135–39.

114. Hodgson, "Editor's Introduction: Strauss's Theological Development," xxix–xxxi.

115. Ibid., xxx.

116. Schweitzer, *The Quest of the Historical Jesus,* 69; Karl Barth, *Protestant Theology in the Nineteenth Century: Its Background & History* (1959; reprint, Valley Forge, Pa.: Judson Press, 1976), 542.

117. Barth, *Protestant Theology in the Nineteenth Century,* 543.

118. Strauss, *The Life of Jesus Critically Examined,* 778.

119. Ibid., 780.
120. For a right-Hegelian critique of Strauss's non-hypostatized panentheism, see Gabler, *Die Hegelsche Philosophie*, 89–215.
121. Strauss, *The Life of Jesus Critically Examined*, 780–82.
122. See Klaus Koch, *The Growth of the Biblical Tradition: The Form-Critical Method* (London: Adam & Charles Black, 1969); Rudolf Bultmann, *The History of the Synoptic Tradition*, trans. John Marsh (New York: Harper & Row, 1963), 2–7, 39–54; Martin Kahler, *The So-Called Historical Jesus and the Historic, Biblical Christ*, trans. and ed. Carl E. Braaten (1896; reprint, Philadelphia: Fortress Press, 1964); Carl Braaten and Roy Harrisville, eds., *The Historical Jesus and the Kerygmatic Christ* (Nashville: Abingdon Press, 1964); John Dominic Crossan, *The Historical Jesus: The Life of a Mediterranean Jewish Peasant* (New York: HarperCollins, 1992).
123. For discussions of the left-Hegelian attacks on Strauss, see Toews, *Hegelianism*, 282–87; and Brazill, *The Young Hegelians*, 179–213.
124. See A. E. Biedermann, *Christliche Dogmatik*, 2 vols. (Berlin: Verlag von Georg Reimer, 1884–1885); idem, "Schleiermacher," in *Ausgewählte Vorträge und Aufsätze*, ed. J. Kradolfer (Berlin: Georg Reimer, 1885), 188–98.
125. See Isaak August Dorner, *Divine Immutability*, trans. Robert R. Williams and Claude Welch (Minneapolis: Fortress Press, 1994); idem, *A System of Christian Doctrine*, 4 vols., trans. Alfred Cave and J. S. Banks (Edinburgh: T. & T. Clark, 1888).
126. Strauss, *The Christ of Faith and the Jesus of History*, 169. Strauss's 1864 edition was published under the title, *The Life of Jesus for the German People*; see discussion in Ziegler, *David Friedrich Strauss*, vol. 2, 589–91.
127. Strauss, *The Old Faith and the New*, 127; on Schleiermacher's theology, see 47–59.
128. Keck, "Editor's Introduction," xcii.
129. On Ritschl's life and career, see Otto Ritschl, *Albrecht Ritschls Leben*, 2 vols. (Freiburg: J. C. B. Mohr, 1892, 1896); see also Albert Temple Swing, *The Theology of Albrecht Ritschl*, trans. Alice Mead Swing (New York: Longmans, Green & Co., 1901), 10–22; Rolf Schafer, *Ritschl* (Tübingen: J. C. B. Mohr, 1968); Philip Hefner, "Albrecht Ritschl: An Introduction," in Albrecht Ritschl, *Three Essays*, trans. and ed. Philip Hefner (Philadelphia: Fortress Press, 1972), 1–50.
130. See Hefner, "Albrecht Ritschl: An Introduction," 7–10; Hodgson, *The Formation of Historical Theology*, 62, 67, 277; and Philip Hefner, *Faith and the Vitalities of History: A Theological Study Based on the Work of Albrecht Ritschl* (New York: Harper & Row, 1966), 70–90.
131. For a discussion of Baur's analysis of the synoptic problem and his response to Ritschl after Ritschl adopted the theory of Markan priority, see Hodgson, *The Formation of Historical Theology*, 214–17.
132. See Albrecht Ritschl, *Die Entstehung der altkatholischen Kirche* (Bonn: Adolph Marcus, 1850).
133. On Baur's Hegelianism, see Barth, *Protestant Theology in the Nineteenth Century*, 499–507; Rupp, *Christologies and Cultures*, 146–47; Hodgson, *The Formation of Historical Theology*, 25–27.
134. On the tridimensional structure of Hegel's dialectic, which, playing out the simultaneous meanings of the concept of *Aufhebung*, always involves three simultaneous cases of reduplicated relation, see Dieter Henrich, "Formen der Negation in Hegels Logik," in *Seminar: Dialektik in der Philosophie Hegels*, ed. Rolf-Peter Horstmann (Frankfurt: Suhrkamp Taschenbuch Verlag, 1978), 213–29; and Jean Hyppolite, *Genesis and Structure of Hegel's Phenomenology of Spirit*, trans. Samuel Cherniak and John Heckman (Evanston, Ill.: Northwestern University Press, 1974), 3–26, 51–74.
135. F. C. Baur, *Das Christenthum und die christliche Kirche der drei ersten Jahrhunderte* (Tübingen: L. F. Fues, 1853).
136. See Albrecht Ritschl, *Die Entstehung der altkatholischen Kirche: Eine kirchenund dogmengeschichtliche Monographie*, rev. 2d ed. (Bonn: Adolph Marcus, 1857).
137. For example: "Hence the rule may be set up that almost everything else in the Old Testament

is, for our Christian usage, but the husk or wrapping of its prophecy, and that whatever is most definitely Jewish has least value"; Schleiermacher, *The Christian Faith*, 62.

138. For text and discussion of Harnack's proposal to "make a clean sweep here" and remove the Old Testament from the Christian scriptures, see Hans-Joachim Kraus, *Geschichte der historisch-kritischen Erforschung des Alten Testaments* (Neukirchen-Vluyn: Neukirchener Verlag, 1969), 384–90.

139. See Martin Luther, "The Babylonian Captivity of the Church," in *Martin Luther's Basic Theological Writings*, ed. Timothy F. Lull (Minneapolis: Fortress Press, 1989), 267–313.

140. Albrecht Ritschl, *The Christian Doctrine of Justification and Reconciliation*, ed. H. R. Mackintosh and A. B. Macaulay (Edinburgh: T. & T. Clark, 1902), 619.

141. Ibid., 205.

142. Ibid., 3.

143. Ibid., 1–2.

144. Schleiermacher, *The Christian Faith*, 52.

145. Ritschl, *The Christian Doctrine*, 8–9.

146. Ibid., 10; closing quote from Albrecht Ritschl, "Instruction in the Christian Religion," reprinted in Ritschl, *Three Essays*, 229.

147. Ibid., 11–13; see Ritschl, "Instruction in the Christian Religion," 232–40.

148. Ritschl, *The Christian Doctrine*, 20–21.

149. See Albrecht Ritschl, "Theology and Metaphysics," reprinted in Ritschl, *Three Essays*, 149–217.

150. In Barth's words, "the very epitome of the national-liberal German bourgeois of the age of Bismarck." Barth, *Protestant Theology in the Nineteenth Century*, 656.

151. On the origins and character of social Christian theology, see Gary Dorrien, *Soul in Society: The Making and Renewal of Social Christianity* (Minneapolis: Fortress Press, 1995).

152. On Harnack's life and career, see Agnes von Zahn-Harnack, *Adolf von Harnack* (Berlin: Walter de Gruyter & Company, 1936, 2d ed. 1951); Wilhelm Pauck, "The Significance of Adolf von Harnack among Church Historians," *Union Theological Seminary Quarterly Review*, Special Issue (January 1954), 13–24; G. Wayne Glick, *The Reality of Christianity: A Study of Adolf von Harnack as Historian and Theologian* (New York: Harper & Row, 1967).

153. Adolf von Harnack, *What Is Christianity?* trans. Thomas Bailey Saunders (1900; reprint, Philadelphia: Fortress Press, 1986), 8.

154. Ibid., 11.

155. See von Zahn-Harnack, *Adolf von Harnack*, 130–33.

156. Ibid., 130–31; Wilhelm Pauck, *Harnack and Troeltsch: Two Historical Theologians* (New York: Oxford University Press, 1968), 33–34; see Adolf von Harnack, "The Present State of Research in Early Church History," in *Adolf von Harnack: Liberal Theology at its Height*, ed. Martin Rumscheidt (Minneapolis: Fortress Press, 1991), 182–93.

157. Harnack, *What Is Christianity?* 20–21.

158. Ibid., 23–25.

159. Ibid., 27–28.

160. Ibid., 30, 51–52; see Harnack, "The Two-Fold Gospel in the New Testament," in Rumscheidt, ed., *Adolf von Harnack: Liberal Theology at its Height*, 146–54.

161. Ibid., 56.

162. Ibid., 162; see Harnack, "Christianity and History," in Rumscheidt, ed., *Adolf von Harnack: Liberal Theology at its Height*, 63–77.

163. See Wilhelm Herrmann, *The Communion of the Christian with God: A Discussion in Agreement with the View of Luther*, trans. J. Sandys Stanyon (London: Williams and Norgate, 1895); A. E. Garvie, *The Ritschlian Theology* (Edinburgh: T. & T. Clark, 1899); William Adams Brown, *The Essence of Christianity: A Study in the History of Definition* (New York: Charles Scribner's Sons, 1902).

164. See Adolf von Harnack and Wilhelm Herrmann, *Essays on the Social Gospel*, trans. G. M. Craik (New York: G. P. Putnam's Sons, 1907), 9–21, 66–91.

165. See Harnack, *What Is Christianity?* 210.

166. See Adolf von Harnack, *History of Dogma*, vol. 1, trans. Neil Buchanan (Boston: Little, Brown, & Co., 1905), 41–136; idem, *What Is Christianity?* 190–245; idem, *The Apostles' Creed*, trans. Thomas Bailey Saunders (London: A. & C. Black, 1901); on the controversy over Harnack's criticism of the Apostles' Creed, see von Zahn-Harnack, *Adolf von Harnack*, 144–60.

167. Adolf von Harnack, *Marcion, das Evangelium vom fremden Gott* (Leipzig: J. C. Hinrichs Verlag, 1921), 217–20.

168. Henry P. van Dusen, *The Vindication of Liberal Theology: A Tract for the Times* (New York: Charles Scribner's Sons, 1963), 41.

169. See William Adams Brown, *A Teacher and His Times: A Story of Two Worlds* (New York: Charles Scribner's Sons, 1940); Samuel McCrea Cavert, "William Adams Brown: Servant of the Church of Christ," in *The Church Through Half a Century: Essays in Honor of William Adams Brown*, ed. Samuel McCrea Cavert and Henry Pitney van Dusen (New York: Charles Scribner's Sons, 1936), 5–38.

170. William Adams Brown, *Christ the Vitalizing Principle of Christian Theology* (New York: W. C. Martin, 1898).

171. See Gary Dorrien, *Reconstructing the Common Good: Theology and the Social Order* (Maryknoll, N.Y.: Orbis Books, 1990), 16–47.

172. Walter Rauschenbusch, *Christianizing the Social Order* (New York: Macmillan Co., 1912), 89–90.

173. Walter Rauschenbusch, *A Theology for the Social Gospel* (1917; reprint, Nashville: Abingdon Press, 1987), 25.

174. Walter Rauschenbusch, "A Conquering Idea," in *Walter Rauschenbusch: Selected Writings*, ed. Winthrop Hudson (New York: Paulist Press, 1984), 71–74; see Rauschenbusch, *Christianizing the Social Order*, 93–94.

175. See Shailer Mathews, *The Social Gospel* (New York: Macmillan Co., 1910), 121–22; Harry Emerson Fosdick, *Christianity and Progress* (New York: Fleming H. Revell Co., 1922), 119, 167–206.

176. Brown, *Christ the Vitalizing Principle of Christian Theology*, 23.

177. See Johannes Weiss, *Jesus' Proclamation of the Kingdom of God*, trans. D. Larrimore Holland and Richard H. Hiers (Philadelphia: Fortress Press, 1971); idem, *The History of Primitive Christianity*, 2 vols., trans. and ed. Frederick C. Grant (New York: Wilson-Erickson, 1937); Schweitzer, *The Quest of the Historical Jesus*, 330–97.

178. Rudolf Bultmann, "Introduction," in Harnack, *What Is Christianity?* x.

179. Walter Rauschenbusch, *Christianity and the Social Crisis* (New York: Macmillan Co., 1907), 63.

180. Van Dusen, *The Vindication of Liberal Theology*, 41.

181. Harry Emerson Fosdick, *The Modern Use of the Bible* (1924; reprint, New York: Macmillan Co., 1945), title to chap. 4, p. 97.

182. See William Newton Clarke, *An Outline of Christian Theology* (New York: Charles Scribner's Sons, 1906); A. C. Knudson, *The Doctrine of God* (Nashville: Abingdon Press, 1930); Eugene W. Lyman, *Theology and Human Problems* (Boston: Pilgrim Press, 1910); Lyman, *The Meaning and Truth of Religion* (New York: Charles Scribner's Sons, 1933).

183. William Adams Brown, "The Old Theology and the New," *Harvard Theological Review*, vol. 4, no. 1 (January 1911):1; idem, *The Essence of Christianity*, 1–42; idem, *Beliefs That Matter* (New York: Charles Scribner's Sons, 1930), 66–87.

184. Auguste Sabatier, *Outlines of a Philosophy of Religion based on Psychology and History* (New York: James Pott & Co., 1910), 35, 56.

185. Ibid., 168; for his developed Christology, see Auguste Sabatier, *Religions of Authority and the Religion of the Spirit*, trans. Louise Seymour Houghton (New York: McClure, Phillips & Co., 1904), 255–300.

186. Brown, "The Old Theology and the New," 15–16, 19.

187. William Adams Brown, *Pathways to Certainty* (New York: Charles Scribner's Sons, 1930), 40; idem, *God at Work: A Study of the Supernatural* (New York: Charles Scribner's Sons, 1933); 23–50.

188. Shailer Mathews, *The Social Teachings of Jesus* (New York: Macmillan Co., 1897).

189. Shailer Mathews, *The Messianic Hope in the New Testament* (Chicago: University of Chicago Press, 1905), 82.

190. Shailer Mathews, *The Gospel and the Modern Man* (New York: Macmillan Co., 1910), 111.

191. Ibid., 112; see Shailer Mathews, *The Church and the Changing Order* (New York: Macmillan Co., 1907), 171–75.

192. Mathews, *The Social Gospel*, 121–22.

193. Shailer Mathews, *The Individual and the Social Gospel* (New York: Missionary Education Movement of the United States and Canada, 1914), 68.

194. Shailer Mathews, "Theology and the Social Mind," *The Biblical World* 46 (October 1915):204.

195. Ibid., 206–48; see Shailer Mathews, "Theology from the Point of View of Social Psychology," *The Journal of Religion*, vol. 3, no. 4 (July 1923):337–51.

196. Ibid., 247.

197. Shailer Mathews, *The Faith of Modernism* (1924; reprint, New York: AMS Press, 1969), 4–16, 31.

198. Ibid., 23.

199. Shailer Mathews, *The Growth of the Idea of God* (New York: Macmillan Co., 1931), 214.

200. See Henry Nelson Wieman, *Religious Experience and Scientific Method* (1926; reprint, Carbondale, Ill.: Southern Illinois University Press, 1971); idem, *The Wrestle of Religion with Truth* (New York: Macmillan Co., 1927); idem, *The Source of Human Good* (Chicago: University of Chicago Press, 1946); idem, *Man's Ultimate Commitment* (Carbondale, Ill.: Southern Illinois University Press, 1958).

201. See Shailer Mathews, *The Atonement and the Social Process* (New York: Macmillan Co., 1930).

202. Mathews, *The Growth of the Idea of God*, 218–19.

203. See George Burman Foster, *The Finality of the Christian Religion* (Chicago: University of Chicago Press, 1906); Foster, *Christianity in its Modern Expression*, ed. Douglas Clyde Macintosh (New York: Macmillan Co., 1921).

204. Douglas Clyde Macintosh, ed., *Religious Realism* (New York: Macmillan Co., 1931), vi.

205. Macintosh, *Theology as an Empirical Science*, 2.

206. Douglas Clyde Macintosh, "Toward a New Untraditional Orthodoxy," *Contemporary American Theology: Theological Autobiographies*, vol. 1, ed. Vergilius Ferm (New York: Round Table Press, 1932), 307.

207. See Douglas Clyde Macintosh, *The Problem of Knowledge* (New York: Macmillan Co., 1915); idem, *The Problem of Religious Knowledge* (New York: Harper & Brothers, 1940).

208. Macintosh, "Toward a New Untraditional Orthodoxy," 306; see idem, "Experimental Realism in Theology," in *Religious Realism*, 307–409.

209. Macintosh, *Theology as an Empirical Science*, 26.

210. Ibid., 16–18.

211. Ibid., 19.

212. See Ernst Troeltsch, *The Christian Faith*, ed. Gertrud von le Fort, trans. Garrett E. Paul (1925; reprint, Minneapolis: Fortress Press, 1991); idem, *Religion in History*, trans. James Luther Adams and Walter F. Bense (Minneapolis: Fortress Press, 1991); idem, *Die Absolutheit der Christentums und die Religionsgeschichte* (1902; reprint, Tübingen: J. C. B. Mohr [Paul Siebeck], 1912).

213. Macintosh, *Theology as an Empirical Science*, 21.

214. Ibid., 25, 45.

215. Ibid., 29; see Macintosh, "Experimental Realism in Theology," 383–95.

216. Macintosh, *Theology as an Empirical Science*, 42; see Macintosh, *The Problem of Religious Knowledge*, 170–75, 188–213.

217. Macintosh, *Theology as an Empirical Science*, 142–44.

218. Douglas Clyde Macintosh, *The Reasonableness of Christianity* (New York: Charles Scribner's Sons, 1926), 46.
219. Macintosh, "Toward a New Untraditional Orthodoxy," 312.
220. Macintosh, *The Reasonableness of Christianity,* 48, 50.
221. Macintosh, "Toward a New Untraditional Orthodoxy," 311.
222. Macintosh, *The Reasonableness of Christianity,* 135–38; see idem, *Personal Religion* (New York: Charles Scribner's Sons, 1942), 139–48.
223. See Foster, *Christianity in its Modern Expression,* 7–9, 153–58; idem, *The Finality of the Christian Religion,* 510–18; Macintosh, "Toward a New Untraditional Orthodoxy," 310–11.
224. Max Carl Otto, Henry Nelson Wieman, and D. C. Macintosh, *Is There a God?* (Chicago: Willett, Clark and Co., 1932), 140; Macintosh, "Toward a New Untraditional Orthodoxy," 316–18.
225. Macintosh, *Personal Religion,* xii.

Notes to Chapter 2.
The Word as Myth: Neoorthodoxy

1. Quoted in Eberhard Busch, *Karl Barth: His Life from Letters and Autobiographical Texts* (London: SCM Press, 1976), 40.
2. Karl Barth, Preface to the First Edition, *The Epistle to the Romans,* 6th ed., trans. Edwyn C. Hoskyns (1933; reprint, London: Oxford University Press, 1975), 1.
3. "Absorbed Herrmann" quote in appendix to *Karl Barth-Rudolf Bultmann Letters, 1922–1966,* trans. and ed. Geoffrey W. Bromiley (1971; reprint, Grand Rapids: Wm. B. Eerdmans Publishing Co., 1981), 153; "remedies" and "swamp" quotes in Busch, *Karl Barth,* 43–44.
4. See Jochen Fähler, *Der Ausbruch des I. Weltkreiges in Karl Barths Predigten 1913–1915* (Bern: Peter Lang, 1979); Karl Barth and Eduard Thurneysen, *Suchet Gott, so werdet ihr legen!* (Bern: G. A. Baschlin, 1917).
5. See Herman Kutter, *Social Democracy: Does it Mean Darkness or Light?* (Letchworth: Garden City Press, 1910); idem, *They Must; or, God and the Social Democracy* (Chicago: Co-operative Printing Co., 1906); Leonhard Ragaz, *Der Kampf um das Reich Gottes in Blumhardt Vater und Sonhund Weiter!* (Erlenbach-Zurich: Rotapfel Verlag, 1922); idem, *Le Message revolutionaire* (Zurich: Neuchatel, 1941); idem, *Israel, Judaism and Christianity* (London: Victor Gollanez, 1947); Busch, *Karl Barth,* 76; Karl Barth and Eduard Thurneysen, *Revolutionary Theology in the Making: Barth-Thurneysen Correspondence, 1914–1925,* trans. James D. Smart (Richmond: John Knox Press, 1964), 27–32.
6. See Karl Barth, "Jesus Christ and the Movement for Social Justice" (1911), Friedrich-Wilhelm Marquardt, "Socialism in the Theology of Karl Barth," and George Hunsinger, "Conclusion: Toward a Radical Barth," in *Karl Barth and Radical Politics,* trans. and ed. George Hunsinger (Philadelphia: Westminster Press, 1976), 19–46, 47–76, 181–233.
7. See Karl Barth, *Predigten 1913,* ed. Nelly Barth and Gerhard Sauter (Zurich: TVZ, 1976), 67–68, 166–68, 213–20. For discussions of Barth's sermons during this period, see Fähler, *Der Ausbruch des 1. Weltkrieges in Karl Barths Predigten,* Bruce L. McCormack, *Karl Barth's Critically Realistic Dialectical Theology: Its Genesis and Development, 1909–1936* (Oxford: Clarendon Press, 1995), 92–107.
8. Barth's October 1, 1914 letter to Martin Rade quoted in McCormack, *Karl Barth's Critically Realistic Dialectical Theology,* 114; quote on the German manifesto in Busch, *Karl Barth,* 81.
9. Karl Barth, *The Theology of Schleiermacher,* trans. Geoffrey W. Bromiley (Grand Rapids: Wm. B. Eerdmans Publishing Co., 1982), 262–65. Busch, *Karl Barth,* 81–82; Terrence N. Tice, "Interviews with Karl Barth and Reflections on His Interpretations of Schleiermacher," *Barth and Schleiermacher: Beyond the Impasse?* ed. James O. Duke and Robert F. Streetman (Philadelphia: Fortress Press, 1988), 46–47.
10. Barth, *Predigten 1913,* 252; Thurneysen quote in Busch, *Karl Barth,* 97.
11. See Karl Barth, 1916 address, "The Strange New World Within the Bible," reprinted in Barth,

The Word of God and the Word of Man, trans. Douglas Horton (1928; reprint, Gloucester, Mass.: Peter Smith, 1978), 28–50.

12. January 1, 1916 letter to Thurneysen, in Barth-Thurneysen, *Revolutionary Theology in the Making*, 36.

13. Quote on Beck in Barth-Thurneysen, *Revolutionary Theology in the Making*, 38; "inexorable logic" quote in Barth, "The Strange New World Within the Bible," 34.

14. Barth, "The Strange New World Within the Bible," 39–43.

15. Ibid., 44.

16. November 11, 1918 letter to Thurneysen, in Barth-Thurneysen, *Revolutionary Theology in the Making*, 45; report on Romans notebook in ibid., 38. For the entire correspondence between Barth and Thurneysen during this period, see Eduard Thurneysen, ed., *Karl Barth-Eduard Thurneysen: Briefwechsel, i. 1913–1921* (Zurich: TVZ, 1973), 145–60.

17. See Barth's September 27, 1917 letter to Thurneysen in Barth-Thurneysen, *Revolutionary Theology in the Making*, 43.

18. Karl Barth, *Der Römerbrief* (Bern: G. A. Baschlin, 1919; reprint, Zurich: Evangelischer Verlag, 1963), 1–22, 46–51.

19. Ibid., 321–27.

20. Hans Urs von Balthasar, *The Theology of Karl Barth*, trans. John Drury (1962; reprint, New York: Holt, Rinehart and Winston, 1971), 48–52.

21. Barth, Preface to the First Edition, *The Epistle to the Romans*, 1.

22. Barth, *Der Römerbrief*, 67–75, 105, 308. For a genetic analysis of these themes in Barth's first edition *Romans*, see McCormack, *Karl Barth's Critically Realistic Dialectical Theology*, 142–45.

23. Adam quoted in John McConnachie, "The Teaching of Karl Barth: A New Positive Movement in German Theology," *The Hibbert Journal*, no. 25 (April 1927): 385–86; and McConnachie, *The Significance of Karl Barth* (London: Hodder and Stoughton, 1931), 43; Barth "church tower" quote in Karl Barth, *Die christliche Dogmatik im Entwurf, I: Die Lehre vom Worte Gottes. Prolegomena zur christlichen Dogmatik* (Munich: Christian Kaiser Verlag, 1927), ix. See Emil Brunner, "*Der Römerbrief* von Karl Barth," *Kirchenblatt für die Reformierte Schweiz* 34(1919):29–32; Philipp Bachmann, "Der Römerbrief verdeutscht und vergegenwärtigt: Ein Wort zu K. Barths Römerbrief," *Neue Kirchliche Zeitschrift* 32(1921):518–20.

24. See Franz Overbeck, *Christentum und Kultur*, ed. Carl Albrecht Bernoulli (Basel: Benno Schwabe & Co., 1919); and Barth's 1920 pamphlet on Overbeck, "On the Inner Situation of Christianity," reprinted as "Unsettled Questions for Theology Today" in Karl Barth, *Theology and Church: Shorter Writings, 1920–1928*, trans. Louise Pettibone Smith (1928; reprint, New York: Harper & Row, 1962), 55–73. For an account of Overbeck's influence on Barth, see Eberhard Jüngel, *Karl Barth, A Theological Legacy*, trans. Garrett E. Paul (Philadelphia: Westminster Press, 1986), 54–65.

25. See Søren Kierkegaard, *Attack Upon "Christendom,"* trans. Walter Lowrie (Princeton, N. J.: Princeton University Press, 1944); Herbert M. Garelick, *The Anti-Christianity of Kierkegaard* (The Hague: Martinus Nijhoff, 1965).

26. See Barth, "Unsettled Questions for Theology Today," 60–73; and Barth, April 1920 address to Aarau Student Conference, reprinted as "Biblical Questions, Insights, and Vistas" in Barth, *The Word of God and the Word of Man*, 60–76; closing quote in April 20, 1920 letter to Thurneysen in Barth-Thurneysen, *Revolutionary Theology in the Making*, 50.

27. Barth, "Biblical Questions, Insights, and Vistas," 74; see Brunner, "*Der Römerbrief* von Karl Barth," 29–32.

28. Barth, September 1919 Tambach address to Conference on Religion and Social Relations, reprinted as "The Christian's Place in Society" in Barth, *The Word of God and the Word of Man*, 282–83.

29. Barth, "Biblical Questions, Insights, and Vistas," 80.

30. Barth, *Epistle to the Romans*, 38.

31. See Eduard Thurneysen, *Dostoiewski* (Munich: Chr. Kaiser Verlag, 1921); Thurneysen, *Christoph Blumhardt* (Munich: Chr. Kaiser Verlag, 1926). Barth later recalled that it was Thur-

neysen "who first put me on the trail of Blumhardt and Kutter and then also of Dostoevsky, without whose discovery I would not have been able to write either the first or the second draft of the commentary on Romans" (Barth-Thurneysen, *Revolutionary Theology in the Making*, 72).

32. Barth, *Epistle to the Romans*, 28.
33. Ibid., 176–77.
34. Ibid., 141–42.
35. Ibid., 43.
36. Ibid., 36.
37. Ibid., 98. See Søren Kierkegaard, *Concluding Unscientific Postscript*, trans. David F. Swenson (Princeton, N. J.: Princeton University Press, 1941), 169–224; idem, *Training in Christianity*, trans. Walter Lowrie (Princeton, N. J.: Princeton University Press, 1947), 79–144.
38. Ibid., 98.
39. For discussions of the early Barth's rhetorical Expressionism, see Hans Frei, "An Afterword: Eberhard Busch's Biography of Karl Barth," in *Karl Barth in Re-View, Posthumous Works Reviewed and Assessed*, ed. H.-Martin Rumscheidt (Pittsburgh: Pickwick Press, 1981), 98–102; Stephen H. Webb, *Re-Figuring Theology: The Rhetoric of Karl Barth* (Albany, N.Y.: State University of New York Press, 1991), 1–18, 47–81.
40. Barth, *Epistle to the Romans*, 30.
41. Ibid., 29.
42. Ibid., 225.
43. Barth, Preface to the Second Edition, *The Epistle to the Romans*, 10.
44. Barth, *Epistle to the Romans*, 42.
45. April 20, 1920 letter to Thurneysen in Barth-Thurneysen, *Revolutionary Theology in the Making*, 50; Adolf Jülicher, "A Modern Interpreter of Paul," review of Barth's first edition *Romans*, reprinted in James M. Robinson, ed., *The Beginnings of Dialectic Theology* (Richmond: John Knox Press, 1968), 72–81; see Friedrich Gogarten, "The Holy Egoism of the Christian: An Answer to Jülicher's Essay: 'A Modern Interpreter of Paul,'" reprinted in Robinson, *The Beginnings of Dialectic Theology*, 82–87.
46. See Adolf von Harnack, *Marcion, das Evangelium vom fremden Gott* (Leipzig: J. C. Hinrichs Verlag, 1921).
47. Barth, Preface to the Second Edition, 13.
48. Barth, Preface to the Third Edition, 18.
49. Barth, Preface to the Fourth Edition, 21–22; idem, Preface to the Fifth Edition, 25–26, quote on 25.
50. Rudolf Bultmann, "Ethical and Mystical Religion in Primitive Christianity," 1920 essay reprinted in Robinson, *The Beginnings of Dialectic Theology*, 221–35, quote on 230.
51. Rudolf Bultmann, "Karl Barth's *Epistle to the Romans* in its Second Edition," 1922 review article reprinted in Robinson, *The Beginnings of Dialectic Theology*, 117.
52. Ibid., 120.
53. Barth, Preface to the Third Edition, 19.
54. Barth, *Epistle to the Romans*, 278.
55. Adolf von Harnack, "Fifteen Questions to Those Among the Theologians Who Are Contemptuous of the Scientific Theology," reprinted in Robinson, *The Beginnings of Dialectic Theology*, 165–66; "just staggering" reaction quoted in Agnes von Zahn-Harnack, *Adolf von Harnack* (Berlin: Walter de Gruyter & Co., 1951), 415.
56. *Zwischen den Zeiten* was edited by Merz and coedited by Barth, Gogarten, and Thurneysen. See Barth-Thurneysen, *Revolutionary Theology in the Making*, 113–14.
57. Harnack, "Fifteen Questions," 166.
58. Karl Barth, "Fifteen Answers to Professor von Harnack," reprinted in Robinson, *The Beginnings of Dialectic Theology*, 167–68.
59. Ibid., 170.

60. Karl Barth, "An Answer to Professor von Harnack's Open Letter," reprinted in Robinson, *The Beginnings of Dialectic Theology*, 176.

61. Adolf von Harnack, "An Open Letter to Professor Karl Barth," reprinted in Robinson, *The Beginnings of Dialectic Theology*, 174.

62. Barth, "An Answer to Professor von Harnack's Open Letter," 181.

63. Karl Barth, *The Göttingen Dogmatics: Instruction in the Christian Religion*, vol. 1, trans. Geoffrey W. Bromiley (Grand Rapids: Wm. B. Eerdmans Publishing Co., 1991), 148.

64. Barth, "An Answer to Professor von Harnack's Open Letter," 180.

65. Barth, *Göttingen Dogmatics*, 222–23.

66. Karl Barth, "Autobiographische Skizzen Karl Barths aus den Fakultatsalben der Ev.- Theo. Fakultat in Munster," reprinted in Barth-Bultmann letters, 156; "work began" quote in Busch, *Karl Barth*, 126.

67. Barth-Thurneysen, *Revolutionary Theology in the Making*, 176.

68. Quoted in Busch, *Karl Barth*, 138.

69. Karl Barth, "Foreword," in Heinrich Heppe, *Reformed Dogmatics* (Grand Rapids: Wm. B. Eerdmans Publishing Co., 1978), v.

70. See H. Schmid, *The Doctrinal Theology of the Evangelical Lutheran Church* (Philadelphia: Fortress Press, 1899).

71. Karl Barth and Eduard Thurneysen, *Briefwechsel Karl Barth-Eduard Thurneysen, II: 1921–1930* (Zurich: Evangelischer Verlag, 1974), 328–29.

72. Quoted in appendix to Barth-Bultmann letters, 158.

73. For Barth's account of his preference for realistic novels, see Busch, *Karl Barth*, 312–13; discussion in Webb, *Re-Figuring Theology*, 154–57.

74. Von Balthasar, *The Theology of Karl Barth*, 80.

75. For an example of Barth's confirmation of this reading, see his preface to the second edition (1958) of Karl Barth, *Anselm: Fides Quaerens Intellectum*, trans. Ian W. Robertson (London: SCM Press, 1960), 11: "Only a comparatively few commentators, for example Hans Urs von Balthasar, have realized that my interest in Anselm was never a side-issue for me or . . . realized how much it has influenced me or been absorbed into my own line of thinking." For a standard neoorthodox treatment of Barth's movement "from dialectical to dogmatic thinking," see Thomas F. Torrance, *Karl Barth: An Introduction to His Early Theology, 1910–1931* [London: SCM Press, 1962], 48–132).

76. Barth, *Anselm: Fides Quaerens Intellectum*, 18.

77. Ibid., 29.

78. Ibid., 26–27.

79. Karl Barth, *Church Dogmatics: The Doctrine of the Word of God*, vol. 1, bk. 1, trans. G. T. Thomson (Edinburgh: T. & T. Clark, 1936), ix–x.

80. Barth, *Göttingen Dogmatics*, 235.

81. Ibid., 58–59.

82. Ibid., 43–314.

83. See Ingrid Spieckermann, *Gotteserkenntnis: Ein Beitrag zur Grundfrage der neuen Theologie Karl Barths* (Munich: Chr. Kaiser Verlag, 1985); Michael Beintker, *Die Dialektik in der 'dialektischen Theologie' Karl Barths* (Munich: Chr. Kaiser Verlag, 1987); Eberhard Mechels, *Analogie bei Erich Przywara und Karl Barth: Das Verhältnis von Offenbarungstheologie und Metaphysik* (Neukirchen-Vluyn: Neukirchener Verlag, 1974); McCormack, *Karl Barth's Critically Realistic Dialectical Theology*.

84. See McCormack, *Karl Barth's Critically Realistic Dialectical Theology*, 14–23, 327–449.

85. Barth, *Church Dogmatics*, 1:1, ix–xii.

86. Ibid., 86.

87. See G. C. Berkouwer, *The Triumph of Grace in the Theology of Karl Barth*, trans. Harry R. Boer (Grand Rapids: Wm. B. Eerdmans Publishing Co., 1956); Robert W. Jenson, *Alpha and Omega: A Study in the Theology of Karl Barth* (New York: Thomas Nelson & Sons, 1963).

88. Barth, *Church Dogmatics,* 1:1, 123–24.

89. Ibid., 134–35.

90. Quoted in Busch, *Karl Barth,* 212.

91. Karl Barth, *Church Dogmatics: The Doctrine of God,* vol. 2, bk. 1, ed. G. W. Bromiley and T. F. Torrance, trans. T. H. L. Parker et al. (Edinburgh: T. & T. Clark, 1957), 4–7, quote on 7. In this volume, Barth also withdrew his previous charge about the Catholic *analogia entis* being the "invention of anti-Christ"; see discussion on 82–83.

92. Paul Tillich and Reinhold Niebuhr repeatedly criticized Barth's "immunization" strategy on these grounds and connected it to his purported disengagement from politics. See Tillich, *A History of Christian Thought: From Its Judaic and Hellenistic Origins to Existentialism,* ed. Carl E. Braaten (New York: Simon & Schuster, 1968), 535–39; Niebuhr, "An Answer to Karl Barth," *The Christian Century* 56 (February 1949), 234–36.

93. Dietrich Bonhoeffer, *Letters and Papers from Prison,* ed. Eberhard Bethge, trans. Reginald Fuller et al. (1953; reprint, New York: Macmillan Co., 1978), 286.

94. See Karl Barth, "An Introductory Essay," introduction to Ludwig Feuerbach, *The Essence of Christianity,* trans. George Eliot (New York: Harper & Row, 1957), x–xxxii; Barth, "Ludwig Feuerbach," 1920 lecture reprinted in Barth, *Theology and Church,* 217–37; Barth, *Protestant Theology in the Nineteenth Century: Its Background and History* (1959; reprint, Valley Forge, Pa.: Judson Press, 1976), 534–40.

95. See Barth, *Church Dogmatics,* vol. 2, bk. 1, 620–21.

96. See Karl Barth, *The German Church Conflict,* trans. P. T. A. Parker (Richmond: John Knox Press, 1965), 13–46; Barth-Bultmann letters, 78–79. For the text of the Barmen Declaration, see Arthur C. Cochrane, *The Church's Confession under Hitler* (1962; reprint, Pittsburgh: Pickwick Press, 1976), 237–47.

97. The Confessing Church grew out of the Pastors' Emergency League founded by Martin Niemoller in 1933. For accounts of its history, see Cochrane, *The Church's Confession under Hitler;* and Ernst Christian Helmreich, *The German Churches under Hitler: Background, Struggle, and Epilogue* (Detroit: Wayne State University Press, 1979). On Barth's later relations with the Confessing movement after his dismissal from Bonn, see Barth, *The German Church Conflict,* 47–76.

98. Karl Barth, "How My Mind Has Changed," 1938 autobiographical essay in *The Christian Century,* reprinted in Barth, *How I Changed My Mind* (Richmond: John Knox Press, 1966), 41–42. See Robert P. Ericksen, *Theologians under Hitler: Gerhard Kittel/Paul Althaus/Emanuel Hirsch* (New Haven, Conn.: Yale University Press, 1985), 120–97.

99. Emil Brunner, *Natural Theology: Comprising 'Nature and Grace' and the Reply 'No!' by Dr. Karl Barth,* trans. Peter Fraenkel (London: Geoffrey Bles, Centenary Press, 1946), 32–33.

100. For the full text of Barth's six-part response to Brunner, see ibid. For a recent reprinting of the preface and sections 2 and 3 of this text, see Karl Barth, "No! Answer to Emil Brunner," in *Karl Barth: Theologian of Freedom,* ed. Clifford Green (Minneapolis: Fortress Press, 1991), 151–67, quote on 164.

101. Emil Brunner, *The Christian Doctrine of God: Dogmatics,* vol. 1, trans. Olive Wyon (Philadelphia: Westminster Press, 1949), 235–36; Barth, *How I Changed My Mind,* 42.

102. See his 1924 article, "Liberal Theology and the Latest Theological Movement," reprinted in Rudolf Bultmann, *Faith and Understanding,* trans. Louise Pettibone Smith (1969; reprint, Philadelphia: Fortress Press, 1987), 36.

103. Rudolf Bultmann, *The History of the Synoptic Tradition,* trans. John Marsh (New York: Harper & Row, 1963).

104. April 28, 1927 letter to Bultmann in Barth-Bultmann letters, 32–33.

105. See Barth, *Die christliche Dogmatik im Entwurf,* vii–x. Barth apparently sent a copy of this work to Bultmann in 1927.

106. June 8, 1928 letter to Barth in Barth-Bultmann letters, 38–39.

107. June 12, 1928 letter to Bultmann in ibid., 40–42.

108. February 5, 1930 letter to Bultmann in ibid., 49–50.

109. Ibid., 50.

110. See the exchange of letters in ibid., 51–65. Though his account says nothing about this incident, Busch observes that Barth repeatedly deflected Bultmann's requests for an in-depth, in-
person exchange of views; see Busch, *Karl Barth*, 195.

111. June 20, 1931 letter to Bultmann in Barth-Bultmann letters, 65.

112. May 27, 1931 letter to Bultmann in ibid., 58.

113. July 7, 1934 letter to Barth in ibid., 75.

114. December 10, 1935 letter to Barth and December 22, 1935 letter to Bultmann in ibid., 82–85.
Barth's implicit reproach to Bultmann for taking the Hitler oath was matched by Tillich's criticism of Barth for opposing Hitler too narrowly and too late. In the first year of Nazi rule,
Tillich explained, Barth accepted Hitler's accession to power "and did not speak against it in
the name of religion, although there were many occasions for doing so." Barth and the
churches kept quiet, for example, when the first attacks on the Jews began in April 1933.
"They did not speak up until they themselves were attacked by Hitler," Tillich recalled. "This
is one of the great shortcomings of the German churches, but also of Karl Barth. But then
Barth became the leader of the inner-churchly resistance against National Socialism" (Tillich,
A History of Christian Thought, 538–39). Tillich's moral awareness and courage clearly surpassed that of Barth during this period, but Tillich also was slow to recognize the seriousness
of the Nazi threat in the early 1930s (see Gary Dorrien, *Reconstructing the Common Good:
Theology and the Social Order* [Maryknoll, N.Y.: Orbis Books, 1990], 65–66).

115. See Rudolf Bultmann, "The Significance of the Historical Jesus for the Theology of Paul" and
"The Christology of the New Testament," reprinted in Bultmann, *Faith and Understanding*,
220–46, 262–85; Bultmann, "Ethical and Mystical Religion in Primitive Christianity," 224–25.

116. Rudolf Bultmann, *Jesus and the Word*, trans. Louise Pettibone Smith and Erminie Huntress
Lantero (New York: Charles Scribner's Sons, 1958), 8.

117. See Bultmann, "Liberal Theology and the Latest Theological Movement," 29–45.

118. Rudolf Bultmann, "New Testament and Mythology," reprinted in Bultmann, *New Testament
and Mythology and Other Basic Writings*, trans. and ed. Schubert M. Ogden (Philadelphia:
Fortress Press, 1984), 1. This is a cleaner and more recent translation than the translation by
Reginald H. Fuller that is featured in the volume edited by Hans Werner Bartsch, *Kerygma
and Myth: A Theological Debate* (London: SPCK, 1954), 1–44. Ogden's translation will be used
here except when otherwise indicated.

119. See Wilhelm Herrmann, *The Communion of the Christian with God*, 2d English ed., trans. J.
Sandys Stanyon (Philadelphia: Fortress Press, 1971), 57–124.

120. Bultmann, "New Testament and Mythology," 12.

121. Rudolf Bultmann, "Religion and Culture," (1920), reprinted in Robinson, *The Beginnings of
Dialectic Theology*, 211.

122. See Bultmann, "Autobiographical Reflections of Rudolf Bultmann," in *The Theology of Rudolf
Bultmann*, ed. Charles W. Kegley (New York: Harper & Row, 1966), xix–xxi; Bultmann, "Ethical and Mystical Religion in Primitive Christianity," 221–25. For his mature reflections on
Christian origins, see Rudolf Bultmann, *Primitive Christianity in Its Contemporary Setting*,
trans. Reginald H. Fuller (Philadelphia: Fortress Press, 1956).

123. Bultmann, "New Testament and Mythology," 42.

124. Rudolf Bultmann, *Jesus Christ and Mythology* (New York: Charles Scribner's Sons, 1958), 18.

125. Bultmann, "New Testament and Mythology," 9.

126. Ibid., 9.

127. Bultmann, *Jesus Christ and Mythology*, 19.

128. Bultmann, "New Testament and Mythology," 10.

129. Bultmann, *Jesus Christ and Mythology*, 18.

130. Bultmann, "New Testament and Mythology," 33.

131. Ibid., 34–35. See Rudolf Bultmann, *The Presence of Eternity: History and Eschatology* (1957;
reprint, Westport, Conn.: Greenwood Press, 1975), 38–55.

132. Bultmann, *Jesus Christ and Mythology*, 15–16.

133. Bultmann, "New Testament and Mythology," 39.

134. Bultmann, *Jesus Christ and Mythology*, 71; see Rudolf Bultmann, *Theology of the New Testament*, vol. 1, trans. Kendrick Grobel (New York: Charles Scribner's Sons, 1951), 314–29.

135. Ibid., 84. On this theme, see Herrmann, *The Communion of the Christian with God*, 146–201.

136. See especially Hans-Werner Bartsch, *Kerygma and Myth*, vol. 1; idem, ed., *Kerygma and Myth: A Theological Debate*, vol. 2, trans. Reginald H. Fuller (London: SPCK, 1962); idem, ed., *Kerygma und Mythos*, vol. 2 (Hamburg: Herbert Reich-Evangelischer Verlag, 1952); idem, ed., *Kerygma und Mythos*, vol. 3 (Hamburg: Herbert Reich-Evangelischer Verlag, 1954); Carl E. Braaten and Roy A. Harrisville, eds., *Kerygma and History: A Symposium on the Theology of Rudolf Bultmann* (New York: Abingdon Press, 1962); John Macquarrie, *The Scope of Demythologizing: Bultmann and his Critics* (New York: Harper & Brothers, 1960); Burton Throckmorton, *The New Testament and Mythology* (Philadelphia: Westminster Press, 1959).

137. See Ernst Kinder, ed., *Ein Wort lutherischer Theologie zur Entmythologisierung* (Munich: Evangelischer Pressverband fur Bayern, 1952); bishops quoted in Hans-Werner Bartsch, "The Present State of the Debate," (1954), in Bartsch, ed., *Kerygma and Myth*, 2:1–2.

138. See Heinrich Fries, *Bultmann, Barth, und die katholische Theologie* (Stuttgart: Schwabenverlag, 1955); Rene Marle, S.J., *Bultmann et l'interpretation du Nouveau Testament* (Aubier: Editions Montaigne, 1956); L. Malevez, S.J., *The Christian Message and Myth: The Theology of Rudolf Bultmann*, trans. Olive Wyon (London: SCM Press, 1958). The fifth volume of the German *Kerygma and Myth* series contained contributions to the demythologizing debate by Catholic scholars Fries, Karl Adam, Adam Fechter, A. Kolping, Jerome Hamer, Rudolf Schnackenburg, and others; see Bartsch, ed., *Kerygma und Mythos*, vol. 5 (Hamburg: Herbert Reich-Evangelischer Verlag, 1955).

139. Julius Schniewind, "A Reply to Bultmann," in Bartsch, *Kerygma and Myth*, 1:66.

140. Helmut Thielicke, "The Restatement of New Testament Mythology," in ibid., 138–74.

141. Austin Farrer, "An English Appreciation," in ibid., 212–23.

142. Friedrich Schumann, "Can the Event of Jesus Christ be Demythologized?" in ibid., 175–90.

143. John Macquarrie, *An Existentialist Theology: A Comparison of Heidegger and Bultmann* (New York: Macmillan Co., 1955), 246.

144. Cited in Bartsch, "The Present State of the Debate," 21–26.

145. Fritz Buri, "Entmythologisierung oder Entkerygmatisierung der Theologie," in Bartsch, *Kerygma und Mythos*, 2:85–101; Buri, "Das Problem der ausgebliebenen Parusie," *Schweizerische theologische Umschau* (October–December 1946), 97–120.

146. Karl Jaspers, "Myth and Religion," and "The Issues Clarified," reprinted in Karl Jaspers and Rudolf Bultmann, *Myth and Christianity: An Inquiry into the Possibility of Religion Without Myth* (New York: Noonday Press, 1958), 3–56, 72–116.

147. Rudolf Bultmann, "A Reply to the Theses of J. Schniewind," in Bartsch, *Kerygma and Myth*, 1:117–18.

148. Bavarian radio discussion quoted in Bartsch, "The Present State of the Debate," 28.

149. Quoted in ibid., 74.

150. Martin Kähler, *The So-called Historical Jesus and the Historic Biblical Christ*, trans. Carl E. Braaten (Philadelphia: Fortress Press, 1988), 43, 46. Kähler studied under Richard Rothe at Heidelberg, under the mediating theologian Julius Müller and August Tholuck at Halle, and under F. C. Baur and the biblical realist J. T. Beck (whose writings greatly influenced Barth in his early crisis theology years) at Tübingen. Kähler later remarked that it was largely to Beck that he owed his appreciation for the revelatory power of scripture. For Barth's similar assessment, see Barth-Thurneysen, *Revolutionary Theology in the Making*, 38, 42; and Barth, *Protestant Theology in the Nineteenth Century*, 616–24.

151. See Martin Kähler, *Dogmatische Zeitfragen: Angewandte Dogmen*, vol. 2, 2d ed. (Leipzig: A. Deichert, 1908); Kähler, *Die Wissenschaft der christlichen Lehre*, 2d ed. (Leipzig: A Deichert, 1893).

152. Kähler, *The So-called Historical Jesus,* 46, 57.

153. See Herrmann, *The Communion of the Christian With God,* 71–101; Wilhelm Herrmann, *Die Religion im Verhältnis zum Welterkennen und zur Sittlichkeit* (Halle: Niemeyer, 1879).

154. Kähler, *The So-called Historical Jesus,* 117–37; see Carl E. Braaten, "Martin Kähler on the Historic Biblical Christ," in *The Historical Jesus and the Kerygmatic Christ: Essays on the New Quest of the Historical Jesus,* ed. Carl E. Braaten and Roy A. Harrisville (New York: Abingdon Press, 1964), 94–99.

155. Kähler, *The So-called Historical Jesus,* 63.

156. Ibid., 131.

157. Ibid., 66.

158. Karl Barth, *Church Dogmatics: The Doctrine of the Word of God,* vol. 1, bk. 2, trans. G. T. Thomson and Harold Knight (Edinburgh: T. & T. Clark, 1956), 64–65. Kähler recognized that the gospels are "testimonies not sources," Barth continued. "There is no reason why historico-critical Bible research should not contribute to the investigation and exposition of this historical Christ of the New Testament, instead of—proceeding every whit as arbitrary, whether the science is history or theology—chasing the ghost of an historical Jesus in the vacuum behind the New Testament."

159. Carl E. Braaten, "Revelation, History, and Faith in Martin Kähler," introduction to English edition of Kähler, *The So-called Historical Jesus,* 15.

160. For example, see Bartsch, "The Present State of the Debate," 72–77.

161. Rudolf Bultmann, "The Case for Demythologization," in Jaspers-Bultmann, *Myth and Christianity,* 60.

162. Rudolf Bultmann, "Preaching: Genuine and Secularized," in *Religion and Culture: Essays in Honor of Paul Tillich,* ed. Walter Leibrecht (New York: Harper & Brothers, 1959), 240.

163. Karl Barth, "Rudolf Bultmann—An Attempt to Understand Him," in Bartsch, *Kerygma and Myth,* 2:92.

164. Ibid., 97.

165. Bultmann, "A Reply to the Theses of J. Schniewind," 107.

166. Bultmann, "New Testament and Mythology," in Bartsch, *Kerygma and Myth* (Fuller translation), 1:41.

167. Barth, "Rudolf Bultmann—An Attempt to Understand Him," 100–101; see Bultmann, *"Karl Barth, The Resurrection of the Dead,"* in Bultmann, *Faith and Understanding,* 66–94.

168. Ibid., 101–2.

169. Ibid., 102, 108.

170. Ibid., 116.

171. Ibid., 127. See November 11–15, 1952 letter to Barth in Barth-Bultmann letters, 87–104.

172. See Friedrich Gogarten, *Entmythologisierung und Kirche* (Stuttgart: Friedrich Vorwerk Verlag, 1953); Bartsch, "The Present State of the Debate"; Bartsch, *Kann man von Bultmanns Exegese predigen?* (Hamburg: Herbert Reich-Evangelischer Verlag, 1955); Christian Hartlich and Walter Sachs, *Der Ursprung des Mythosbegriffes in der modernen Bibelwissenschaft* (Tübingen: J. C. B. Mohr, 1952); Schubert M. Ogden, *Christ Without Myth: A Study Based on the Theology of Rudolf Bultmann* (New York: Harper & Row, 1961).

173. See Karl Barth, *Church Dogmatics: The Doctrine of Creation,* vol. 3, bk. 2, trans. Harold Knight et al. (Edinburgh: T. & T. Clark, 1960), 442–54; Barth, *Church Dogmatics: The Doctrine of Reconciliation,* vol. 4, bk. 1, trans. G. W. Bromiley (Edinburgh: T. & T. Clark, 1956), 767–69.

174. Barth, *Church Dogmatics,* 4:1, ix–x; see James D. Smart, *The Divided Mind of Modern Theology: Karl Barth and Rudolf Bultmann, 1908–1933* (Philadelphia: Westminster Press, 1967); Helmut Gollwitzer, *The Existence of God as Confessed by Faith* (Philadelphia: Westminster Press, 1965).

175. See Heinrich Ott, *Geschichte und Heilsgeschichte in der Theologie Rudolf Bultmanns* (Tübingen: J. C. B. Mohr, 1955); Ott, "Objectification and Existentialism," in Bartsch, *Kerygma and*

Myth, 2:306–35; Hermann Diem, *Dogmatics,* trans. Harold Knight (Philadelphia: Westminster Press, 1959); Helmut Thielicke, "The Restatement of New Testament Mythology."

176. See Emil Brunner, *The Christian Doctrine of Creation and Redemption: Dogmatics: vol. 2,* trans. Olive Wyon (Philadelphia: Westminster Press, 1952), 263–70.

177. See Søren Kierkegaard, *Philosophical Fragments,* trans. Howard V. Hong (Princeton, N. J.: Princeton University Press, 1962), 11–60; idem, *Concluding Unscientific Postscript,* 169–224.

178. Emil Brunner, *Truth as Encounter,* trans. Amandus W. Loos and David Cairns (Philadelphia: Westminster Press, 1964), 21, 24.

179. See Harold E. Hatt, *Encountering Truth: A New Understanding of How Revelation as Encounter Yields Doctrine* (Nashville: Abingdon Press, 1966); Martin Buber, *I and Thou,* trans. Walter Kaufman (New York: Charles Scribner's Sons, 1970); Paul King Jewett, *Emil Brunner's Concept of Revelation* (London: James Clarke, 1954).

180. Brunner, *Truth as Encounter,* 44; for a similarly harsh assessment of Barth's doctrine of election, see Brunner, *The Christian Doctrine of God,* 346–52.

181. See Rudolf Bultmann, "What Does it Mean to Speak of God?" in Bultmann, *Faith and Understanding,* 53–65.

182. Brunner, *Truth as Encounter,* 49.

183. Emil Brunner, *Revelation and Reason: The Christian Doctrine of Faith and Knowledge,* trans. Olive Wyon (Philadelphia: Westminster Press, 1946), 399–400.

184. Ibid., 406–7. Brunner acknowledged elsewhere that if one accepts Bultmann's definition of myth—to "speak of God in a human way"—then the Christian kerygma cannot be separated from myth, since the Bible everywhere speaks of God in a human way (see Brunner, *The Christian Doctrine of Creation and Redemption,* 268–70). For an earlier assessment of the problem of Christian myth, see Brunner, *The Mediator: A Study of the Central Doctrine of the Christian Faith,* trans. Olive Wyon (1927; reprint, Philadelphia: Westminster Press, 1947), 377–96.

185. See Gustaf Aulén, *The Drama and the Symbols: A Book on Images of God and the Problems They Raise,* trans. Sydney Linton (Philadelphia: Fortress Press, 1970), 125–30; Kinder, ed., *Ein Wort lutherischer Theologie zur Entmythologisierung;* Paul Althaus, *The So-called Kerygma and the Historical Jesus,* trans. David Cairns (Edinburgh: Oliver & Boyd, 1959).

186. See H. P. Owen, *Revelation and Existence: A Study in the Theology of Rudolf Bultmann* (Cardiff: University of Wales Press, 1957), 9–14, 37–47, 99–110; Macquarrie, *An Existentialist Theology,* 29–134.

187. Bultmann, *Jesus Christ and Mythology,* 68.

188. See Philip A. Rolnick, *Analogical Possibilities: How Words Refer to God* (Atlanta: Scholars Press, 1993); Ralph McInerny, *The Logic of Analogy* (The Hague: Nijhoff, 1961); William Hordern, *Speaking of God: The Nature and Purpose of Theological Language* (New York: Macmillan Co., 1964), 66–67, 125–32; Janet Martin Soskice, *Metaphor and Religious Language* (Oxford: Clarendon Press, 1985), 64–66.

189. Paul Tillich, *On the Boundary: An Autobiographical Sketch* (New York: Charles Scribner's Sons, 1966), 21–22. For an early version of this reminiscence, see Tillich, *The Interpretation of History,* trans. N. A. Rasetzki and Elsa L. Talmey (New York: Charles Scribner's Sons, 1936), 3–76.

190. See Paul Tillich, "Critical and Positive Paradox: A Discussion with Karl Barth and Friedrich Gogarten," in Robinson, *The Beginnings of Dialectic Theology,* 133–41; Tillich, "Autobiographical Reflections," in *The Theology of Paul Tillich,* ed. Charles W. Kegley and Robert W. Bretall (New York: Macmillan Co., 1952), 8–9.

191. Karl Barth, "The Paradoxical Nature of the 'Positive Paradox': Answers and Questions to Paul Tillich," in Robinson, *The Beginnings of Dialectic Theology,* 147. See Tillich, "Answer to Karl Barth," 155–58; and Friedrich Gogarten, "The Intellectual Situation of the Theologian: Another Answer to Paul Tillich," 159–62, in ibid.

192. See Paul Tillich, "Denker der Zeit, Karl Barth," *Vossische Zeitung* (January 20, 1926); Tillich,

The Religious Situation, trans. H. Richard Niebuhr (1932; reprint, Cleveland: Meridian Books/World Publishing Co., 1956), 214–17.

193. See Paul Tillich, "Logos und Mythos der Technik," *Logos* 16(1927):356–65; Tillich, "Mythos und Mythologie," in *Die Religion in Geschichte und Gegenwart,* 2d ed., vol. 4 (Tübingen: J. C. B. Mohr, 1930), 664–69; Tillich, *The Socialist Decision,* trans. Franklin Sherman (1933; reprint, New York: Harper & Row, 1977); Tillich, *The Protestant Era,* trans. James Luther Adams (London: Nisbet & Co., 1951); Wilhelm and Marion Pauck, *Paul Tillich: His Life and Thought* (New York: Harper & Row, 1976).

194. Paul Tillich, "The Present Theological Situation in Light of the Continental European Development," *Theology Today* 6 (October 1949):306.

195. Paul Tillich, *Religionsphilosophie,* in *Lehrbuch der Philosophie,* ed. M. Dessoir (Berlin: Ullstein, 1925), reprinted in *What Is Religion?* trans. James Luther Adams (New York: Harper & Row, 1969), 101–5.

196. Paul Tillich, "The Religious Symbol," in *Symbolism in Religion and Literature,* ed. Rollo May (New York: George Braziller, 1960), 84. For earlier versions, see Tillich, "The Religious Symbol," *The Journal of Liberal Religion* 2 (1940):13–33; and Tillich, "Das religiöse Symbol," *Blätter für deutsche Philosophie,* vol. 1, 1928.

197. See Ernst Cassirer, *The Philosophy of Symbolic Forms, Volume One: Language; Volume Two: Mythical Thought,* trans. Ralph Manheim (New Haven, Conn.: Yale University Press, 1953, 1955).

198. Tillich, "The Religious Symbol," 87.

199. See Paul Tillich, *Theology of Culture* (New York: Oxford University Press, 1959), 36–38.

200. Tillich, "The Religious Symbol," 87.

201. Ibid., 89.

202. Paul Tillich, *Dynamics of Faith* (New York: Harper & Brothers, 1957), 49–50.

203. Paul Tillich, *Systematic Theology,* vol. 2 (Chicago: University of Chicago Press, 1957), 152.

204. Tillich, *Dynamics of Faith,* 50. See Tillich, *Biblical Religion and the Search for Ultimate Reality* (Chicago: University of Chicago Press, 1955), 78–85.

205. Tillich, *Systematic Theology,* 2:152.

206. Paul Tillich, "The Meaning and Justification of Religious Symbols," in *Religious Experience and Truth,* ed. Sidney Hook (New York: New York University Press, 1961), 4; see Tillich, *Theology of Culture,* 53–67.

207. Ibid., 10.

208. Tillich, "The Religious Symbol," 91.

209. See Paul Tillich, *Systematic Theology,* vol. 1 (Chicago: University of Chicago Press, 1951), 271–89; idem, *The Interpretation of History,* 77–122.

210. Tillich, *Systematic Theology,* 2:29.

211. Ibid.

212. Tillich, *Theology of Culture,* 3–7.

213. Ibid., 7–8.

214. Reinhold Niebuhr, *An Interpretation of Christian Ethics* (1935; reprint, San Francisco: Harper & Row, 1963), 2–3.

215. Ibid., 2.

216. Ibid., 2.

217. Ibid., 7.

218. See Nicolas Berdyaev, *Freedom and the Spirit,* trans. Oliver Fielding Clarke (New York: Charles Scribner's Sons, 1935), 69–70.

219. Niebuhr, *An Interpretation of Christian Ethics,* 7.

220. Reinhold Niebuhr, "The Truth in Myths," in *The Nature of Religious Experience: Essays in Honor of Douglas Clyde Macintosh,* ed. J. S. Bixler et al. (New York: Harper & Brothers, 1937), 123.

221. Niebuhr, *An Interpretation of Christian Ethics,* 4–8.

222. Niebuhr, "The Truth in Myths," 121.

223. Ibid., 121–22.

224. Reinhold Niebuhr, *Beyond Tragedy: Essays on the Christian Interpretation of History* (New York: Charles Scribner's Sons, 1951), 20–21.

225. Niebuhr, *An Interpretation of Christian Ethics*, 53–54; Niebuhr, *The Nature and Destiny of Man*, vol. 1 (New York: Charles Scribner's Sons, 1941), 265–80. Parts of this section are drawn from my chapter on Christian realism in Dorrien, *Soul In Society: The Making and Renewal of Social Christianity* (Minneapolis: Fortress Press, 1995), 95–97.

226. Niebuhr, "The Truth in Myths," 128.

227. Niebuhr, *The Nature and Destiny of Man*, 1:178–86.

228. Reinhold Niebuhr, *The Self and the Dramas of History* (New York: Charles Scribner's Sons, 1955), 97.

229. Niebuhr, "The Truth in Myths," 133.

230. Ibid., 133.

231. Reinhold Niebuhr, "The Quality of Our Lives," *The Christian Century* 77 (May 11, 1960): 568.

232. See Moltmann's interview with Teofilo Cabestrero in Cabestrero, ed., *Faith: Conversations with Contemporary Theologians* (Maryknoll, N.Y.: Orbis Books, 1980), 121–22; and Moltmann's exchange of letters with Barth reprinted in Jürgen Fangmeier and Hinrich Stoevesandt, eds., *Karl Barth Letters, 1961–1968*, trans. Geoffrey W. Bromiley (Grand Rapids: Wm. B. Eerdmans Publishing Co., 1981), 174–76, 348–49.

233. Langdon Gilkey, "Dissolution and Reconstruction in Theology," *The Christian Century* 82 (February 3, 1965):135.

Notes to Chapter 3.
Beyond Neoorthodoxy: The Sacred Dimension

1. Brevard S. Childs, *Biblical Theology in Crisis* (Philadelphia: Westminster Press, 1970), 17.

2. See Bernhard W. Anderson, *Rediscovering the Bible* (New York: Association Press, 1951); H. H. Rowley, *The Relevance of the Bible* (New York: Macmillan Co., 1944); H. H. Rowley, *The Unity of the Bible* (Philadelphia: Westminster Press, 1955); Alan Richardson, "The Nature of the Biblical Theology," *Theology* 39 (1939):166–76; Alan Richardson, *A Preface to Bible Study* (Philadelphia: Westminster Press, 1943); Paul S. Minear, *Eyes of Faith: A Study in the Biblical Point of View* (Philadelphia: Westminster Press, 1946); Otto Piper, "The Bible as 'Holy History,'" *The Christian Century* 63 (1946):362–72; Floyd V. Filson, *The New Testament Against Its Environment* (London: SCM Press, 1941).

3. See James D. Smart, "The Death and Rebirth of Old Testament Theology," *Journal of Religion* 23(1943):1–11, 125–36; idem, *The Interpretation of Scripture* (Philadelphia: Westminster Press, 1961); Joseph Haroutunian, "Recent Theology and the Biblical Mind," *Journal of Bible and Religion* 8 (1940):15–25.

4. H. H. Rowley, *The Re-Discovery of the Old Testament* (Philadelphia: Westminster Press, 1946), 58.

5. G. Ernest Wright, *God Who Acts: Biblical Theology as Recital* (1952; reprint, London: SCM Press, 1958), 29.

6. Ibid., 124.

7. G. Ernest Wright, *The Challenge of Israel's Faith* (Chicago: University of Chicago Press, 1944), chap. 3.

8. Wright, *God Who Acts*, 125.

9. See G. Ernest Wright, *The Old Testament Against Its Environment* (Chicago: University of Chicago Press, 1950).

10. Ernst Cassirer, *An Essay on Man* (New Haven, Conn.: Yale University Press, 1944), 82–83.

11. Wright, *God Who Acts*, 125–26.

12. Ibid., 127.
13. See William F. Albright, *The Archaeology of Palestine* (New York: Penguin Books, 1949); idem, *The Biblical Period;* idem, *From the Stone Age to Christianity,* 2d ed. (New York: Doubleday Anchor Books, 1957); idem, *Archaeology and the Religion of Israel,* 5th ed. (New York: Doubleday Anchor Books, 1969); idem, *Yahweh and the Gods of Canaan* (New York: Doubleday & Co., 1968); idem, *The Biblical Period from Abraham to Ezra* (New York: Harper & Row, 1963); G. Ernest Wright, *Biblical Archaeology* (Philadelphia: Westminster Press, 1962).
14. G. Ernest Wright, "How Did Early Israel Differ from Her Neighbors?" *The Biblical Archaeologist* 6, (1943):6.
15. Wright, *God Who Acts,* 127.
16. Anderson, *Rediscovering the Bible,* 35; idem, *Understanding the Old Testament* (New York: Prentice-Hall, 1957), 37–41.
17. Among the various collections of Biblical Theology movement articles that develop these themes, see Alan Richardson and Wolfgang Schweitzer, eds., *Biblical Authority for Today* (Philadelphia: Westminster Press, 1951); and Berhard W. Anderson, ed., *The Old Testament and Christian Faith* (New York: Harper & Row, 1963).
18. See Walther Eichrodt, *Theology of the Old Testament,* 2 vols., trans. J. A. Baker (Philadelphia: Westminster Press, 1961, 1967).
19. For his account of "the cracking of the walls" of the Biblical Theology movement, see Childs, *Biblical Theology in Crisis,* 61–87.
20. Langdon Gilkey, "Introduction: A Retrospective Glance at My Work," in *The Whirlwind in Culture: Frontiers in Theology,* ed. Donald W. Musser and Joseph L. Price (Bloomington, Ind.: Meyer-Stone Books, 1988), 3–4.
21. Langdon Gilkey, *Shantung Compound: The Story of Men and Women Under Pressure* (New York: Harper & Row, 1966), 92.
22. Ibid., 232.
23. Ibid.
24. See Langdon Gilkey, "An Appreciation of Karl Barth," in *How Karl Barth Changed My Mind,* ed. Donald K. McKim (Grand Rapids: Wm. B. Eerdmans Publishing Co., 1986), 151–52.
25. Gilkey, "A Retrospective Glance at My Work," 15.
26. William Adams Brown, "The Old Theology and the New," *The Harvard Theological Review* 4 (January 1911):15–16; quoted in Langdon Gilkey, *Maker of Heaven and Earth: A Study of the Christian Doctrine of Creation* (Garden City, N.Y.: Doubleday & Co., 1959), 20–21.
27. Gilkey, *Maker of Heaven and Earth,* 27.
28. Ibid., 29–30.
29. Ibid., 260–61.
30. Ibid., 268–69.
31. Barth explained that he admired Tillich's work, for example, "but I do not think he is writing Christian theology. . . . If I understand myself as a creature, then I understand my limits and He who limits me: God the Creator. We are either in this circle of knowledge or we are not. That is the question of revelation or faith." (Quoted in John D. Godsey, ed., *Karl Barth's Table Talk,* Scottish Journal of Theology Occasional Papers, no. 10 [Edinburgh: Oliver and Boyd, 1963], 29.)
32. Gilkey, *Maker of Heaven and Earth,* 270.
33. See Karl Barth, *Church Dogmatics: The Doctrine of the Word of God,* vol. 1, bk. 1 trans. G. T. Thomson (Edinburgh: T. & T. Clark, 1936), 111–24.
34. Gilkey, *Maker of Heaven and Earth,* 271.
35. Ibid., 280–81.
36. Ibid., 281.
37. Ibid., 283.
38. Ibid., 291.
39. Gilkey's reading of Aquinas as an ontological theologian was problematic. It was in the

Augustinian tradition (from Augustine to the thirteenth-century Franciscan Scholastics) that theologians developed the ontological approach in which God is conceived as the presupposition of the question of God. Augustinians such as Alexander of Hales and Bonaventura argued that God is not subject to doubt because God is the necessary presupposition of all thought. Aquinas was critically responding to a centuries-long tradition of ontological reasoning when he allowed that there is, indeed, an identity of predicate and subject in the divine reality, since "God is His own being." Aquinas rejected the ontological claim to immediate knowledge of God, however. For him, the principle of the identity of thought and being in divine reality did not imply that God was not subject to doubt. He argued that since we do not know what God is in Godself, our knowledge of God is attainable only through God's effects. And because God can be known only through God's effects, human knowledge of God is not immediate, but must be mediated through authority. Tillich aptly observed that with this argument, Aquinas cut the nerve of the ontological approach. See Thomas Aquinas, *Summa Theologica*, 1, Q. 12: "How God Is Known By Us," in *Basic Writings of Saint Thomas Aquinas,* ed. Anton C. Pegis, (New York: Random House, 1944), 91–111; Paul Tillich, *Theology of Culture* (New York: Oxford University Press, 1959), 12–19.

40. Paul Tillich, *Systematic Theology,* vol. 2 (Chicago: University of Chicago Press, 1957), 9. Tillich's argument in this section marked a retreat from his claim in volume 1 that "The statement that God is being-itself is a nonsymbolic statement. It does not point beyond itself. It means what it says directly and properly" (see Tillich, *Systematic Theology,* 1:238–39).

41. Gilkey, *Maker of Heaven and Earth,* 293.

42. Ibid., 293–94.

43. Langdon Gilkey, "Neo-Orthodoxy," in *A Handbook of Christian Theology: Definition Essays on Concepts and Movements of Thought in Contemporary Protestantism,* ed. Marvin Halverson and Arthur A. Cohen (Cleveland: World Publishing Co., 1958), 259; Gilkey, *How the Church Can Minister to the World Without Losing Itself* (New York: Harper & Row, 1964), 105.

44. Gilkey, "Neo-Orthodoxy," 259–60.

45. Gilkey, *How the Church Can Minister to the World Without Losing Itself,* 84.

46. Ibid., 77.

47. James Branton, "Our Present Situation in Biblical Theology," *Religion in Life* 26 (1956–1957):12–13.

48. Winston L. King, "Some Ambiguities in Biblical Theology," *Religion in Life* 27 (1957–1958):95.

49. For example, see Alan Richardson, *The Miracle-Stories of the Gospels* (London: SCM Press, 1941), 127–31; Anderson, *Understanding the Old Testament,* 44.

50. Langdon Gilkey, "Cosmology, Ontology, and the Travail of Biblical Language," *The Journal of Religion* 41 (July 1961):196.

51. Ibid., 197.

52. Ibid., 199.

53. Anderson, *Understanding the Old Testament,* 47–49.

54. G. E. Wright, *Books of the Acts of God* (Garden City, N.Y.: Doubleday & Co., 1959), 86.

55. Gilkey, "Cosmology, Ontology, and the Travail of Biblical Language," 199.

56. Gilkey, "Cosmology, Ontology, and the Travail of Biblical Language," 202; see Wright, *Books of the Acts of God,* 73–74.

57. Ibid., 203.

58. Gilkey, *How the Church Can Minister to the World Without Losing Itself,* 75, 84.

59. Langdon Gilkey, "The Concept of Providence in Contemporary Theology," *The Journal of Religion* 43 (July 1963):182.

60. Ibid., 183.

61. Ibid.; see Jürgen Moltmann, *Theology of Hope: On the Ground and the Implications of a Christian Eschatology,* trans. James W. Leitch (London: SCM Press, 1967), 316.

62. Karl Barth, *Church Dogmatics: The Doctrine of Creation,* vol. 3, bk. 3, trans. G. W. Bromiley

and R. J. Ehrlich (Edinburgh: T. & T. Clark, 1961), on divine providence, 3–288; on God and nothingness, 289–368.

63. Gilkey, "An Appreciation of Karl Barth," 152.
64. James Barr, "The Multiplex Nature of the Old Testament Tradition," reprinted in Barr, *Old and New in Interpretation: A Study of the Two Testaments* (New York: Harper & Row, 1966), 18; see James Barr, "Revelation Through History in the Old Testament and in Modern Theology, *Princeton Seminary Bulletin* 56 (1963):4–14.
65. James Barr, "The Concepts of History and Revelation," reprinted in Barr, *Old and New in Interpretation,* 69, 74.
66. James Barr, *The Semantics of Biblical Language* (London: Oxford University Press, 1961), 194. Barr's critique focused on writings by A. G. Hebert, Thomas F. Torrance, A. Weiser, and others.
67. Childs, *The Crisis of Biblical Theology,* 72.
68. Langdon Gilkey, "Dissolution and Reconstruction in Theology," *The Christian Century* 82 (February 3, 1965):135; closing quote in Gilkey, *Gilkey on Tillich* (New York: Crossroad, 1990), xiii.
69. Gilkey, "Dissolution and Reconstruction in Theology," 135.
70. Ibid., 135–36.
71. Langdon Gilkey, *Naming the Whirlwind: The Renewal of God-Language* (Indianapolis: Bobbs-Merrill, 1969), 39.
72. Gilkey, "Dissolution and Reconstruction in Theology," 136–37.
73. Ibid., 137.
74. Ibid.
75. See Gilkey, *Shantung Compound,* 233.
76. Gilkey, "Dissolution and Reconstruction in Theology," 138.
77. Ibid.

Notes to Chapter 4.
Renaming the Whirlwind: God Beyond Being

1. See Dietrich Bonhoeffer, *Letters and Papers from Prison,* ed. Eberhard Bethge (1953; reprint, New York: Macmillan Co., 1978), 278–86, 310–12, 324–29; Langdon B. Gilkey, "A New Linguistic Madness," in *New Theology No. 2,* ed. Martin E. Marty and Dean G. Peerman (New York: Macmillan Co., 1965), 39–49.
2. Langdon Gilkey, *Naming the Whirlwind: The Renewal of God-Language* (Indianapolis: Bobbs-Merrill Co., 1969), 5.
3. Ibid., 20, 234.
4. See Edmund Husserl, *Ideas: General Introduction to Pure Phenomenology,* trans. W. R. Boyce Gibson (1931; reprint, New York: Humanities Press, 1969); Martin Heidegger, *Being and Time,* trans. John Macquarrie and Edward Robinson (New York: Harper & Row, 1962); idem, *An Introduction to Metaphysics,* trans. Ralph Manheim (New Haven, Conn.: Yale University Press, 1959*);* Marvin Farber, *The Foundation of Phenomenology: Edmund Husserl and the Quest for a Rigorous Science of Philosophy* (Albany, N.Y.: State University of New York Press, 1943).
5. See Alice Ambrose, "Linguistic Approaches to Philosophical Problems," in *The Linguistic Turn: Recent Essays in Philosophical Method,* ed. Richard Rorty (Chicago: University of Chicago Press, 1967), 147–55; A. J. Ayer, *Language, Truth and Logic* (London: Gollancz, 1946).
6. Gilkey, *Naming the Whirlwind,* 188–90. See Langdon Gilkey, "Social and Intellectual Sources of Contemporary Protestant Theology in America," *Daedalus* 96 (Winter 1967):69–98.
7. See Thomas J. J. Altizer and William Hamilton, eds., *Radical Theology and the Death of God* (Indianapolis: Bobbs-Merrill Company, 1966); Thomas J. J. Altizer, *The Gospel of Christian Atheism* (Philadelphia: Westminster Press, 1966); William Hamilton, *The New Essence of Chris-*

tianity (New York: Association Press, 1961); Paul van Buren, *The Secular Meaning of the Gospel* (New York: Macmillan Co., 1963); Gabriel Vahanian, *The Death of God* (New York: G. Braziller, 1961); Langdon Gilkey, "Secularism's Impact on Contemporary Theology," *Christianity and Crisis* (April 5, 1965), reprinted in C. W. Christian and Glenn R. Wittig, eds., *Radical Theology: Phase Two* (New York: J. B. Lippincott Co., 1967), 17–23.

8. Gilkey, *Naming the Whirlwind*, 251–54; see Langdon Gilkey, "Unbelief and the Secular Spirit," in *The Presence and Absence of God*, ed. C. F. Mooney (New York: Fordham University Press, 1969), 50–68.

9. See Paul Ricoeur, *The Symbolism of Evil*, trans. Emerson Buchanan (New York: Harper & Row, 1967), esp. 165: "What is myth if it is not gnosis? Once more we are brought back to the function of the symbol. The symbol, we have said, opens up and discloses a dimension of experience that, without it, would remain closed and hidden."

10. Gilkey, *Naming the Whirlwind*, 282, 296.

11. Ibid., 306–14.

12. Ibid., 330.

13. See Jean-Paul Sartre, *Essays in Existentialism*, ed. Wade Baskin (1965; reprint, Seacaucus, N.J.: Citadel Press, 1974); Norman O. Brown, *Life Against Death: The Psychoanalytical Meaning of History* (1959; reprint, Middletown, Conn.: Wesleyan University Press, 1985); Walter Kaufmann, *Nietzsche: Philosopher, Psychologist, Antichrist* (Princeton: Princeton University Press, 1974); Henri de Lubac, S.J., *The Drama of Atheist Humanism*, trans. Edith M. Riley (1950; reprint, New York: World Publishing Co., 1971).

14. Gilkey, *Naming the Whirlwind*, 401.

15. Ibid., 419.

16. Friedrich Schleiermacher, *The Christian Faith*, trans. H. R. Mackintosh and J. S. Stewart (Edinburgh: T. & T. Clark, 1928), 44–52, 194–200.

17. For example, Clifford Geertz, *The Interpretation of Cultures* (New York: Basic Books, 1973); George Herbert Mead, *Selected Writings* (Indianapolis: Bobbs-Merrill Company, 1964); Herbert Blumer, *Symbolic Interactionism: Perspective and Method* (1969; reprint, Berkeley: University of California Press, 1986).

18. Ricoeur, *The Symbolism of Evil*, 5.

19. Langdon Gilkey, "Modern Myth-Making and the Possibilities of Twentieth-Century Theology," in *Theology of Renewal*, vol. 1, ed. L. K. Shook (Montreal: Palm Publishers, 1968), 283.

20. See especially Reinhold Niebuhr, "The Truth in Myths," in *The Nature of Religious Experience*, ed. J. S. Bixler (New York: Harper & Brothers, 1937), 117–35; Paul Tillich, *Dynamics of Faith* (New York: Harper & Brothers, 1957), 48–54; Rudolf Bultmann, *New Testament and Mythology and Other Basic Writings*, trans. Schubert M. Ogden (Philadelphia: Fortress Press, 1984), 1–44.

21. Gilkey, "Modern Myth-Making," 286; reworked discussion in Langdon Gilkey, *Religion and the Scientific Future* (New York: Harper & Row, 1970), 66–67.

22. See Mircea Eliade, *A History of Religious Ideas*, vol. 1: *From the Stone Age to the Eleusinian Mysteries*, trans. Willard R. Trask (Chicago: University of Chicago Press, 1978); idem, *The Sacred and the Profane: The Nature of Religion*, trans. Willard R. Trask (1959; reprint, San Diego: Harcourt Brace & Co., 1987); idem, *Myth and Reality*, trans. Willard R. Trask (New York: Harper & Row, 1963).

23. Langdon Gilkey, *Catholicism Confronts Modernity: A Protestant View* (New York: Seabury Press, 1975), 86; see Langdon Gilkey, *Nature, Reality, and the Sacred: The Nexus of Science and Religion* (Minneapolis: Fortress Press, 1993), 17–33.

24. Mircea Eliade, *The Myth of the Eternal Return: Or, Cosmos and History*, trans. Willard R. Trask (1954; reprint, Princeton, N. J.: Princeton University Press, 1974).

25. Gilkey, "Modern Myth-Making," 287.

26. Ibid., 290–91.

27. Ibid., 301–2.

28. Gilkey, *Religion and the Scientific Future*, 78.
29. See Reinhold Niebuhr, *Moral Man and Immoral Society: A Study in Ethics and Politics* (1932; reprint, New York: Charles Scribner's Sons, 1947); idem, *The Self and the Dramas of History* (New York: Charles Scribner's Sons, 1955).
30. Gilkey, *Religion and the Scientific Future*, 62.
31. Gilkey, *Catholicism Confronts Modernity*, 100.
32. Gilkey, "Modern Myth-Making," 310; see Gilkey, *Nature, Reality, and the Sacred*, 150–53.
33. Gilkey, *Religion and the Scientific Future*, 103–4.
34. Gilkey, *Naming the Whirlwind*, 93.
35. See Jürgen Moltmann, *Theology of Hope: On the Ground and the Implications of a Christian Eschatology*, trans. James W. Leitch (New York: Harper & Row, 1967); Wolfhart Pannenberg, "Focal Essay: The Revelation of God in Jesus of Nazareth," in *New Frontiers in Theology, III: Theology as History*, ed. James M. Robinson and John B. Cobb (New York: Harper & Row, 1967), 101–34; Van Austin Harvey, *The Historian and the Believer: The Morality of Historical Knowledge and Christian Belief* (New York: Macmillan Co., 1966); Richard R. Niebuhr, *Resurrection and Historical Reason: A Study of Theological Method* (New York: Charles Scribner's Sons, 1957).
36. Gilkey, *Catholicism Confronts Modernity*, 85.
37. Langdon Gilkey, *Reaping the Whirlwind: A Christian Interpretation of History* (New York: Seabury Press, 1976), 48.
38. See Paul Tillich, *Systematic Theology*, vol. 1 (Chicago: University of Chicago Press, 1951), 79–81, 235–89.
39. Gilkey, *Reaping the Whirlwind*, 370.
40. Ibid., 49–52.
41. Ibid., 52–53.
42. Ibid., 55–59.
43. An instructive example is Richard Rorty's article, "Thugs and Theorists: A Reply to Bernstein," *Political Theory* 15 (November 1987):564–80, in which the noted relativist and "liberal ironist" passionately defends his social democratic politics from various criticisms. Rorty's customary manner of bemused detachment disappears when the "truth" of his political position is questioned.
44. As in the religious character of much environmentalist literature. See Charlene Spretnak, *The Spiritual Dimension of Green Politics* (Santa Fe: Bear & Co., 1986); Charlene Spretnak and Fritjof Capra, *Green Politics: The Global Promise* (New York: E. P. Dutton, 1984).
45. Gilkey, *Reaping the Whirlwind*, 118–21.
46. This is also a major theme of transcendental Thomist theology, especially in the work of Karl Rahner. See Rahner, *Spirit in the World*, trans. William Dych (New York: Herder & Herder, 1968); and Rahner, *Foundations of Christian Faith: An Introduction to the Idea of Christianity*, trans. William Dych (New York: Seabury Press, 1978).
47. Gilkey, *Reaping the Whirlwind*, 122.
48. Ibid., 151; see Paul Tillich, *Theology of Culture* (New York: Oxford University Press, 1959), 40–51.
49. See Reinhold Niebuhr, *Beyond Tragedy: Essays on the Christian Interpretation of History* (1937; reprint, New York: Charles Scribner's Sons, 1951), 1–24; idem, *Faith and History: A Comparison of Christian and Modern Views of History* (New York: Charles Scribner's Sons, 1949), 103–37.
50. Gilkey, *Reaping the Whirlwind*, 151–53; see Niebuhr, *Faith and History*, 118–19; Niebuhr, "The Truth in Myths," 133.
51. See Augustine, *On Nature and Grace*, in *Basic Writings of Saint Augustine*, trans. P. Holmes (New York: Random House, 1948), 521–82; John Calvin, *Institutes of the Christian Religion*, vol. 1, trans. Ford Lewis Battles (Philadelphia: Westminster Press, 1975), 35–68, 197–238.
52. Gilkey, *Reaping the Whirlwind*, 218.

53. See Schleiermacher, *The Christian Faith*, 211–32, 725–26; Albrecht Ritschl, *The Christian Doctrine of Justification and Reconciliation*, trans. H. R. Mackintosh and others (Edinburgh: T. & T. Clark, 1900), 135–38, 303–18; Karl Barth, *The Epistle to the Romans*, trans. Edwyn C. Hoskyns (1933; reprint, London: Oxford University Press, 1975), 43; James M. Robinson, ed., *The Beginnings of Dialectic Theology*, trans. Keith R. Crim and Louis De Grazia (Richmond: John Knox Press, 1968).

54. Moltmann, *Theology of Hope*, 16; Wolfhart Pannenberg, *Theology and the Kingdom of God* (Philadelphia: Westminster Press, 1969), 70; idem, "Theology as Eschatology," in *The Future of Hope*, ed. Frederick Herzog (New York: Herder & Herder, 1970), 10–11.

55. Gilkey, *Reaping the Whirlwind*, 234; Moltmann, *Theology of Hope*, 16.

56. See Langdon Gilkey, "The Universal and Immediate Presence of God," 81–109.

57. Gilkey, *Reaping the Whirlwind*, 234.

58. Ibid., 243.

59. See Alfred North Whitehead, *Process and Reality: An Essay in Cosmology* (New York: Macmillan Co., 1929), 27–45; idem, *Modes of Thought* (1938; reprint, New York: Free Press, 1966).

60. Gilkey, *Reaping the Whirlwind*, 251.

61. See Norman Pittenger, *The Lure of Divine Love: Human Experience and Christian Faith in a Process Perspective* (New York: Pilgrim Press, 1979); Charles Hartshorne, *The Divine Relativity: A Social Conception of God* (1948; reprint, New Haven, Conn.: Yale University Press, 1976).

62. Whitehead, *Process and Reality*, 519–33.

63. See Alfred North Whitehead, *Religion in the Making* (1926; reprint, New York: New American Library, 1974), 143–51.

64. Gilkey, *Reaping the Whirlwind*, 249; see Gilkey, *Nature, Reality, and the Sacred*, 202–4.

65. Ibid., 249.

66. Ibid., 253.

67. See Walter Rauschenbusch, *Christianity and the Social Crisis* (1907; reprint, Louisville, Ky.: Westminster John Knox Press, 1991), 420–21; Rauschenbusch, *Christianizing the Social Order* (New York: Macmillan Co., 1912), 458–76; Rauschenbusch, *A Theology for the Social Gospel* (1917; reprint, Nashville: Abingdon Press, 1987), 131–45.

68. Reinhold Niebuhr, *An Interpretation of Christian Ethics* (1935; reprint, San Francisco: Harper & Row, 1963), 58–61.

69. Ibid., 53.

70. Calvin, *Institutes of the Christian Religion*, 1:201–37.

71. Niebuhr, *An Interpretation of Christian Ethics*, 60.

72. Gilkey, *Reaping the Whirlwind*, 266.

73. Ibid., 279.

74. Ibid., 305; see Gilkey, *Nature, Reality, and the Sacred*, 201–2.

75. Langdon Gilkey, *Message and Existence: An Introduction to Christian Theology* (New York: Seabury Press, 1981), 91.

76. Gilkey, *Reaping the Whirlwind*, 305.

77. Gilkey, *Message and Existence*, 96.

78. Gilkey, *Reaping the Whirlwind*, 306.

79. One important recent exception to this trend is Rosemary R. Ruether's appropriation of process thought in her ecofeminist work, *Gaia & God: An Ecofeminist Theology of Earth Healing* (San Francisco: HarperCollins, 1992), 246–53.

80. On process theology, see John B. Cobb, Jr., *A Christian Natural Theology: Based on the Thought of Alfred North Whitehead* (Philadelphia: Westminster Press, 1976); idem, *Process Theology as Political Theology* (Philadelphia: Westminster Press, 1982); John B. Cobb, Jr. and David Ray Griffin, *Process Theology: An Introductory Exposition* (Philadelphia: Westminster Press, 1967).

81. On this point, see Eugene TeSelle, "Being in History," *The Journal of Religion* 58 (July 1978):305.

82. Edward Farley, Review of *Reaping the Whirlwind*, in *Religious Studies Review* 4 (October 1978):236.
83. See W. Norman Pittenger, *The Word Incarnate: A Study of the Doctrine of the Person of Christ* (Digswell Place, England: James Nisbet & Co., 1959); John B. Cobb, Jr., *Christ in a Pluralistic Age* (Philadelphia: Westminster Press, 1975); Schubert M. Ogden, *The Point of Christology* (San Francisco: Harper & Row, 1982); Marjorie Suchocki, *God-Christ-Church: A Practical Guide to Process Theology* (New York: Crossroad, 1989).
84. Farley, review of *Reaping the Whirlwind*, 237.
85. Langdon Gilkey, "Theology for a Time of Troubles," reprinted in *Theologians in Transition: The Christian Century "How My Mind Has Changed" Series*, ed. James M. Wall (New York: Crossroad, 1981), 31.
86. Langdon Gilkey, *Gilkey on Tillich* (New York: Crossroad, 1990), xiv.
87. See Langdon Gilkey, "Theology and Culture: Reflections on the Conference," *Criterion* (Autumn 1989):3. Tillich took up a serious interest in the theology of world religions near the end of his life; see Paul Tillich, *Christianity and the Encounter of World Religions* (1963; reprint, Minneapolis: Fortress Press, 1994).
88. Author's conversation with Langdon Gilkey, May 27, 1988.
89. Gilkey, *Message and Existence*, 1–2.
90. Ibid., 3.
91. Langdon Gilkey, *Society and the Sacred: Toward a Theology of Culture in Decline* (New York: Crossroad, 1981), 4–5.
92. Ibid., 22.
93. See Tillich, *Theology of Culture*, 3–9, 40–51; Paul Tillich, *What Is Religion?* (1969; reprint, New York: Harper & Row, 1973), 159–81.
94. Gilkey, *Society and the Sacred*, 25.
95. See Ernst Troeltsch, *The Absoluteness of Christianity and the History of Religions*, trans. David Reid (1902; reprint, Richmond: John Knox Press, 1971); G. W. F. Hegel, *Phenomenology of Spirit*, trans. A. V. Miller (Oxford: Clarendon Press, 1977).
96. Gilkey, *Through the Tempest*, 153.
97. See Karl Rahner, *Theological Investigations*, vol. 5, trans. Karl H. Kruger (Baltimore: Helicon Press, 1966), 115–34; Rahner, *Theological Investigations*, vol. 12, trans. David Bourke (New York: Seabury Press, 1974), 161–78; Rahner, *Theological Investigations*, vol. 14, trans David Bourke (New York: Seabury Press, 1976) 280–94; Rahner, *Foundations of Christian Faith*, 311–21; George Rupp, *Christologies and Cultures: Toward a Typology of Religious Worldviews* (The Hague: Mouton & Co., 1974).
98. Langdon Gilkey, "Plurality and Its Theological Implications," in *The Myth of Christian Uniqueness: Toward a Pluralistic Theology of Religions*, ed. John Hick and Paul F. Knitter (Maryknoll, N.Y.: Orbis Books, 1987), 38–42; quote in Langdon Gilkey, "Introduction: A Retrospective Glance at My Work," in *The Whirlwind in Culture: Frontiers in Theology*, ed. Donald W. Musser and Joseph L. Price (Bloomington, Ind.: Meyer-Stone Books, 1988), 34.
99. Gilkey, *Society and the Sacred*, 14.
100. See Frithjof Schuon, *The Transcendental Unity of Religions* (New York: Harper & Row, 1975); Raimundo Panikkar, *The Unknown Christ of Hinduism* (Maryknoll, N.Y.: Orbis Books, 1981); Huston Smith, *Beyond the Post-Modern Mind* (New York: Crossroad, 1982); Wilfred Cantwell Smith, *Toward a World Theology: Faith and the Comparative History of Religion* (Philadelphia: Westminster Press, 1981); John Hick, *An Interpretation of Religion: Human Responses to the Transcendent* (New Haven, Conn.: Yale University Press, 1989); Paul F. Knitter, *No Other Name?: A Critical Survey of Christian Attititudes Toward the World Religions* (Maryknoll, N.Y.: Orbis Books, 1985).
101. Gilkey, "Introduction: A Retrospective Glance at My Work," 34–35; Gilkey, "Plurality and Its Theological Implications," 41–42.
102. Author's conversation with Langdon Gilkey, October 22, 1987.

103. Gilkey, "Introduction: A Retrospective Glance at My Work," 35; see idem, "Plurality and Its Theological Implications," 46–49.

104. Gilkey, *Through the Tempest*, 154–55.

105. See John B. Cobb, Jr., *Beyond Dialogue: Toward a Mutual Transformation of Christianity and Buddhism* (Philadelphia: Fortress Press, 1982); Hans Küng, et al., *Christianity and World Religions: Paths of Dialogue with Islam, Hinduism, and Buddhism*, trans. Peter Heinegg (1986; reprint, Maryknoll, N.Y.: Orbis Books, 1993); Kenneth Cragg, *The Christ and the Faiths* (Philadelphia: Westminster Press, 1986); Leonard Swidler, ed., *Toward a Universal Theology of Religion* (Maryknoll, N.Y.: Orbis Books, 1987).

106. Gilkey, *Through the Tempest*, 155.

107. See Masao Abe, *Zen and Western Thought* (Honolulu: University of Hawaii Press, 1985), 171–85.

108. Gilkey, *Society and the Sacred*, 128.

109. Ibid., 134.

110. Ibid., 135–36.

111. Gilkey, *Through the Tempest*, 95.

112. Ibid., 97.

113. Ibid., 109.

114. Bonhoeffer, *Letters and Papers from Prison*, 360–61.

115. Gilkey, *Society and the Sacred*, 136.

116. Gilkey, *Through the Tempest*, 108–9.

117. Gilkey, "Plurality and Its Theological Implications," 50.

Notes to Chapter 5.
Return of the Repressed: Postmodernism and the Sacred

1. See Auguste Comte, *System of Positive Polity* (London: Burt Franklin, 1875), 21–29; John Stuart Mill, *Auguste Comte and Positivism* (Ann Arbor: University of Michigan Press, 1961).

2. Dietrich Bonhoeffer, *Letters and Papers from Prison*, trans. Reginald Fuller and John Bowden (New York: Macmillan Co., 1972), 324–29.

3. Schubert M. Ogden, *Christ Without Myth: A Study Based on the Theology of Rudolf Bultmann* (1961; reprint, Dallas: SMU Press, 1979), 146.

4. See Fritz Buri, "Entmythologisierung oder Entkerygmatisierung der Theologie," in *Kerygma und Mythos*, vol. 2, ed. Hans-Werner Bartsch (Hamburg: Herbert Reich-Evangelischer Verlag, 1952), 85–101; Buri, "Theologie und Philosophie," *Theologische Zeitschrift* (March-April 1952): 128–30.

5. Rudolf Bultmann, "New Testament and Mythology," in *Kerygma and Myth: A Theological Debate*, vol. 1, ed. Hans-Werner Bartsch and trans. Reginald H. Fuller (London: SPCK, 1954), 41; idem, *Theology of the New Testament*, vol. 1, trans. Kendrick Grobel (New York: Charles Scribner's Sons, 1951), 191.

6. Ogden, *Christ Without Myth*, 146–47.

7. Ibid., 151.

8. Ibid., 162.

9. See Frederick Denison Maurice, *The Kingdom of Christ*, 2 vols. (London: SCM Press, 1958); idem, *Theological Essays* (New York: Harper & Brothers, 1957), 82–100.

10. Schubert M. Ogden, *The Reality of God and Other Essays* (New York: Harper & Row, 1966), 104; see idem, *The Point of Christology* (San Francisco: Harper & Row, 1982), 10–13.

11. See Gilbert Ryle, *The Concept of Mind* (London: Hutchinson & Co., 1949), 7–8.

12. Ogden, *The Reality of God*, 106.

13. Ibid.

14. See Carl G. Hempel, "The Empiricist Criterion of Meaning," and A. J. Ayer, "Verification and

Experience," in *Logical Positivism*, ed. A. J. Ayer (New York: Free Press, 1959), 108–32, 228–46.

15. See Michael Polanyi, *Personal Knowledge: Towards a Post-Critical Philosophy* (Chicago: University of Chicago Press, 1962); Richard Rorty, *Objectivity, Relativism, and Truth: Philosophical Papers*, vol. 1 (New York: Cambridge University Press, 1991); idem, *Contingency, Irony, and Solidarity* (New York: Cambridge University Press, 1989).

16. Stephen Toulmin, *The Uses of Argument* (Cambridge, England: Cambridge University Press, 1958), 30–43.

17. Ibid., 38.

18. Ogden, *The Reality of God*, 112.

19. Ibid., 116.

20. Ibid., 117.

21. Ibid.

22. See Schubert M. Ogden, *On Theology* (San Francisco: Harper & Row, 1986), 69–93.

23. See Karl Jaspers, *The Origin and Goal of History*, trans. Michael Bullock (New Haven, Conn.: Yale University Press, 1953), 1–27.

24. John B. Cobb, Jr., *The Structure of Christian Existence* (Philadelphia: Westminster Press, 1972), 41–42.

25. Ibid., 43.

26. John B. Cobb, Jr., "Christianity and Myth," *The Journal of Bible and Religion* 33 (October 1965):316.

27. See Harvey Cox, *The Secular City—Urbanization and Secularization in Theological Perspective* (New York: Macmillan Co., 1965); Friedrich Gogarten, *Verhängnis und Hoffnung der Neuzeit, Die Säkularisierung als Theologisches Problem* (Stuttgart: Friedrich Vorwerk, 1953); idem, *Der Mensch zwischen Gott und Welt, Eine Untersuchung über Gesetz und Evangelium* (Heidelberg: Lambert Schneider, 1952); John B. Cobb, Jr., *Liberal Christianity at the Crossroads* (Philadelphia: Westminster Press, 1973).

28. Cobb, "Christianity and Myth," 317.

29. Ibid., 317; see John B. Cobb, Jr., *God and the World* (Philadelphia: Westminster Press, 1969), 19–41.

30. See John B. Cobb, Jr., *A Christian Natural Theology: Based on the Thought of Alfred North Whitehead* (Philadelphia: Westminster Press, 1976); idem, *Christ in a Pluralistic Age* (Philadelphia: Westminster Press, 1975).

31. See Gustavo Gutiérrez, *A Theology of Liberation: History, Politics and Salvation*, trans. Caridad Inda and John Eagleson (Maryknoll, N.Y.: Orbis Books, 1973); James H. Cone, *A Black Theology of Liberation* (1970; reprint, Maryknoll, N.Y.: Orbis Books, 1990).

32. For more extensive discussions of these themes, see Gary Dorrien, *Reconstructing the Common Good: Theology and the Social Order* (Maryknoll, N.Y.: Orbis Books, 1990), 101–75; Dorrien, *Soul in Society: The Making and Renewal of Social Christianity* (Minneapolis: Fortress Press, 1995), 221–81.

33. Ogden, *Christ Without Myth*, "Afterward—1978," 184.

34. Author's conversation with John B. Cobb, Jr., November 18, 1994; see Cobb, "A Critical View of Inherited Theology," in *Theologians in Transition*, ed. James M. Wall (New York: Crossroad, 1981), 74–81.

35. See John B. Cobb, Jr., *Sustainability: Economics, Ecology, and Justice* (Maryknoll, N.Y.: Orbis Books, 1992); idem, *Sustaining the Common Good: A Christian Perspective on the Global Economy* (Cleveland: Pilgrim Press, 1994).

36. Bonhoeffer, *Letters and Papers from Prison*, 327–28.

37. See Joseph Campbell, *The Mythic Image* (Princeton, N. J.: Princeton University Press, 1974); idem, *Transformations of Myth Through Time* (New York: Harper & Row, 1990); Joseph Campbell, with Bill Moyers, *The Power of Myth* (New York: Anchor Books, 1988); M. Scott

Peck, *The Road Less Traveled: A New Psychology of Love, Traditional Values and Spiritual Growth* (New York: Simon & Schuster, 1982).

38. See Robert L. Moore, ed., *Carl Jung and Christian Spirituality* (New York: Paulist Press, 1988); Wallace B. Clift, *Jung and Christianity: The Challenge of Reconciliation* (New York: Crossroad, 1988); Raymond Hostie, *Religion and the Psychology of C. G. Jung* (New York: Sheed and Ward, 1957); James Heisig, *Imago Dei: A Study of C. G. Jung's Psychology of Religion* (Lewisburg, Va.: Bucknell University Press, 1979); Peter Homans, *Jung in Context: Modernity and the Making of a Psychology* (Chicago: University of Chicago Press, 1979); Ann and Barry Ulanov, *Religion and the Unconscious* (Philadelphia: Westminster Press, 1975); Clifford A. Brown, *Jung's Hermeneutic of Doctrine* (Chicago: Scholars Press, 1981); Frank M. Bockus, "The Archetypal Self: Theological Values in Jung's Psychology," in *The Dialogue Between Theology and Psychology,* ed. Peter Homans (Chicago: University of Chicago Press, 1968), 221–48.

39. See Noam Chomsky, *Aspects of the Theory of Syntax* (Cambridge: MIT Press, 1965); Robin Fox, *Encounter with Anthropology* (London: Peregrine, 1975); Niko Tinbergen, *The Study of Instinct* (London: Oxford University Press, 1951).

40. See Ernst Cassirer, *The Philosophy of Symbolic Forms: Language,* vol. 1 trans. Ralph Manheim (New Haven, Conn.: Yale University Press, 1953); Claude Levi-Strauss, *Structural Anthropology,* trans. Claire Jacobson and Brooke Grundfest Schoepf (New York: Basic Books, 1963); Mircea Eliade, *The Sacred and the Profane: The Nature of Religion,* trans. Willard R. Trask (New York: Harcourt Brace & Co., 1959).

41. Anthony Stevens, *Archetypes: A Natural History of the Self* (New York: William Morrow and Co., 1982).

42. See Don S. Browning, *Religious Thought and the Modern Psychologies: A Critical Conversation in the Theology of Culture* (Philadelphia: Fortress Press, 1987), 161–203; James Olney, *Metaphors of Self* (Princeton, N. J.: Princeton University Press, 1972), 85–110.

43. C. G. Jung, *Memories, Dreams, Reflections,* ed. Aniela Jaffe, and trans. Richard and Clara Winston (New York: Random House, 1963), 3.

44. See Reuben Fine, *A History of Psychoanalysis* (New York: Columbia University Press, 1979), 81–88; Paul Roazen, *Freud and His Followers* (New York: New York University Press, 1984), 223–96.

45. C. G. Jung, *Symbols of Transformation: An Analysis of the Prelude to a Case of Schizophrenia,* trans. R. F. C. Hull (Princeton, N. J.: Princeton University Press, 1967), xxiii.

46. C. G. Jung, *The Archetypes and the Collective Unconscious,* trans. R. F. C. Hull (Princeton, N. J.: Princeton University Press, 1968), 50–53; see Jung, *Symbols of Transformation,* 101–2; Jung, *The Symbolic Life,* trans. R. F. C. Hull (Princeton, N. J.: Princeton University Press, 1954), 41–42.

47. C. G. Jung, *The Structure and Dynamics of the Psyche,* trans. R. F. C. Hull (Princeton, N. J.: Princeton University Press, 1969), 158.

48. Jung, *The Archetypes and the Collective Unconscious,* 3–4.

49. Paul Tillich, "The Relation of Religion and Health: Historical Considerations and Theoretical Questions," *The Review of Religion* (May 1946):380.

50. C. G. Jung, *Psychology and Religion* (New Haven, Conn.: Yale University Press, 1938), 63.

51. See Browning, *Religious Thought and the Modern Psychologies,* 170–72.

52. Philip Rieff, *The Triumph of the Therapeutic* (New York: Harper & Row, 1966), 122.

53. C. G. Jung, *Letters,* trans. R. F. C. Hull (Princeton, N. J.: Princeton University Press, 1975), 7; see C. G. Jung, *Psychology and Western Religion,* trans. R. F. C. Hull (Princeton, N. J.: Princeton University Press, 1984), 221–23.

54. C. G. Jung, *Mysterium Coniunctionis: An Inquiry into the Separation and Synthesis of Psychic Opposites in Alchemy,* trans. R. F. C. Hull (Princeton, N. J.: Princeton University Press, 1970), 336 n. 297.

55. C. G. Jung, *Civilization in Transition,* trans. R. F. C. Hull (Princeton, N. J.: Princeton University Press, 1964), 120–21.

56. C. G. Jung, *Two Essays on Analytical Psychology,* trans. R. F. C. Hull (Princeton, N. J.: Princeton University Press, 1966), 221.
57. Ibid., 238.
58. Jung, *Civilization in Transition,* 463.
59. See especially C. G. Jung, *Answer to Job,* trans. R. F..C. Hull (Princeton, N. J.: Princeton University Press, 1969); and Jung, *Psychology and Western Religion.*
60. Quoted in Clift, *Jung and Christianity,* 3–4.
61. See Jung, *The Symbolic Life,* 707.
62. Jung, *Two Essays on Analytical Psychology,* 70.
63. C. G. Jung, *Psychology and Religion: West and East,* trans. R. F. C. Hull (New York: Pantheon Books, 1958), 455.
64. C. G. Jung, *Psychology and Alchemy,* trans. R. F. C. Hull (Princeton, N. J.: Princeton University Press, 1968), 15.
65. Jung, *Psychology and Religion: West and East,* 273.
66. Ibid., 157.
67. Jung, *Psychology and Alchemy,* 19; see Jung, *Psychology and Religion: West and East,* 157.
68. C. G. Jung, *Aion: Researches into the Phenomenology of the Self,* trans. R. F. C. Hull (Princeton, N. J.: Princeton University Press, 1968), 36.
69. Jung, *Psychology and Alchemy,* 17.
70. C. G. Jung, Foreword to D. T. Suzuki, *An Introduction to Zen Buddhism* (New York: Grove Press, 1964), 26.
71. C. G. Jung, "Differences between East and West," in *The Portable Jung,* ed. Joseph Campbell (New York: Viking, 1971), 490; see C. G. Jung, *Modern Man in Search of a Soul,* trans. W. S. Dell and Cary F. Baynes (London: Kegan Paul, Trench, Trubner & Co., 1933).
72. Jung, *Memories, Dreams, Reflections,* 69.
73. Jung, *Psychology and Religion: West and East,* 153.
74. Ibid., 88.
75. Jung, *Memories, Dreams, Reflections,* 340.
76. See Morton Kelsey, *Christo-Psychology* (New York: Crossroad, 1982); idem, "Rediscovering the Priesthood through the Unconscious," in Moore, ed., *Carl Jung and Christian Spirituality,* 133–45; Clift, *Jung and Christianity,* 115–49.
77. See Morton Kelsey, *Myth, History & Faith: The Mysteries of Christian Myth and Imagination* (Rockport, Mass.: Element, 1991); idem, *Encounter with God* (Minneapolis: Bethany Fellowship, 1972); idem, *The Other Side of Silence: A Guide to Christian Meditation* (New York: Paulist Press, 1976); John Sanford, *Healing and Wholeness* (New York: Paulist Press, 1977); idem, *The Kingdom Within* (New York: J. B. Lippincott Co., 1970).
78. Jung, *Aion,* 68.
79. James E. Loder, *The Transforming Moment* (Colorado Springs, Colo.: Helmers & Howard, 1989), 138–39.
80. Ibid., 139–40.
81. See Ann Ulanov, *The Feminine in Jungian Psychology and Christian Theology* (Evanston: Northwestern University Press, 1971); June Singer, *Boundaries of the Soul: The Practice of Jung's Psychology* (New York: Anchor Books, 1972); Emma Jung, *Animus and Anima* (New York: Analytical Psychology Club of New York, 1957).
82. William G. Doty, *Mythography: The Study of Myths and Rituals* (Tuscaloosa, Ala.: University of Alabama Press, 1986), 153; see Eric Gould, *Mythical Intentions in Modern Literature* (Princeton: Princeton University Press, 1981).
83. Jacques Derrida, *Margins of Philosophy,* trans. Alan Bass (Chicago: University of Chicago Press, 1982), 3–27; see idem, *Of Grammatology,* trans. Gayatri Chakravorty Spivak (Baltimore: Johns Hopkins University Press, 1976); idem, *Speech and Phenomena and Other Essays on Husserl's Theory of Signs,* trans. David B. Allison (Evanston, Ill.: Northwestern University Press,

1973); Wesley A Kort, *Bound to Differ: The Dynamics of Theological Discourses* (University Park, Pa.: Pennsylvania State University Press, 1992), 30–36.

84. See Gould, *Mythical Intentions in Modern Literature*, 69.

85. Doty, *Mythography*, 241; Gould, *Mythical Intentions in Modern Literature*, 33.

86. Jean-Francois Lyotard, *The Postmodern Condition: A Report on Knowledge*, trans. Geoff Bennington and Brian Massumi (Minneapolis: University of Minnesota Press, 1988), xxiv.

87. See Steven Best and Douglas Kellner, *Postmodern Theory: Critical Interrogations* (New York: Guilford Press, 1991); Frederic Jameson, *Postmodernism: Or, the Cultural Logic of Late Capitalism* (Durham, N. C.: Duke University Press, 1991); Art Berman, *From the New Criticism to Deconstruction: The Reception of Structuralism and Post-Structuralism* (Urbana, Ill.: University of Illinois Press, 1988); John McGowan, *Postmodernism and Its Critics* (Ithaca, N.Y.: Cornell University Press, 1991).

88. David Ray Griffin, *God and Religion in the Postmodern World: Essays in Postmodern Theology* (Albany, N.Y.: State University of New York Press, 1989), ix–xii. For a protest that "reconstructive postmodernism" is not postmodern at all, see Carl Raschke, "Fire and Roses: Or the Problem of Postmodern Religious Thinking," *Shadow of Spirit: Postmodernism and Religion,* ed. Philippa Berry and Andrew Wernick (London: Routledge & Kegan Paul, 1992), 94–100.

89. See Thomas J. J. Altizer, et al., eds., *Deconstruction and Theology* (New York: Crossroad, 1982); Carl Raschke, *The Alchemy of the Word: Language and the End of Theology* (Missoula, Mont.: Scholars Press, 1979); Mark C. Taylor, *Erring: A Postmodern A/theology* (Chicago: University of Chicago Press, 1984); idem, *Altarity* (Chicago: University of Chicago Press, 1987); Charles E. Winquist, *Desiring Theology* (Chicago: University of Chicago Press, 1995).

90. Friedrich Nietzsche, "Twilight of the Idols," in *The Portable Nietzsche*, trans. and ed. Walter Kaufmann (New York: Viking Press, 1954), 485–86.

91. Carl A. Raschke, "The Deconstruction of God," in Altizer et al., *Deconstruction and Theology*, 2.

92. Friedrich Nietzsche, *The Gay Science*, trans. Walter Kaufmann (New York: Random House, 1974), 299.

93. See Mark C. Taylor, *Deconstructing Theology* (New York: Crossroad, 1982), 91.

94. See Richard Rorty, *Philosophy and the Mirror of Nature* (Princeton: Princeton University Press, 1979), 357–94.

95. Raschke, "The Deconstruction of God," 6–7.

96. Derrida, *Grammatology*, 50.

97. Raschke, "The Deconstruction of God," 9–10.

98. See Derrida, *Margins of Philosophy*, 19–27; Jacques Derrida, *Positions*, trans. Alan Bass (Chicago: University of Chicago Press, 1981), 93–94.

99. Taylor, *Deconstructing Theology*, 91.

100. Raschke, "The Deconstruction of God," 3; see Thomas J. J. Altizer, "History as Apocalypse," in Altizer et al., *Deconstruction and Theology*, 168–76.

101. See Harold Bloom et al., *Deconstructionism and Criticism* (New York: Continuum, 1994); Jonathan Culler, *On Deconstruction: Theory and Criticism After Structuralism* (Ithaca, N.Y.: Cornell University Press, 1982); Vincent B. Leitch, *Deconstructive Criticism: An Advanced Introduction* (New York: Columbia University Press, 1983); John Sallis, ed., *Deconstruction and Philosophy: The Texts of Jacques Derrida* (Chicago: University of Chicago Press, 1987).

102. Raschke, "The Deconstruction of God," 27; see Robert P. Scharlemann, "The Being of God When God Is Not Being God: Deconstructing the History of Theism," in Altizer et al., *Deconstruction and Theology*, 79–108.

103. Raschke, "The Deconstruction of God," 28; see James Hillmann, *The Dream and the Underworld* (New York: Harper & Row, 1979), 45.

104. For a spirited polemic against deconstruction that assumes a negative answer to this question, see Colin Falck, *Myth, Truth and Literature: Towards a True Post-Modernism* (Cam-

bridge: Cambridge University Press, 1989). Falck's defense of a fictive mythopoetic position is otherwise similar to the Gould/Doty concept of mythicity.

105. Gould, *Mythical Intentions in Modern Literature,* 44.

106. Doty, *Mythography,* 242–45.

107. See Gayatri Chakravorty Spivak, *In Other Worlds: Essays in Cultural Politics* (New York: Routledge & Kegan Paul, 1988); Michel Foucault, *Madness and Civilization,* trans. Richard Howard (New York: Random House, 1965); idem, *Discipline and Punish: The Birth of the Prison,* trans. Alan Sheridan (New York: Pantheon Books, 1977).

108. See Michel Foucault, *The Order of Things: An Archaeology of the Human Sciences,* trans. Alan Sheridan-Smith (New York: Random House, 1970); idem, *Power/Knowledge: Selected Interviews and Other Writings, 1972–1977,* ed. Colin Gordon (New York: Pantheon Books, 1980).

109. See Jacques Derrida, "The Question of Style," in *The New Nietzsche,* ed. David Allison (New York: Delta Books, 1977), 179; on the politics and theory of feminist postmodernism, see Elaine Marks and Isabelle de Courtivron, eds., *New French Feminisms* (New York: Schocken Books, 1980); Linda J. Nicholson, ed., *Feminism/Postmodernism* (New York: Routledge & Kegan Paul, 1990).

110. See Letty M. Russell, *Human Liberation in a Feminist Perspective—A Theology* (Philadelphia: Westminster Press, 1974); Patricia Wilson-Kastner, *Faith, Feminism and the Christ* (Philadelphia: Fortress Press, 1983); Anne Carr, *Transforming Grace: Christian Tradition and Women's Experience* (San Francisco: Harper & Row, 1988); Catherine Mowry LaCugna, *God for Us: The Trinity and Christian Life* (San Francisco: HarperSanFrancisco, 1991).

111. See Rosemary Radford Ruether, *Sexism and God-Talk: Toward a Feminist Theology* (Boston: Beacon Press, 1983); Elisabeth Schüssler Fiorenza, *In Memory of Her: A Feminist Theological Reconstruction of Christian Origins* (New York: Crossroad, 1983); Carter Heyward, *Touching Our Strength: The Erotic as Power and the Love of God* (San Francisco: HarperSanFrancisco, 1989).

112. Mary Daly, *Beyond God the Father: Toward a Philosophy of Women's Liberation* (Boston: Beacon Press, 1973), 8.

113. Mary Daly, *Gyn/Ecology: The Metaethics of Radical Feminism* (Boston: Beacon Press, 1978), 39.

114. Daly, *Beyond God the Father,* 44–45.

115. Ibid., 45.

116. Ibid., 47.

117. Mary Daly, *Outercourse: The Be-Dazzling Voyage* (San Francisco: HarperSanFrancisco, 1992), 1.

118. Daly, "Original Reintroduction," in *Beyond God the Father* (1985), xx.

119. Daly, "Original Reintroduction," xxv.

120. Ibid., xix.

121. Daly, *Beyond God the Father,* 171; see Daly, *Gyn/Ecology,* 27–29; Mary Daly, *Pure Lust: Elemental Feminist Philosophy* (Boston: Beacon Press, 1984).

122. Daly, "Original Reintroduction," xviii.

123. Ruether, *Sexism and God-Talk,* 263.

124. See Daly, *Outercourse,* esp. 1–13, 256–58.

125. Ruether, *Sexism and God-Talk,* 229–30; see Rosemary Radford Ruether, *Gaia and God: An Ecofeminist Theology of Earth Healing* (San Francisco: HarperCollins, 1992), 147–48.

126. Audre Lord, "An Open Letter to Mary Daly," in *This Bridge Called My Back: Writings by Radical Women of Color,* ed. Cherrie Moraga and Gloria Anzaldua (New York: Kitchen Table Women of Color Press, 1983), 94–97.

127. Sheila Greeve Davaney, "The Limits of the Appeal to Women's Experience," in *Shaping New Vision: Gender and Values in American Culture,* ed. Clarissa W. Atkinson, Constance H. Buchanan, and Margaret R. Miles (Ann Arbor, Mich.: UMI Research Press, 1987); see Davaney, "Problems with Feminist Theory: Historicity and the Search for Sure Foundations," in *Embodied Love: Sensuality and Relationship as Feminist Values,* ed. Paula M. Cooey, Sharon A.

Farmer, and Mary Ellen Ross (San Francisco: Harper & Row, 1987), 79–95; Daly, *Pure Lust,* 26–27, 87–89.

128. Ellen T. Armour, "Questioning 'Woman' in Feminist/Womanist Theology," in *Transfigurations: Theology and the French Feminists,* ed. C. W. Maggie Kim, Susan M. St. Ville, and Susan M. Simonaitis (Minneapolis: Fortress Press, 1993), 148–50.

129. Daly, *Outercourse,* 341.

130. Nancy Hartsock, "Foucault on Power: A Theory for Women," in Nicholson, ed., *Feminism/Postmodernism,* 163.

131. Mary McClintock Fulkerson, *Changing the Subject: Women's Discourses and Feminist Theology* (Minneapolis: Fortress Press, 1994), 3.

132. Ibid., 9.

133. Sharon D. Welch, "Sporting Power: American Feminism, French Feminisms, and an Ethic of Conflict," in Kim et al., *Transfigurations,* 171–98.

134. See Sharon D. Welch, *A Feminist Ethic of Risk* (Minneapolis: Fortress Press, 1990).

135. Rebecca S. Chopp, "From Patriarchy Into Freedom: A Conversation between American Feminist Theology and French Feminism," in Kim et al., *Transfigurations,* 45.

136. Sharon D. Welch, *Communities of Resistance and Solidarity: A Feminist Theology of Liberation* (Maryknoll, N.Y.: Orbis Books, 1985), 70–72.

137. Fulkerson, *Changing the Subject,* ix.

138. On the difference between belief-problematizing "progressive" theology and oppression-problematizing liberation theology, see Gustavo Gutiérrez, *The Power of the Poor in History,* trans. Robert R. Barr (Maryknoll, N. Y.:Orbis Books, 1983), 169–221.

139. Fulkerson, *Changing the Subject,* 7.

140. Ibid., 372.

141. For a programmatic argument that develops this thesis, see Rebecca S. Chopp, *The Power to Speak: Feminism, Language, God* (New York: Crossroad, 1991).

142. Fulkerson, *Changing the Subject,* 375.

143. Sallie McFague, *Models of God: Theology for an Ecological, Nuclear Age* (Philadelphia: Fortress Press, 1987), xi–xii.

144. Sallie McFague, *Metaphorical Theology: Models of God in Religious Language* (Philadelphia: Fortress Press, 1982), 145.

145. McFague, *Models of God,* xii; see McFague, *Metaphorical Theology,* 147.

146. Ibid., xii–xiv, 7.

147. Ibid., 25.

148. See Martin Heidegger, *On Time and Being,* trans. Joan Stambaugh (New York: Harper & Row, 1972), 55–73; Herman Rapaport, *Heidegger and Derrida* (Lincoln, Nebr.: University of Nebraska Press, 1989); Charles Spinosa, "Derrida and Heidegger: Iterability and *Ereignis,*" in *Heidegger: A Critical Reader,* ed. Hubert L. Dreyfus and Harrison Hall (Cambridge, England: Basil Blackwell, 1992), 270–97.

149. McFague, *Models of God,* 26.

150. Ibid., 27.

151. See McFague, *Metaphorical Theology,* 24–28.

152. See Gordon D. Kaufman, *An Essay on Theological Method* (Missoula, Mont.: Scholars Press, 1979); idem, *The Theological Imagination: Constructing the Concept of God* (Philadelphia: Westminster Press, 1981); idem, *In Face of Mystery: A Constructive Theology* (Cambridge: Harvard University Press, 1993).

153. McFague, *Models of God,* 61.

154. Quoted in Ellen K. Coughlin, "Christianity and Ecology: Scholars of 'Religion and the Environment' Re-examine God's Relationship to the Physical World," *The Chronicle of Higher Education* 41 (July 20, 1994):A14.

155. McFague, *Models of God,* 84.

156. Ibid., 183.

157. Ibid., 185.
158. Sallie McFague, *The Body of God: An Ecological Theology* (Minneapolis: Fortress Press, 1993), 65.
159. Ibid., viii, xi.
160. On Teilhard's remythologization of nature, see Claude Stewart, *Nature in Grace: A Study of the Theology of Nature* (Macon, Ga.: Mercer University Press, 1983); Pierre Teilhard de Chardin, *Christianity and Evolution* (London: Collins, 1971).
161. McFague, *The Body of God*, 179.
162. See McFague, *Metaphorical Theology*, viii.
163. McFague, *The Body of God*, 179.
164. McFague follows here the account of the differences between "modern" and "postmodern" science presented by Ian Barbour, *Religion in an Age of Science*, vol. 1 (New York: Harper & Row, 1990). See also Arthur Peacocke, *Theology for a Scientific Age: Being and Becoming—Natural, Divine, and Human* (Minneapolis: Fortress Press, 1993); and John Polkinghorne, *Science and Providence: God's Interaction with the World* (Boston: New Science Library, 1989).
165. See Thomas S. Kuhn, *The Structure of Scientific Revolutions* (Chicago: University of Chicago Press, 1970); Kurt Hubner, *Critique of Scientific Reason*, trans. Paul R. Dixon, Jr. and Hollis M. Dixon (Chicago: University of Chicago Press, 1983).
166. McFague, *The Body of God*, 81.
167. See Alfred North Whitehead, *Process and Reality: An Essay in Cosmology* (1929; reprint, New York: Free Press, 1978); Charles Hartshorne, *The Logic of Perfection: And Other Essays in Neoclassical Metaphysics* (LaSalle, Ill.: Open Court, 1962).
168. See Charles Hartshorne, *Man's Vision of God* (Chicago: Willett Clark & Co., 1941), 209; Tyron Inbody, "Myth in Contemporary Theology: The Irreconcilable Issue," *Anglican Theological Review* 57:139–57; John Knox, *Myth and Truth* (Charlottesville, Va.: University Press of Virginia, 1964).
169. Quoted in Inbody, "Myth in Contemporary Theology," 157.
170. R. G. Collingwood, *An Essay on Metaphysics* (London: Oxford University Press, 1940), 34–48; Inbody, "Myth in Contemporary Theology," 155–57.
171. McFague, *The Body of God*, 65.
172. Ibid., 154.

Notes to Chapter 6.
Dialectics of Word and Spirit: Christ as True Myth

1. See Karl Barth, *Church Dogmatics: The Doctrine of Creation*, vol. 3, bk. 4, trans. A. T. Mackay et al. (Edinburgh: T. & T. Clark, 1961), 116–240. Barth insisted that the man's "primacy of service" implies no superiority on his part (the English translators distorted his meaning by speaking of "false superiority," whereas Barth's German text is categorical that man is not superior to woman in any way; see p. 171). He could see no way around the biblical teaching, however, that woman is "second in sequence, but only in sequence."
2. See Karl Barth, *Church Dogmatics: The Doctrine of Creation*, vol. 3, bk. 2, trans. Harold Knight and others (Edinburgh: T. & T. Clark, 1960), ix–x; see Barth, "Church and Culture," in Barth, *Theology and Church: Shorter Writings, 1920–1928*, trans. Louise Pettibone Smith (New York: Harper & Row, 1962), 334–54.
3. On reading Barth as the intiator of a postmodern paradigm in theology, see Hans Küng, *Theology for the Third Millenium: An Ecumenical View*, trans. Peter Heinegg (New York: Doubleday, 1988), 259–84.
4. Quoted in John D. Godsey, ed., *Karl Barth's Table Talk* (Edinburgh: Tweeddale Court, Scottish Journal of Theology Occasional Papers, no. 10, 1963), 33; on Barth's multiple modes of thought, see George Hunsinger, *How to Read Karl Barth: The Shape of His Theology* (New York: Oxford University Press, 1991).

5. See Luce Irigaray, *Speculum of the Other Woman,* trans. Gillian C. Gill (Ithaca, N.Y.: Cornell University Press, 1985); Irigaray, *This Sex Which Is Not One,* trans. Catherine Porter (Ithaca, N.Y.: Cornell University Press, 1985); Julia Kristeva, *Desire in Language: A Semiotic Approach to Literature and Art,* trans. Thomas Gora, Alice Jardine, and Leon S. Roudiez (New York: Columbia University Press, 1980); Serene Jones, "This God Which Is Not One: Irigaray and Barth on the Divine," in *Transfigurations: Theology and the French Feminists,* ed. C. W. Maggie Kim, Susan M. St. Ville, and Susan M. Simonaitis (Minneapolis: Fortress Press, 1993), 109–41.

6. Barth, *Church Dogmatics,* vol. 3, bk. 2, 447. On the analogy of truth, see Karl Barth, *Church Dogmatics: The Doctrine of God,* vol. 2, bk. 1, trans. T. H. L. Parker et al. (Edinburgh: T. & T. Clark, 1957), 230–36.

7. See Karl Barth, *Church Dogmatics: The Doctrine of Creation,* vol. 3, bk. 1, trans. J. W. Edwards et al. (Edinburgh: T. & T. Clark, 1958), 79–89.

8. Barth, *Church Dogmatics,* vol. 3, bk. 2, 446–47.

9. Ibid., ix.

10. Barth, *Church Dogmatics,* vol. 3, bk. 1, 82.

11. Ibid.

12. Ibid., 85–86.

13. Ibid., 87. See Hans W. Frei, *The Eclipse of Biblical Narrative: A Study in Eighteenth and Nineteenth Century Hermeneutics* (New Haven, Conn.: Yale University Press, 1974), 130–36, 307–24; idem, *The Identity of Jesus Christ: The Hermeneutical Bases of Dogmatic Theology* (Philadelphia: Fortress Press, 1975), 49–52, 102–5, 139–52.

14. Frei, *The Identity of Jesus Christ,* 59, 108, quote on 51.

15. Ibid., 140–47. On narrative theology, see Stanley Hauerwas and L. Gregory Jones, eds., *Why Narrative?: Readings in Narrative Theology* (Grand Rapids: Wm. B. Eerdmans Publishing Co., 1989); Ronald F. Thiemann, *Revelation and Theology: The Gospel as Narrated Promise* (Notre Dam, Ind.: University of Notre Dame Press, 1985); Gabriel Fackre, *The Christian Story: A Pastoral Systematics,* 2 vols. (Grand Rapids: Wm. B. Eerdmans Publishing Co., 1984, 1987).

16. See Hans-Georg Gadamer, *Truth and Method,* 2d ed., trans. Joel Weinsheimer and Donald G. Marshall (1960; reprint, New York: Crossroad, 1989).

17. Karl Barth, *Church Dogmatics: The Doctrine of the Word of God,* vol. 1, bk. 2, trans. G. T. Thomson and Harold Knight (Edinburgh: T. & T. Clark, 1956), 470–71.

18. Karl Barth, "Rudolf Bultmann—An Attempt to Understand Him," in *Kerygma and Myth: A Theological Debate,* vol. 2, ed. Hans-Werner Bartsch, trans. Reginald H. Fuller (London: SPCK, 1962), 123.

19. Barth, *Church Dogmatics,* vol. 1, bk. 2, 735; see Karl Barth, *Credo,* trans. J. S. McNab (New York: Charles Scribner's Sons, 1962), 182–84; Hans W. Frei, *Types of Christian Theology,* ed. George Hunsinger and William C. Placher (New Haven, Conn.: Yale University Press, 1992), 78–91; Frei, *The Identity of Jesus Christ,* 137–38.

20. Ibid., 493.

21. Karl Barth, *The Epistle to the Romans,* trans. Edwyn C. Hoskyns (1933; reprint, London: Oxford University Press, 1975), 314.

22. For Barth's discussion of why we cannot believe "and still want to know" (on independent grounds), see Karl Barth, *Church Dogmatics,* vol. 3, bk. 3, trans. G. W. Bromiley and R. J. Ehrlich (Edinburgh: T. & T. Clark, 1961), 403; Barth, *Church Dogmatics,* vol. 3, bk. 1, 109.

23. C. S. Lewis, *Surprised By Joy: The Shape of My Early Life* (1956; reprint, San Diego: Harcourt, Brace & Co., 1984), 236.

24. C. S. Lewis, *God in the Dock: Essays on Theology and Ethics* (Grand Rapids: Wm. B. Eerdmans Publishing Co., 1970), 63–67.

25. Lewis, *Surprised By Joy,* 236.

26. Lewis, *God In the Dock,* 66–67.

27. Letter from C. S. Lewis to Arthur Greeves, quoted in Roger Lancelyn Green and Walter Hooper, *C. S. Lewis: A Biography* (San Diego: Harcourt, Brace & Co., 1974), 117–18.

28. Ibid., 118.

29. James E. Loder, *The Transforming Moment* (Colorado Springs, Colo.: Helmers & Howard, 1989), 152.

30. On the persistently dialectical character of Barth's theology, see Bruce L. McCormack, *Karl Barth's Critically Realistic Dialectical Theology: Its Genesis and Development, 1909–1936* (Oxford: Clarendon Press, 1995), esp. 1–28, 270–74, 453–67.

31. Barth, *Church Dogmatics,* vol. 2, bk. 1, 179–204, quote on 188.

32. Ibid., 194.

33. Ibid., 199.

Index of Authors and Subjects

Maurice, Frederick Denison, 190–91
McCormack, Bruce, 93–94
McFague, Sally: feminist theology of, 2, 213, 219–25; on normative role of myth, 225–28
Mein Kampf, 97
Merz, Georg, 87, 98
metaphorical theology, feminist remythologization and, 220–25
metaphysics: absolute presuppositions and, 226; being, process and providence and, 174–78
Meyer, Heinrich August Wilhelm, 22
Michelet, Karl, 27
Minear, Paul, 128, 131
modernism: liberal theology and, 22–25; neo-orthodoxy and, 62–65; process theology and, 195–96
modern theology: Biblical Theology movement and, 144–48; crisis of belief in, 1; critique of, 229–39; Gilkey's participation in, 166–70; historicism and, 167–68; language of myth and, 164–66; myth and history and, 170–73; process philosophy and, 178–80; Ritschlian school and, 52; sacredness and, 187
Moltmann, Jürgen, 127, 165, 171–72, 230
monistic idealism, Strauss' contribution to, 43–45
Moody, Howard, 135
Moore, Robert, 199
morality: religion founded in, 11; Schleiermacher rejects religion's ties to, 12–15
moral optimism, empirical theology and, 69–70
moral reason, Christianity based in, 10
Moravian Bretheren, 12
Muilenburg, James, 128
Müller, Julius, 256 n.150
Müller, Ottfried, 36
Munger, Theodore, 60
Munzer, Thomas, 84
Myers, Max, 210
mysticism, Biblical Theology movement and, 129–30
myth. *See also* specific types of myth; Baur on symbolism and, 30–31; Brunner on, 115–18, 258 n.184; Bultmann on, 101–7; feminist critique of, 213–17; feminist remythologization and, 219–25; Gilkey's neoorthodox theology and, 137–40; Jung's archetypes and, 202–6; left Hegelianism and, 30–31; liberal theology's rethinking of, 160–66; liberation theology and, 197–99; modern theology and, 170–73, 229–39; Niebuhr on theology as, 122–26; normative role of, 225–28; Ogden on truth and, 188–94; pejorative context for in

scripture, 5–6; postmodern deconstruction of, 209–12, 272 n.104; poststructuralist feminism, 217–19; *Religionsgeschichtliche Schule,* 7–9; sacred and, 7–9; Schleiermacher's rejection of, 14–16; Strauss' proposed destruction of, 29; Tillich on, 118–22
mythical criticism, Strauss' interpretation of, 33–37
"mythical school" bible critics, Strauss and, 32–33

Napoleon Bonaparte, 16–17
nationalism, Christianity and, 50
natural order, feminist resacralization of, 223
nature: liberal theology and, 71–72; modernism and, 64–65; Strauss' deconstruction of gospel narrative and, 32–33
Nazi ideology, Barth's criticism of, 97–98, 101, 255 n.14
Neibuhr, Reinhold: Biblical Theology movement and, 129–30; liberal theology and, 72
neoorthodoxy: Barth's historical criticism and, 77; Biblical Theology movement, 128–32, 233; as Christian existentialism, 149–50; as crisis theology, 78–81; debate concerning truth and, 114–18; decline of, 126–27; Gilkey's theology as, 134–43, 229–30; historicism and, 8; interwar debate on liberal theology and, 86–90; kerygma and existence and, 112–14; kerygma and historical criticism, 111–12; as liberal modernist alternative, 62–65; Niebuhr on, 122–26; origins of, 2–4; Ritschl and, 52; roots of, 73–75; salvation history and, 143–48; secularization and, 152–54; univocal center of, 140–43
New Testament: Harnack on, 55–58; mythical criticism of, 36–37; mythology and, 101–7; pejorative context for myth in, 6; Strauss on mythical elements in, 31–32
Niebuhr, Reinhold, 2–3, 8–9, 253 n.92; criticism of myth by, 161, 164, 166; Gilkey and, 132–41, 179–80; on myth and religion, 122–26, 225; on myth of the Fall, 215; neoorthodoxy and, 126–27, 137; on providence, 176–78; theology of history, 170–73
Niemoller, Martin, 254 n.97
Nietzsche, Friedrich, 80, 159, 184, 210–11, 224
Nitzsch, Immanuel, 46
novum organum theologicum of Macintosh, 68–69

myth   30 Schelling
              Baur
        34 Strauss
        35
        36 Müller

60 Schweitzer
64-5 Mathews
79 Barth
        81
        94-5
        96
        97

99 Bultmann
        100 re Barth + philosophy *
              101 Barth's response *
        102-3
        104 myth
        114
116 Brunner re myth
        Tillich
117 *
118 Tillich - myth

138 v 139
    143
    145-147
    149
152 *
    152-3 *
    154

159
161 - myth-
162
163
167
167
169
171 *

178 *

181 *

182 *
184 *
194

202 Jung
206

221-24 *
225-6 *
    226 'metaphysics'

225-6 process @s3 - Whitehead
      re immanence
      + transcendence *

CPSIA information can be obtained
at www.ICGtesting.com
Printed in the USA
LVHW090226200421
684990LV00018B/90

9 780664 257453